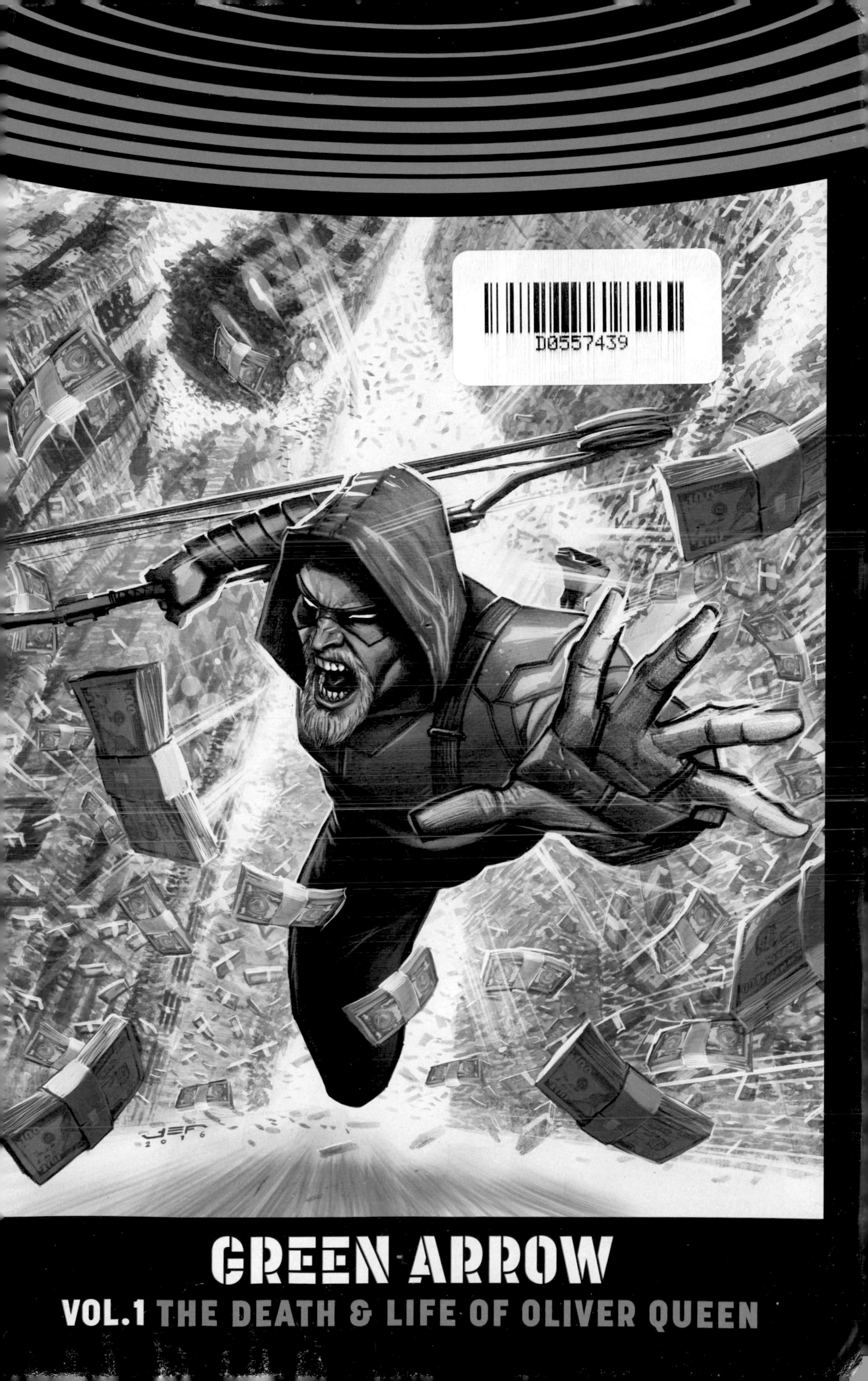

GREEN ARROW

VOL.1 THE DEATH & LIFE OF OLIVER QUEEN

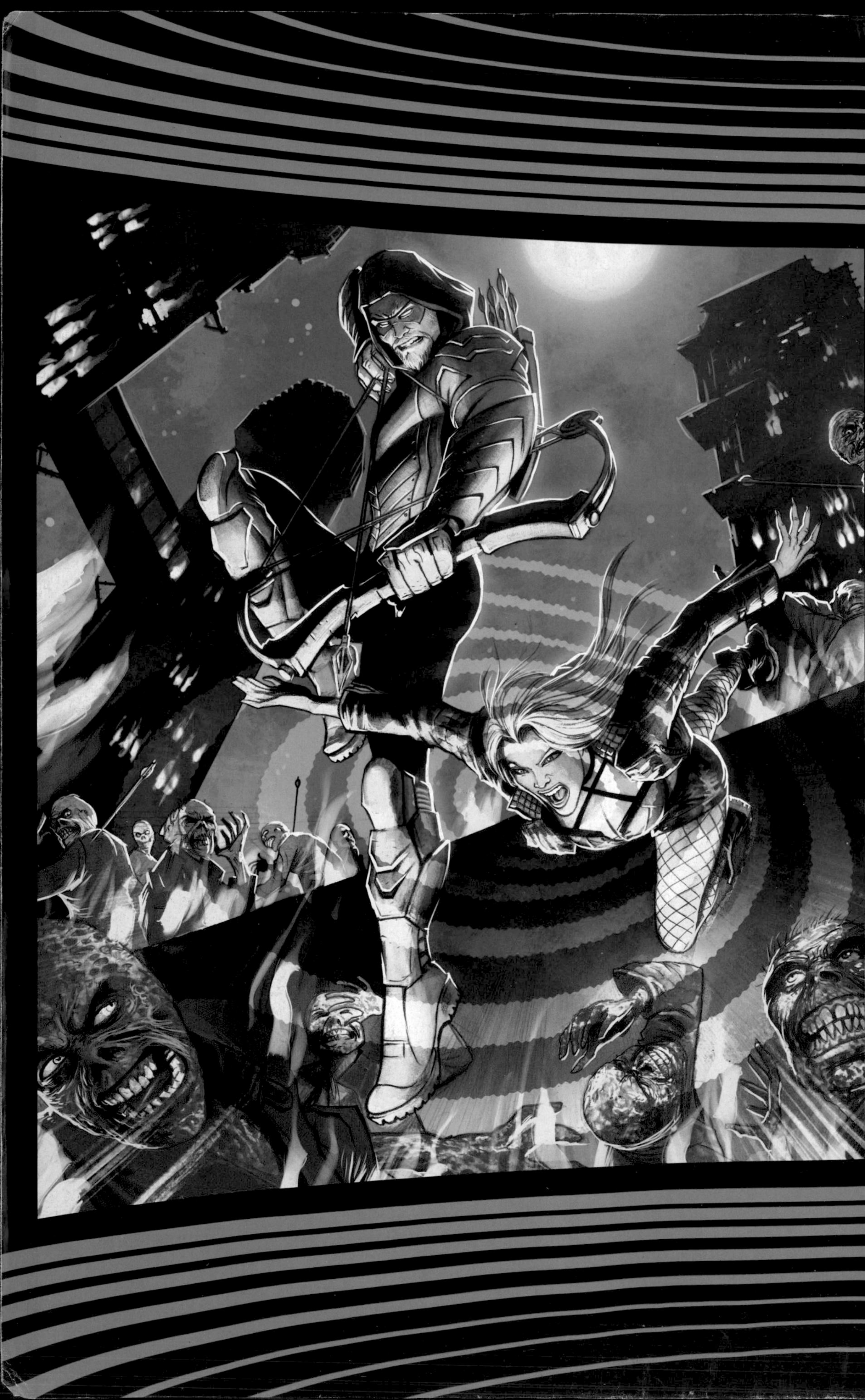

GREEN ARROW

VOL.1 THE DEATH & LIFE OF OLIVER QUEEN

BENJAMIN PERCY
writer

OTTO SCHMIDT
JUAN FERREYRA
artists & colorists

NATE PIEKOS OF BLAMBOT®
letterer

JUAN FERREYRA
series & collection cover artist

ANDY KHOURI Editor - Original Series • **HARVEY RICHARDS** Associate Editor - Original Series • **JEB WOODARD** Group Editor - Collected Editions
STEVE COOK Design Director - Books • **LOUIS PRANDI** Publication Design

BOB HARRAS Senior VP - Editor-in-Chief, DC Comics

DIANE NELSON President • **DAN DiDIO** Publisher • **JIM LEE** Publisher • **GEOFF JOHNS** President & Chief Creative Officer
AMIT DESAI Executive VP - Business & Marketing Strategy, Direct to Consumer & Global Franchise Management
SAM ADES Senior VP - Direct to Consumer • **BOBBIE CHASE** VP - Talent Development • **MARK CHIARELLO** Senior VP - Art, Design & Collected Editions
JOHN CUNNINGHAM Senior VP - Sales & Trade Marketing • **ANNE DePIES** Senior VP - Business Strategy, Finance & Administration
DON FALLETTI VP - Manufacturing Operations • **LAWRENCE GANEM** VP - Editorial Administration & Talent Relations
ALISON GILL Senior VP - Manufacturing & Operations • **HANK KANALZ** Senior VP - Editorial Strategy & Administration
JAY KOGAN VP - Legal Affairs • **THOMAS LOFTUS** VP - Business Affairs • **JACK MAHAN** VP - Business Affairs
NICK J. NAPOLITANO VP - Manufacturing Administration • **EDDIE SCANNELL** VP - Consumer Marketing
COURTNEY SIMMONS Senior VP - Publicity & Communications • **JIM (SKI) SOKOLOWSKI** VP - Comic Book Specialty Sales & Trade Marketing
NANCY SPEARS VP - Mass, Book, Digital Sales & Trade Marketing

GREEN ARROW VOLUME 1: THE DEATH & LIFE OF OLIVER QUEEN

Published by DC Comics. Compilation and all new material Copyright © 2017 DC Comics. All Rights Reserved. Originally published in single magazine form
in GREEN ARROW: REBIRTH 1, GREEN ARROW 1-5. Copyright © 2016 DC Comics. All Rights Reserved. All characters, their distinctive likenesses and related
elements featured in this publication are trademarks of DC Comics. The stories, characters and incidents featured in this publication are entirely fictional.
DC Comics does not read or accept unsolicited submissions of ideas, stories or artwork.

DC Comics, 2900 West Alameda Ave., Burbank, CA 91505
Printed by LSC Communications, Salem, VA, USA 12/23/16. First Printing.
ISBN: 978-1-4012-6781-0

Library of Congress Cataloging-in-Publication Data is available.

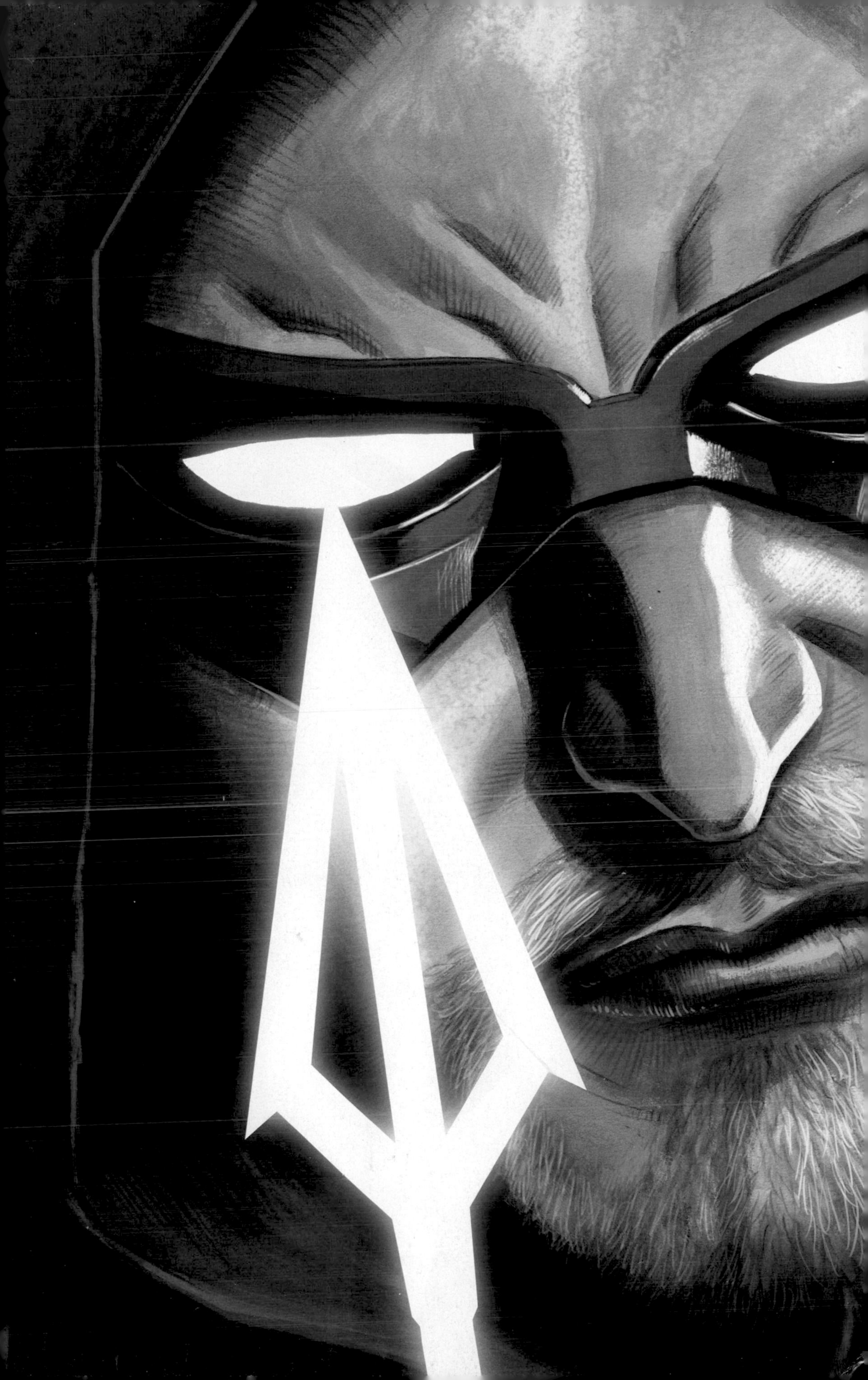

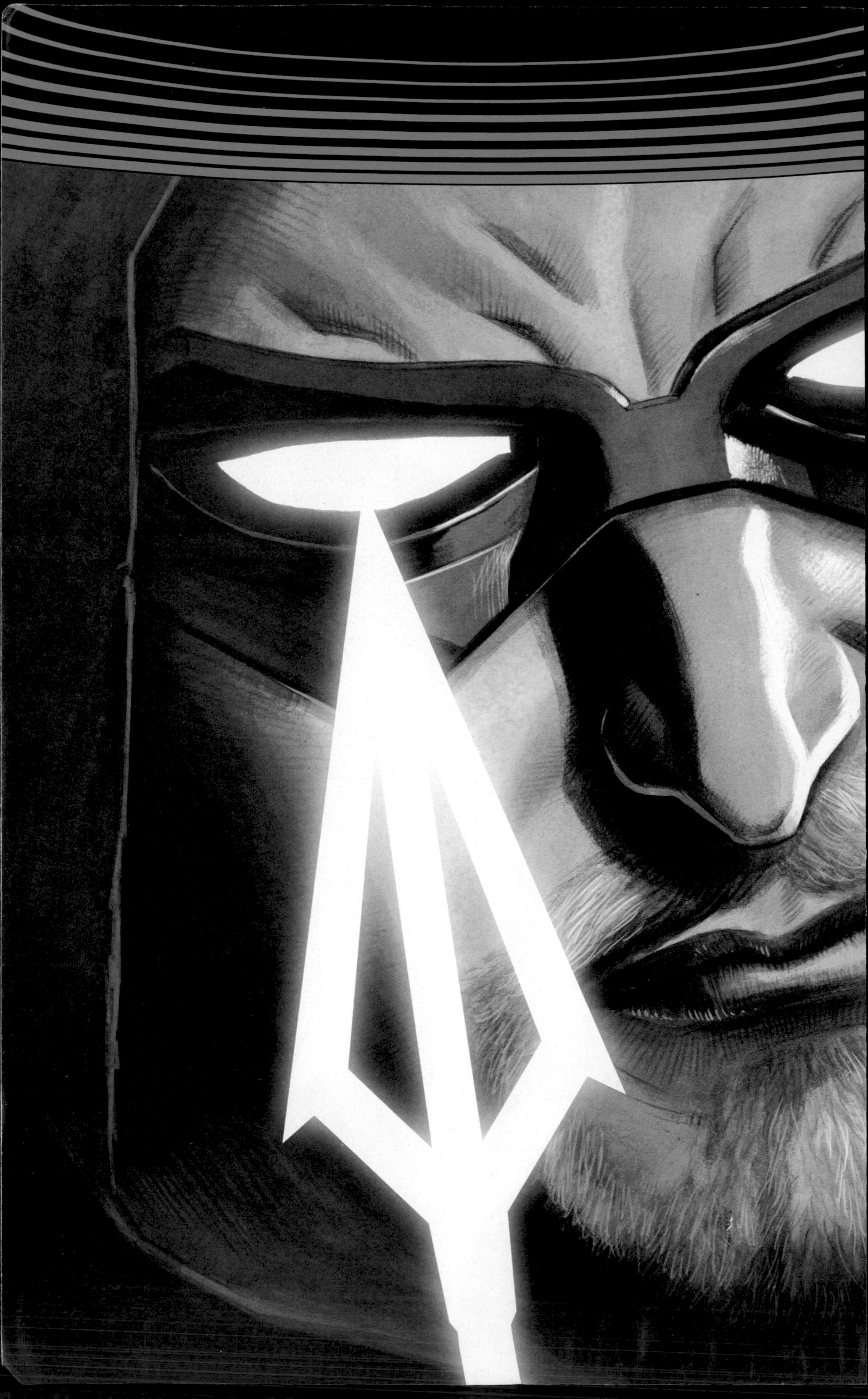

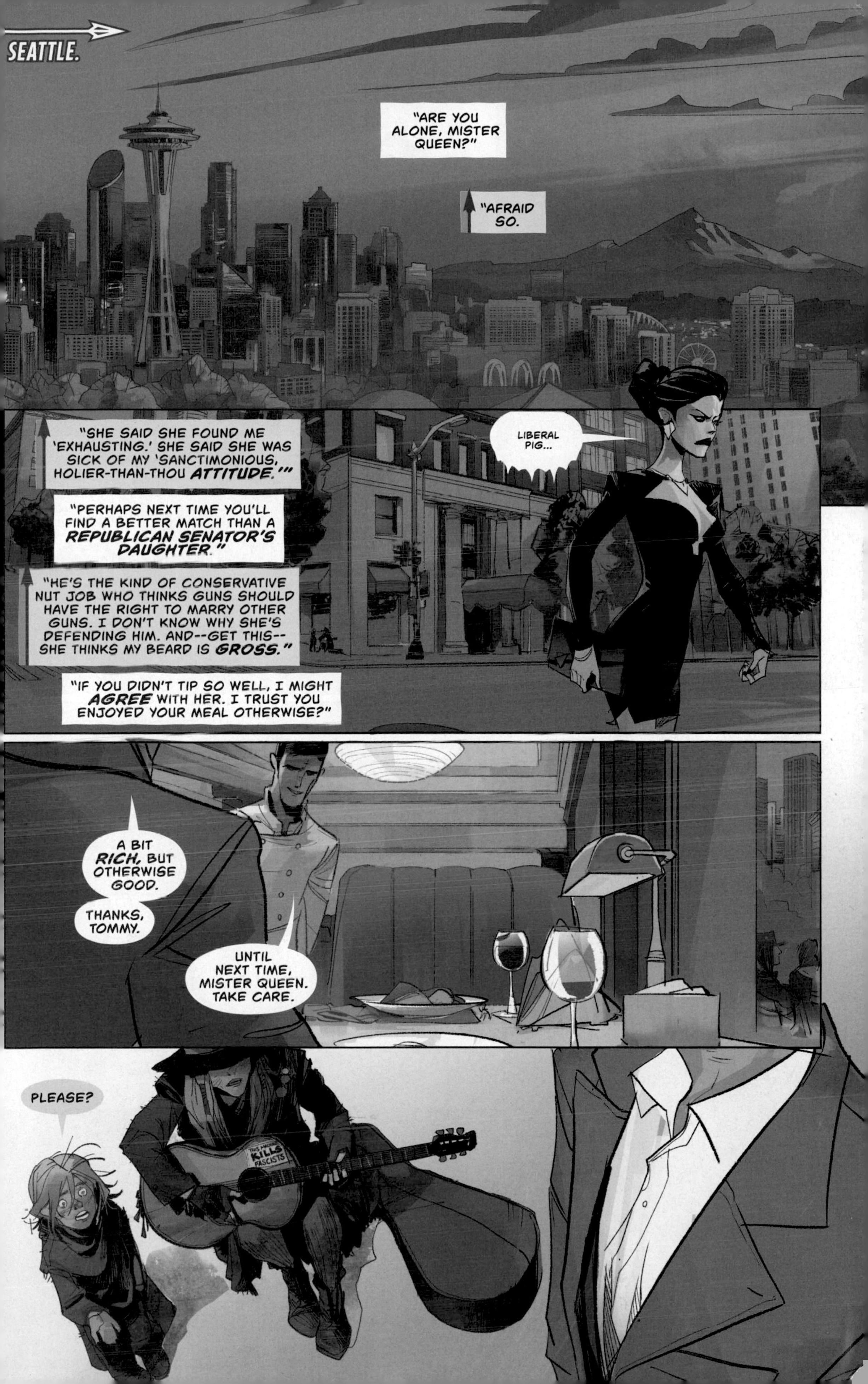
SEATTLE.
"ARE YOU ALONE, MISTER QUEEN?"
"AFRAID SO.
"SHE SAID SHE FOUND ME 'EXHAUSTING.' SHE SAID SHE WAS SICK OF MY 'SANCTIMONIOUS, HOLIER-THAN-THOU ATTITUDE.'"
LIBERAL PIG...
"PERHAPS NEXT TIME YOU'LL FIND A BETTER MATCH THAN A REPUBLICAN SENATOR'S DAUGHTER."
"HE'S THE KIND OF CONSERVATIVE NUT JOB WHO THINKS GUNS SHOULD HAVE THE RIGHT TO MARRY OTHER GUNS. I DON'T KNOW WHY SHE'S DEFENDING HIM. AND--GET THIS--SHE THINKS MY BEARD IS GROSS."
"IF YOU DIDN'T TIP SO WELL, I MIGHT AGREE WITH HER. I TRUST YOU ENJOYED YOUR MEAL OTHERWISE?"
A BIT RICH, BUT OTHERWISE GOOD.
THANKS, TOMMY.
UNTIL NEXT TIME, MISTER QUEEN. TAKE CARE.
PLEASE?
THIS MACHINE KILLS FASCISTS

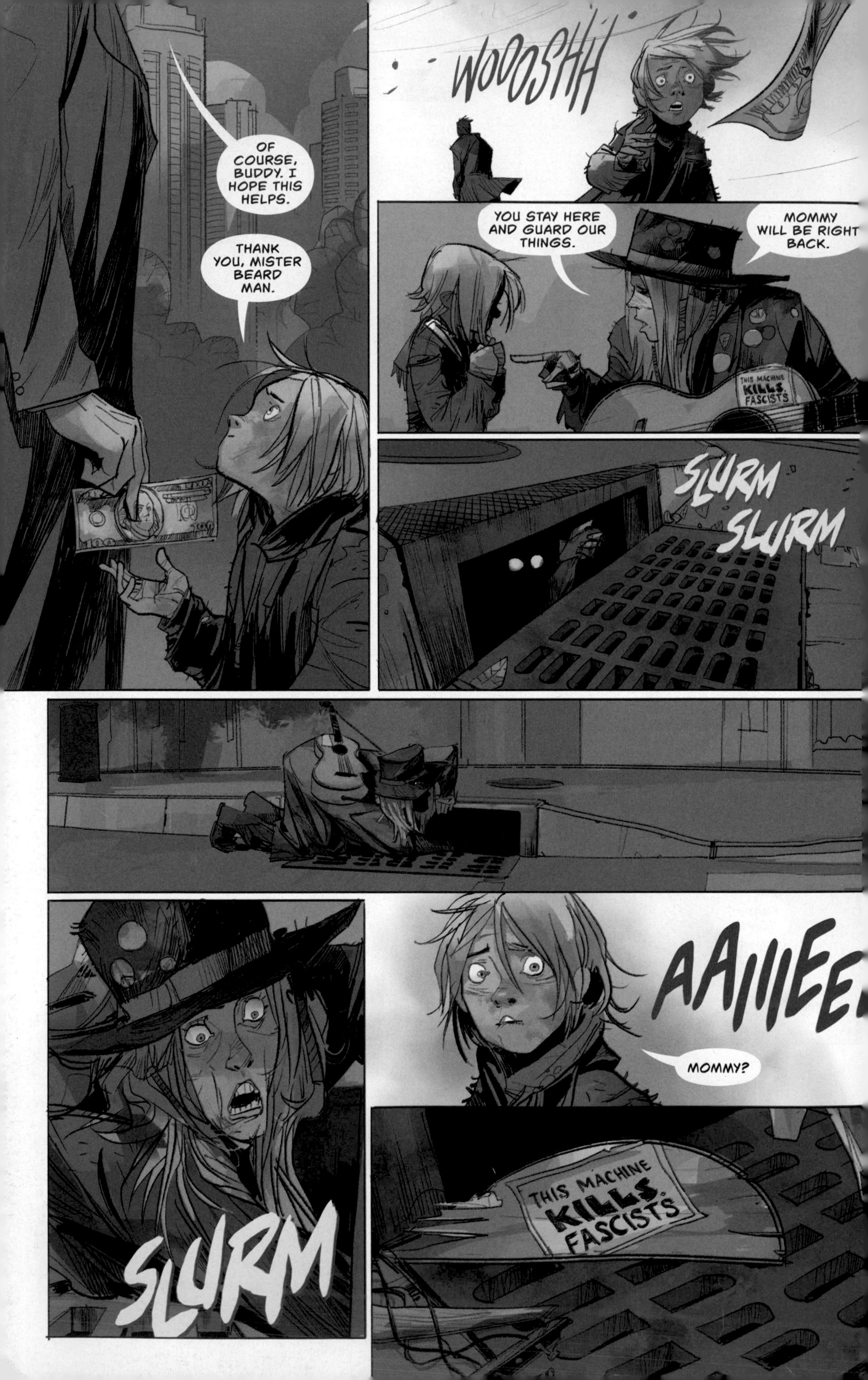
OF COURSE, BUDDY. I HOPE THIS HELPS.
THANK YOU, MISTER BEARD MAN.
WOOOSHH
YOU STAY HERE AND GUARD OUR THINGS.
MOMMY WILL BE RIGHT BACK.
THIS MACHINE KILLS FASCISTS
SLURM
SLURM
SLURM
AAIIIEE
MOMMY?
THIS MACHINE KILLS FASCISTS

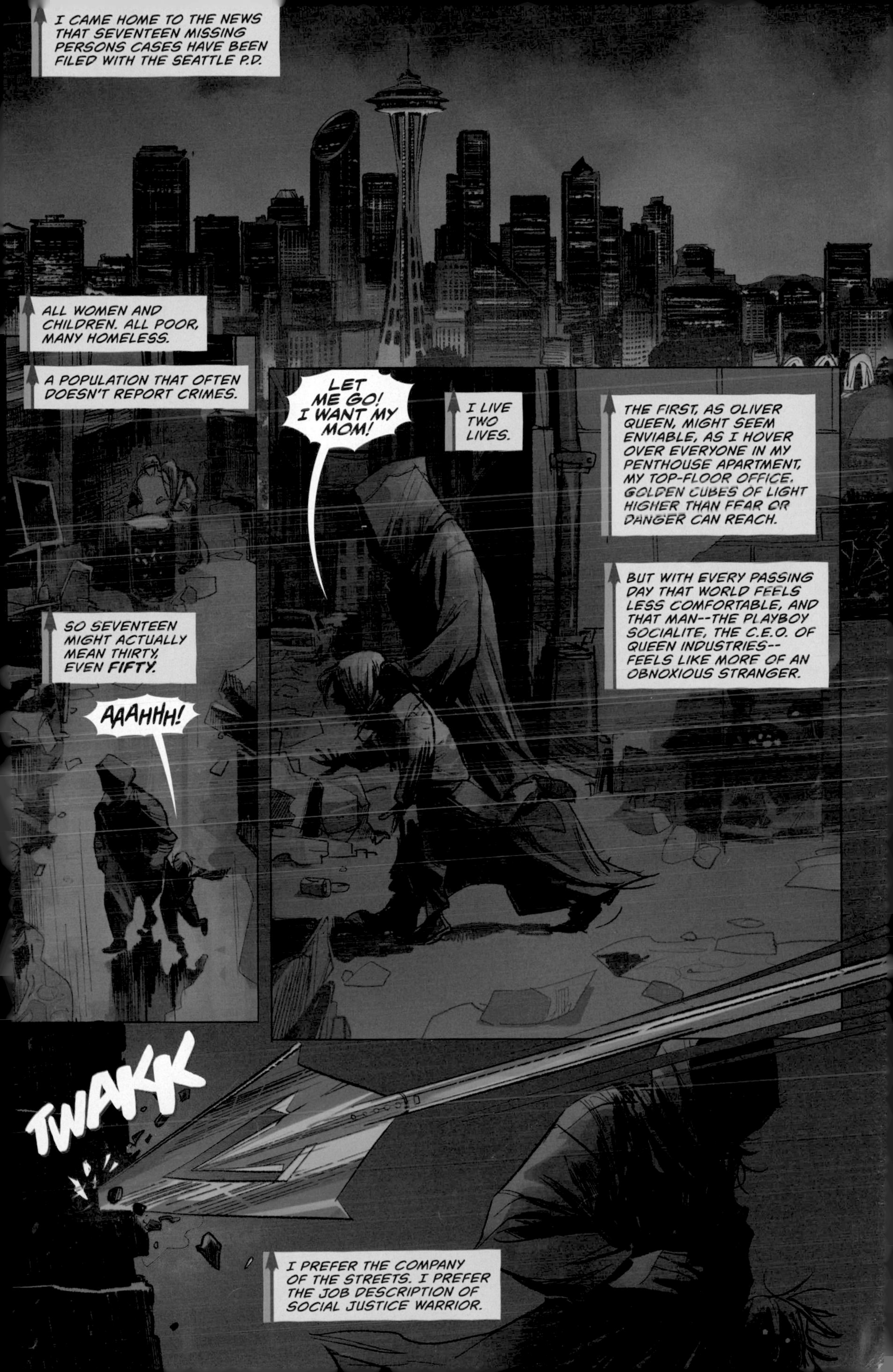
I CAME HOME TO THE NEWS THAT SEVENTEEN MISSING PERSONS CASES HAVE BEEN FILED WITH THE SEATTLE P.D.
ALL WOMEN AND CHILDREN. ALL POOR, MANY HOMELESS.
A POPULATION THAT OFTEN DOESN'T REPORT CRIMES.
SO SEVENTEEN MIGHT ACTUALLY MEAN THIRTY, EVEN FIFTY.
AAAHHH!
LET ME GO! I WANT MY MOM!
I LIVE TWO LIVES.
THE FIRST, AS OLIVER QUEEN, MIGHT SEEM ENVIABLE, AS I HOVER OVER EVERYONE IN MY PENTHOUSE APARTMENT, MY TOP-FLOOR OFFICE. GOLDEN CUBES OF LIGHT HIGHER THAN FEAR OR DANGER CAN REACH.
BUT WITH EVERY PASSING DAY THAT WORLD FEELS LESS COMFORTABLE, AND THAT MAN--THE PLAYBOY SOCIALITE, THE C.E.O. OF QUEEN INDUSTRIES--FEELS LIKE MORE OF AN OBNOXIOUS STRANGER.
TWAKK
I PREFER THE COMPANY OF THE STREETS. I PREFER THE JOB DESCRIPTION OF SOCIAL JUSTICE WARRIOR.

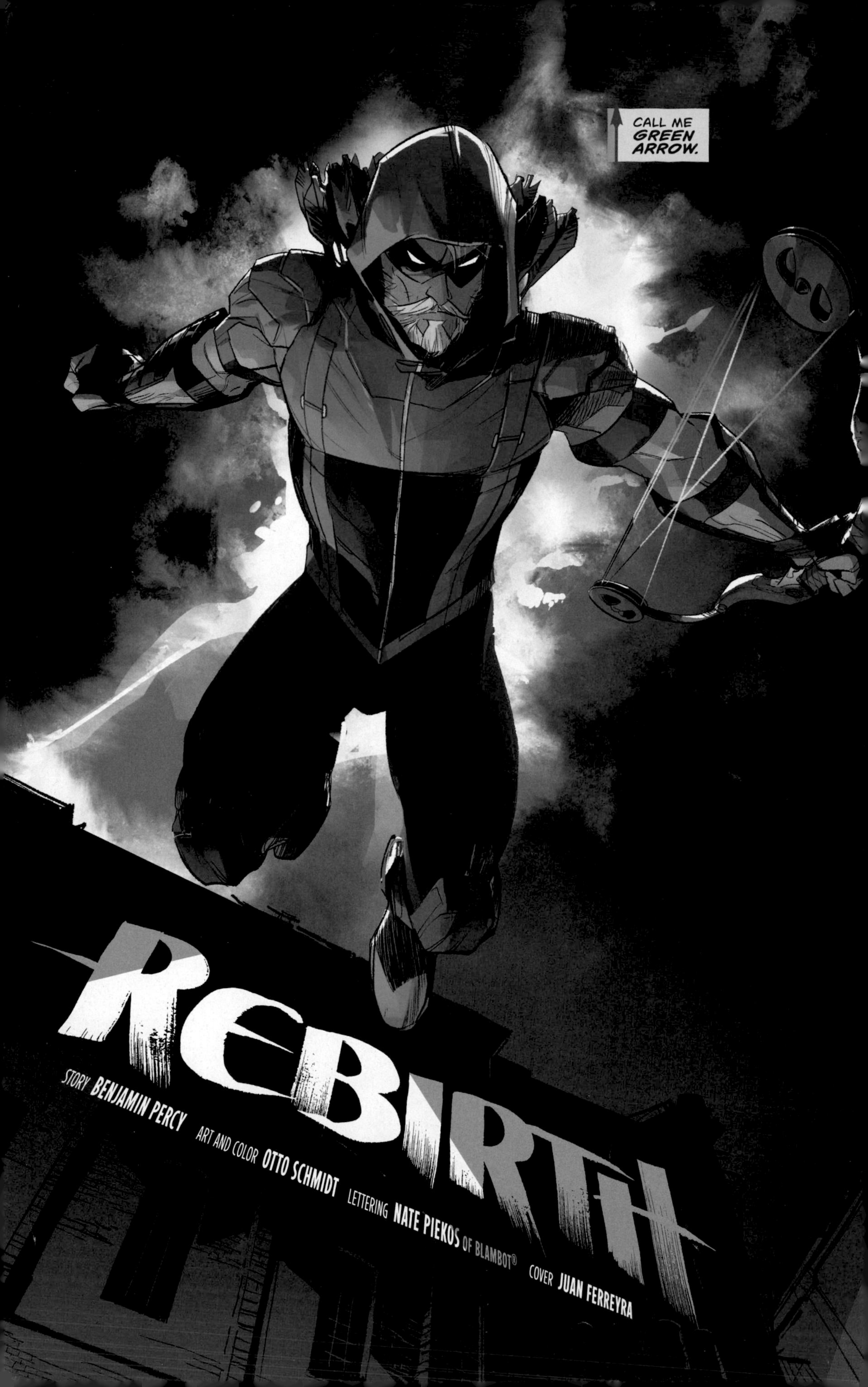

CALL ME GREEN ARROW.
REBIRTH
STORY BENJAMIN PERCY ART AND COLOR OTTO SCHMIDT LETTERING NATE PIEKOS OF BLAMBOT® COVER JUAN FERREYRA

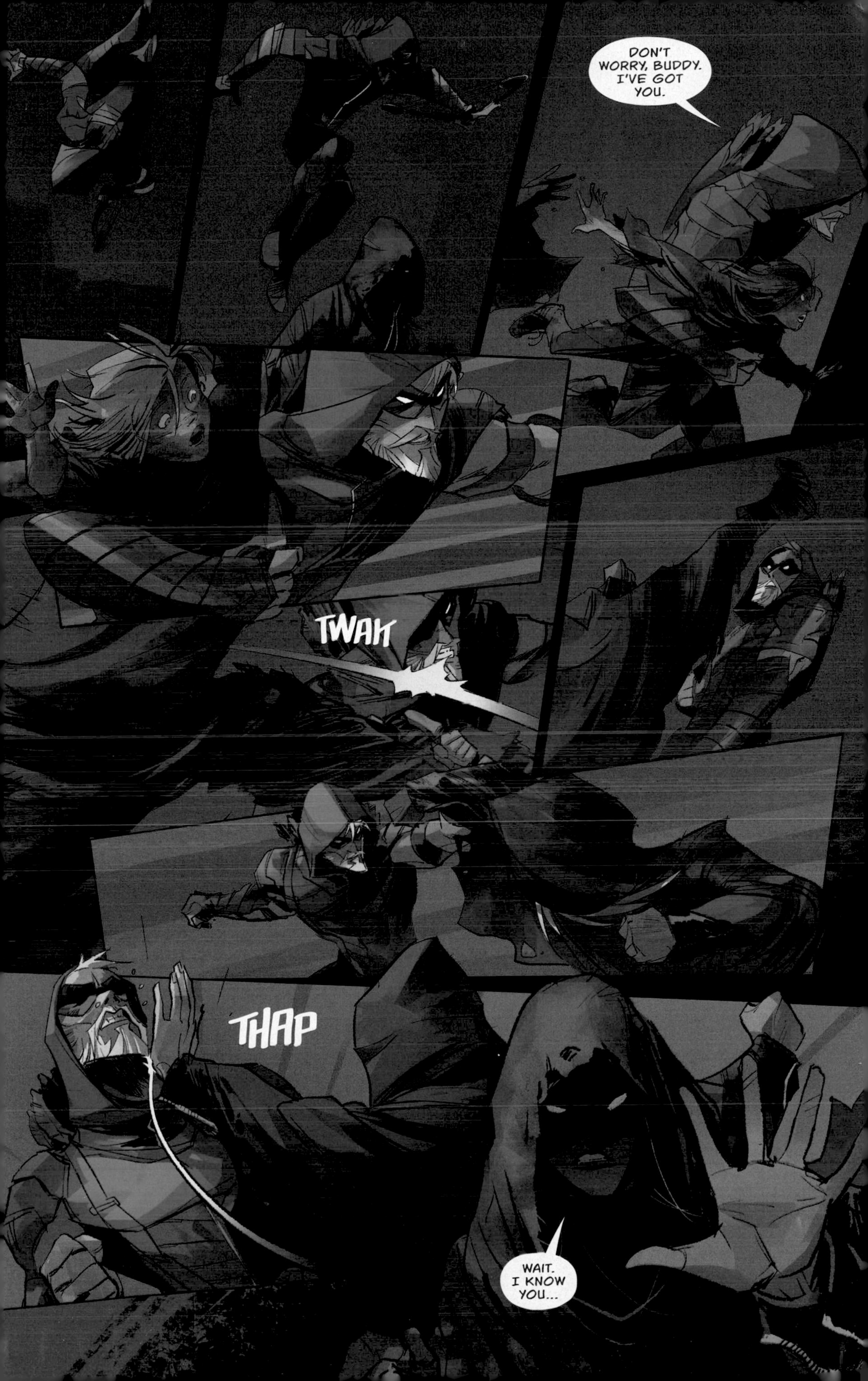
DON'T WORRY, BUDDY. I'VE GOT YOU.
TWAK
THAP
WAIT. I KNOW YOU...

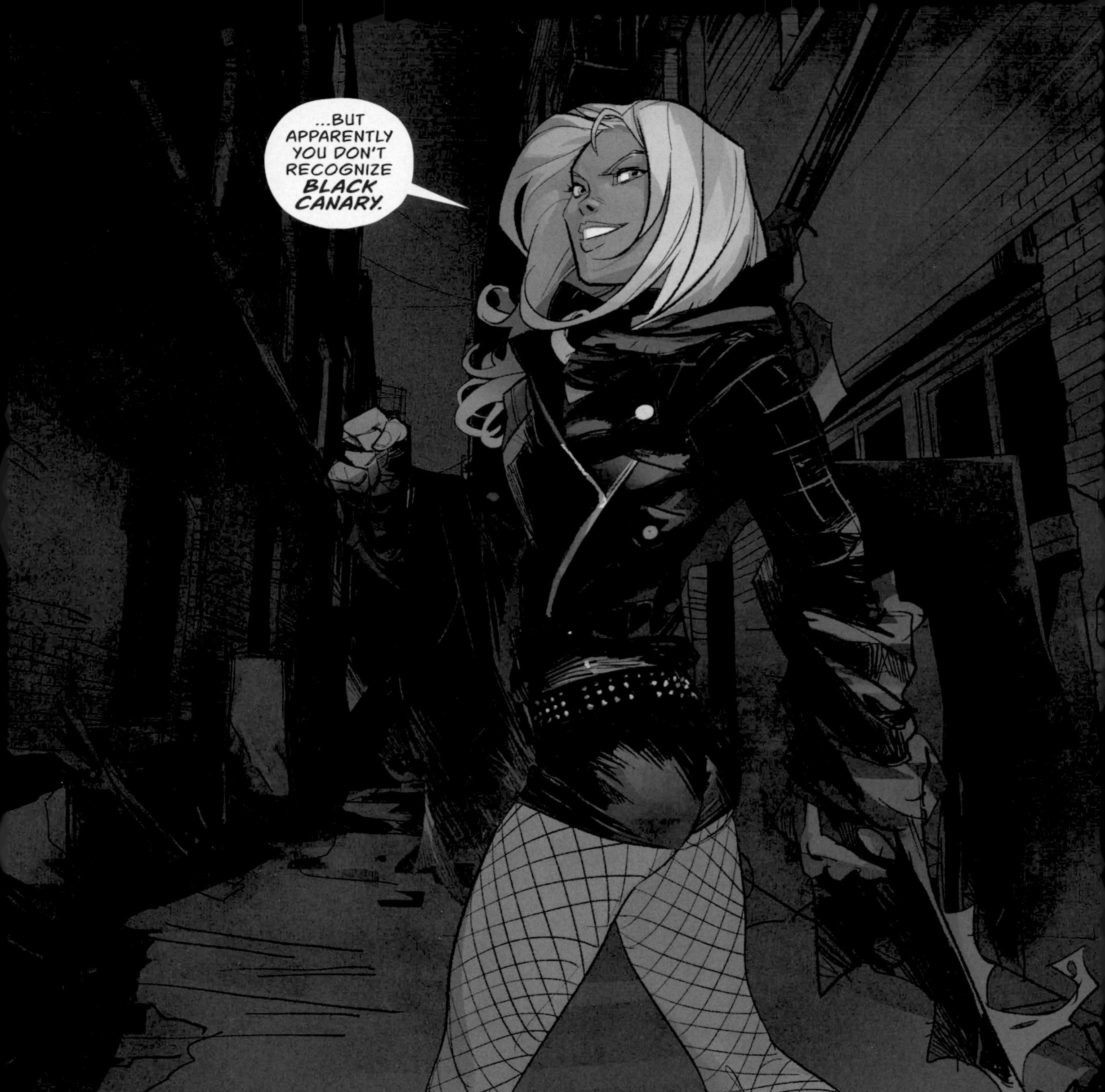
...BUT APPARENTLY YOU DON'T RECOGNIZE BLACK CANARY.

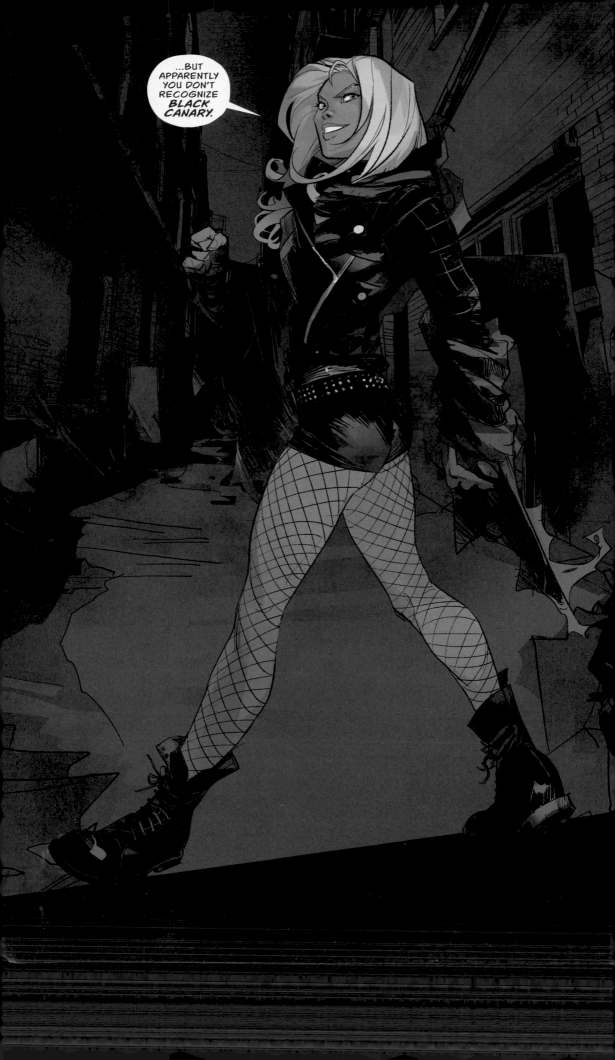

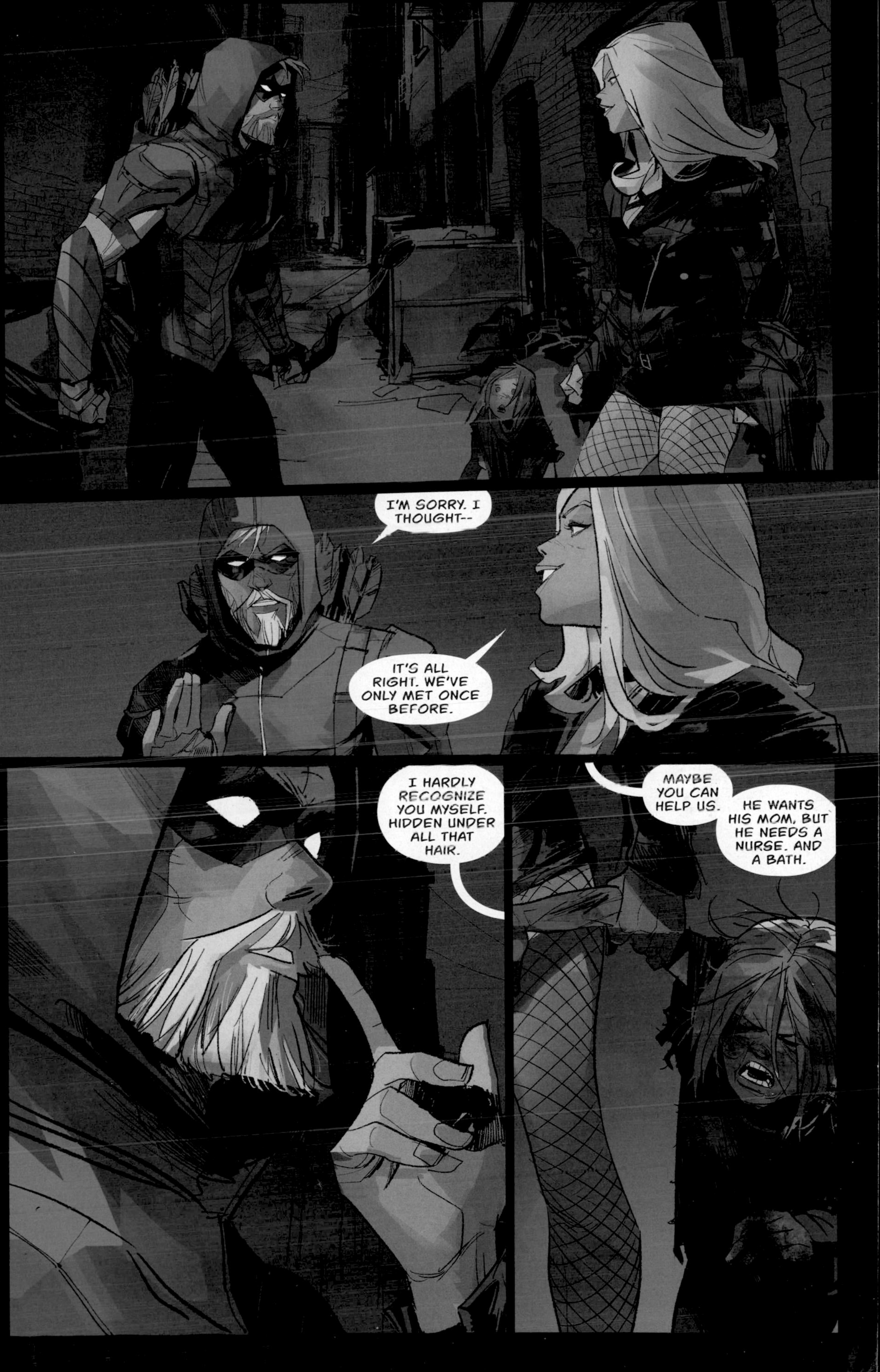
I'M SORRY. I THOUGHT--
IT'S ALL RIGHT. WE'VE ONLY MET ONCE BEFORE.
I HARDLY RECOGNIZE YOU MYSELF. HIDDEN UNDER ALL THAT HAIR.
MAYBE YOU CAN HELP US.
HE WANTS HIS MOM, BUT HE NEEDS A NURSE. AND A BATH.

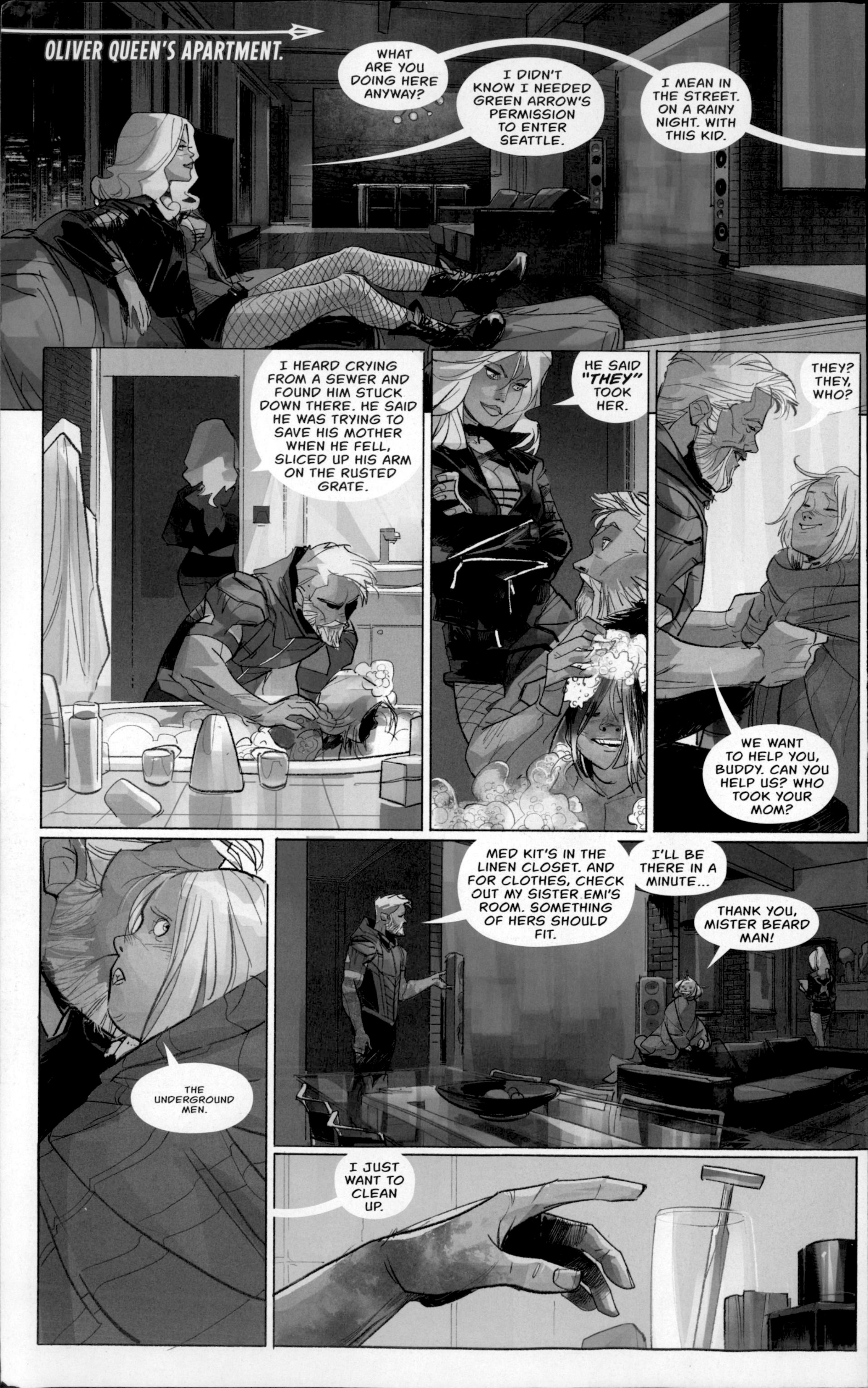
OLIVER QUEEN'S APARTMENT.
WHAT ARE YOU DOING HERE ANYWAY?
I DIDN'T KNOW I NEEDED GREEN ARROW'S PERMISSION TO ENTER SEATTLE.
I MEAN IN THE STREET. ON A RAINY NIGHT. WITH THIS KID.
I HEARD CRYING FROM A SEWER AND FOUND HIM STUCK DOWN THERE. HE SAID HE WAS TRYING TO SAVE HIS MOTHER WHEN HE FELL, SLICED UP HIS ARM ON THE RUSTED GRATE.
HE SAID "THEY" TOOK HER.
THEY? THEY, WHO?
WE WANT TO HELP YOU, BUDDY. CAN YOU HELP US? WHO TOOK YOUR MOM?
THE UNDERGROUND MEN.
MED KIT'S IN THE LINEN CLOSET. AND FOR CLOTHES, CHECK OUT MY SISTER EMI'S ROOM. SOMETHING OF HERS SHOULD FIT.
I'LL BE THERE IN A MINUTE...
THANK YOU, MISTER BEARD MAN!
I JUST WANT TO CLEAN UP.

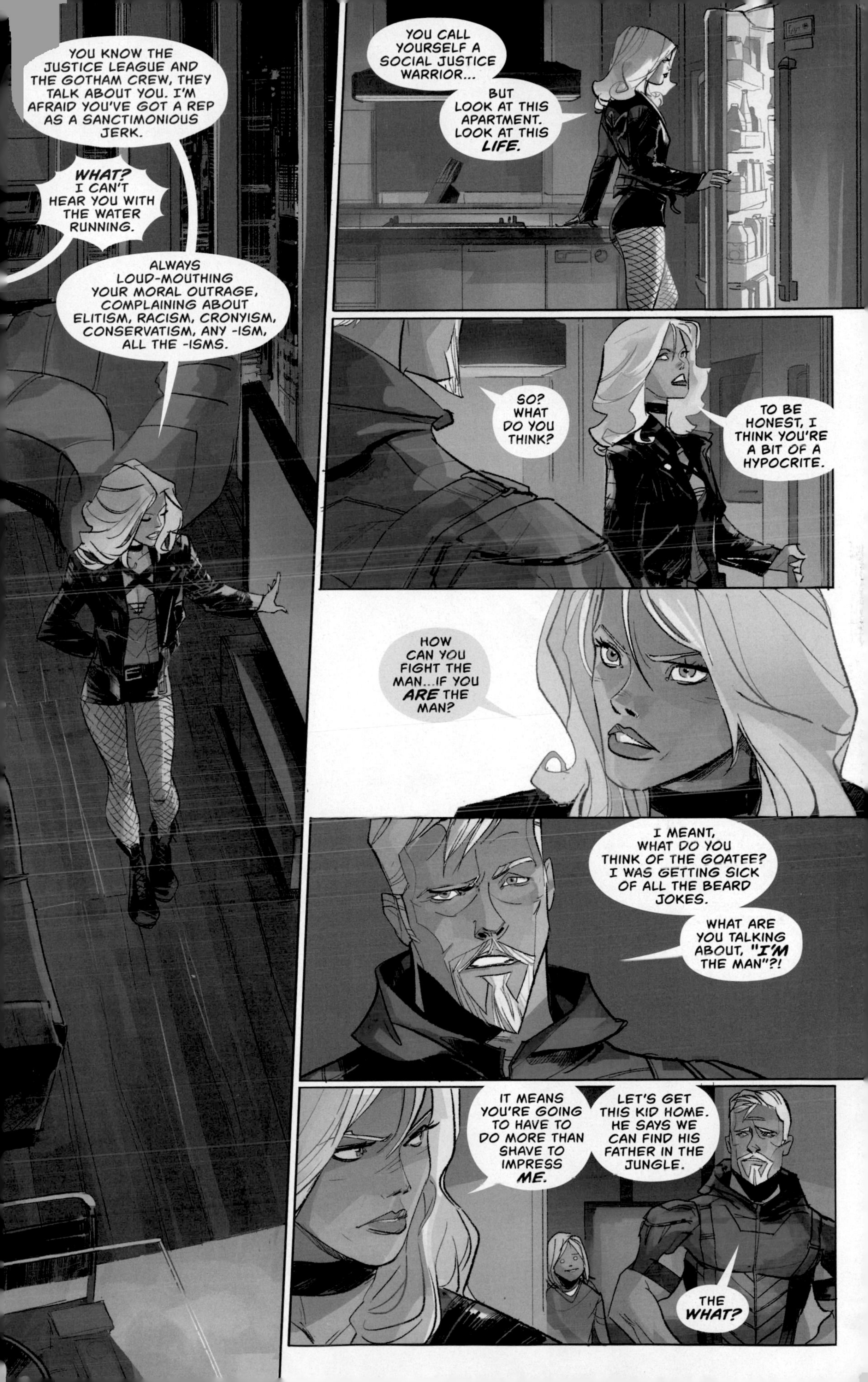
YOU KNOW THE JUSTICE LEAGUE AND THE GOTHAM CREW, THEY TALK ABOUT YOU. I'M AFRAID YOU'VE GOT A REP AS A SANCTIMONIOUS JERK.
WHAT? I CAN'T HEAR YOU WITH THE WATER RUNNING.
ALWAYS LOUD-MOUTHING YOUR MORAL OUTRAGE, COMPLAINING ABOUT ELITISM, RACISM, CRONYISM, CONSERVATISM, ANY -ISM, ALL THE -ISMS.
YOU CALL YOURSELF A SOCIAL JUSTICE WARRIOR...
BUT LOOK AT THIS APARTMENT. LOOK AT THIS *LIFE.*
SO? WHAT DO YOU THINK?
TO BE HONEST, I THINK YOU'RE A BIT OF A HYPOCRITE.
HOW CAN YOU FIGHT THE MAN...IF YOU *ARE* THE MAN?
I MEANT, WHAT DO YOU THINK OF THE GOATEE? I WAS GETTING SICK OF ALL THE BEARD JOKES.
WHAT ARE YOU TALKING ABOUT, "*I'M* THE MAN"?!
IT MEANS YOU'RE GOING TO HAVE TO DO MORE THAN SHAVE TO IMPRESS *ME.*
LET'S GET THIS KID HOME. HE SAYS WE CAN FIND HIS FATHER IN THE JUNGLE.
THE *WHAT?*

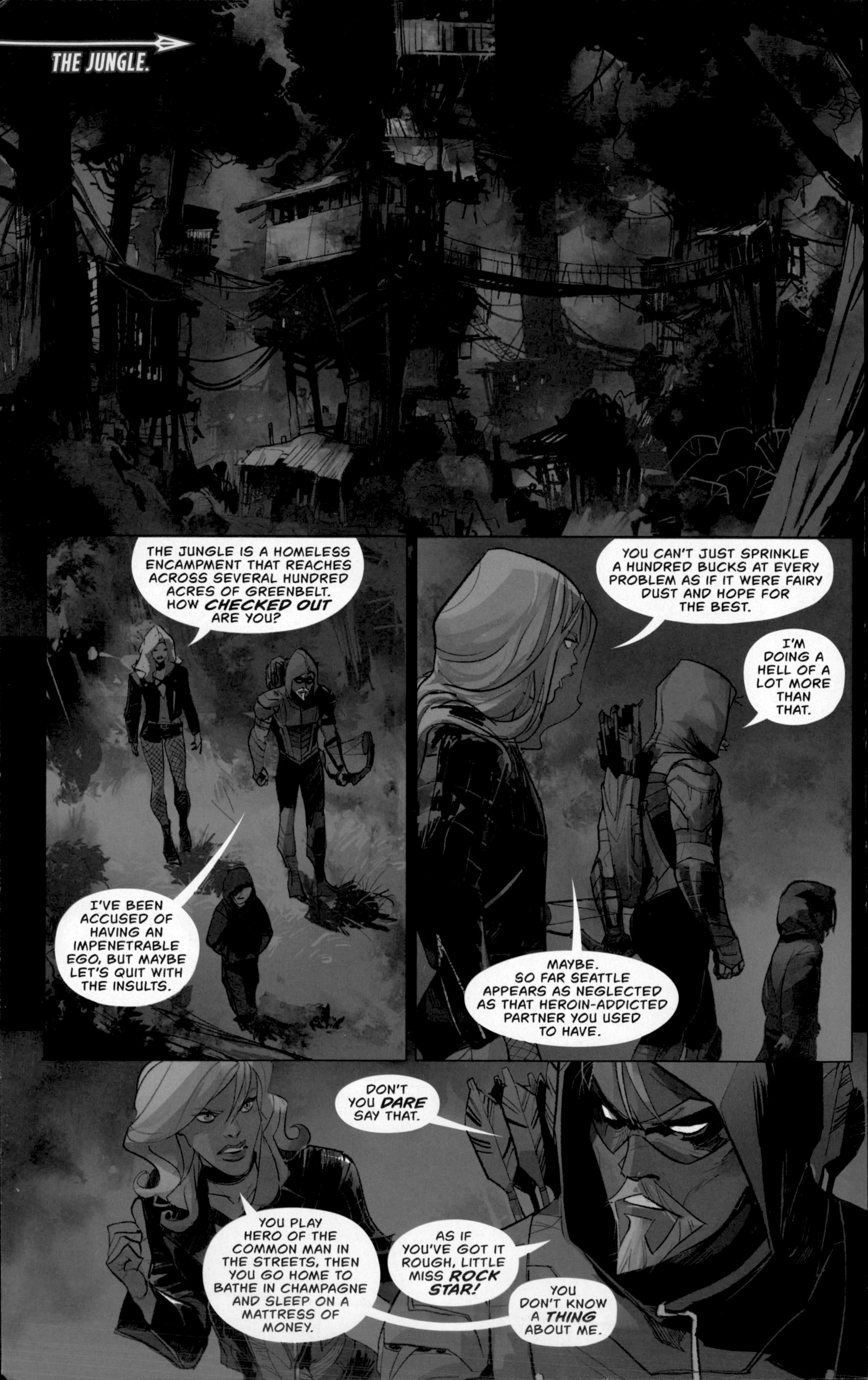
THE JUNGLE.
THE JUNGLE IS A HOMELESS ENCAMPMENT THAT REACHES ACROSS SEVERAL HUNDRED ACRES OF GREENBELT. HOW CHECKED OUT ARE YOU?
I'VE BEEN ACCUSED OF HAVING AN IMPENETRABLE EGO, BUT MAYBE LET'S QUIT WITH THE INSULTS.
YOU CAN'T JUST SPRINKLE A HUNDRED BUCKS AT EVERY PROBLEM AS IF IT WERE FAIRY DUST AND HOPE FOR THE BEST.
I'M DOING A HELL OF A LOT MORE THAN THAT.
MAYBE. SO FAR SEATTLE APPEARS AS NEGLECTED AS THAT HEROIN-ADDICTED PARTNER YOU USED TO HAVE.
DON'T YOU DARE SAY THAT.
YOU PLAY HERO OF THE COMMON MAN IN THE STREETS, THEN YOU GO HOME TO BATHE IN CHAMPAGNE AND SLEEP ON A MATTRESS OF MONEY.
AS IF YOU'VE GOT IT ROUGH, LITTLE MISS ROCK STAR!
YOU DON'T KNOW A THING ABOUT ME.

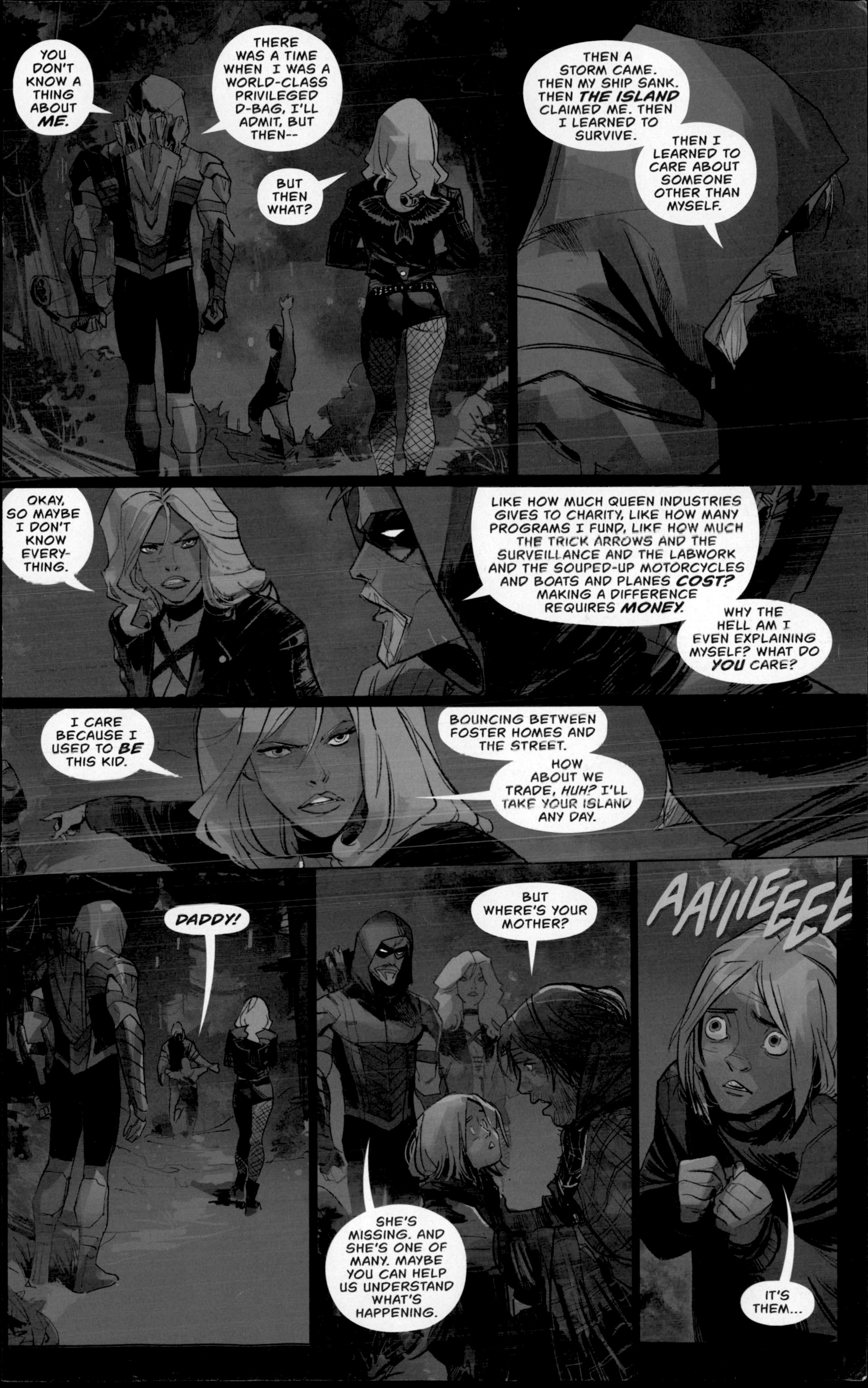
YOU DON'T KNOW A THING ABOUT ME.
THERE WAS A TIME WHEN I WAS A WORLD-CLASS PRIVILEGED D-BAG, I'LL ADMIT, BUT THEN--
BUT THEN WHAT?
THEN A STORM CAME. THEN MY SHIP SANK. THEN THE ISLAND CLAIMED ME. THEN I LEARNED TO SURVIVE.
THEN I LEARNED TO CARE ABOUT SOMEONE OTHER THAN MYSELF.
OKAY, SO MAYBE I DON'T KNOW EVERY-THING.
LIKE HOW MUCH QUEEN INDUSTRIES GIVES TO CHARITY, LIKE HOW MANY PROGRAMS I FUND, LIKE HOW MUCH THE TRICK ARROWS AND THE SURVEILLANCE AND THE LABWORK AND THE SOUPED-UP MOTORCYCLES AND BOATS AND PLANES COST? MAKING A DIFFERENCE REQUIRES MONEY.
WHY THE HELL AM I EVEN EXPLAINING MYSELF? WHAT DO YOU CARE?
I CARE BECAUSE I USED TO BE THIS KID.
BOUNCING BETWEEN FOSTER HOMES AND THE STREET.
HOW ABOUT WE TRADE, HUH? I'LL TAKE YOUR ISLAND ANY DAY.
DADDY!
BUT WHERE'S YOUR MOTHER?
SHE'S MISSING. AND SHE'S ONE OF MANY. MAYBE YOU CAN HELP US UNDERSTAND WHAT'S HAPPENING.
AAIIIEEEE
IT'S THEM...

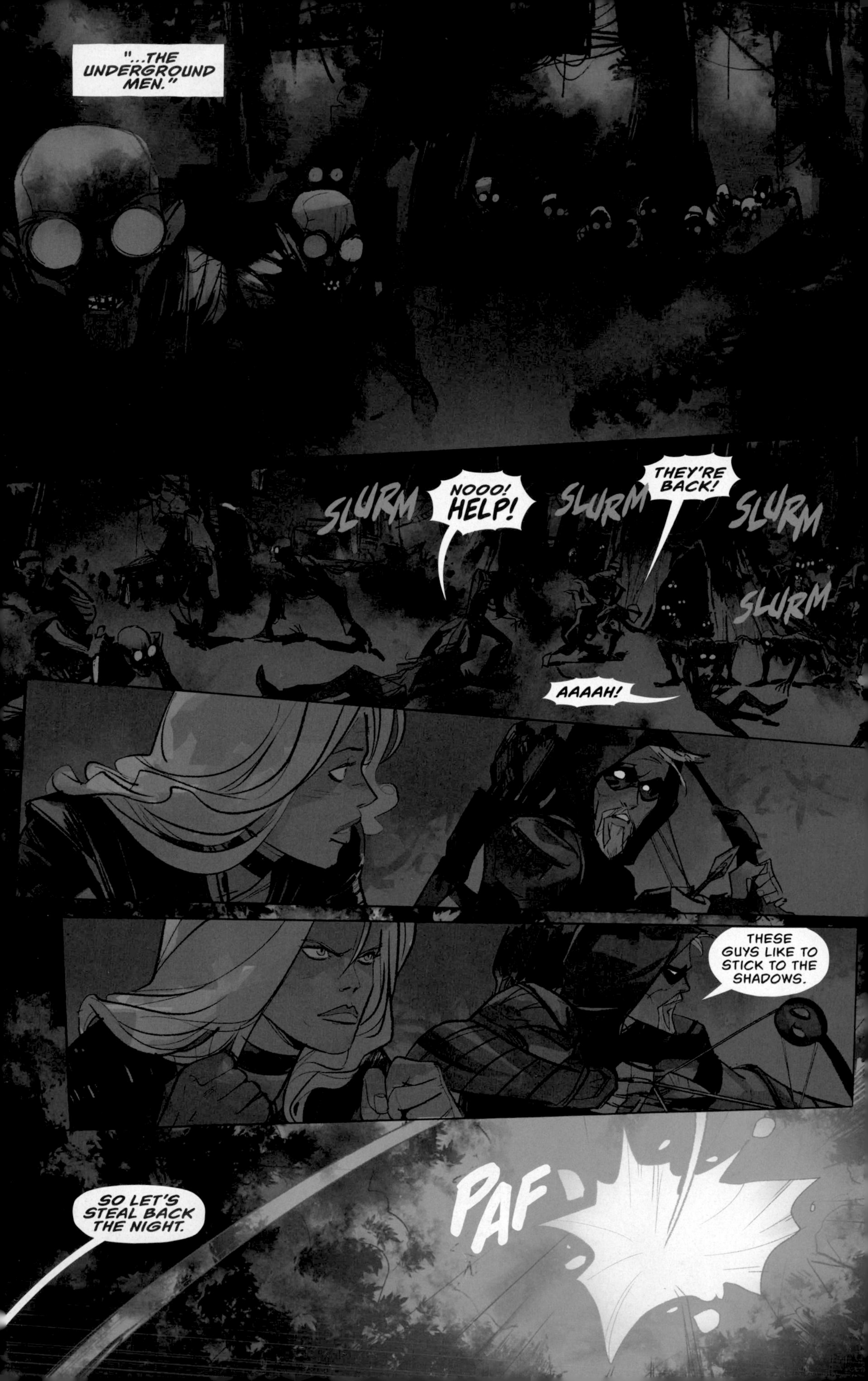
"...THE UNDERGROUND MEN."
SLURM
NOOO! HELP!
SLURM
THEY'RE BACK!
SLURM
SLURM
AAAAH!
THESE GUYS LIKE TO STICK TO THE SHADOWS.
SO LET'S STEAL BACK THE NIGHT.
PAF

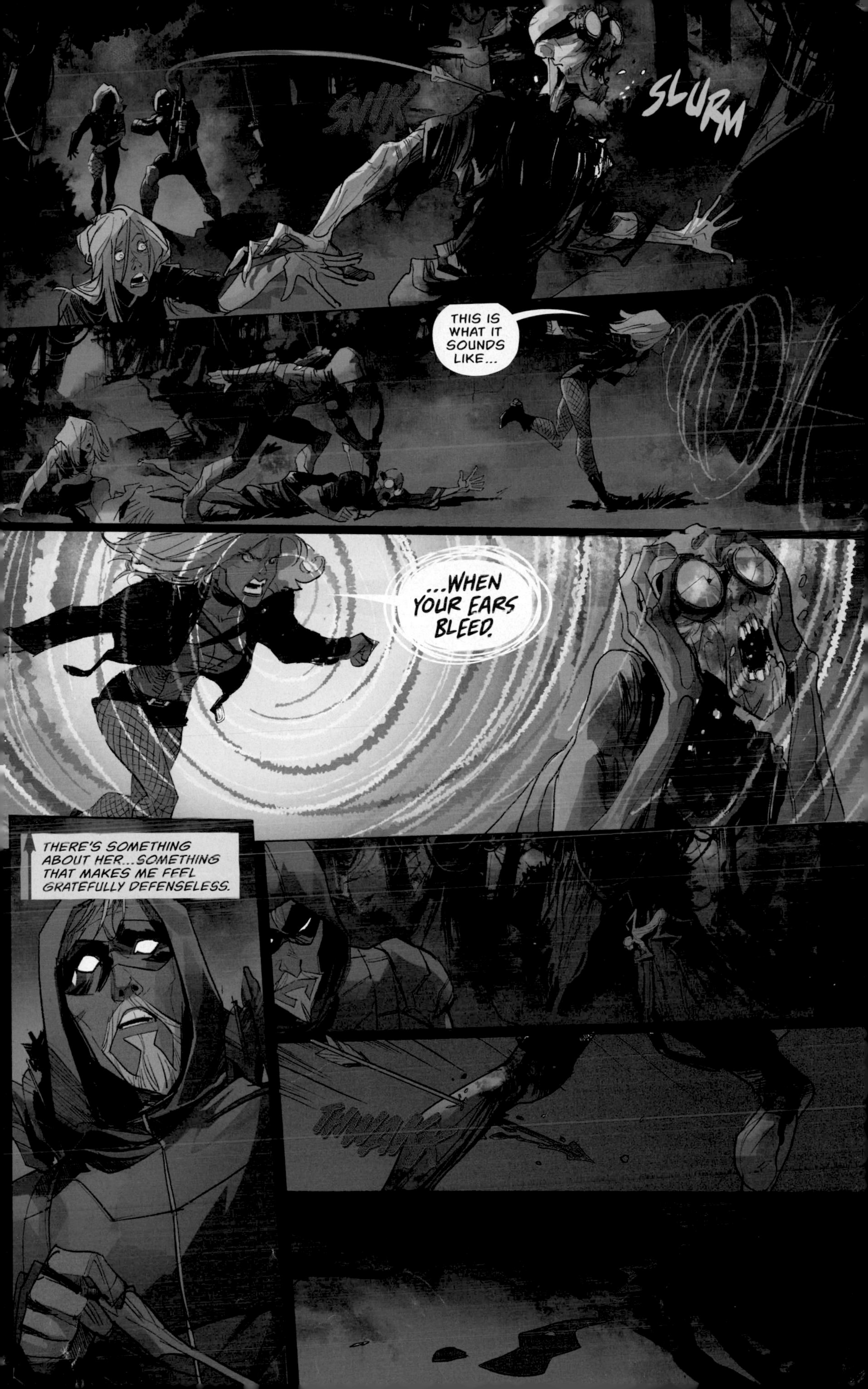
SNIK
SLURM
THIS IS WHAT IT SOUNDS LIKE...
...WHEN YOUR EARS BLEED.
THERE'S SOMETHING ABOUT HER...SOMETHING THAT MAKES ME FFFL GRATEFULLY DEFENSELESS.

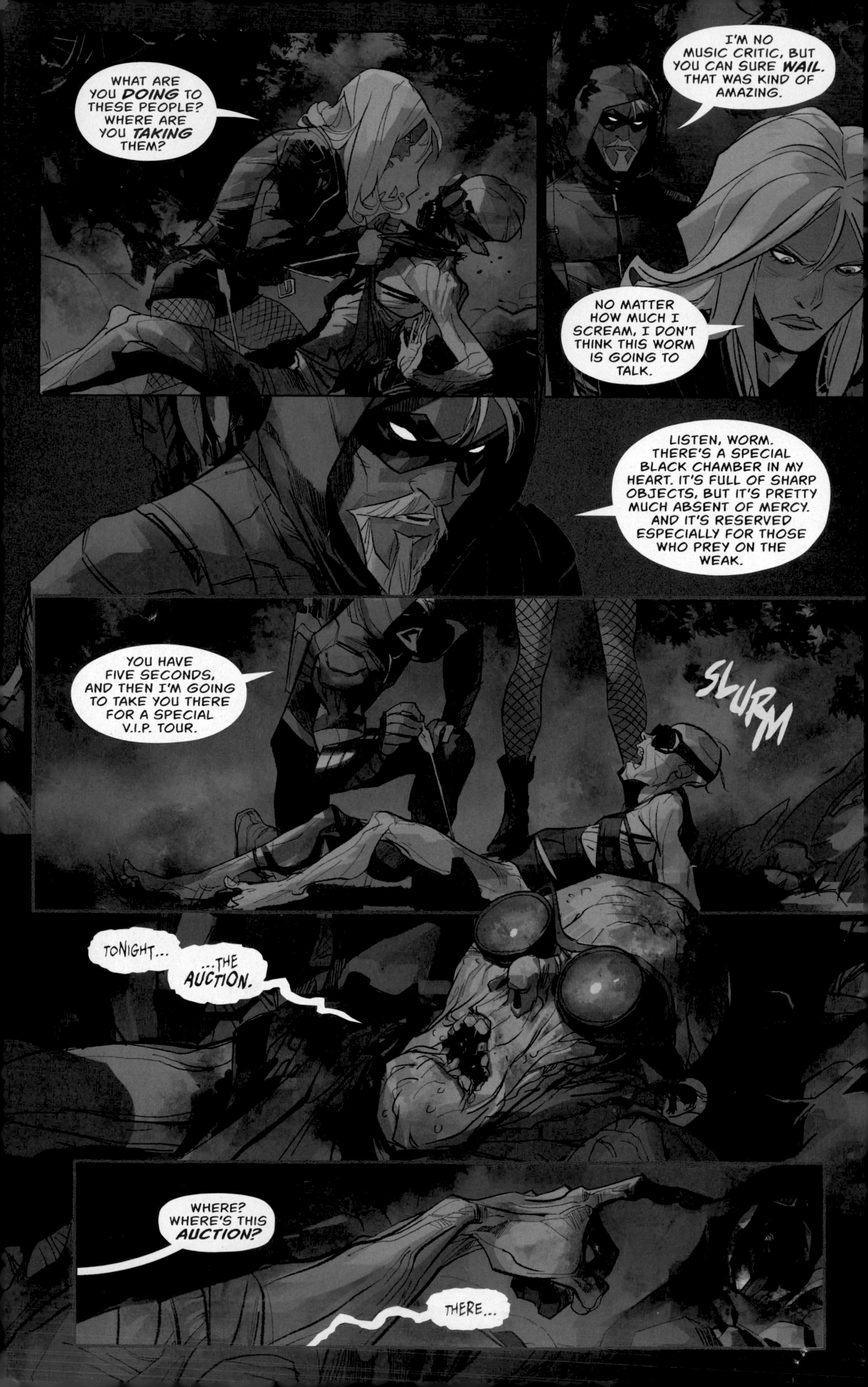
WHAT ARE YOU DOING TO THESE PEOPLE? WHERE ARE YOU TAKING THEM?
I'M NO MUSIC CRITIC, BUT YOU CAN SURE WAIL. THAT WAS KIND OF AMAZING.
NO MATTER HOW MUCH I SCREAM, I DON'T THINK THIS WORM IS GOING TO TALK.
LISTEN, WORM. THERE'S A SPECIAL BLACK CHAMBER IN MY HEART. IT'S FULL OF SHARP OBJECTS, BUT IT'S PRETTY MUCH ABSENT OF MERCY. AND IT'S RESERVED ESPECIALLY FOR THOSE WHO PREY ON THE WEAK.
YOU HAVE FIVE SECONDS, AND THEN I'M GOING TO TAKE YOU THERE FOR A SPECIAL V.I.P. TOUR.
SLURM
TONIGHT...
...THE AUCTION.
WHERE? WHERE'S THIS AUCTION?
THERE...

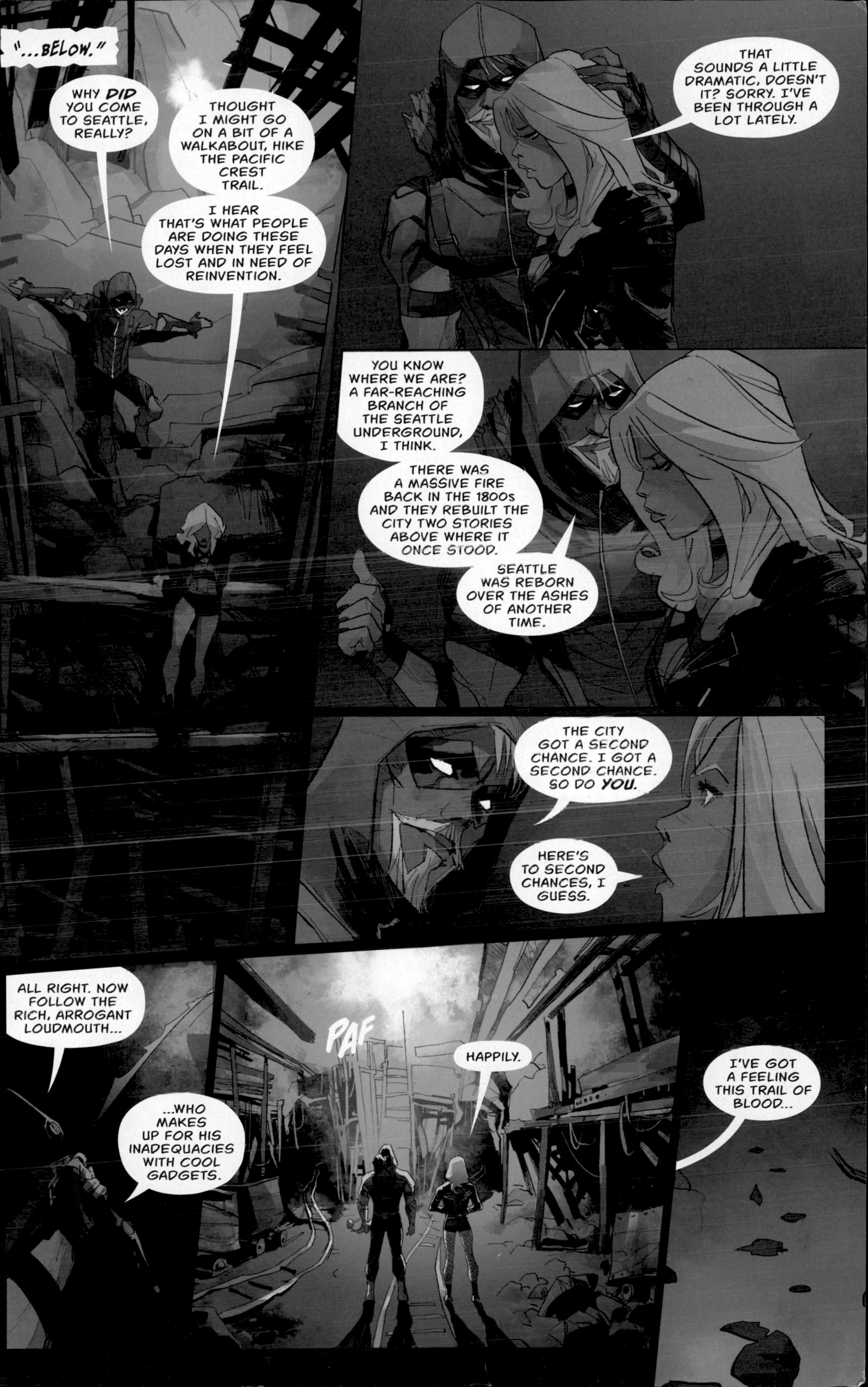
"...BELOW."
WHY DID YOU COME TO SEATTLE, REALLY?
THOUGHT I MIGHT GO ON A BIT OF A WALKABOUT, HIKE THE PACIFIC CREST TRAIL.
I HEAR THAT'S WHAT PEOPLE ARE DOING THESE DAYS WHEN THEY FEEL LOST AND IN NEED OF REINVENTION.
THAT SOUNDS A LITTLE DRAMATIC, DOESN'T IT? SORRY. I'VE BEEN THROUGH A LOT LATELY.
YOU KNOW WHERE WE ARE? A FAR-REACHING BRANCH OF THE SEATTLE UNDERGROUND, I THINK.
THERE WAS A MASSIVE FIRE BACK IN THE 1800s AND THEY REBUILT THE CITY TWO STORIES ABOVE WHERE IT ONCE STOOD.
SEATTLE WAS REBORN OVER THE ASHES OF ANOTHER TIME.
THE CITY GOT A SECOND CHANCE. I GOT A SECOND CHANCE. SO DO YOU.
HERE'S TO SECOND CHANCES, I GUESS.
ALL RIGHT. NOW FOLLOW THE RICH, ARROGANT LOUDMOUTH...
...WHO MAKES UP FOR HIS INADEQUACIES WITH COOL GADGETS.
PAF
HAPPILY.
I'VE GOT A FEELING THIS TRAIL OF BLOOD...

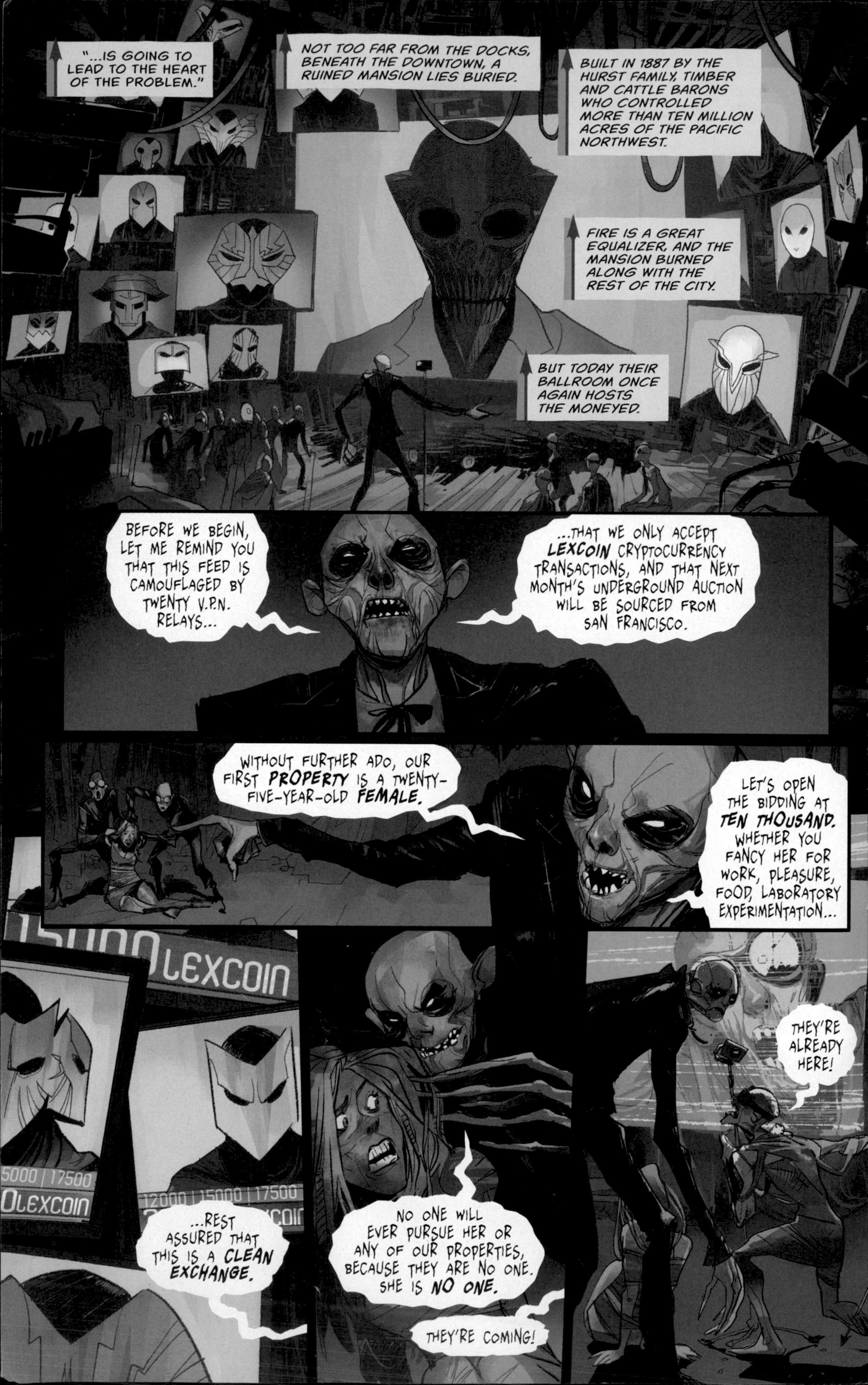
"...IS GOING TO LEAD TO THE HEART OF THE PROBLEM."
NOT TOO FAR FROM THE DOCKS, BENEATH THE DOWNTOWN, A RUINED MANSION LIES BURIED.
BUILT IN 1887 BY THE HURST FAMILY, TIMBER AND CATTLE BARONS WHO CONTROLLED MORE THAN TEN MILLION ACRES OF THE PACIFIC NORTHWEST.
FIRE IS A GREAT EQUALIZER, AND THE MANSION BURNED ALONG WITH THE REST OF THE CITY.
BUT TODAY THEIR BALLROOM ONCE AGAIN HOSTS THE MONEYED.
BEFORE WE BEGIN, LET ME REMIND YOU THAT THIS FEED IS CAMOUFLAGED BY TWENTY V.P.N. RELAYS...
...THAT WE ONLY ACCEPT LEXCOIN CRYPTOCURRENCY TRANSACTIONS, AND THAT NEXT MONTH'S UNDERGROUND AUCTION WILL BE SOURCED FROM SAN FRANCISCO.
WITHOUT FURTHER ADO, OUR FIRST PROPERTY IS A TWENTY-FIVE-YEAR-OLD FEMALE.
LET'S OPEN THE BIDDING AT TEN THOUSAND. WHETHER YOU FANCY HER FOR WORK, PLEASURE, FOOD, LABORATORY EXPERIMENTATION...
LEXCOIN
5000 | 17500
LEXCOIN
12000 | 15000 | 17500
...REST ASSURED THAT THIS IS A CLEAN EXCHANGE.
NO ONE WILL EVER PURSUE HER OR ANY OF OUR PROPERTIES, BECAUSE THEY ARE NO ONE. SHE IS NO ONE.
THEY'RE COMING!
THEY'RE ALREADY HERE!

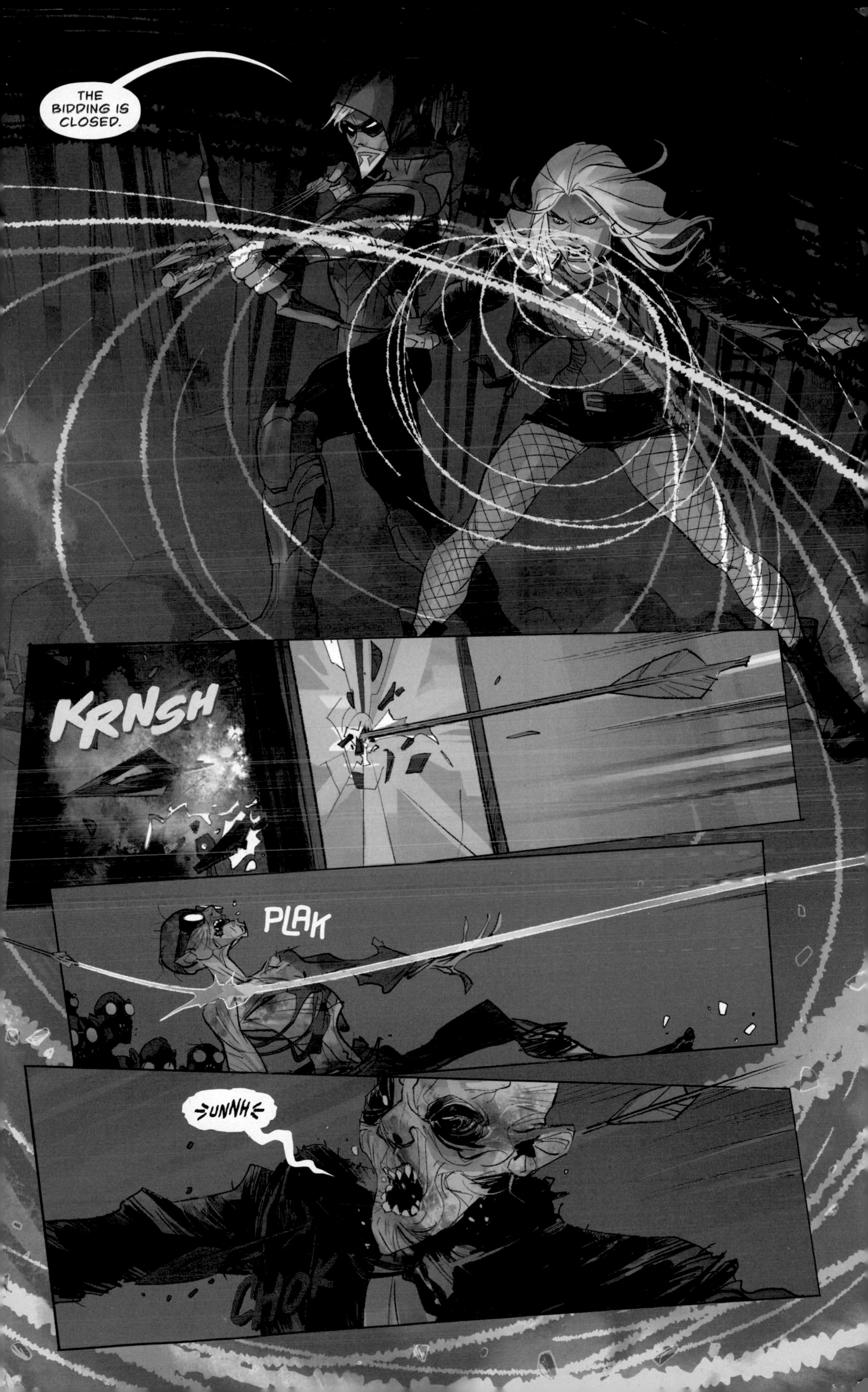
THE BIDDING IS CLOSED.
KRNSH
PLAK
UNNH
CHOK

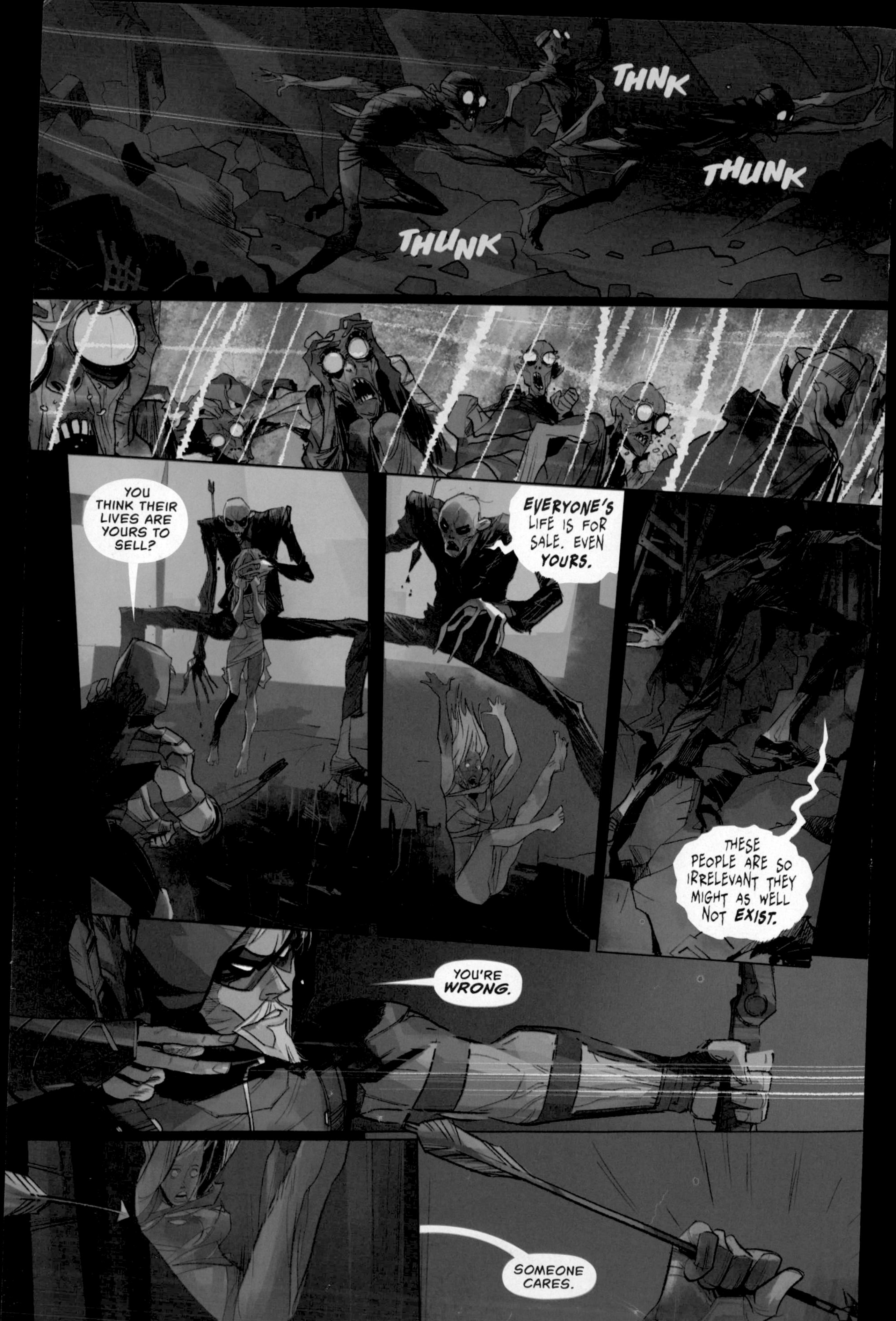
THNK
THUNK
THUNK
YOU THINK THEIR LIVES ARE YOURS TO SELL?
EVERYONE'S LIFE IS FOR SALE. EVEN YOURS.
THESE PEOPLE ARE SO IRRELEVANT THEY MIGHT AS WELL NOT EXIST.
YOU'RE WRONG.
SOMEONE CARES.

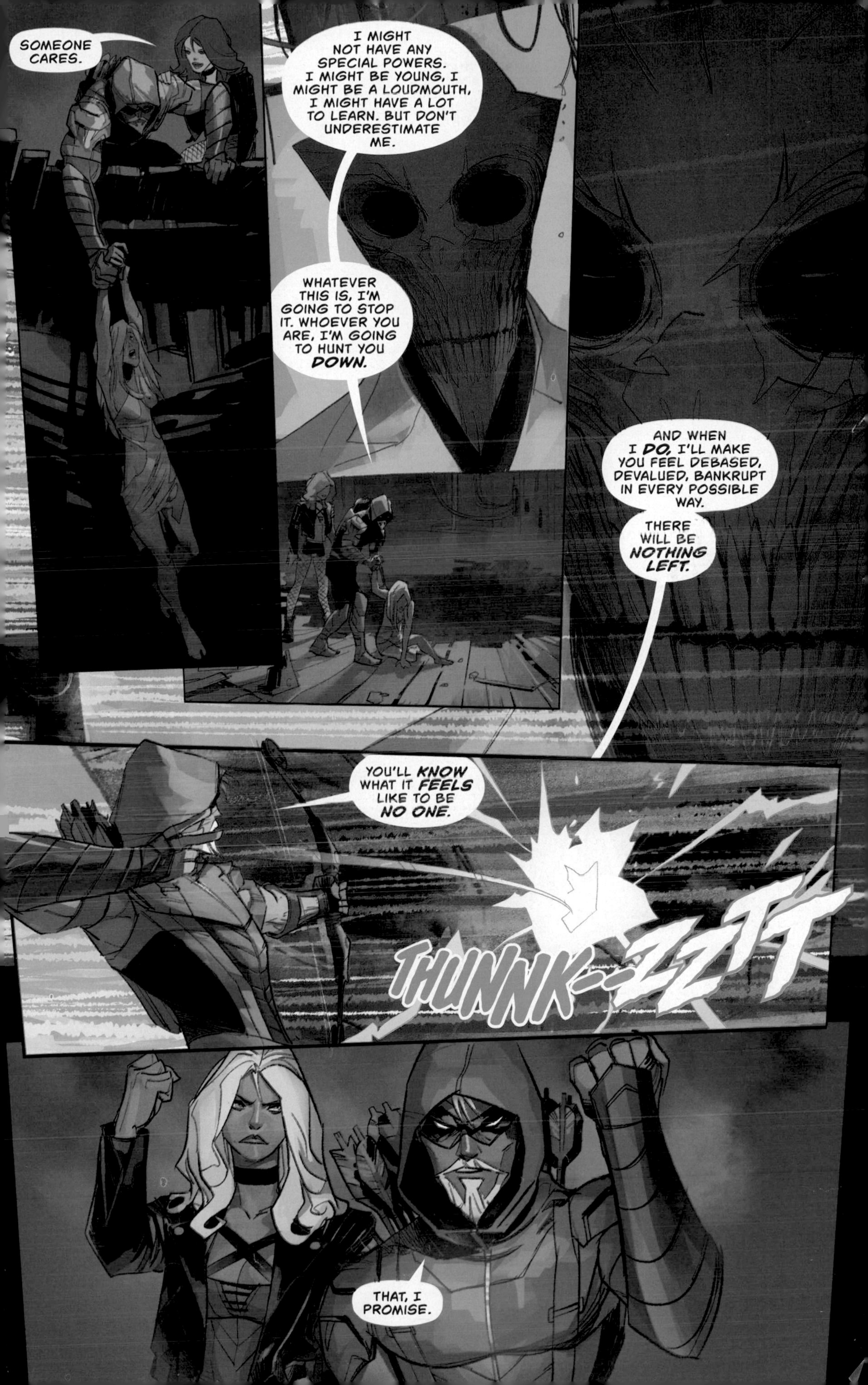
SOMEONE CARES.
I MIGHT NOT HAVE ANY SPECIAL POWERS. I MIGHT BE YOUNG, I MIGHT BE A LOUDMOUTH, I MIGHT HAVE A LOT TO LEARN. BUT DON'T UNDERESTIMATE ME.
WHATEVER THIS IS, I'M GOING TO STOP IT. WHOEVER YOU ARE, I'M GOING TO HUNT YOU **DOWN.**
AND WHEN I **DO,** I'LL MAKE YOU FEEL DEBASED, DEVALUED, BANKRUPT IN EVERY POSSIBLE WAY.
THERE WILL BE **NOTHING LEFT.**
YOU'LL **KNOW** WHAT IT **FEELS** LIKE TO BE **NO ONE.**
THUNNK--ZZTT
THAT, I PROMISE.

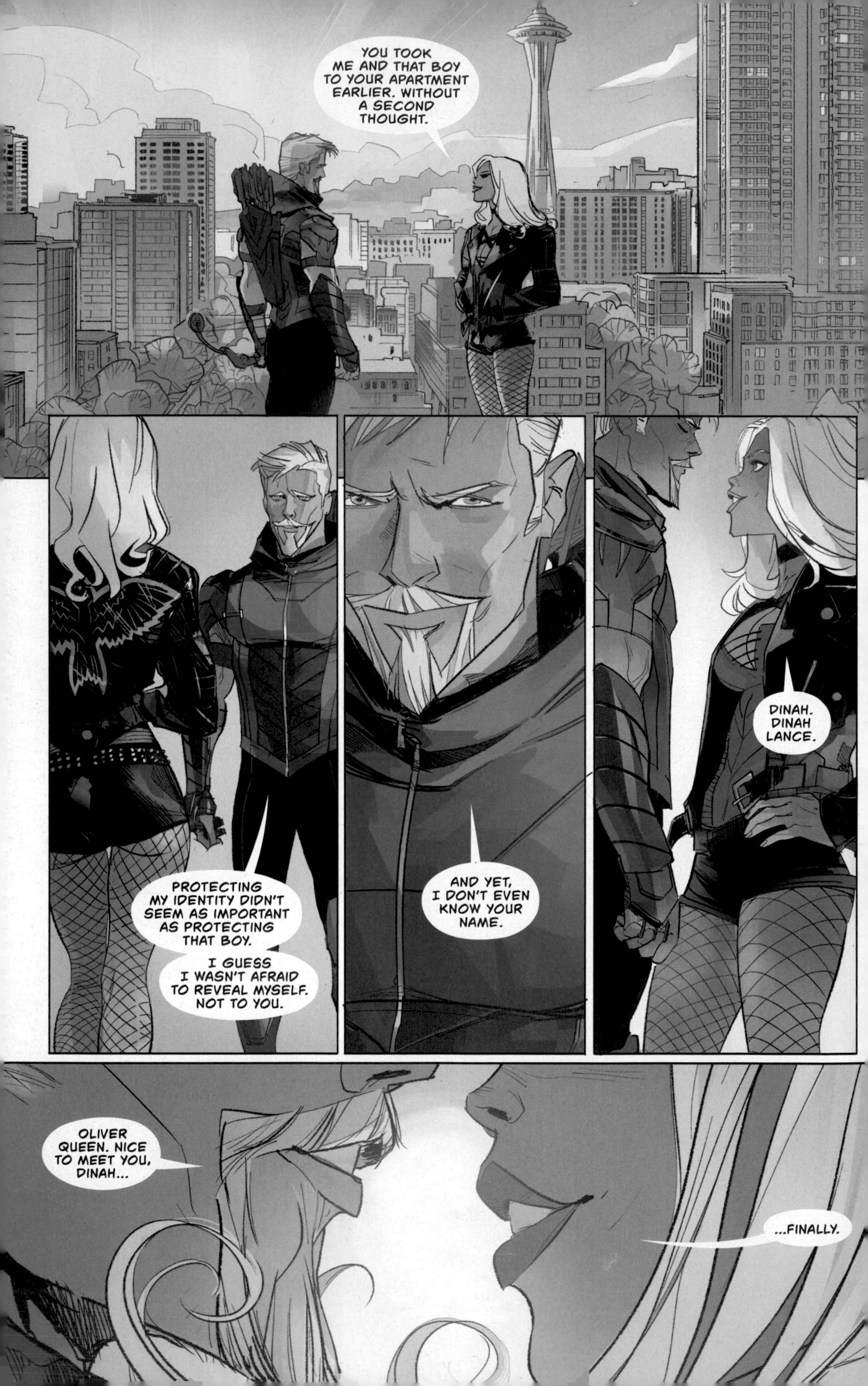
YOU TOOK ME AND THAT BOY TO YOUR APARTMENT EARLIER. WITHOUT A SECOND THOUGHT.
PROTECTING MY IDENTITY DIDN'T SEEM AS IMPORTANT AS PROTECTING THAT BOY.
I GUESS I WASN'T AFRAID TO REVEAL MYSELF. NOT TO YOU.
AND YET, I DON'T EVEN KNOW YOUR NAME.
DINAH. DINAH LANCE.
OLIVER QUEEN. NICE TO MEET YOU, DINAH...
...FINALLY.

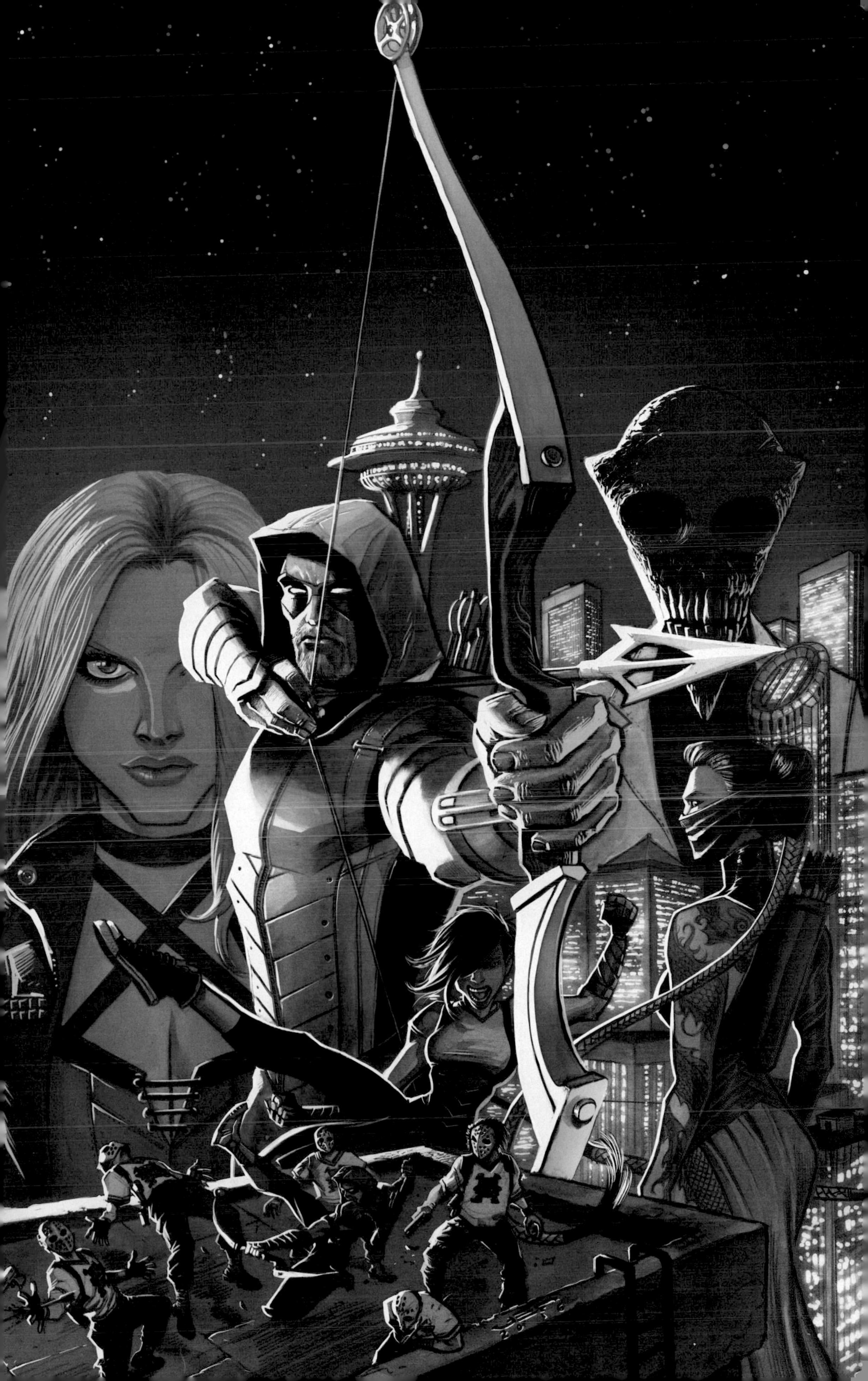

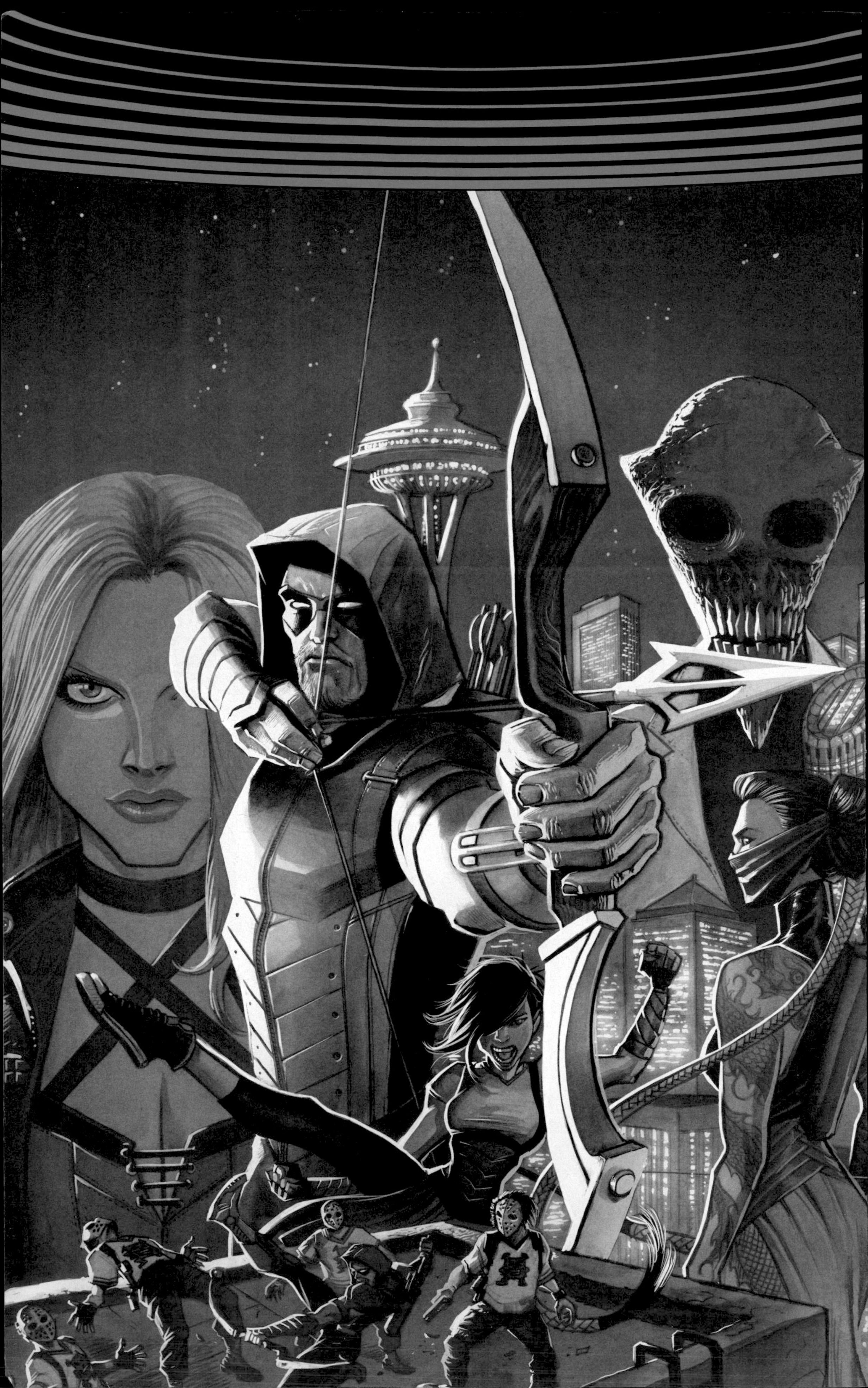

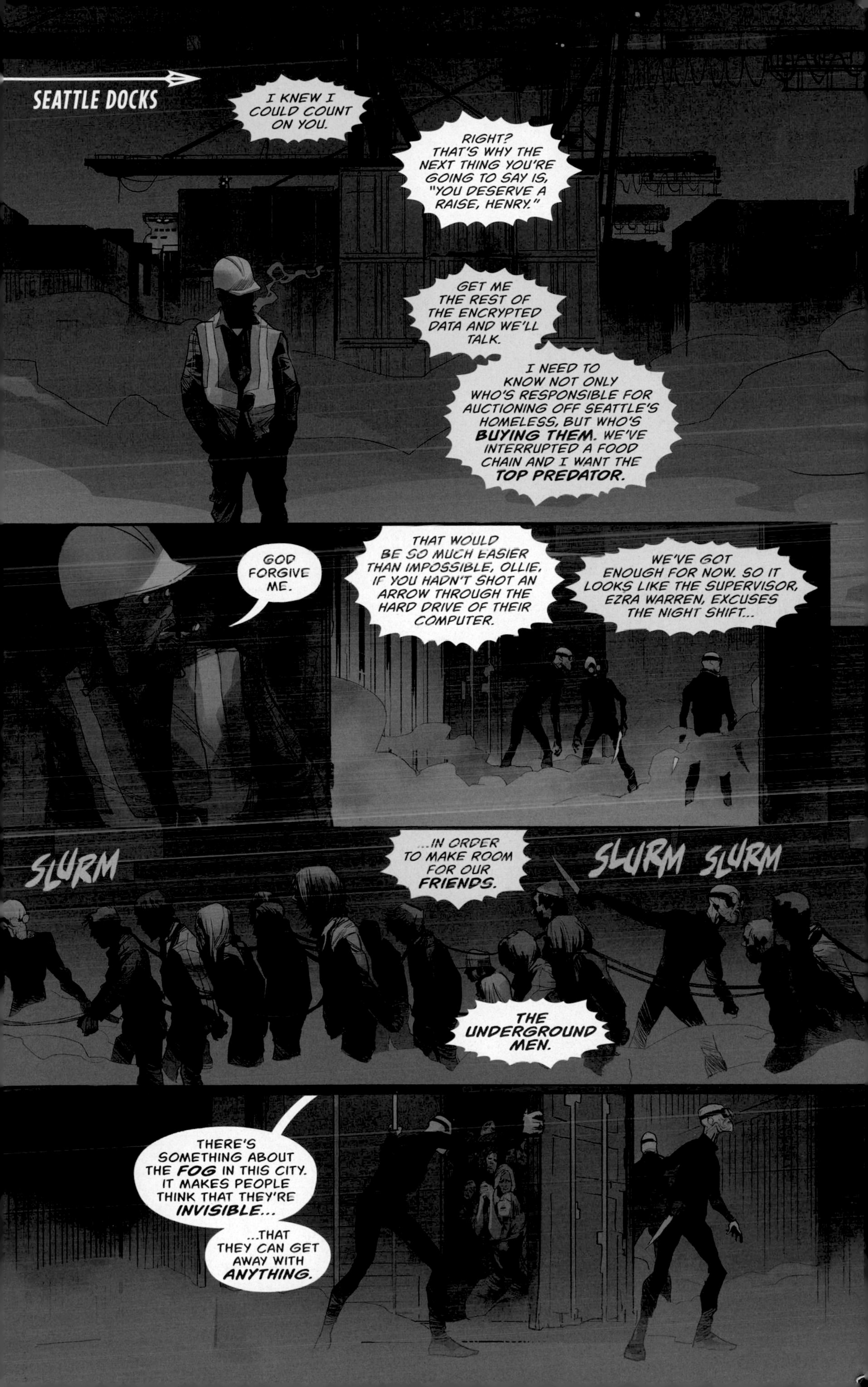
SEATTLE DOCKS
I KNEW I COULD COUNT ON YOU.
RIGHT? THAT'S WHY THE NEXT THING YOU'RE GOING TO SAY IS, "YOU DESERVE A RAISE, HENRY."
GET ME THE REST OF THE ENCRYPTED DATA AND WE'LL TALK.
I NEED TO KNOW NOT ONLY WHO'S RESPONSIBLE FOR AUCTIONING OFF SEATTLE'S HOMELESS, BUT WHO'S BUYING THEM. WE'VE INTERRUPTED A FOOD CHAIN AND I WANT THE TOP PREDATOR.
GOD FORGIVE ME.
THAT WOULD BE SO MUCH EASIER THAN IMPOSSIBLE, OLLIE, IF YOU HADN'T SHOT AN ARROW THROUGH THE HARD DRIVE OF THEIR COMPUTER.
WE'VE GOT ENOUGH FOR NOW. SO IT LOOKS LIKE THE SUPERVISOR, EZRA WARREN, EXCUSES THE NIGHT SHIFT...
SLURM
...IN ORDER TO MAKE ROOM FOR OUR FRIENDS.
SLURM SLURM
THE UNDERGROUND MEN.
THERE'S SOMETHING ABOUT THE FOG IN THIS CITY. IT MAKES PEOPLE THINK THAT THEY'RE INVISIBLE...
...THAT THEY CAN GET AWAY WITH ANYTHING.

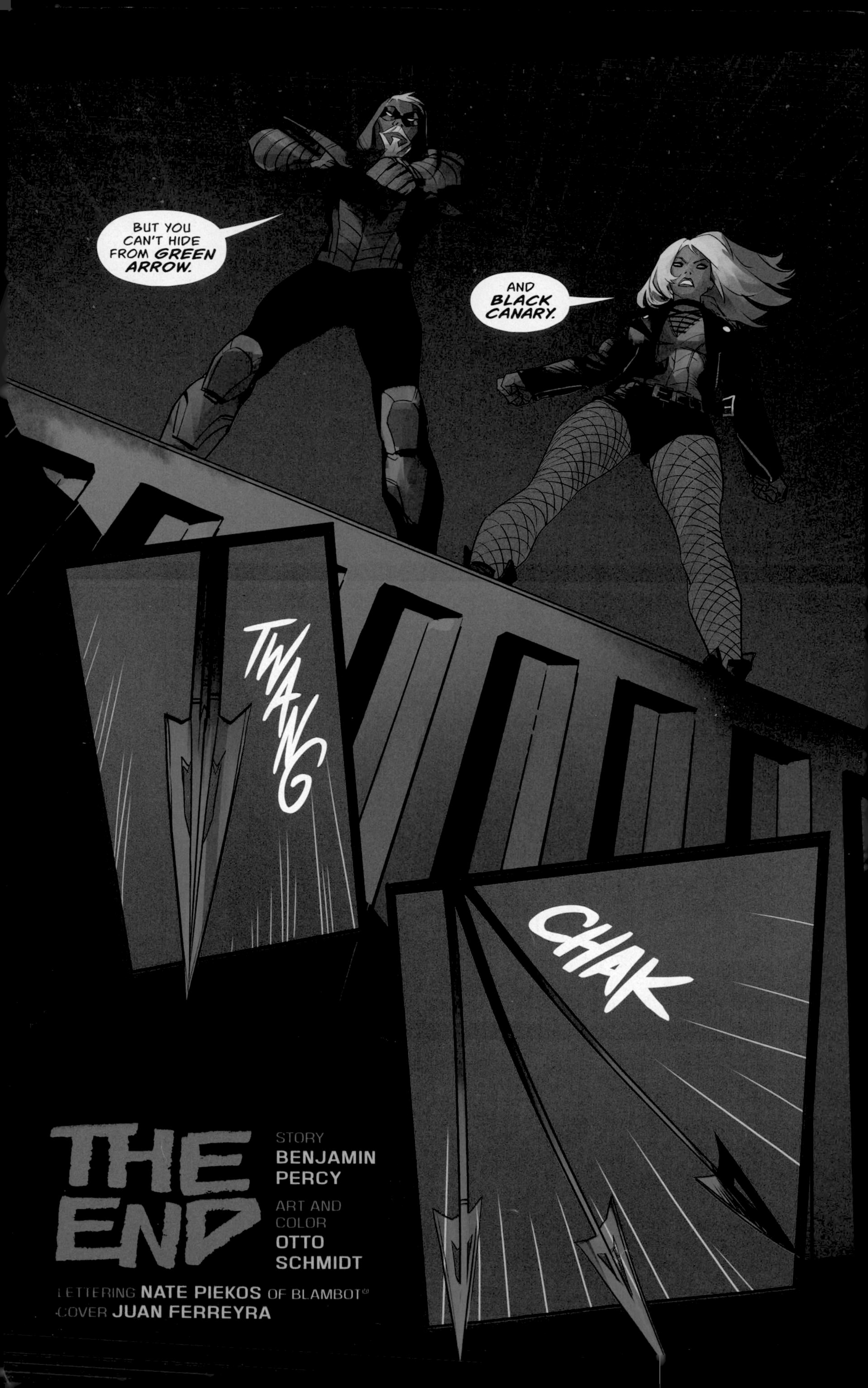
BUT YOU CAN'T HIDE FROM GREEN ARROW.
AND BLACK CANARY.
TWANG
CHAK
THE END
STORY BENJAMIN PERCY
ART AND COLOR OTTO SCHMIDT
LETTERING NATE PIEKOS OF BLAMBOT®
COVER JUAN FERREYRA

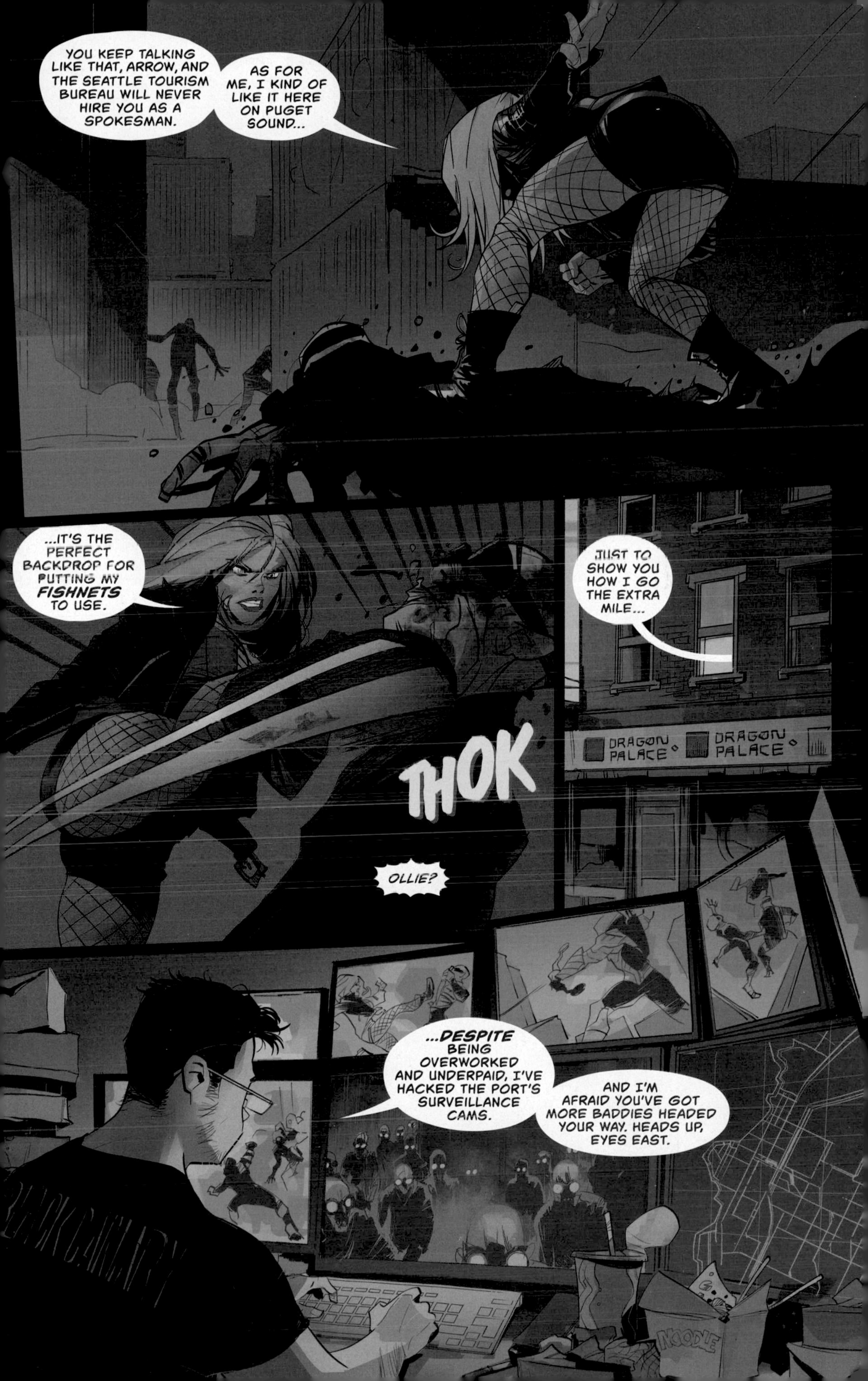
YOU KEEP TALKING LIKE THAT, ARROW, AND THE SEATTLE TOURISM BUREAU WILL NEVER HIRE YOU AS A SPOKESMAN.
AS FOR ME, I KIND OF LIKE IT HERE ON PUGET SOUND...
...IT'S THE PERFECT BACKDROP FOR PUTTING MY FISHNETS TO USE.
THOK
OLLIE?
JUST TO SHOW YOU HOW I GO THE EXTRA MILE...
DRAGON PALACE
DRAGON PALACE
...DESPITE BEING OVERWORKED AND UNDERPAID, I'VE HACKED THE PORT'S SURVEILLANCE CAMS.
AND I'M AFRAID YOU'VE GOT MORE BADDIES HEADED YOUR WAY. HEADS UP, EYES EAST.
NOODLE

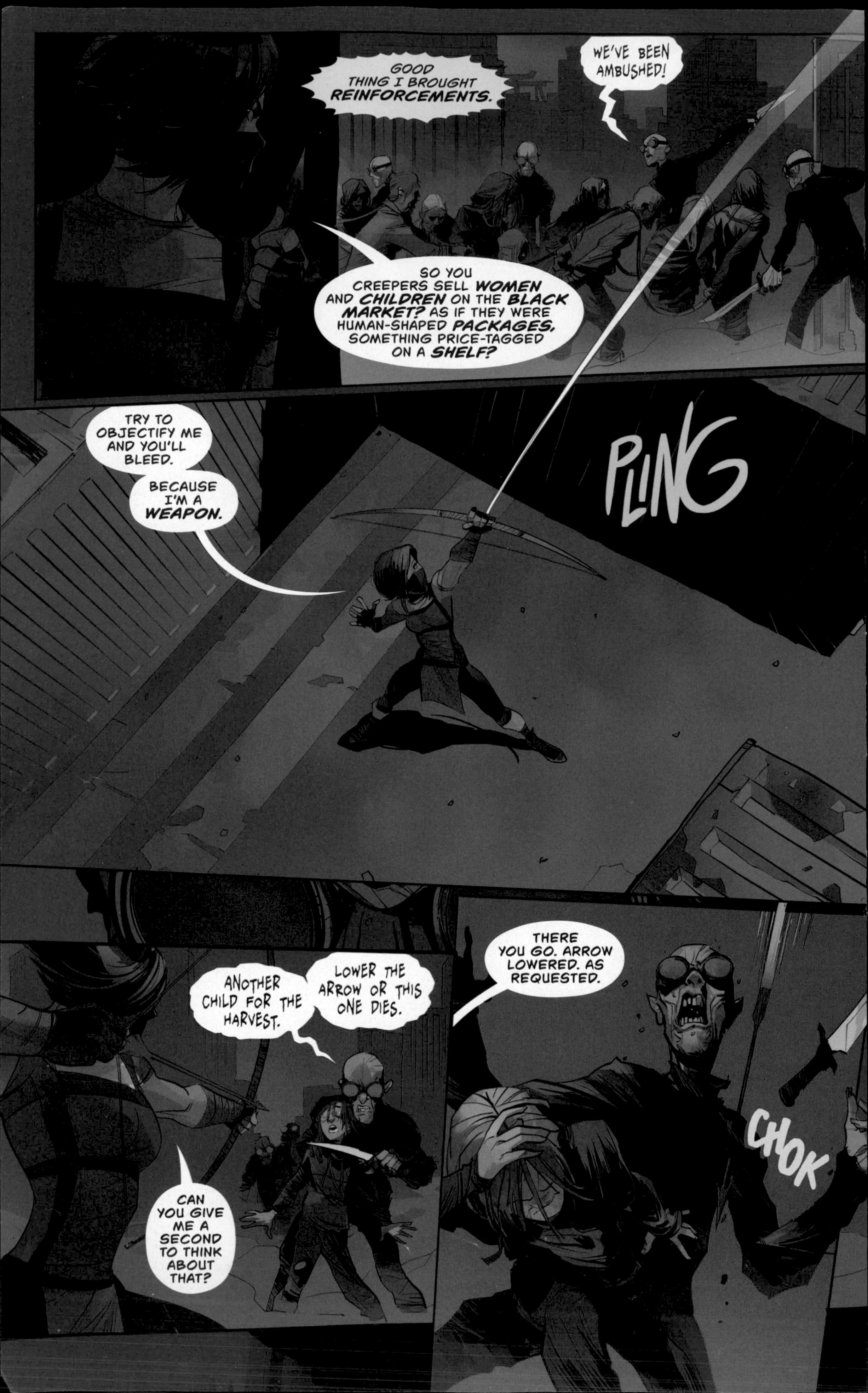
GOOD THING I BROUGHT REINFORCEMENTS.
WE'VE BEEN AMBUSHED!
SO YOU CREEPERS SELL WOMEN AND CHILDREN ON THE BLACK MARKET? AS IF THEY WERE HUMAN-SHAPED PACKAGES, SOMETHING PRICE-TAGGED ON A SHELF?
TRY TO OBJECTIFY ME AND YOU'LL BLEED.
BECAUSE I'M A WEAPON.
PLING
ANOTHER CHILD FOR THE HARVEST.
LOWER THE ARROW OR THIS ONE DIES.
CAN YOU GIVE ME A SECOND TO THINK ABOUT THAT?
THERE YOU GO. ARROW LOWERED. AS REQUESTED.
CHOK

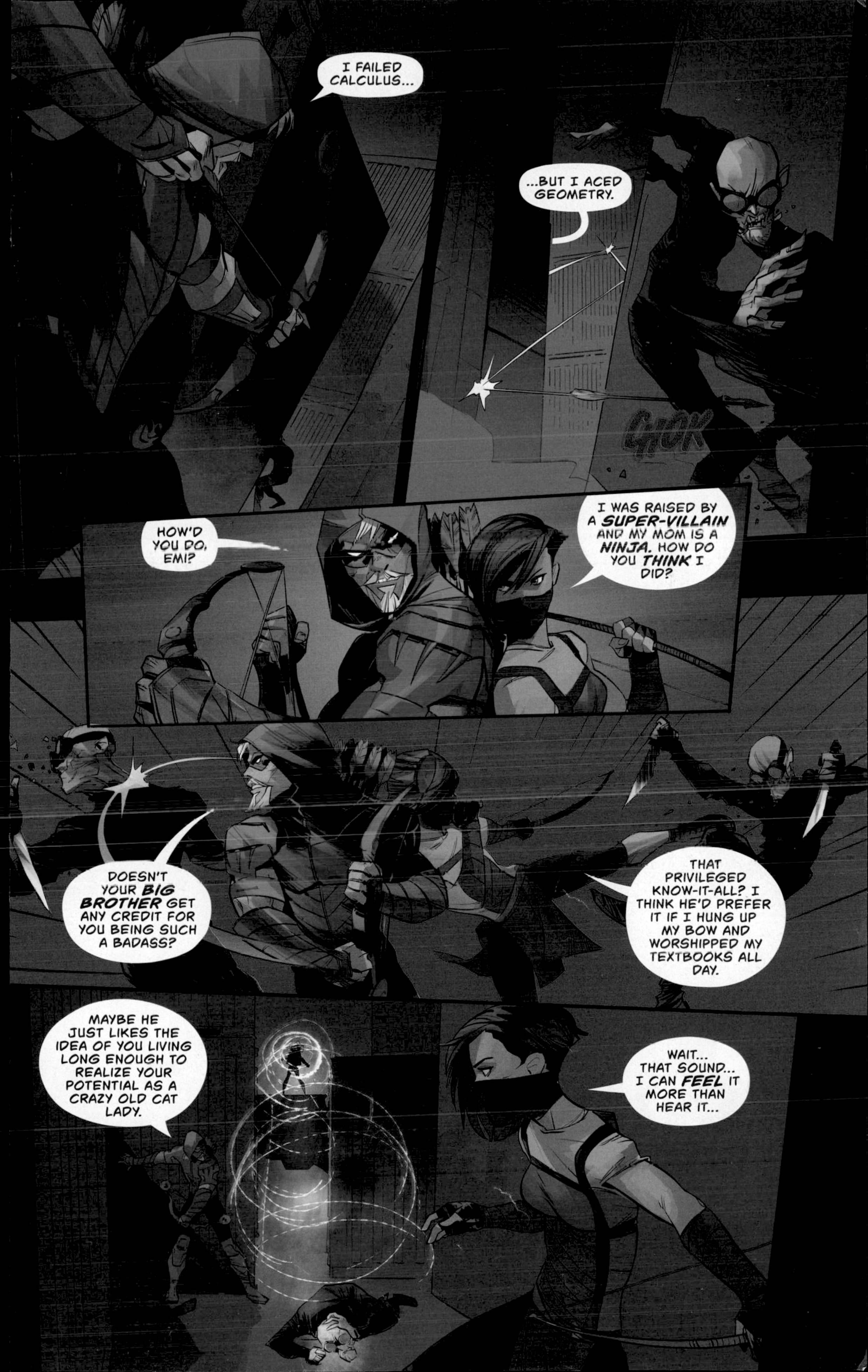
I FAILED CALCULUS...
...BUT I ACED GEOMETRY.
GHOK
HOW'D YOU DO, EMI?
I WAS RAISED BY A SUPER-VILLAIN AND MY MOM IS A NINJA. HOW DO YOU THINK I DID?
DOESN'T YOUR BIG BROTHER GET ANY CREDIT FOR YOU BEING SUCH A BADASS?
THAT PRIVILEGED KNOW-IT-ALL? I THINK HE'D PREFER IT IF I HUNG UP MY BOW AND WORSHIPPED MY TEXTBOOKS ALL DAY.
MAYBE HE JUST LIKES THE IDEA OF YOU LIVING LONG ENOUGH TO REALIZE YOUR POTENTIAL AS A CRAZY OLD CAT LADY.
WAIT... THAT SOUND... I CAN FEEL IT MORE THAN HEAR IT...

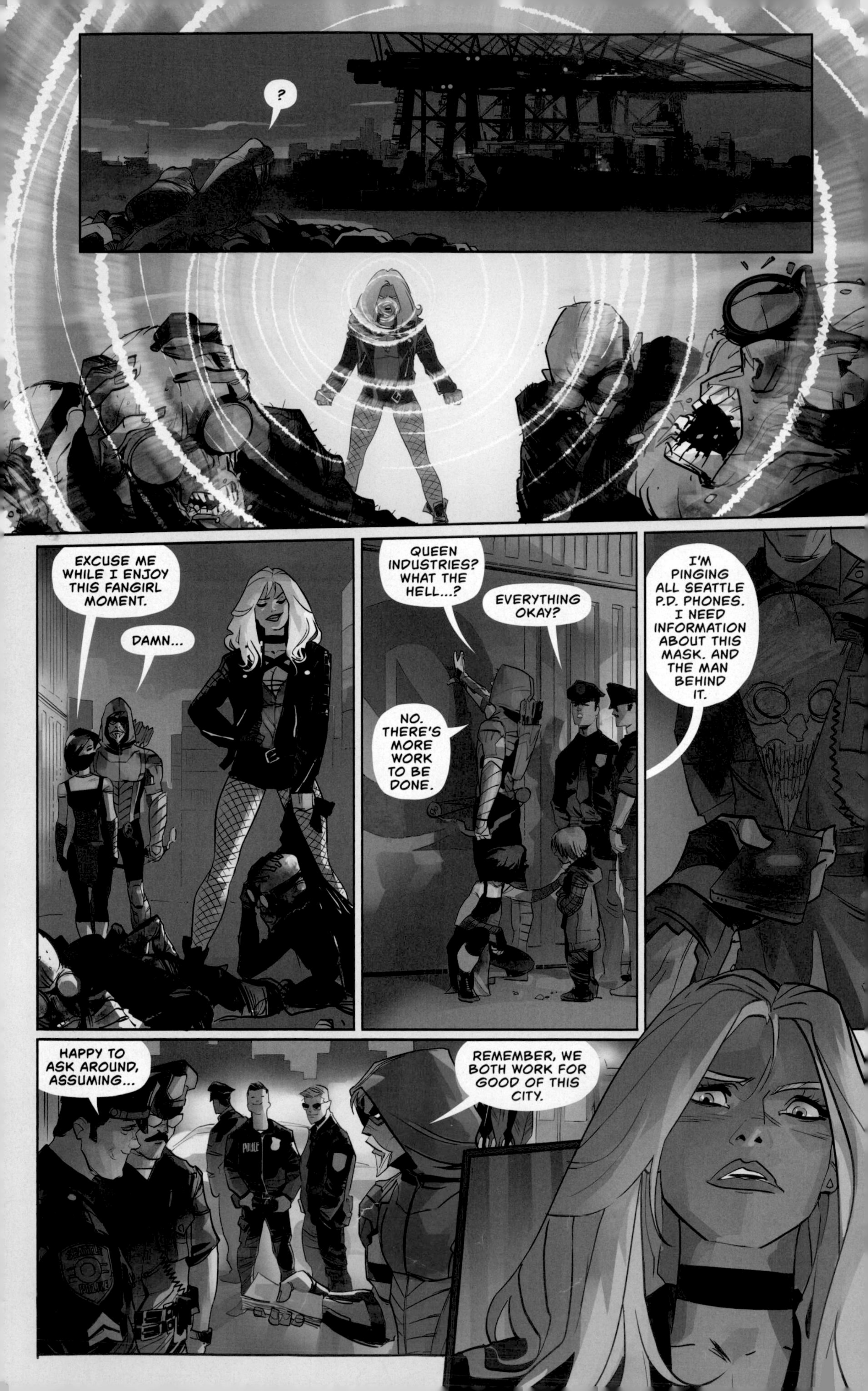
?
EXCUSE ME WHILE I ENJOY THIS FANGIRL MOMENT.
DAMN...
QUEEN INDUSTRIES? WHAT THE HELL...?
EVERYTHING OKAY?
NO. THERE'S MORE WORK TO BE DONE.
I'M PINGING ALL SEATTLE P.D. PHONES. I NEED INFORMATION ABOUT THIS MASK. AND THE MAN BEHIND IT.
HAPPY TO ASK AROUND, ASSUMING...
REMEMBER, WE BOTH WORK FOR GOOD OF THIS CITY.

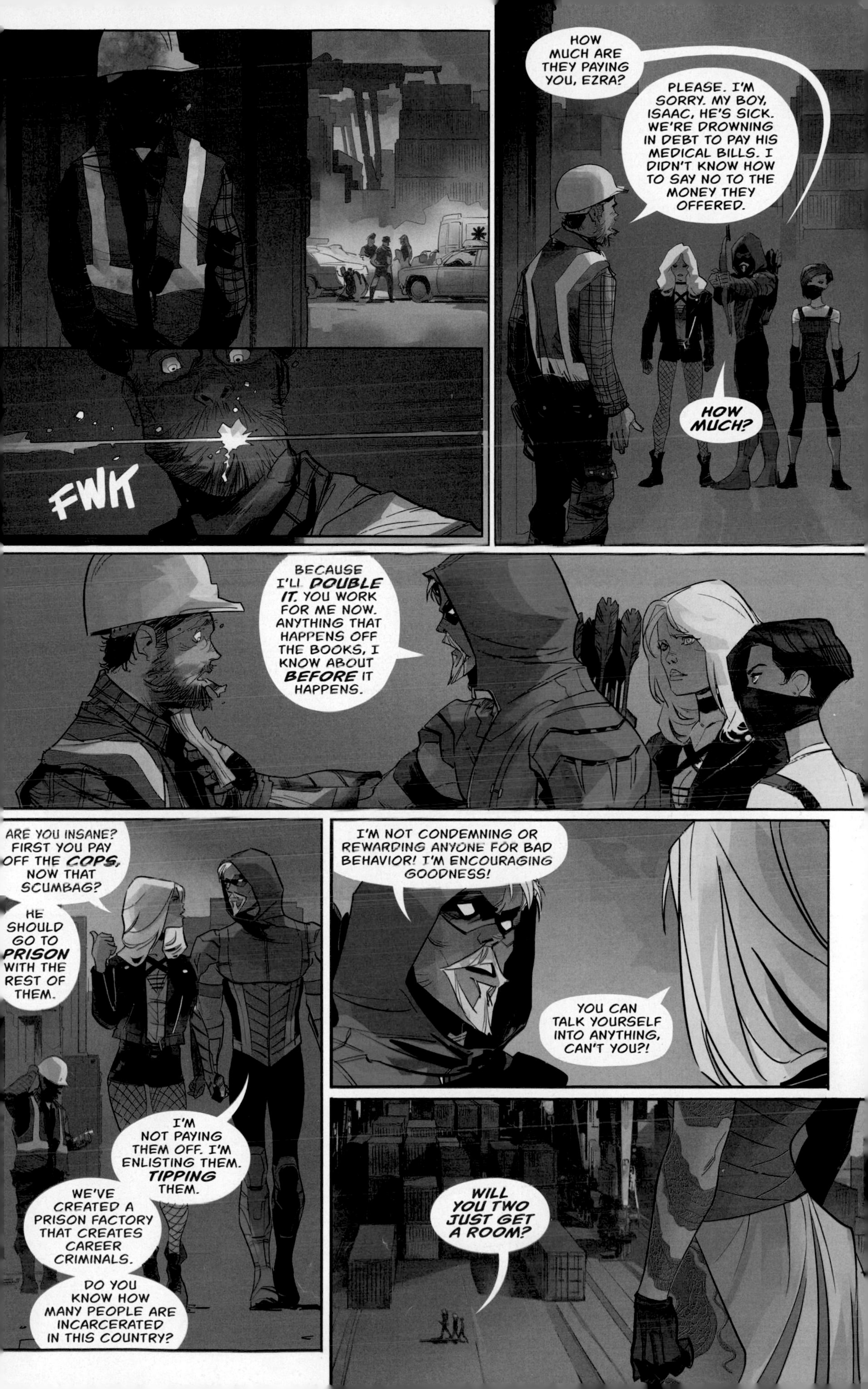
FWK
HOW MUCH ARE THEY PAYING YOU, EZRA?
PLEASE. I'M SORRY. MY BOY, ISAAC, HE'S SICK. WE'RE DROWNING IN DEBT TO PAY HIS MEDICAL BILLS. I DIDN'T KNOW HOW TO SAY NO TO THE MONEY THEY OFFERED.
HOW MUCH?
BECAUSE I'LL DOUBLE IT. YOU WORK FOR ME NOW. ANYTHING THAT HAPPENS OFF THE BOOKS, I KNOW ABOUT BEFORE IT HAPPENS.
ARE YOU INSANE? FIRST YOU PAY OFF THE COPS, NOW THAT SCUMBAG?
HE SHOULD GO TO PRISON WITH THE REST OF THEM.
I'M NOT PAYING THEM OFF. I'M ENLISTING THEM. TIPPING THEM.
WE'VE CREATED A PRISON FACTORY THAT CREATES CAREER CRIMINALS.
DO YOU KNOW HOW MANY PEOPLE ARE INCARCERATED IN THIS COUNTRY?
I'M NOT CONDEMNING OR REWARDING ANYONE FOR BAD BEHAVIOR! I'M ENCOURAGING GOODNESS!
YOU CAN TALK YOURSELF INTO ANYTHING, CAN'T YOU?!
WILL YOU TWO JUST GET A ROOM?

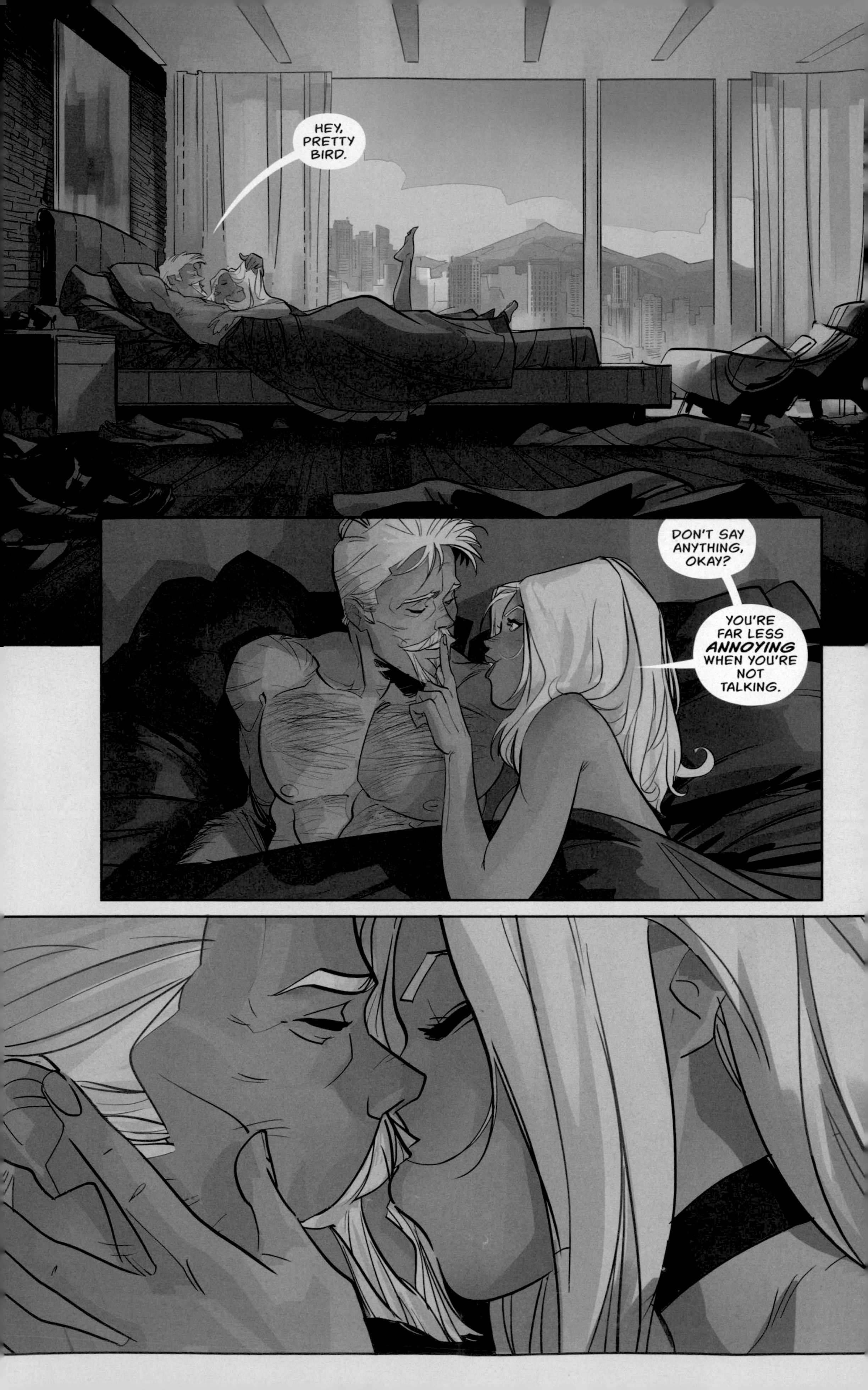
HEY, PRETTY BIRD.
DON'T SAY ANYTHING, OKAY?
YOU'RE FAR LESS ANNOYING WHEN YOU'RE NOT TALKING.

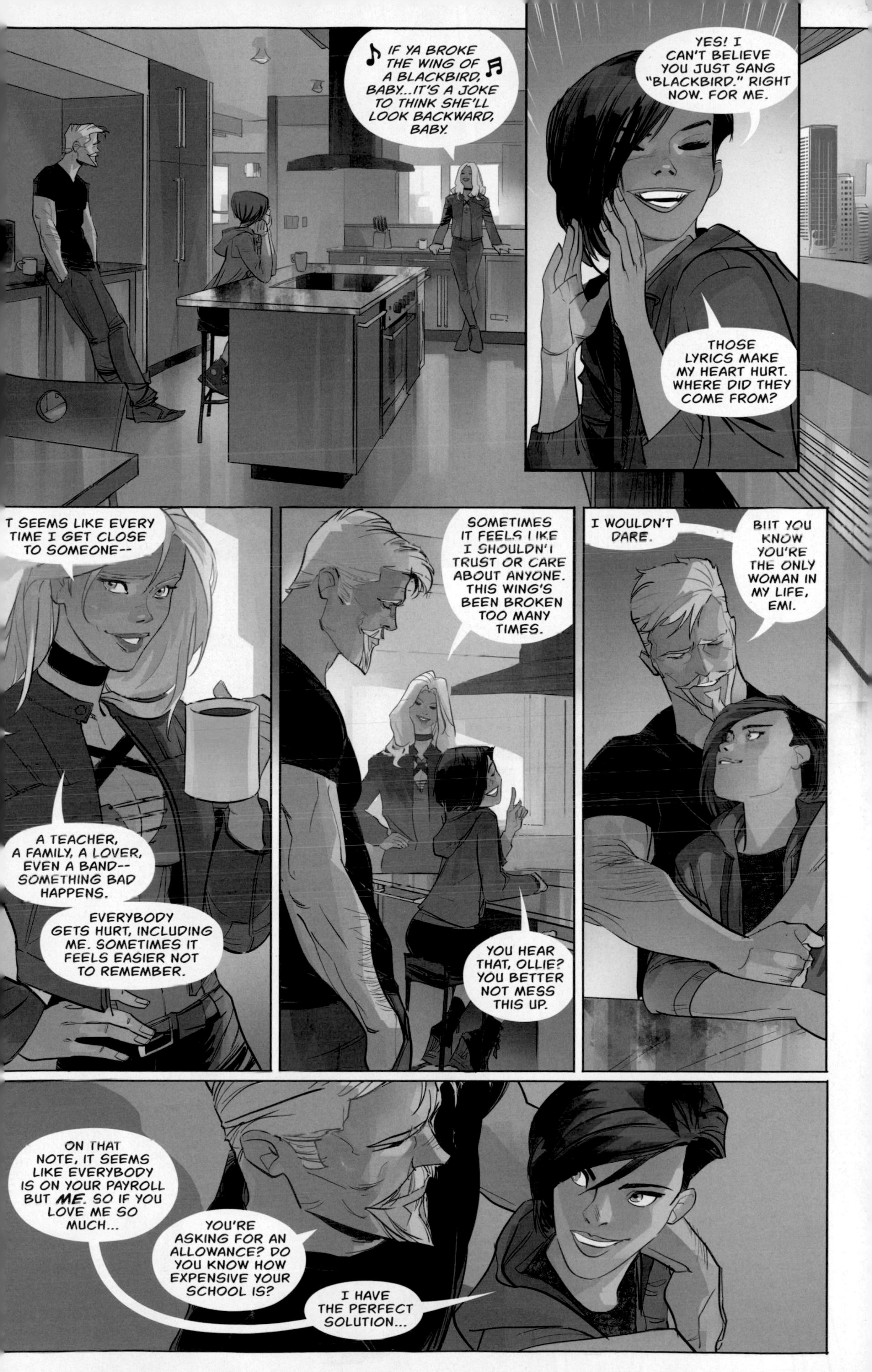
♪ IF YA BROKE THE WING OF A BLACKBIRD, BABY...IT'S A JOKE TO THINK SHE'LL LOOK BACKWARD, BABY. ♫
YES! I CAN'T BELIEVE YOU JUST SANG "BLACKBIRD." RIGHT NOW. FOR ME.
THOSE LYRICS MAKE MY HEART HURT. WHERE DID THEY COME FROM?
T SEEMS LIKE EVERY TIME I GET CLOSE TO SOMEONE--
A TEACHER, A FAMILY, A LOVER, EVEN A BAND--SOMETHING BAD HAPPENS.
EVERYBODY GETS HURT, INCLUDING ME. SOMETIMES IT FEELS EASIER NOT TO REMEMBER.
SOMETIMES IT FEELS LIKE I SHOULDN'T TRUST OR CARE ABOUT ANYONE. THIS WING'S BEEN BROKEN TOO MANY TIMES.
YOU HEAR THAT, OLLIE? YOU BETTER NOT MESS THIS UP.
I WOULDN'T DARE.
BUT YOU KNOW YOU'RE THE ONLY WOMAN IN MY LIFE, EMI.
ON THAT NOTE, IT SEEMS LIKE EVERYBODY IS ON YOUR PAYROLL BUT *ME*. SO IF YOU LOVE ME SO MUCH...
YOU'RE ASKING FOR AN ALLOWANCE? DO YOU KNOW HOW EXPENSIVE YOUR SCHOOL IS?
I HAVE THE PERFECT SOLUTION...

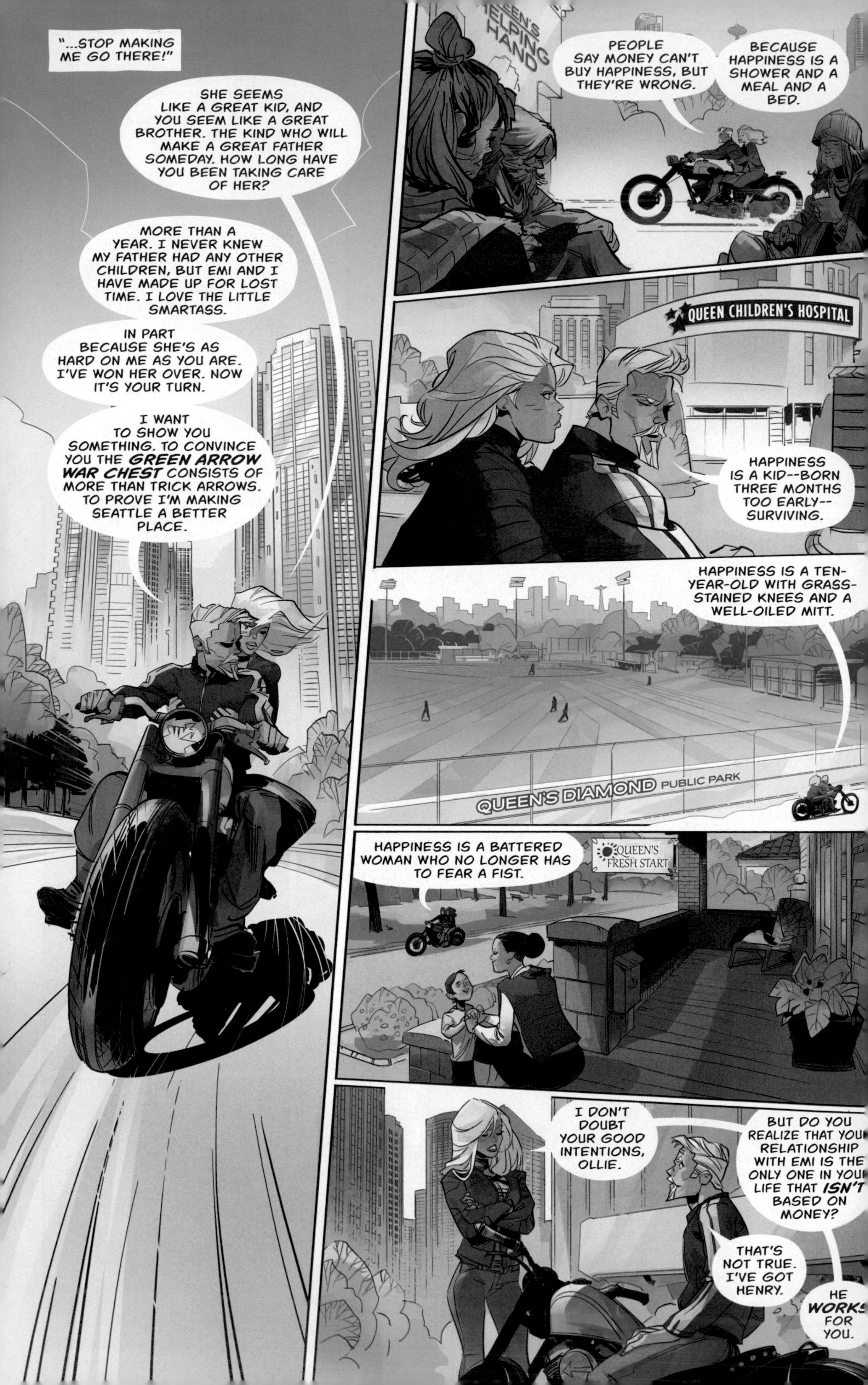
"...STOP MAKING ME GO THERE!"
SHE SEEMS LIKE A GREAT KID, AND YOU SEEM LIKE A GREAT BROTHER. THE KIND WHO WILL MAKE A GREAT FATHER SOMEDAY. HOW LONG HAVE YOU BEEN TAKING CARE OF HER?
MORE THAN A YEAR. I NEVER KNEW MY FATHER HAD ANY OTHER CHILDREN, BUT EMI AND I HAVE MADE UP FOR LOST TIME. I LOVE THE LITTLE SMARTASS.
IN PART BECAUSE SHE'S AS HARD ON ME AS YOU ARE. I'VE WON HER OVER. NOW IT'S YOUR TURN.
I WANT TO SHOW YOU SOMETHING. TO CONVINCE YOU THE **GREEN ARROW WAR CHEST** CONSISTS OF MORE THAN TRICK ARROWS. TO PROVE I'M MAKING SEATTLE A BETTER PLACE.
HELPING HAND
PEOPLE SAY MONEY CAN'T BUY HAPPINESS, BUT THEY'RE WRONG.
BECAUSE HAPPINESS IS A SHOWER AND A MEAL AND A BED.
QUEEN CHILDREN'S HOSPITAL
HAPPINESS IS A KID--BORN THREE MONTHS TOO EARLY--SURVIVING.
HAPPINESS IS A TEN-YEAR-OLD WITH GRASS-STAINED KNEES AND A WELL-OILED MITT.
QUEEN'S DIAMOND PUBLIC PARK
HAPPINESS IS A BATTERED WOMAN WHO NO LONGER HAS TO FEAR A FIST.
QUEEN'S FRESH START
I DON'T DOUBT YOUR GOOD INTENTIONS, OLLIE.
BUT DO YOU REALIZE THAT YOU RELATIONSHIP WITH EMI IS THE ONLY ONE IN YOU LIFE THAT ***ISN'T*** BASED ON MONEY?
THAT'S NOT TRUE. I'VE GOT HENRY.
HE ***WORKS*** FOR YOU.

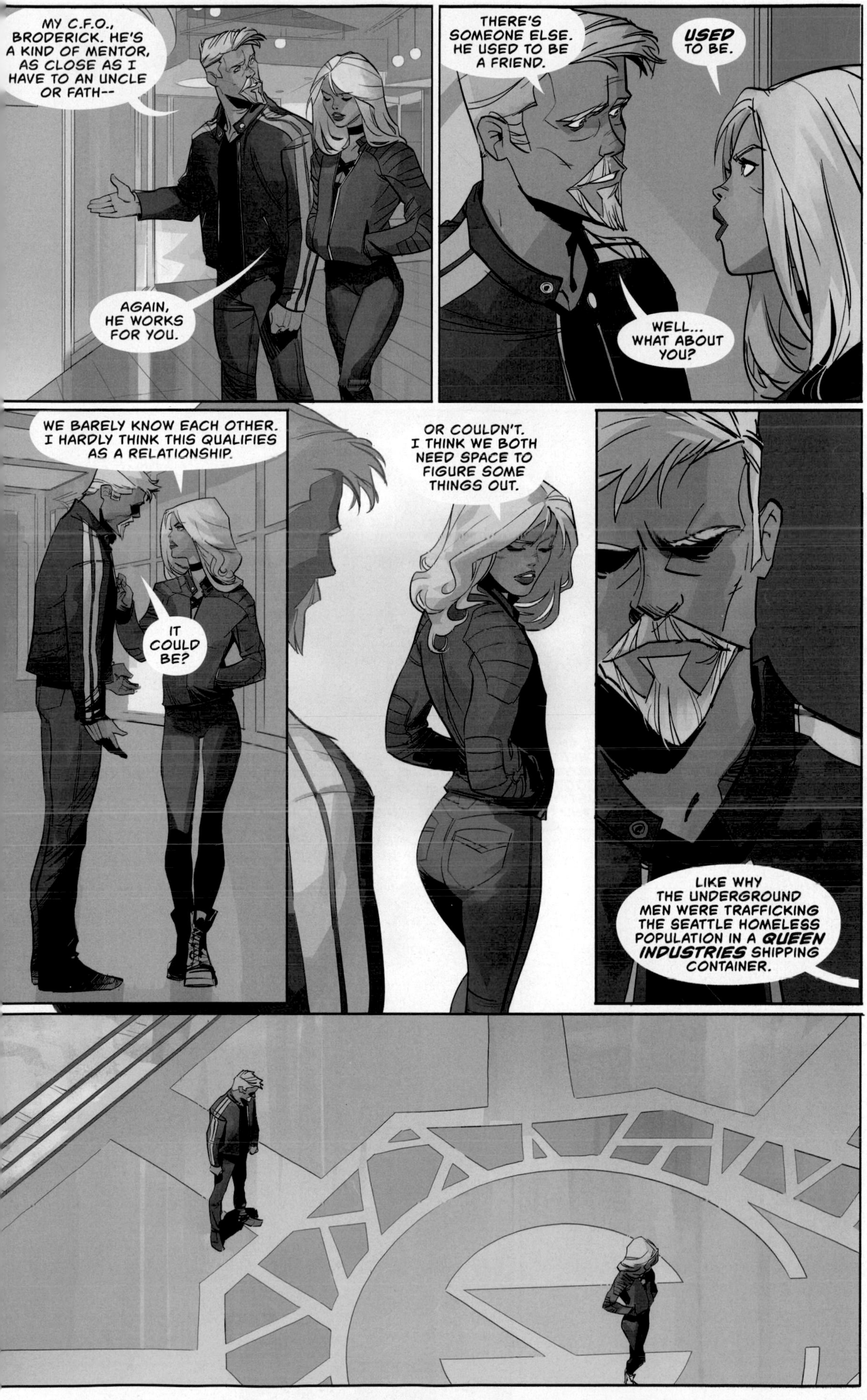

MY C.F.O., BRODERICK. HE'S A KIND OF MENTOR, AS CLOSE AS I HAVE TO AN UNCLE OR FATH--
AGAIN, HE WORKS FOR YOU.
THERE'S SOMEONE ELSE. HE USED TO BE A FRIEND.
USED TO BE.
WELL... WHAT ABOUT YOU?
WE BARELY KNOW EACH OTHER. I HARDLY THINK THIS QUALIFIES AS A RELATIONSHIP.
IT COULD BE?
OR COULDN'T. I THINK WE BOTH NEED SPACE TO FIGURE SOME THINGS OUT.
LIKE WHY THE UNDERGROUND MEN WERE TRAFFICKING THE SEATTLE HOMELESS POPULATION IN A QUEEN INDUSTRIES SHIPPING CONTAINER.

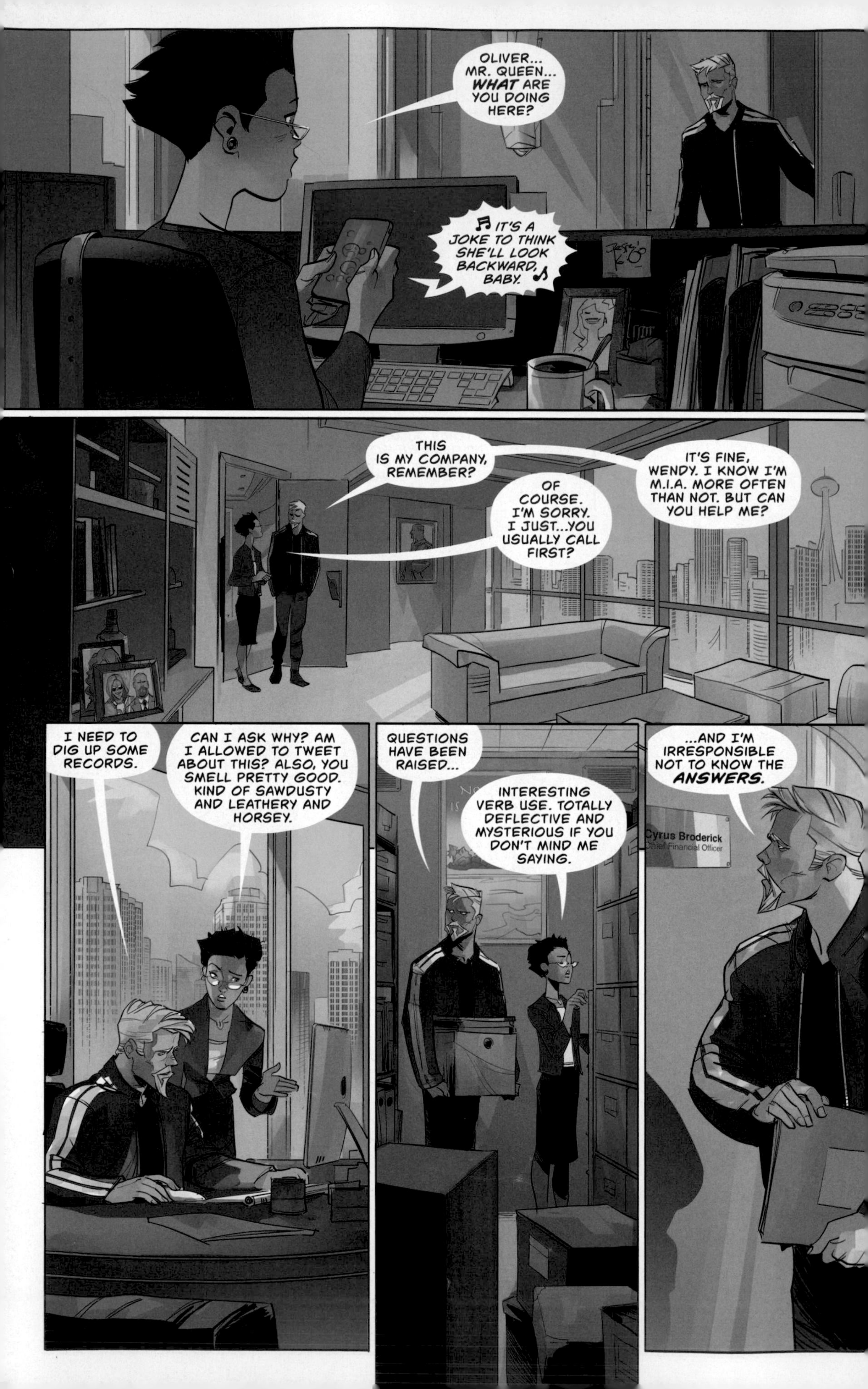

OLIVER... MR. QUEEN... WHAT ARE YOU DOING HERE?
♫ IT'S A JOKE TO THINK SHE'LL LOOK BACKWARD, BABY. ♪
THIS IS MY COMPANY, REMEMBER?
OF COURSE. I'M SORRY. I JUST...YOU USUALLY CALL FIRST?
IT'S FINE, WENDY. I KNOW I'M M.I.A. MORE OFTEN THAN NOT. BUT CAN YOU HELP ME?
I NEED TO DIG UP SOME RECORDS.
CAN I ASK WHY? AM I ALLOWED TO TWEET ABOUT THIS? ALSO, YOU SMELL PRETTY GOOD. KIND OF SAWDUSTY AND LEATHERY AND HORSEY.
QUESTIONS HAVE BEEN RAISED...
INTERESTING VERB USE. TOTALLY DEFLECTIVE AND MYSTERIOUS IF YOU DON'T MIND ME SAYING.
Cyrus Broderick
Chief Financial Officer
...AND I'M IRRESPONSIBLE NOT TO KNOW THE ANSWERS.

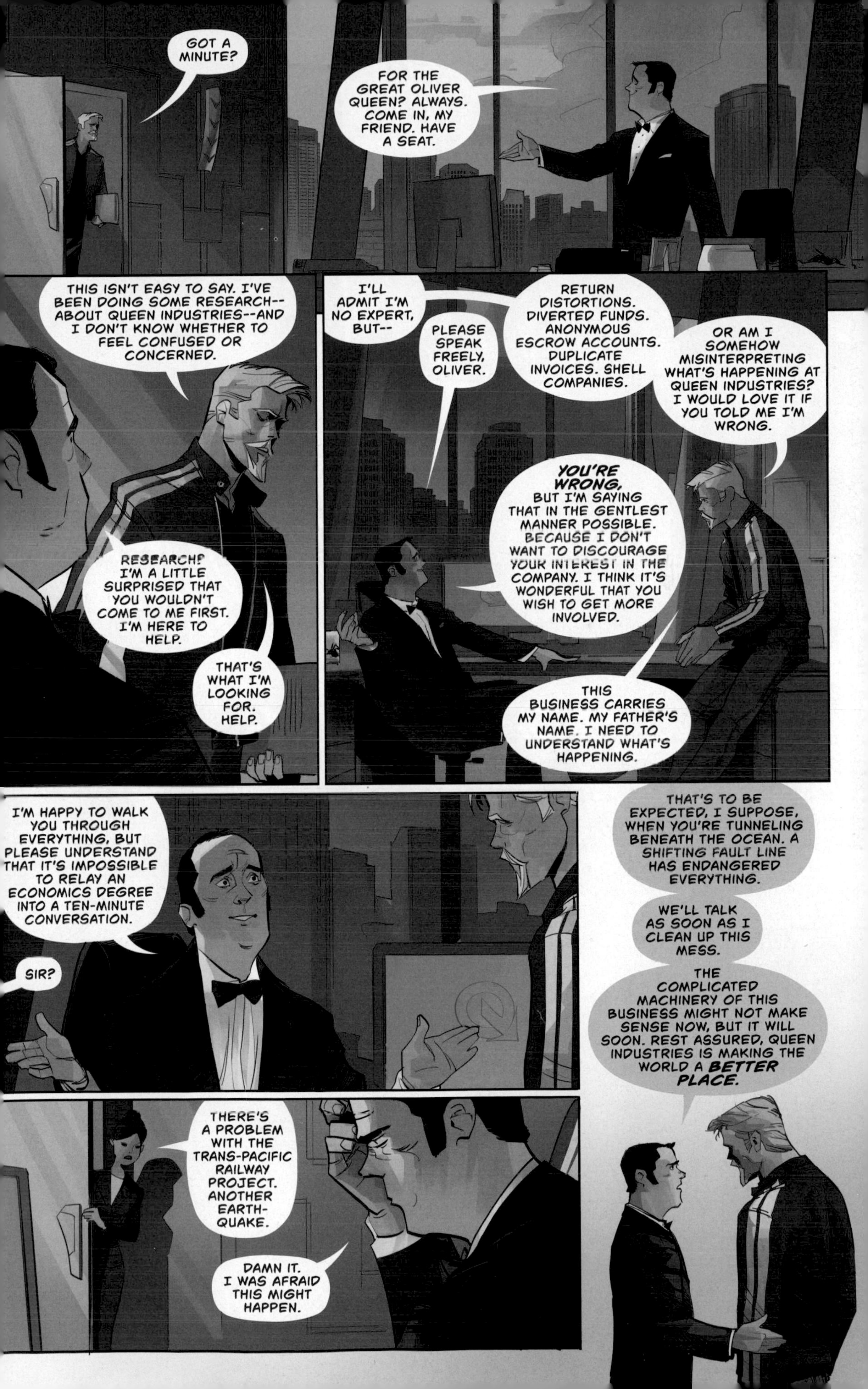
GOT A MINUTE?
FOR THE GREAT OLIVER QUEEN? ALWAYS. COME IN, MY FRIEND. HAVE A SEAT.
THIS ISN'T EASY TO SAY. I'VE BEEN DOING SOME RESEARCH--ABOUT QUEEN INDUSTRIES--AND I DON'T KNOW WHETHER TO FEEL CONFUSED OR CONCERNED.
RESEARCH? I'M A LITTLE SURPRISED THAT YOU WOULDN'T COME TO ME FIRST. I'M HERE TO HELP.
THAT'S WHAT I'M LOOKING FOR. HELP.
I'LL ADMIT I'M NO EXPERT, BUT--
PLEASE SPEAK FREELY, OLIVER.
RETURN DISTORTIONS. DIVERTED FUNDS. ANONYMOUS ESCROW ACCOUNTS. DUPLICATE INVOICES. SHELL COMPANIES.
OR AM I SOMEHOW MISINTERPRETING WHAT'S HAPPENING AT QUEEN INDUSTRIES? I WOULD LOVE IT IF YOU TOLD ME I'M WRONG.
YOU'RE WRONG, BUT I'M SAYING THAT IN THE GENTLEST MANNER POSSIBLE. BECAUSE I DON'T WANT TO DISCOURAGE YOUR INTEREST IN THE COMPANY. I THINK IT'S WONDERFUL THAT YOU WISH TO GET MORE INVOLVED.
THIS BUSINESS CARRIES MY NAME. MY FATHER'S NAME. I NEED TO UNDERSTAND WHAT'S HAPPENING.
I'M HAPPY TO WALK YOU THROUGH EVERYTHING, BUT PLEASE UNDERSTAND THAT IT'S IMPOSSIBLE TO RELAY AN ECONOMICS DEGREE INTO A TEN-MINUTE CONVERSATION.
SIR?
THERE'S A PROBLEM WITH THE TRANS-PACIFIC RAILWAY PROJECT. ANOTHER EARTH-QUAKE.
DAMN IT. I WAS AFRAID THIS MIGHT HAPPEN.
THAT'S TO BE EXPECTED, I SUPPOSE, WHEN YOU'RE TUNNELING BENEATH THE OCEAN. A SHIFTING FAULT LINE HAS ENDANGERED EVERYTHING.
WE'LL TALK AS SOON AS I CLEAN UP THIS MESS.
THE COMPLICATED MACHINERY OF THIS BUSINESS MIGHT NOT MAKE SENSE NOW, BUT IT WILL SOON. REST ASSURED, QUEEN INDUSTRIES IS MAKING THE WORLD A BETTER PLACE.

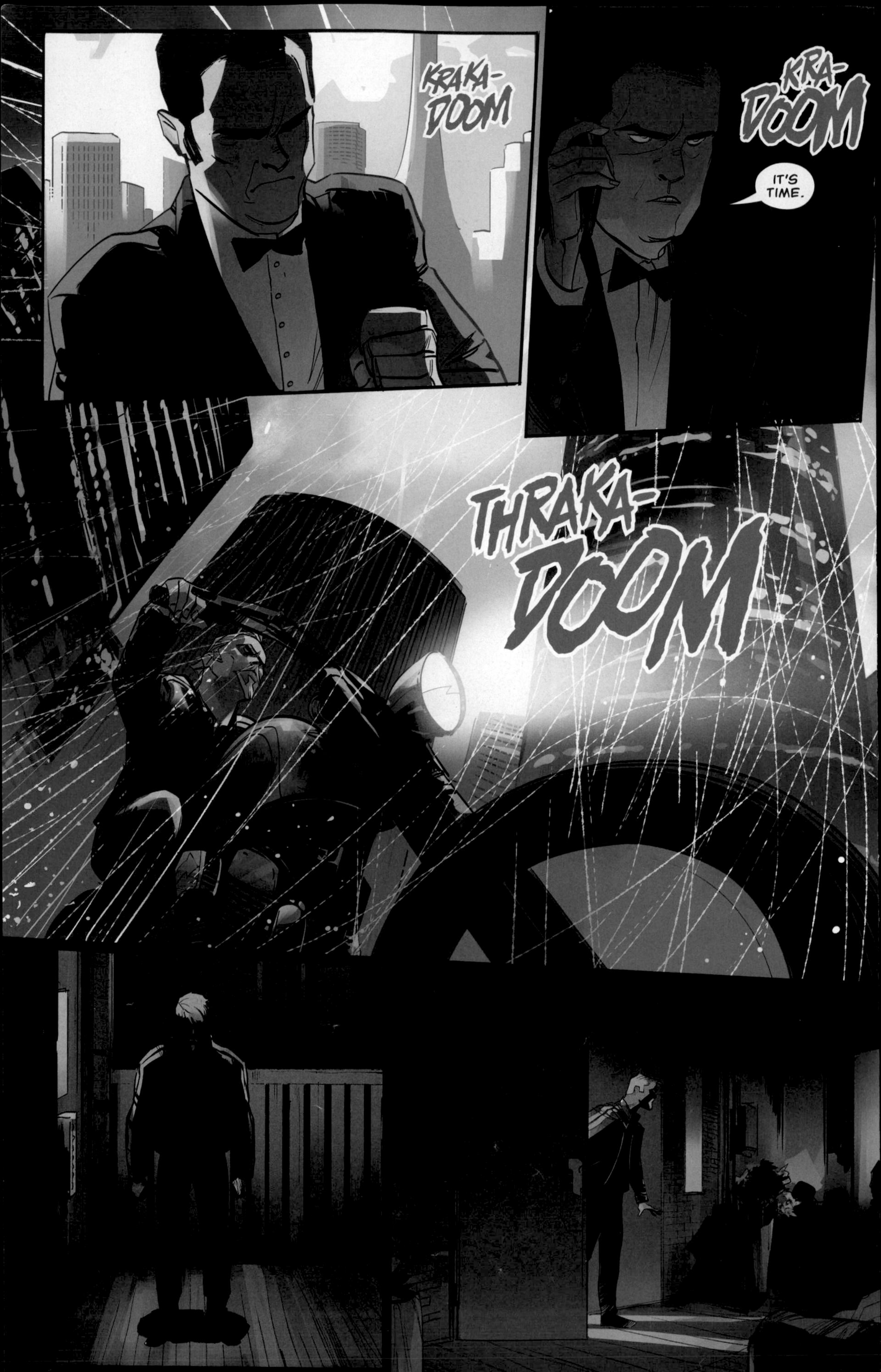
KRAKA-
DOOM
KRA-
DOOM
IT'S TIME.
THRAKA-
DOOM

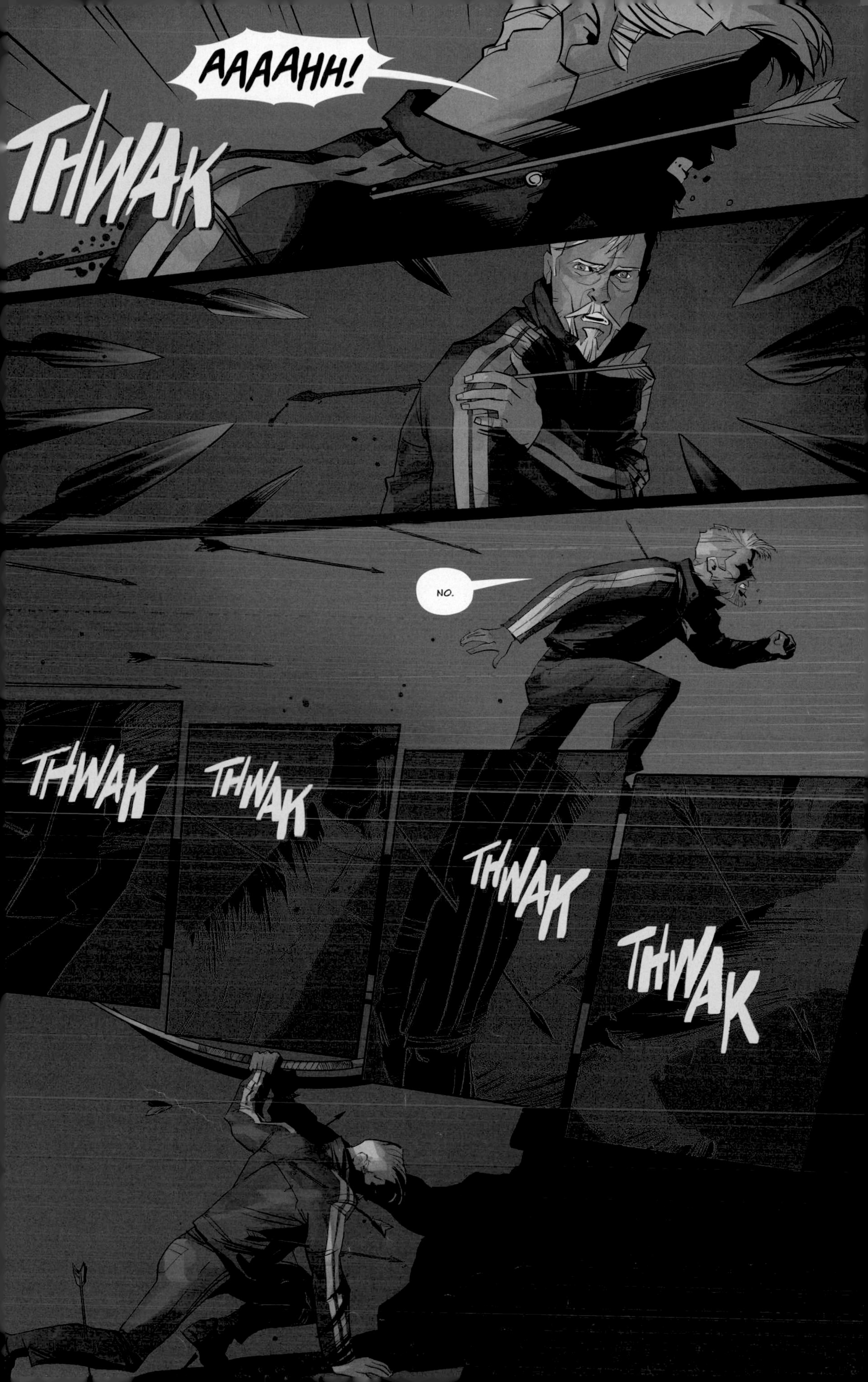
AAAAHH!
THWAK
NO.
THWAK
THWAK
THWAK
THWAK

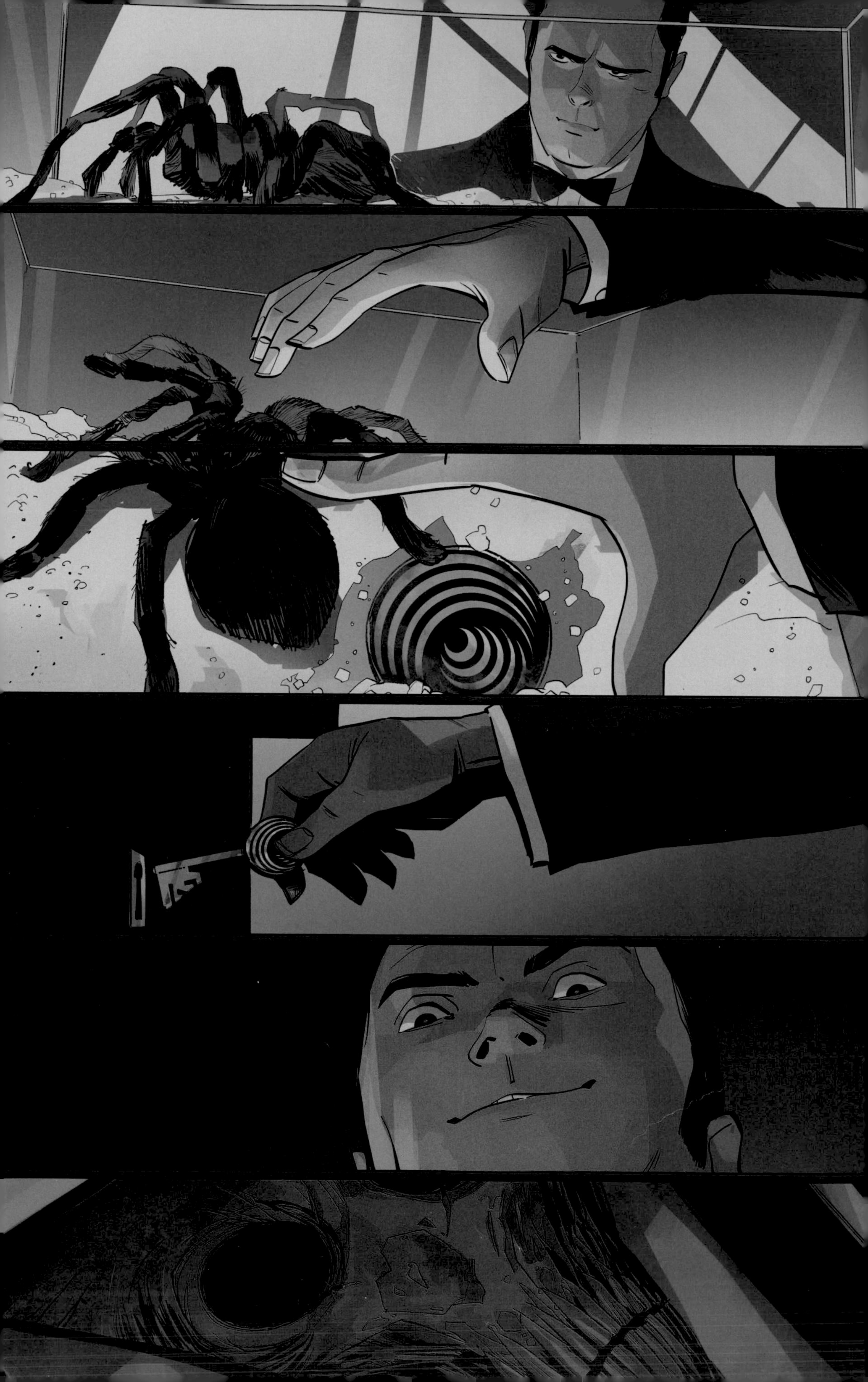

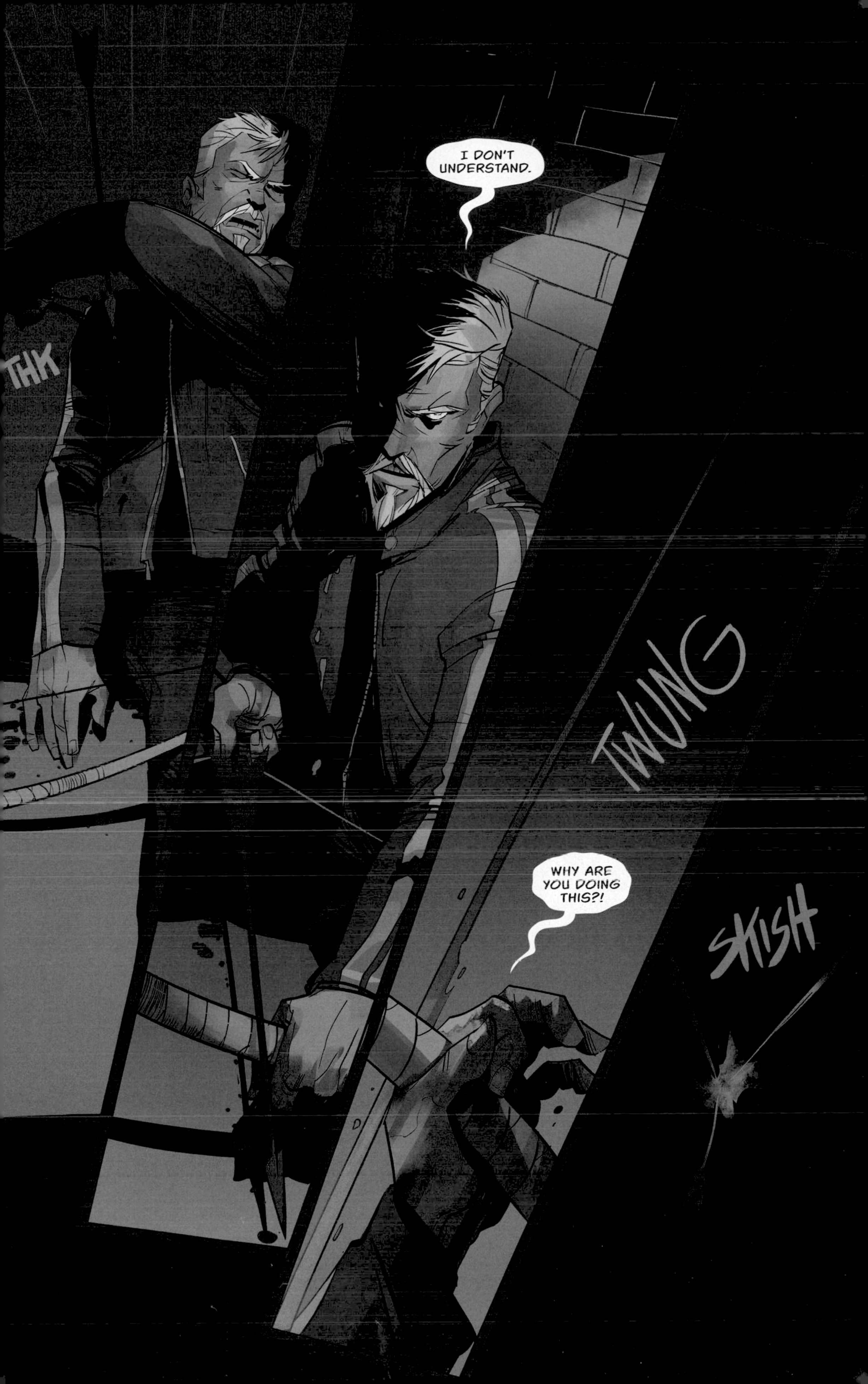
I DON'T UNDERSTAND.
THK
TWUNG
WHY ARE YOU DOING THIS?!
SKISH

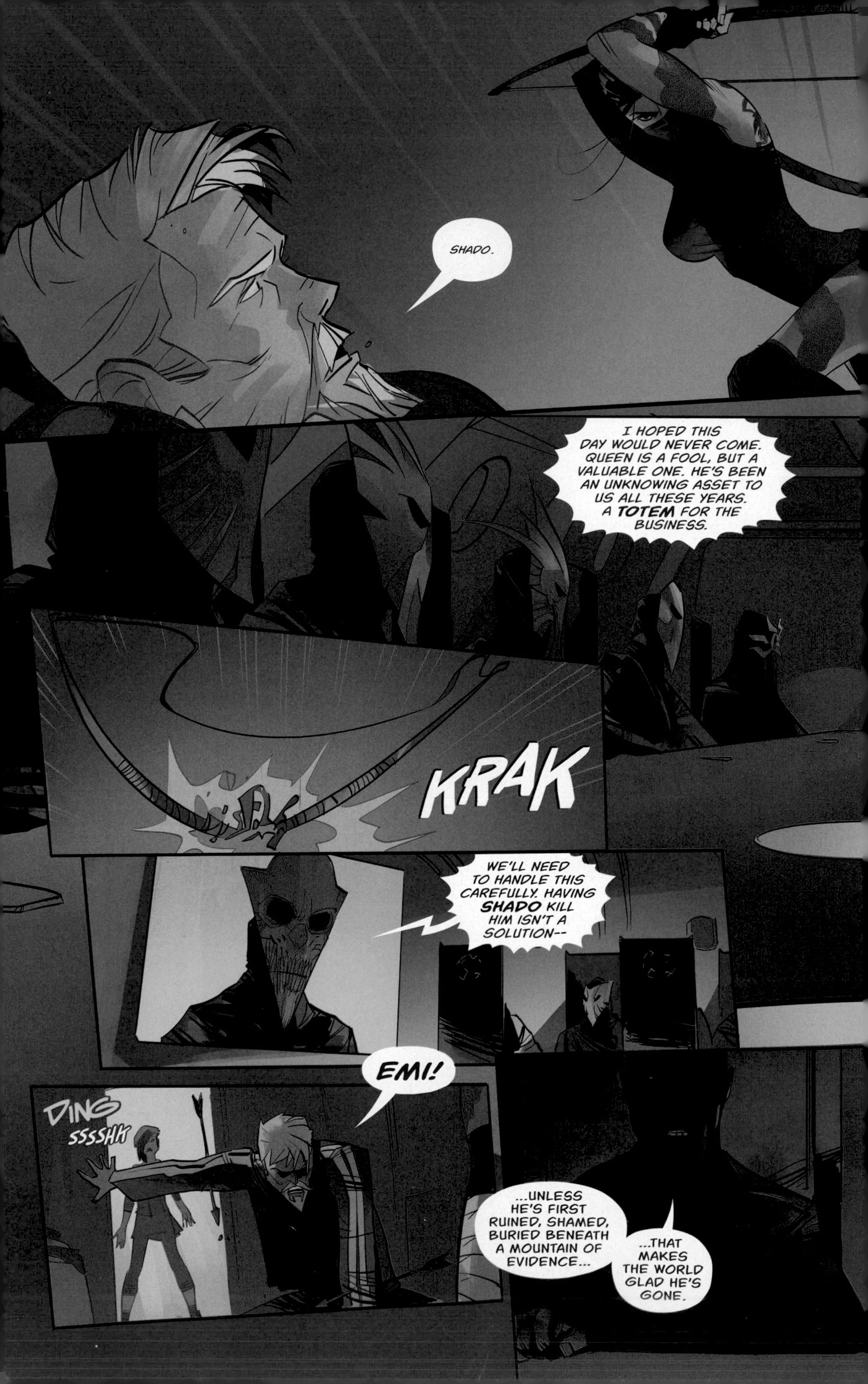
SHADO.
I HOPED THIS DAY WOULD NEVER COME. QUEEN IS A FOOL, BUT A VALUABLE ONE. HE'S BEEN AN UNKNOWING ASSET TO US ALL THESE YEARS. A TOTEM FOR THE BUSINESS.
KRAK
WE'LL NEED TO HANDLE THIS CAREFULLY. HAVING SHADO KILL HIM ISN'T A SOLUTION--
EMI!
DING
SSSSHK
...UNLESS HE'S FIRST RUINED, SHAMED, BURIED BENEATH A MOUNTAIN OF EVIDENCE...
...THAT MAKES THE WORLD GLAD HE'S GONE.

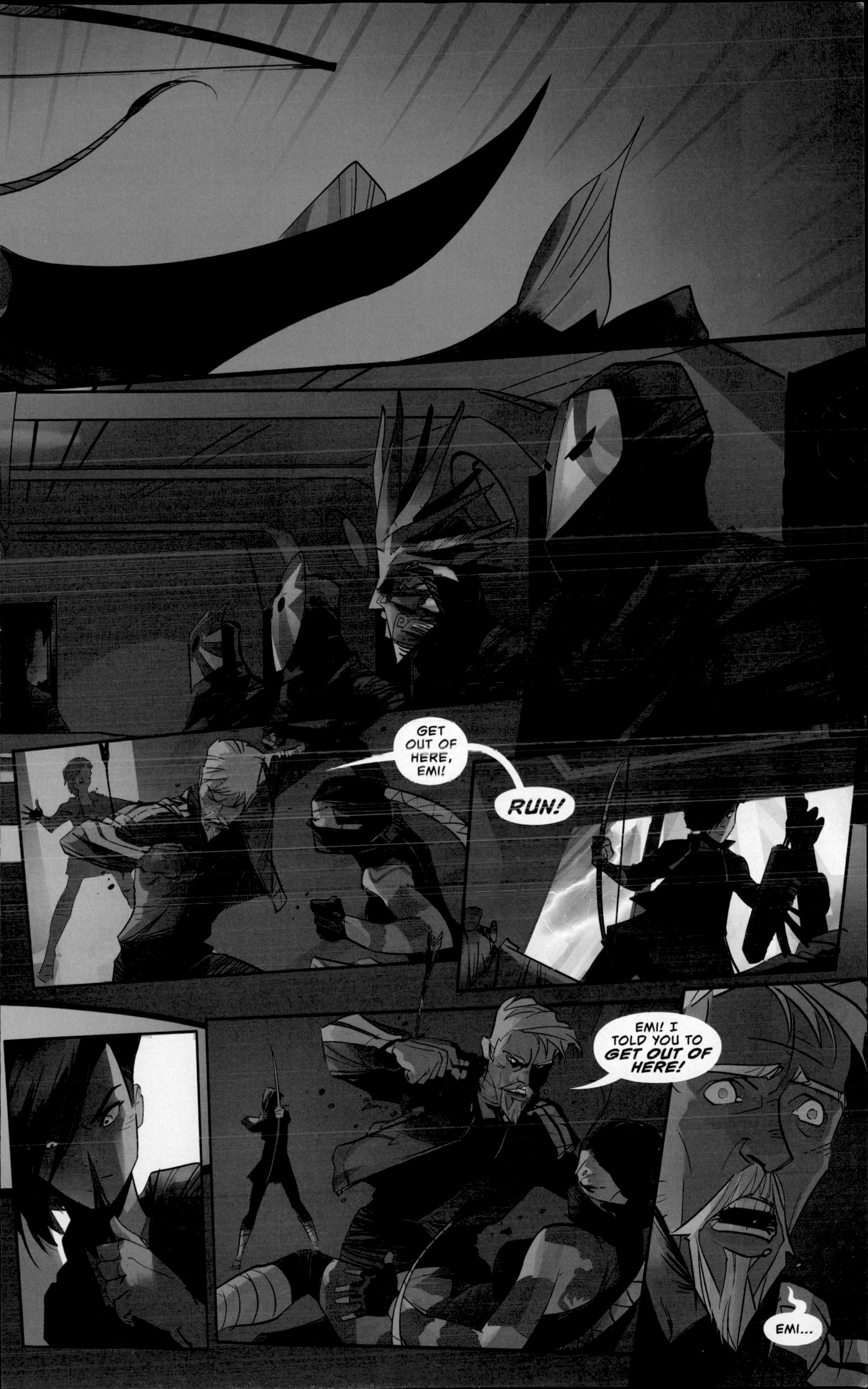
GET OUT OF HERE, EMI!
RUN!
EMI! I TOLD YOU TO GET OUT OF HERE!
EMI...

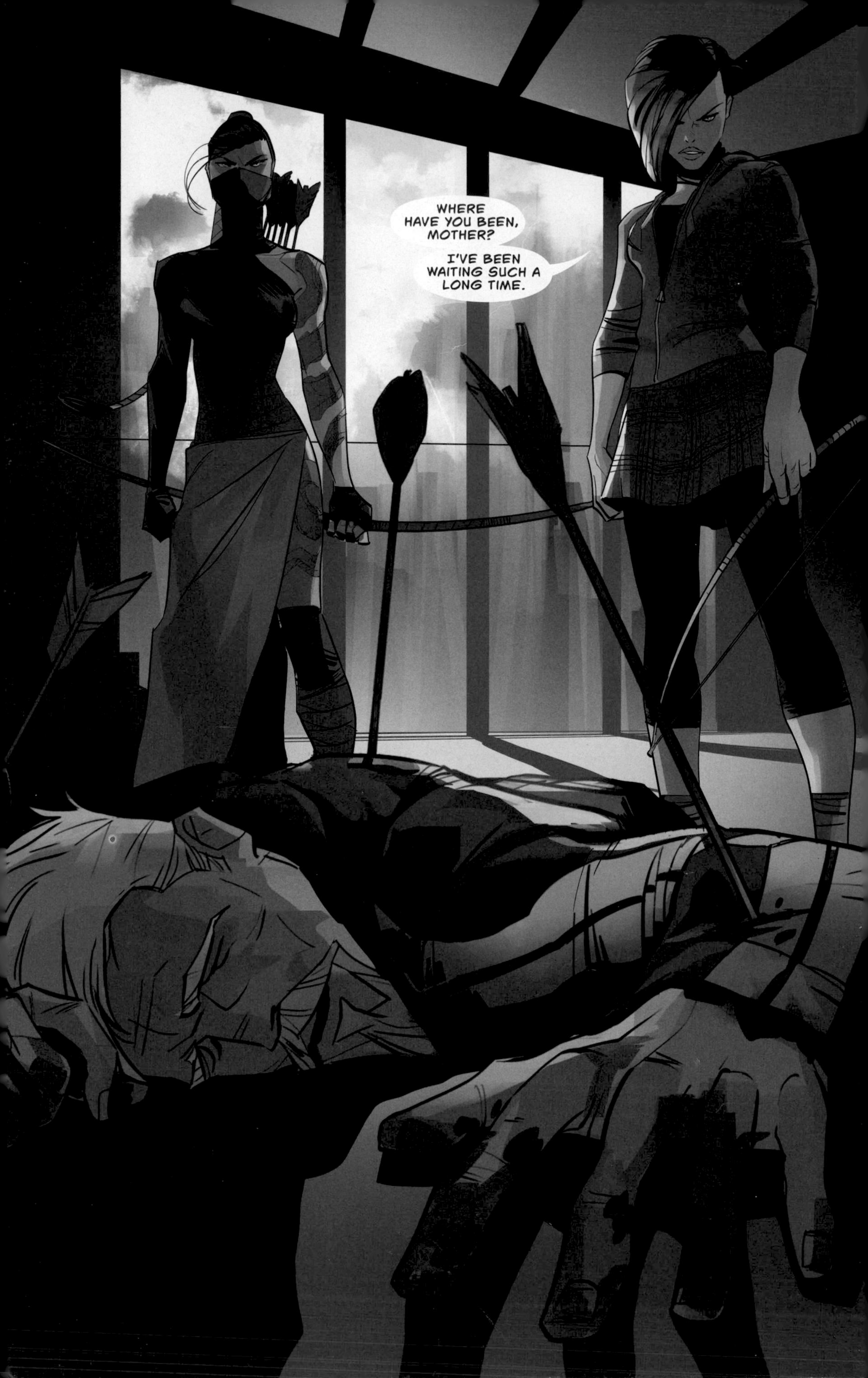
WHERE HAVE YOU BEEN, MOTHER?
I'VE BEEN WAITING SUCH A LONG TIME.

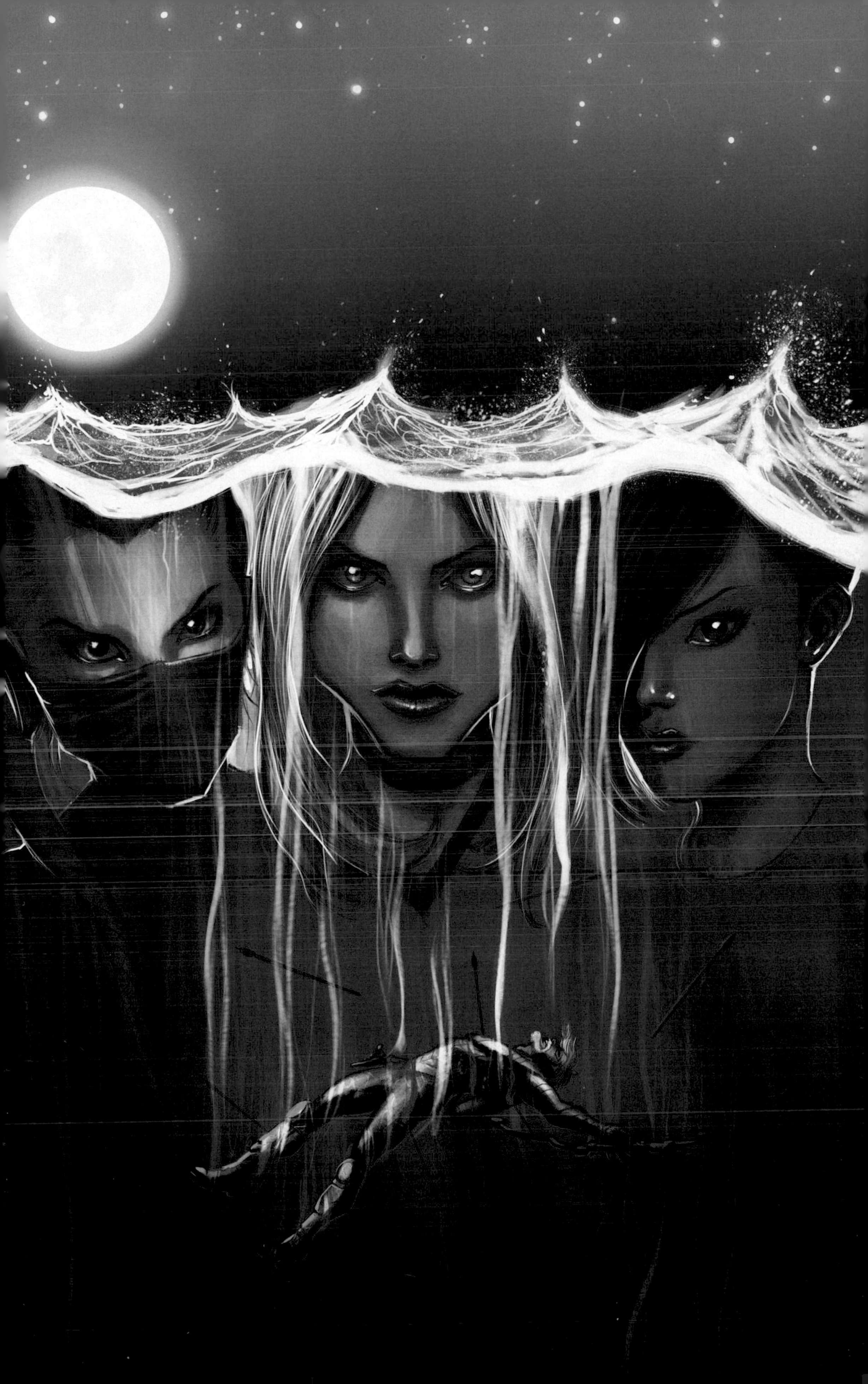

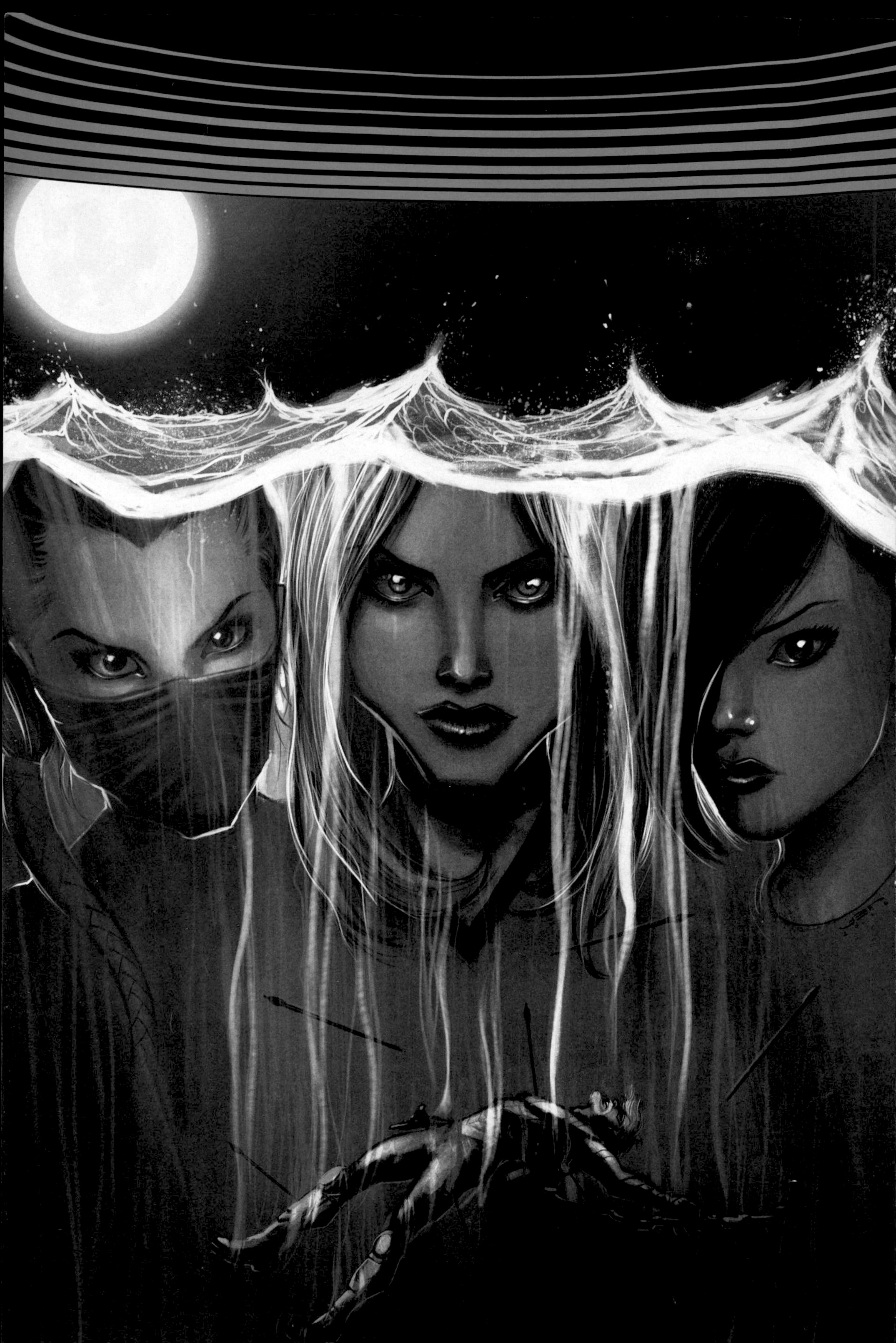

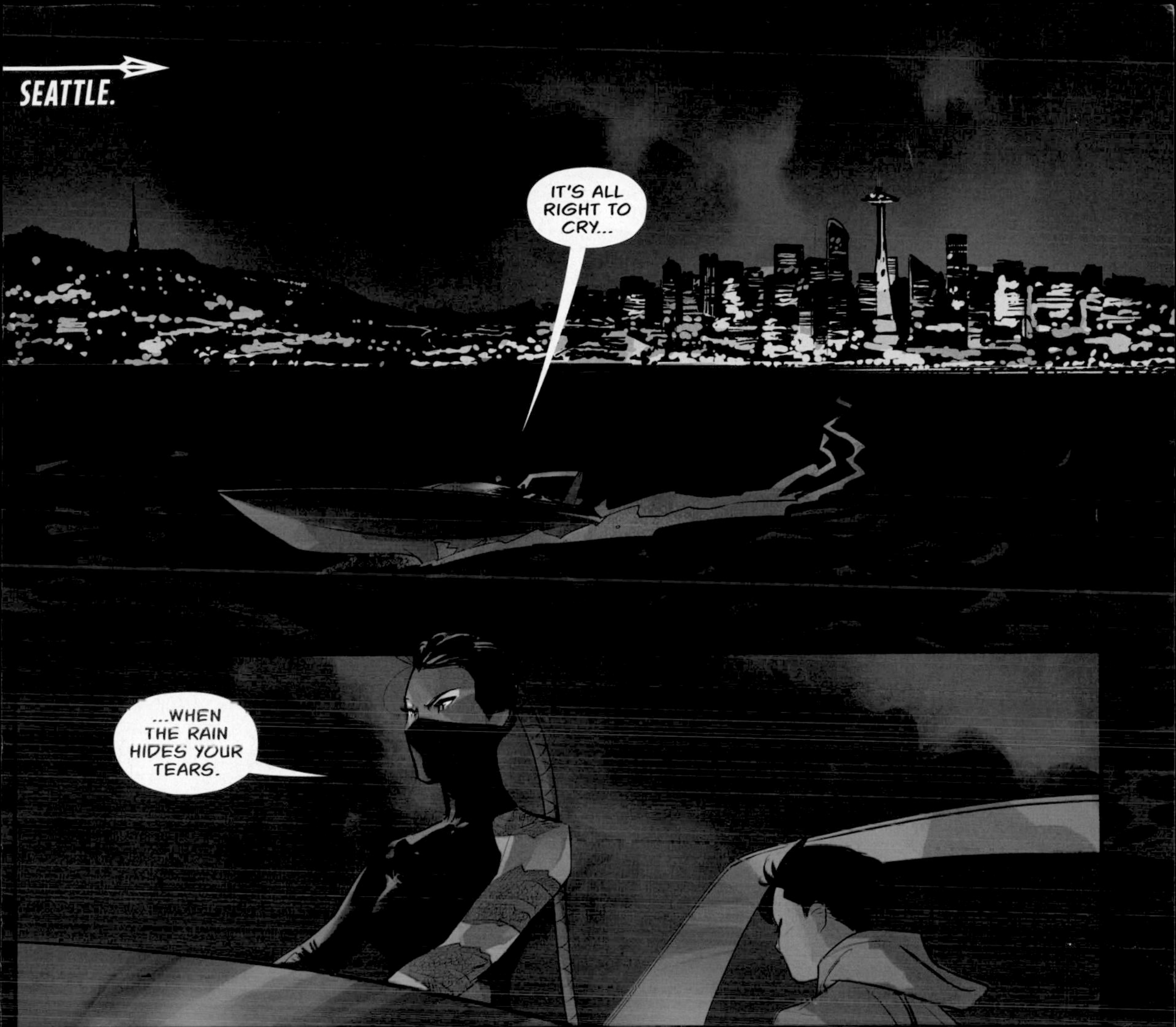
SEATTLE.
IT'S ALL RIGHT TO CRY...
...WHEN THE RAIN HIDES YOUR TEARS.

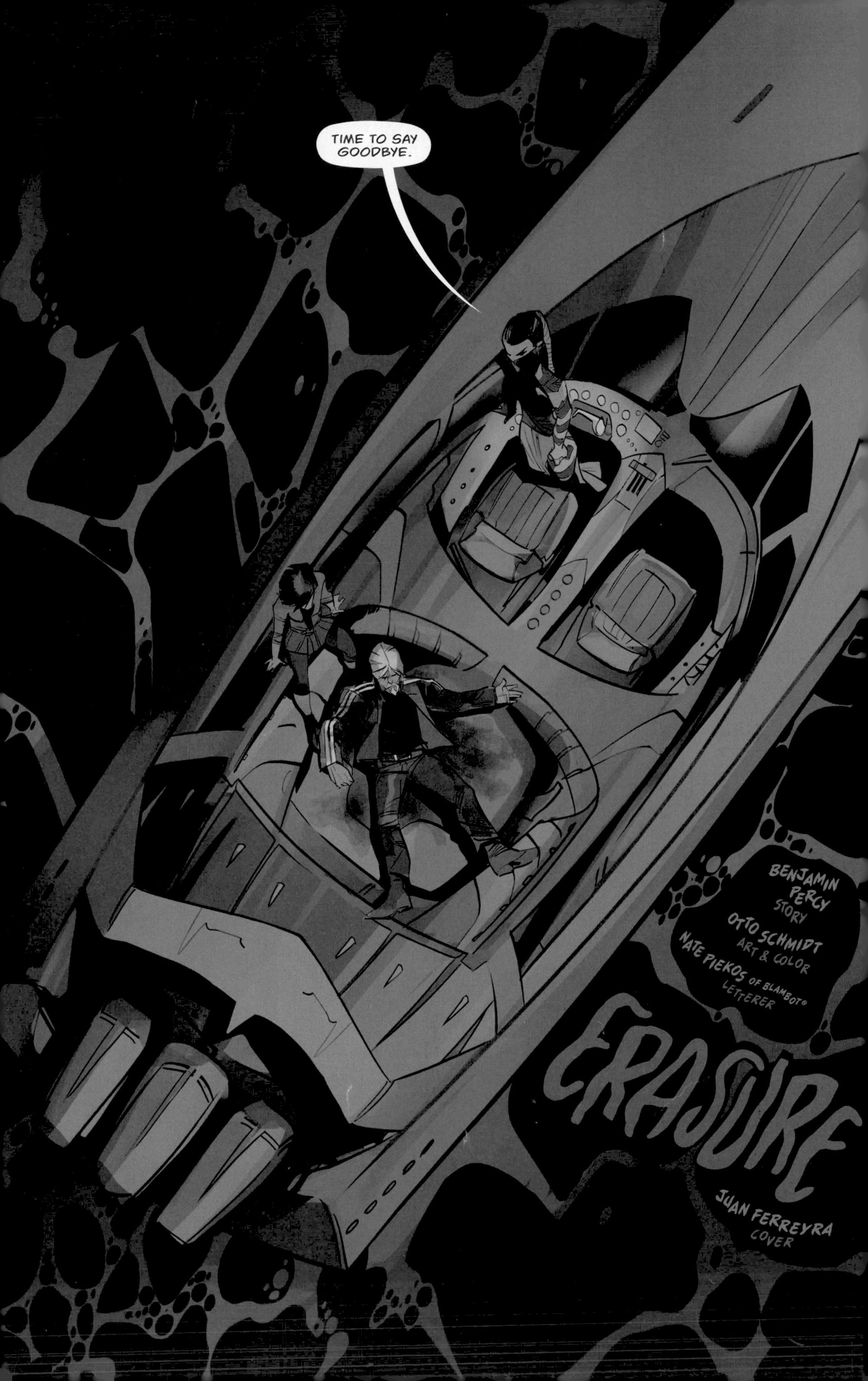
TIME TO SAY GOODBYE.
BENJAMIN PERCY STORY
OTTO SCHMIDT ART & COLOR
NATE PIEKOS OF BLAMBOT® LETTERER
ERASURE
JUAN FERREYRA COVER

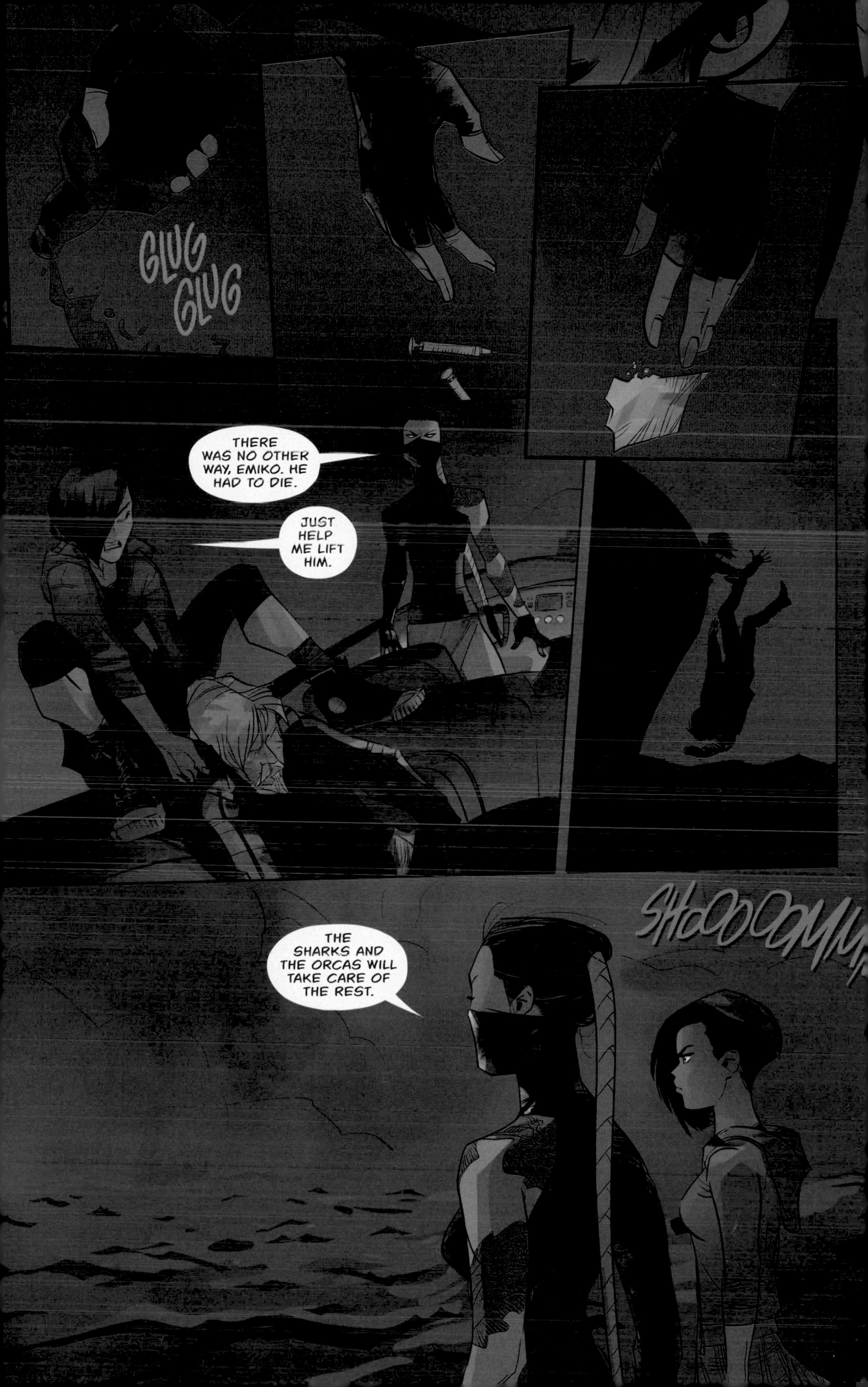
GLUG GLUG
THERE WAS NO OTHER WAY, EMIKO. HE HAD TO DIE.
JUST HELP ME LIFT HIM.
SHOOOOOMM
THE SHARKS AND THE ORCAS WILL TAKE CARE OF THE REST.

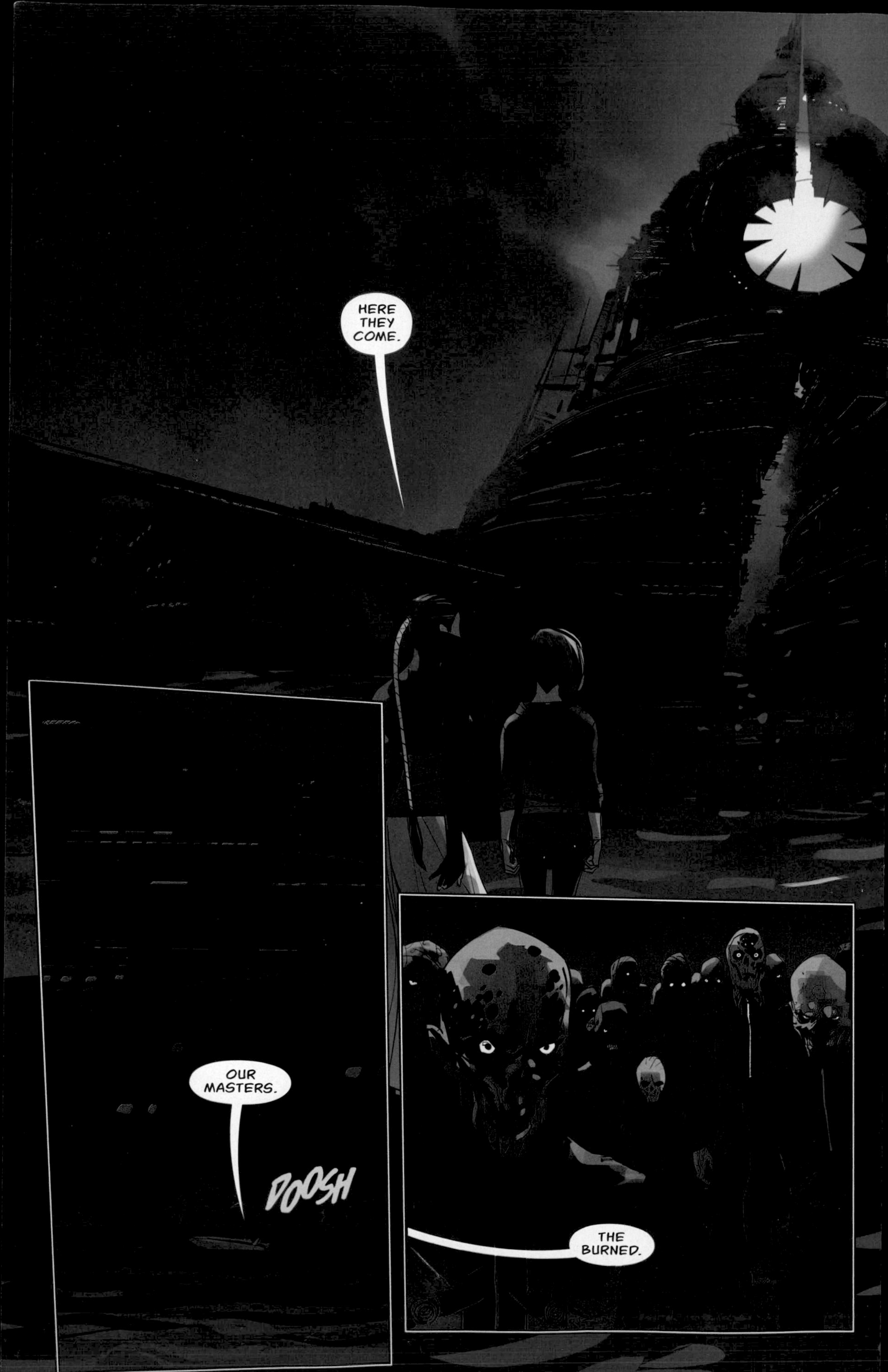
HERE THEY COME.
OUR MASTERS.
DOOSH
THE BURNED.

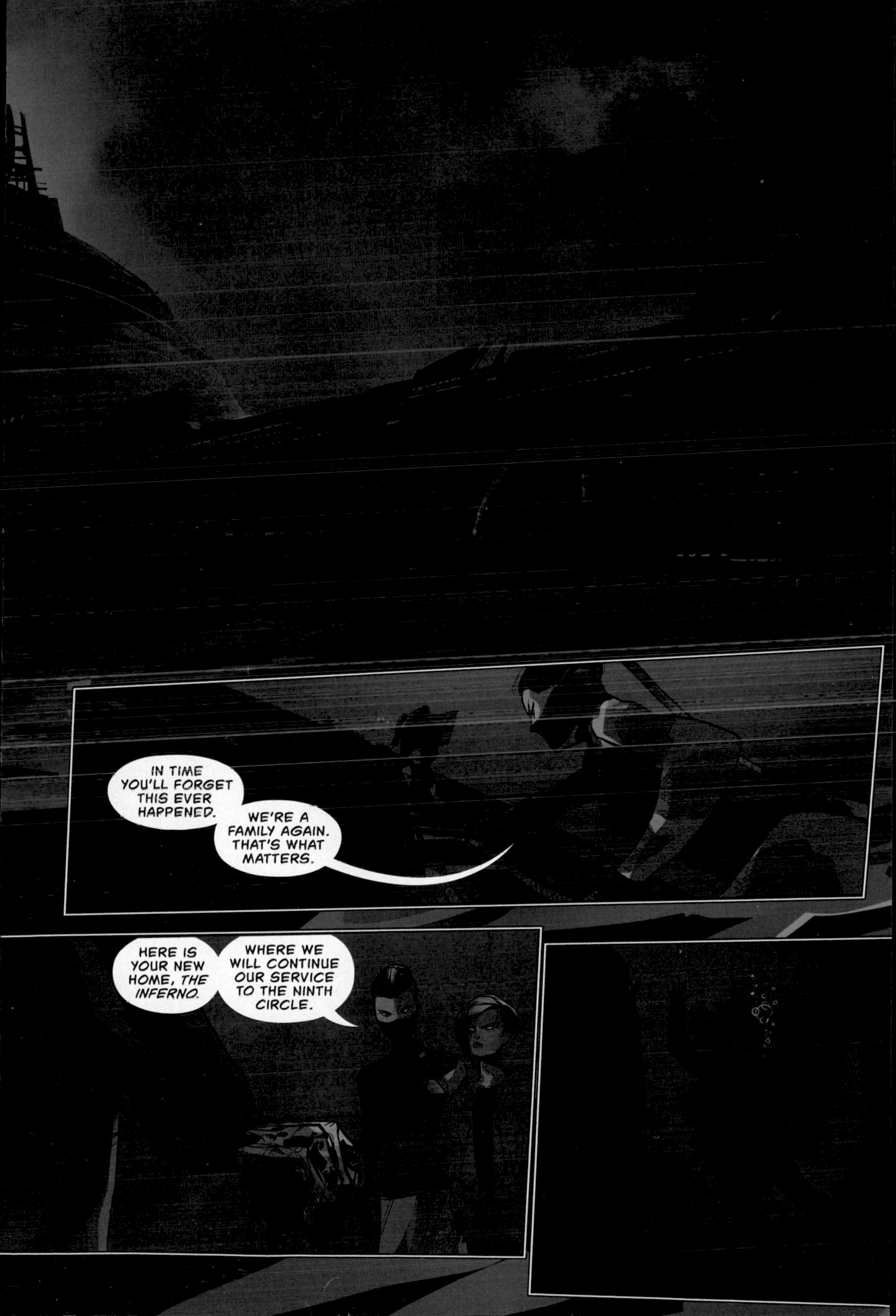
IN TIME YOU'LL FORGET THIS EVER HAPPENED.
WE'RE A FAMILY AGAIN. THAT'S WHAT MATTERS.
HERE IS YOUR NEW HOME, *THE INFERNO*.
WHERE WE WILL CONTINUE OUR SERVICE TO THE NINTH CIRCLE.

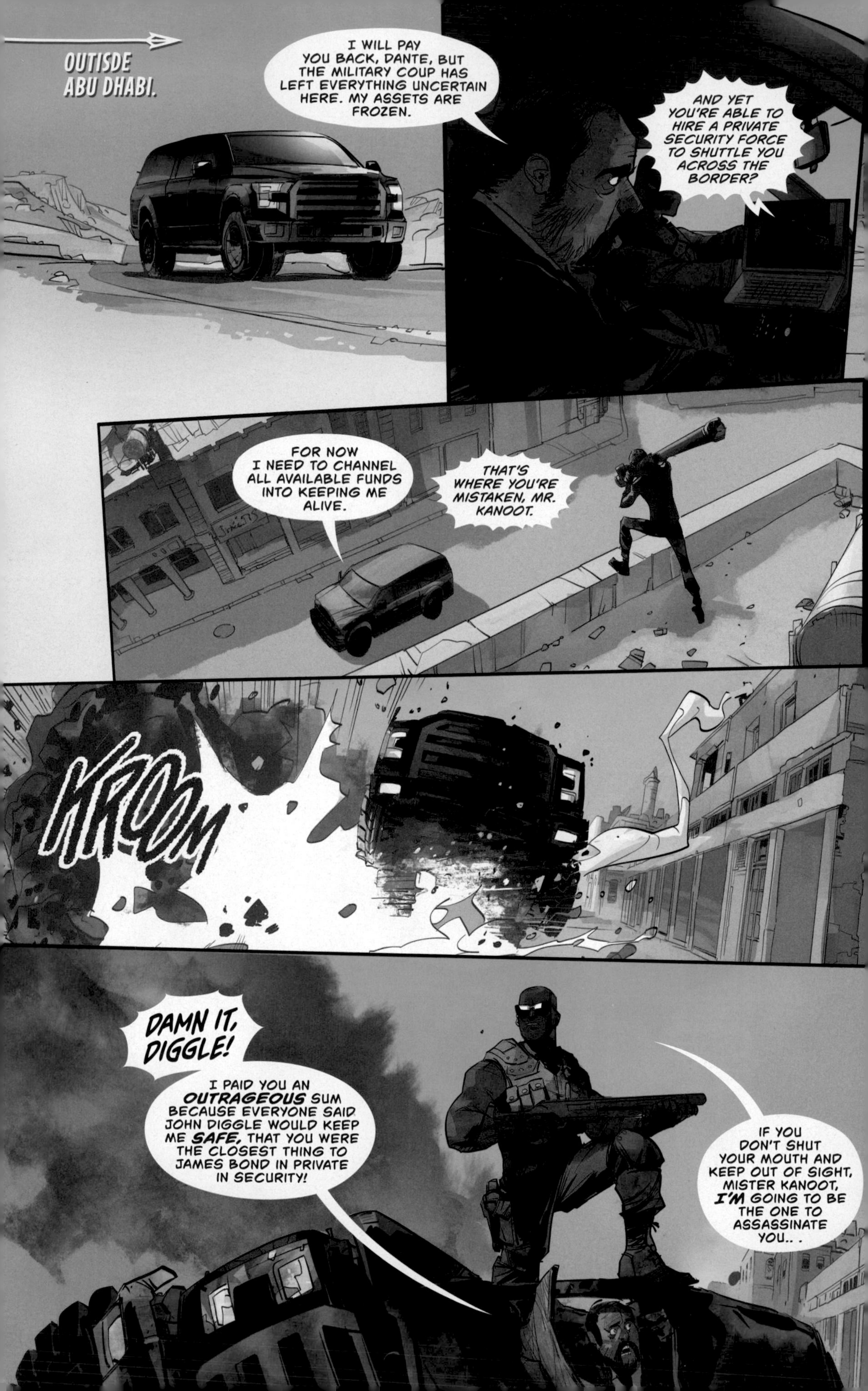
OUTISDE ABU DHABI.
I WILL PAY YOU BACK, DANTE, BUT THE MILITARY COUP HAS LEFT EVERYTHING UNCERTAIN HERE. MY ASSETS ARE FROZEN.
AND YET YOU'RE ABLE TO HIRE A PRIVATE SECURITY FORCE TO SHUTTLE YOU ACROSS THE BORDER?
FOR NOW I NEED TO CHANNEL ALL AVAILABLE FUNDS INTO KEEPING ME ALIVE.
THAT'S WHERE YOU'RE MISTAKEN, MR. KANOOT.
KROOM
DAMN IT, DIGGLE!
I PAID YOU AN OUTRAGEOUS SUM BECAUSE EVERYONE SAID JOHN DIGGLE WOULD KEEP ME SAFE, THAT YOU WERE THE CLOSEST THING TO JAMES BOND IN PRIVATE IN SECURITY!
IF YOU DON'T SHUT YOUR MOUTH AND KEEP OUT OF SIGHT, MISTER KANOOT, I'M GOING TO BE THE ONE TO ASSASSINATE YOU.. .

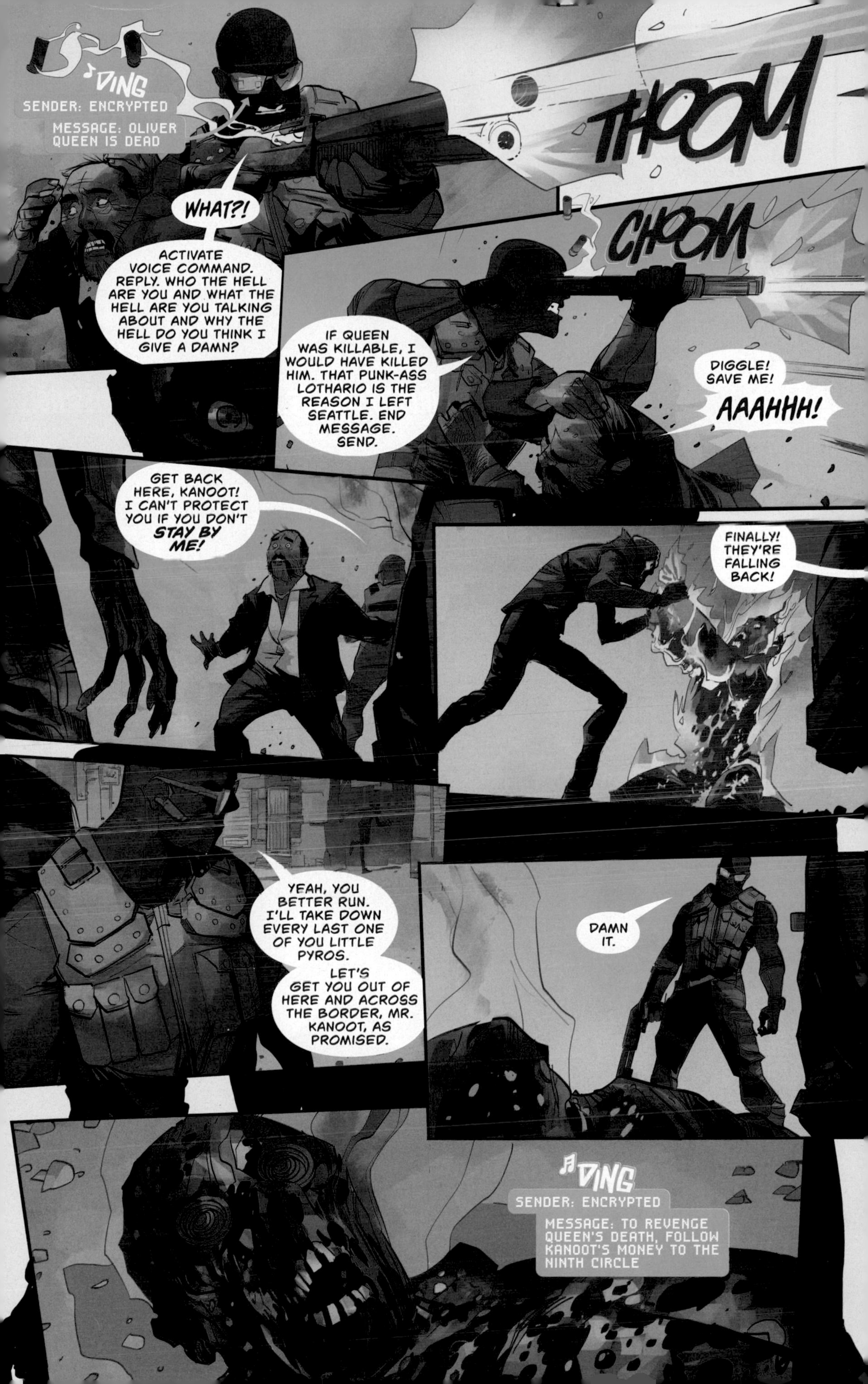
DING
SENDER: ENCRYPTED
MESSAGE: OLIVER QUEEN IS DEAD
THOOM
WHAT?!
ACTIVATE VOICE COMMAND. REPLY. WHO THE HELL ARE YOU AND WHAT THE HELL ARE YOU TALKING ABOUT AND WHY THE HELL DO YOU THINK I GIVE A DAMN?
CHOOM
IF QUEEN WAS KILLABLE, I WOULD HAVE KILLED HIM. THAT PUNK-ASS LOTHARIO IS THE REASON I LEFT SEATTLE. END MESSAGE. SEND.
DIGGLE! SAVE ME! AAAHHH!
GET BACK HERE, KANOOT! I CAN'T PROTECT YOU IF YOU DON'T STAY BY ME!
FINALLY! THEY'RE FALLING BACK!
YEAH, YOU BETTER RUN. I'LL TAKE DOWN EVERY LAST ONE OF YOU LITTLE PYROS.
LET'S GET YOU OUT OF HERE AND ACROSS THE BORDER, MR. KANOOT, AS PROMISED.
DAMN IT.
DING
SENDER: ENCRYPTED
MESSAGE: TO REVENGE QUEEN'S DEATH, FOLLOW KANOOT'S MONEY TO THE NINTH CIRCLE

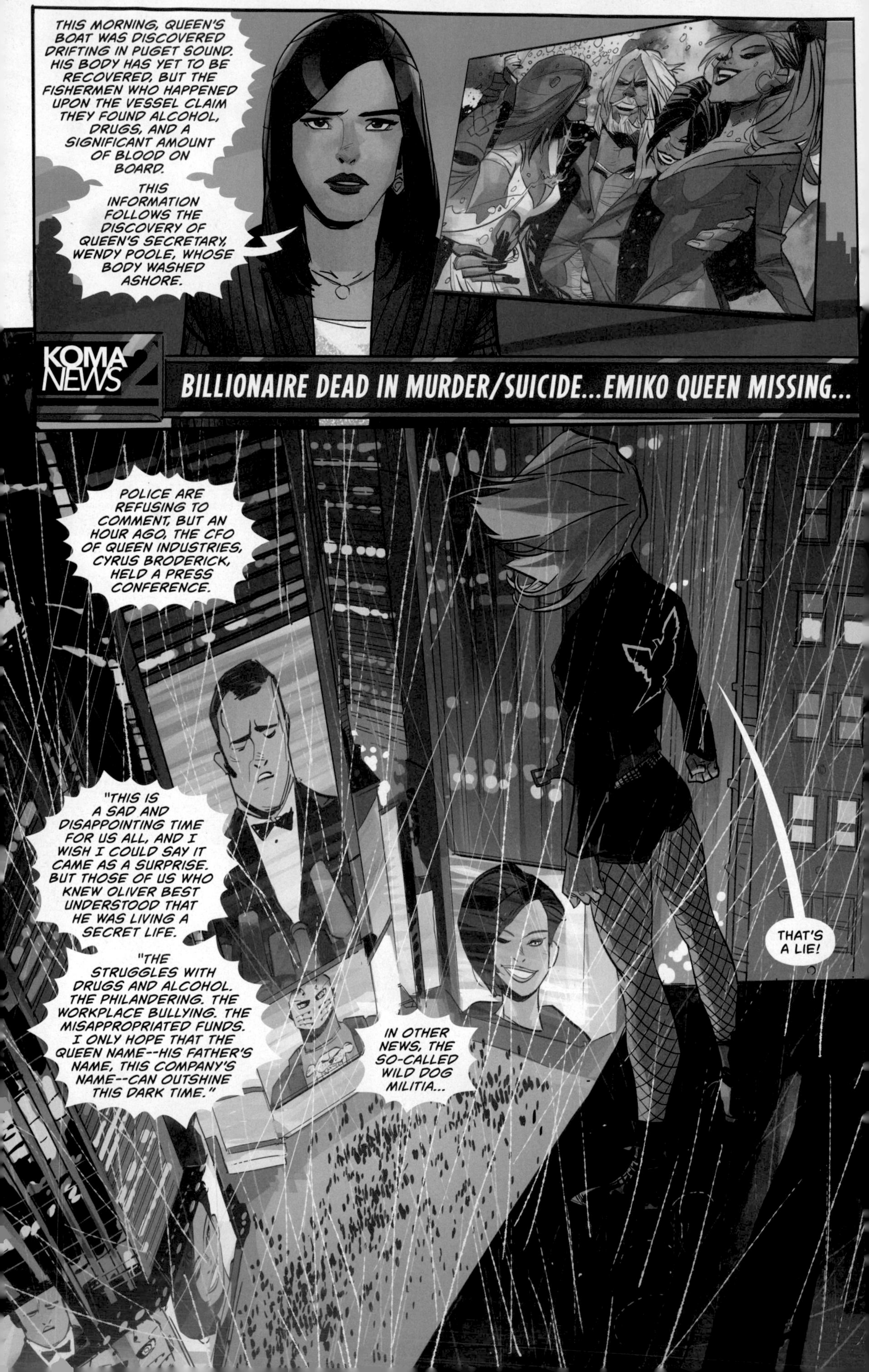
THIS MORNING, QUEEN'S BOAT WAS DISCOVERED DRIFTING IN PUGET SOUND. HIS BODY HAS YET TO BE RECOVERED, BUT THE FISHERMEN WHO HAPPENED UPON THE VESSEL CLAIM THEY FOUND ALCOHOL, DRUGS, AND A SIGNIFICANT AMOUNT OF BLOOD ON BOARD.
THIS INFORMATION FOLLOWS THE DISCOVERY OF QUEEN'S SECRETARY, WENDY POOLE, WHOSE BODY WASHED ASHORE.
KOMA NEWS 2
BILLIONAIRE DEAD IN MURDER/SUICIDE...EMIKO QUEEN MISSING...
POLICE ARE REFUSING TO COMMENT, BUT AN HOUR AGO, THE CFO OF QUEEN INDUSTRIES, CYRUS BRODERICK, HELD A PRESS CONFERENCE.
"THIS IS A SAD AND DISAPPOINTING TIME FOR US ALL, AND I WISH I COULD SAY IT CAME AS A SURPRISE. BUT THOSE OF US WHO KNEW OLIVER BEST UNDERSTOOD THAT HE WAS LIVING A SECRET LIFE.
"THE STRUGGLES WITH DRUGS AND ALCOHOL. THE PHILANDERING. THE WORKPLACE BULLYING. THE MISAPPROPRIATED FUNDS. I ONLY HOPE THAT THE QUEEN NAME--HIS FATHER'S NAME, THIS COMPANY'S NAME--CAN OUTSHINE THIS DARK TIME."
THAT'S A LIE!
IN OTHER NEWS, THE SO-CALLED WILD DOG MILITIA...

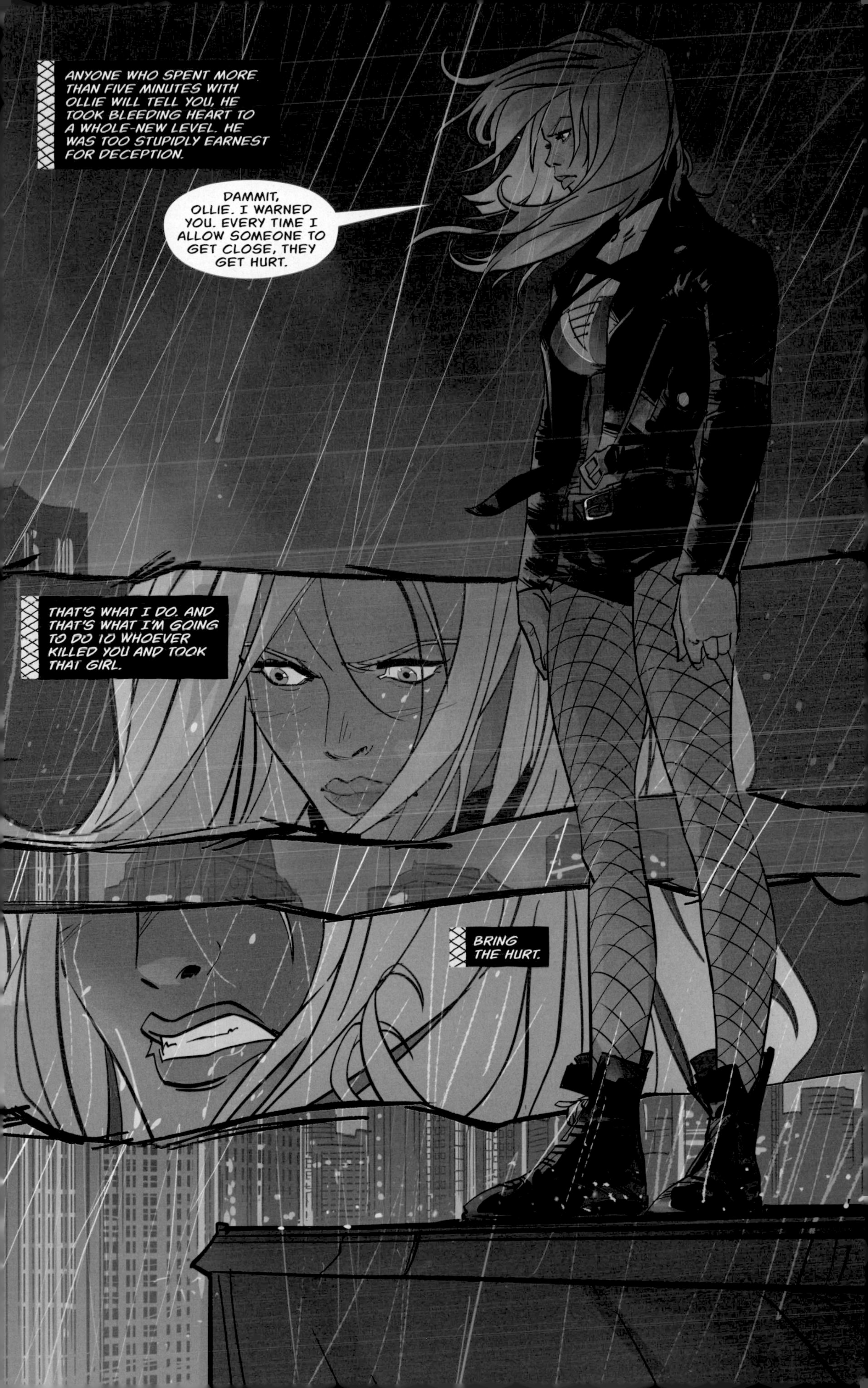
ANYONE WHO SPENT MORE THAN FIVE MINUTES WITH OLLIE WILL TELL YOU, HE TOOK BLEEDING HEART TO A WHOLE-NEW LEVEL. HE WAS TOO STUPIDLY EARNEST FOR DECEPTION.
DAMMIT, OLLIE. I WARNED YOU. EVERY TIME I ALLOW SOMEONE TO GET CLOSE, THEY GET HURT.
THAT'S WHAT I DO. AND THAT'S WHAT I'M GOING TO DO TO WHOEVER KILLED YOU AND TOOK THAT GIRL.
BRING THE HURT.

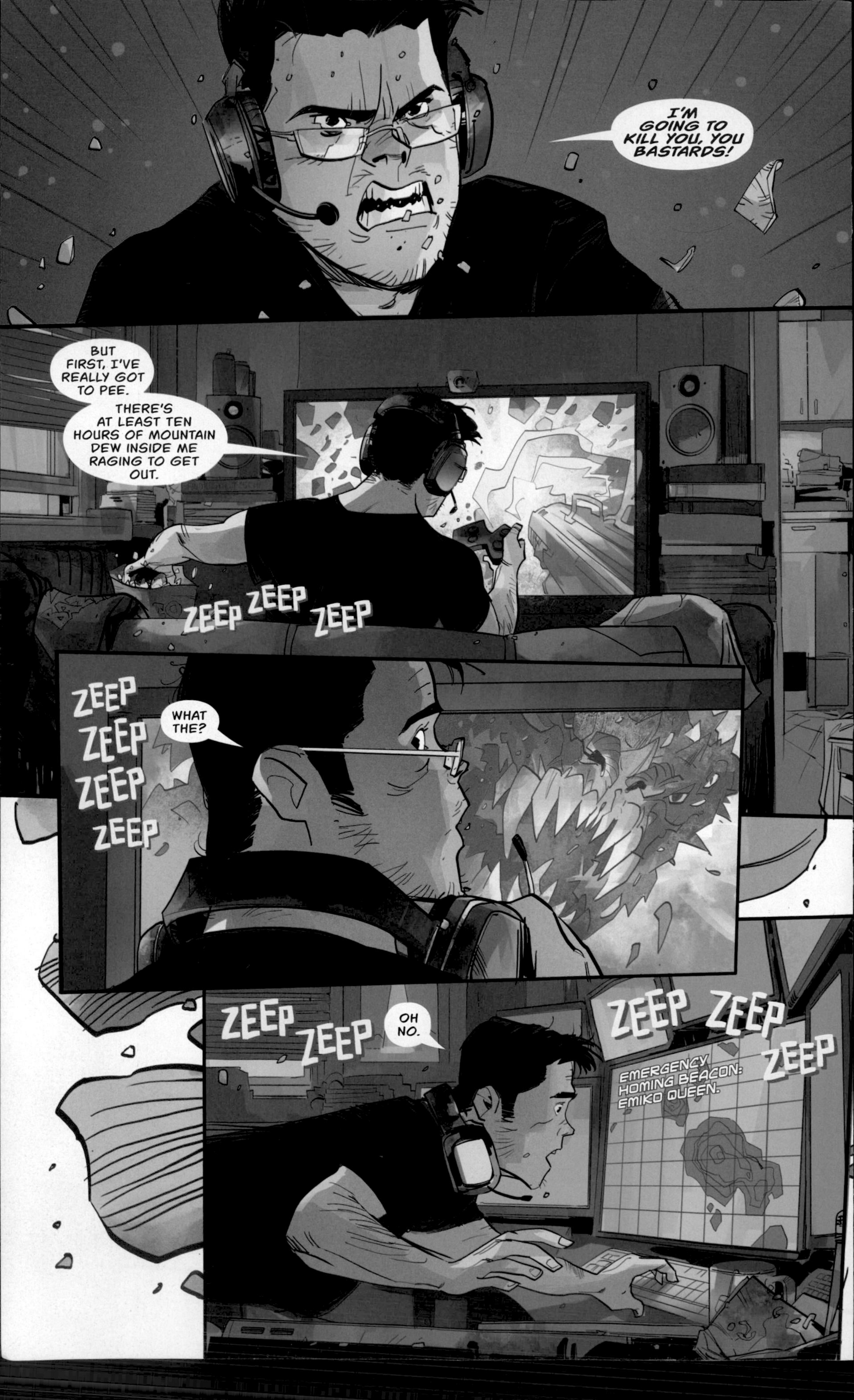
I'M GOING TO KILL YOU, YOU BASTARDS!
BUT FIRST, I'VE REALLY GOT TO PEE.
THERE'S AT LEAST TEN HOURS OF MOUNTAIN DEW INSIDE ME RAGING TO GET OUT.
ZEEP ZEEP ZEEP
ZEEP ZEEP ZEEP ZEEP
WHAT THE?
ZEEP ZEEP
OH NO.
ZEEP ZEEP ZEEP
EMERGENCY HOMING BEACON: EMIKO QUEEN.

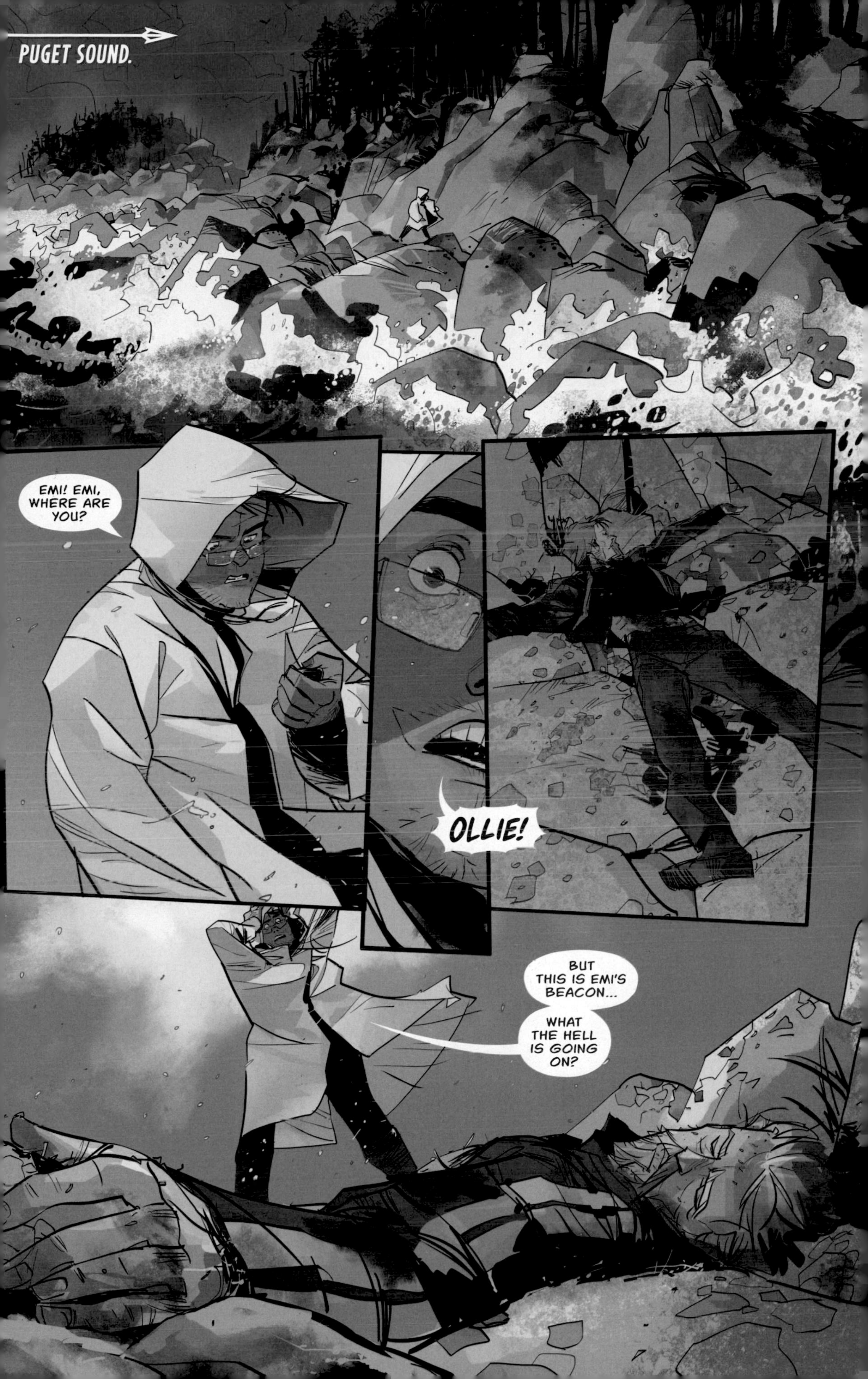
PUGET SOUND.
EMI! EMI, WHERE ARE YOU?
OLLIE!
BUT THIS IS EMI'S BEACON...
WHAT THE HELL IS GOING ON?

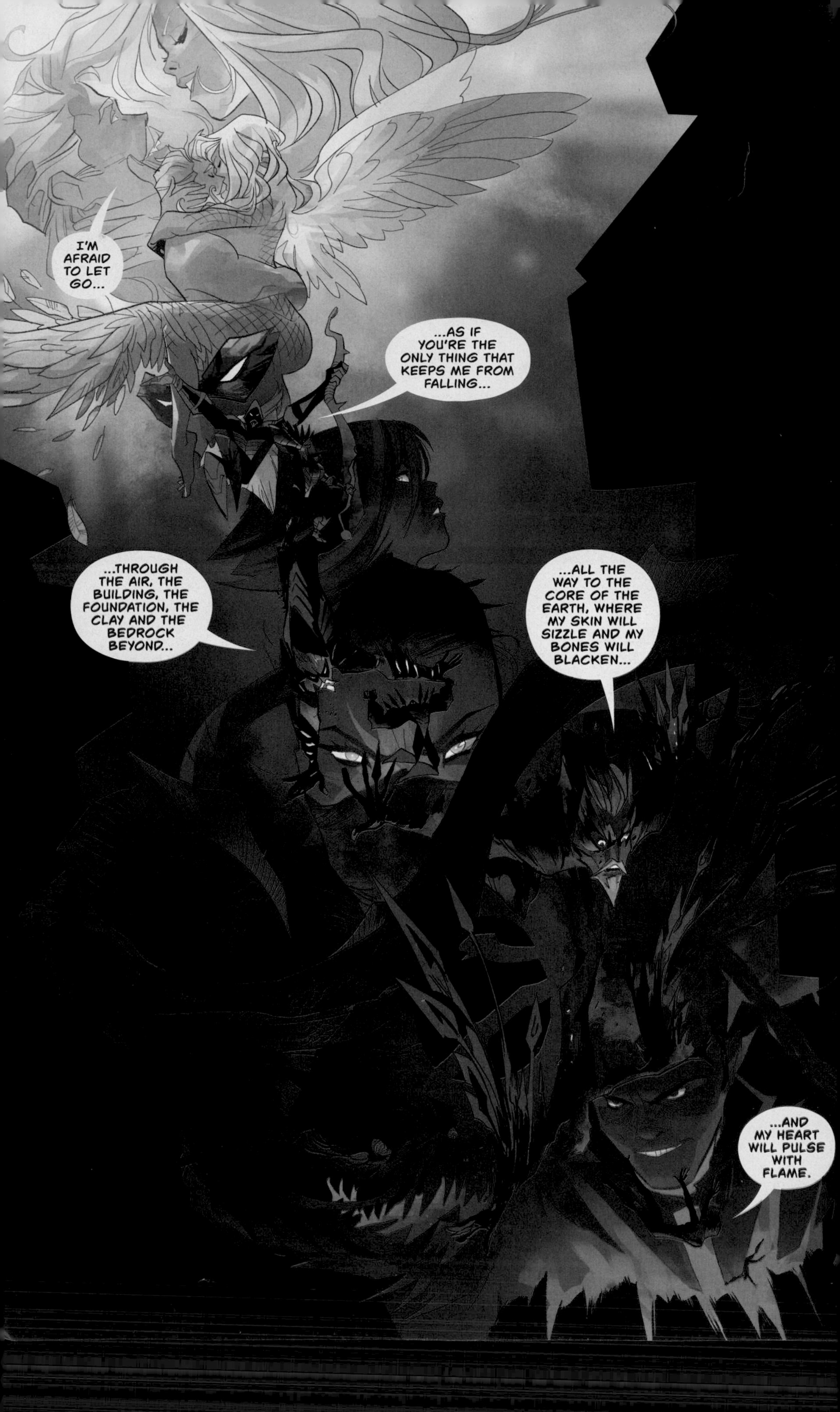

I'M AFRAID TO LET GO...
...AS IF YOU'RE THE ONLY THING THAT KEEPS ME FROM FALLING...
...THROUGH THE AIR, THE BUILDING, THE FOUNDATION, THE CLAY AND THE BEDROCK BEYOND...
...ALL THE WAY TO THE CORE OF THE EARTH, WHERE MY SKIN WILL SIZZLE AND MY BONES WILL BLACKEN...
...AND MY HEART WILL PULSE WITH FLAME.

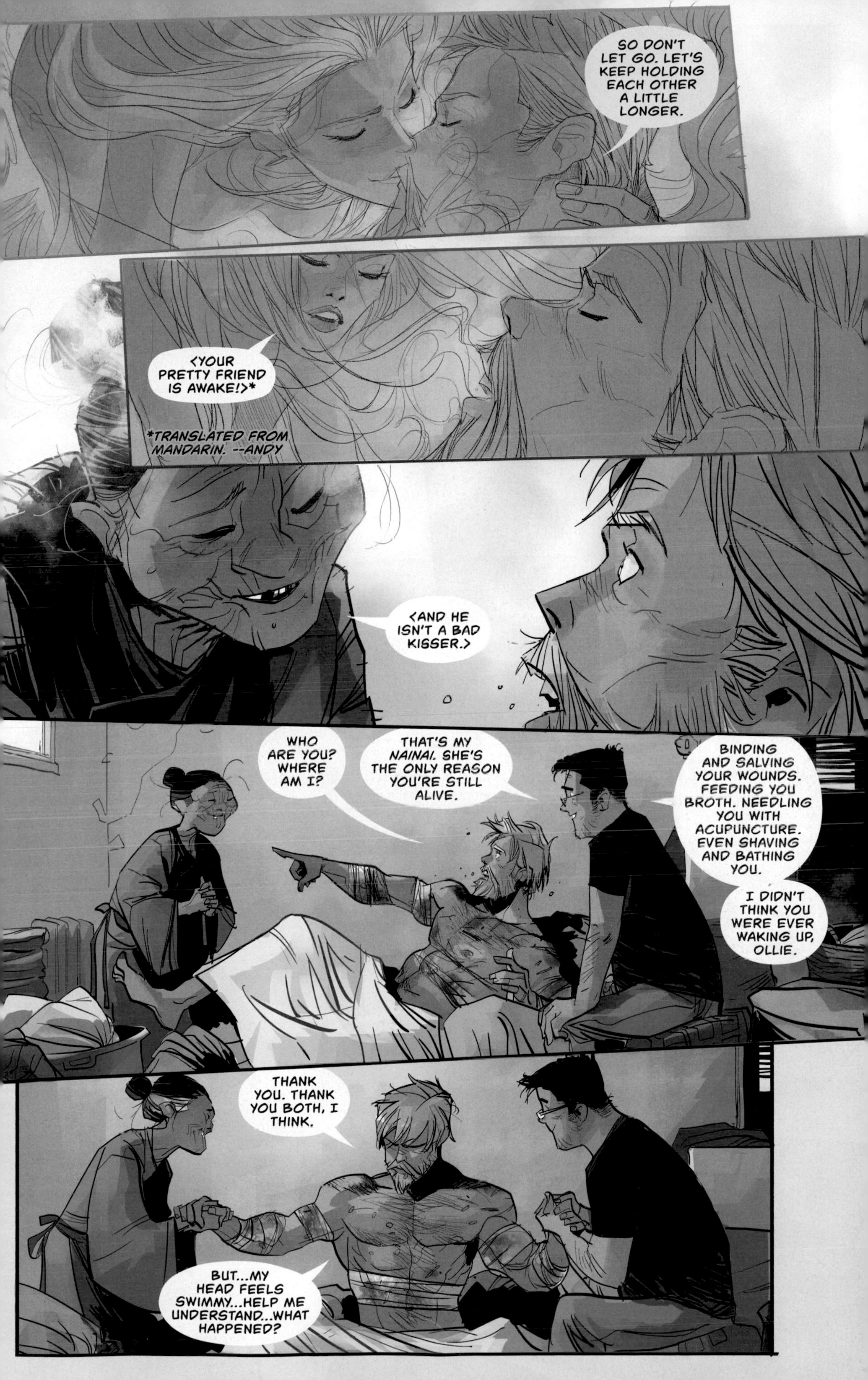
SO DON'T LET GO. LET'S KEEP HOLDING EACH OTHER A LITTLE LONGER.
<YOUR PRETTY FRIEND IS AWAKE!>*
*TRANSLATED FROM MANDARIN. --ANDY
<AND HE ISN'T A BAD KISSER.>
WHO ARE YOU? WHERE AM I?
THAT'S MY *NAINAI*. SHE'S THE ONLY REASON YOU'RE STILL ALIVE.
BINDING AND SALVING YOUR WOUNDS. FEEDING YOU BROTH. NEEDLING YOU WITH ACUPUNCTURE. EVEN SHAVING AND BATHING YOU.
I DIDN'T THINK YOU WERE EVER WAKING UP, OLLIE.
THANK YOU. THANK YOU BOTH, I THINK.
BUT...MY HEAD FEELS SWIMMY...HELP ME UNDERSTAND...WHAT HAPPENED?

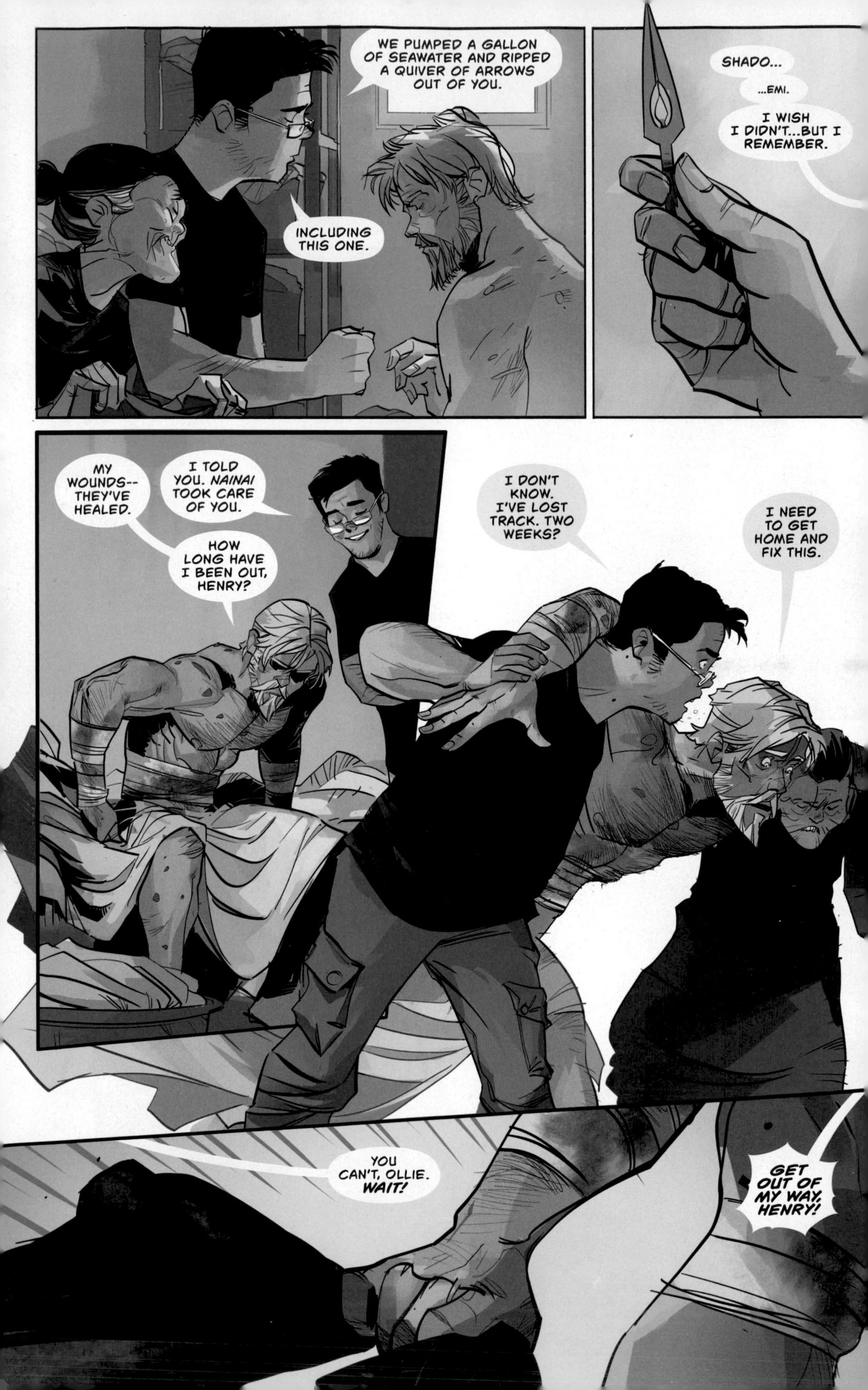
WE PUMPED A GALLON OF SEAWATER AND RIPPED A QUIVER OF ARROWS OUT OF YOU.
INCLUDING THIS ONE.
SHADO...
...EMI.
I WISH I DIDN'T...BUT I REMEMBER.
MY WOUNDS-- THEY'VE HEALED.
I TOLD YOU. *NAINAI* TOOK CARE OF YOU.
HOW LONG HAVE I BEEN OUT, HENRY?
I DON'T KNOW. I'VE LOST TRACK. TWO WEEKS?
I NEED TO GET HOME AND FIX THIS.
YOU CAN'T, OLLIE. *WAIT!*
GET OUT OF MY WAY, HENRY!

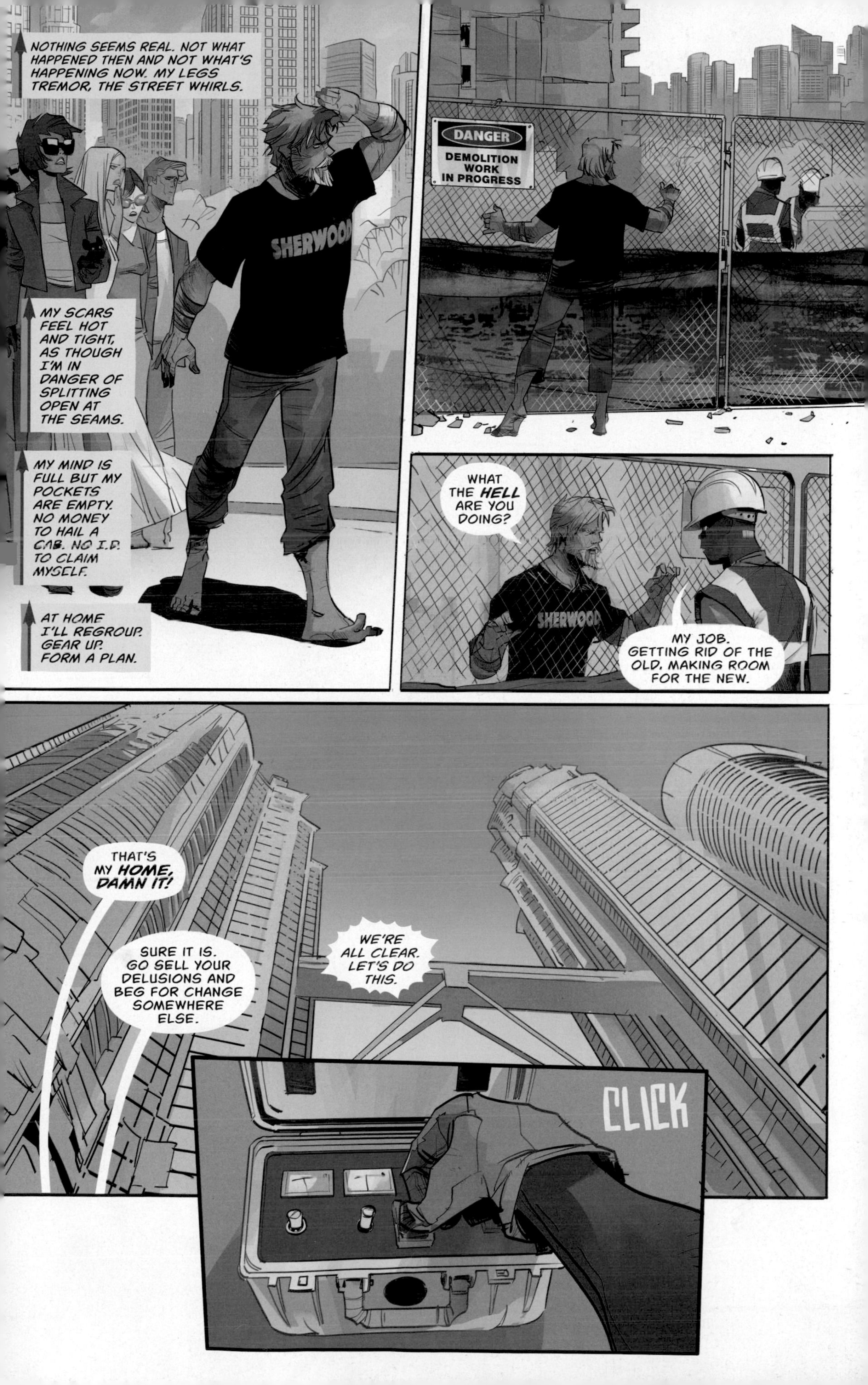
NOTHING SEEMS REAL. NOT WHAT HAPPENED THEN AND NOT WHAT'S HAPPENING NOW. MY LEGS TREMOR, THE STREET WHIRLS.
SHERWOOD
MY SCARS FEEL HOT AND TIGHT, AS THOUGH I'M IN DANGER OF SPLITTING OPEN AT THE SEAMS.
MY MIND IS FULL BUT MY POCKETS ARE EMPTY. NO MONEY TO HAIL A CAB. NO I.D. TO CLAIM MYSELF.
AT HOME I'LL REGROUP. GEAR UP. FORM A PLAN.
DANGER
DEMOLITION WORK IN PROGRESS
WHAT THE HELL ARE YOU DOING?
SHERWOOD
MY JOB. GETTING RID OF THE OLD, MAKING ROOM FOR THE NEW.
THAT'S MY HOME, DAMN IT!
SURE IT IS. GO SELL YOUR DELUSIONS AND BEG FOR CHANGE SOMEWHERE ELSE.
WE'RE ALL CLEAR. LET'S DO THIS.
CLICK

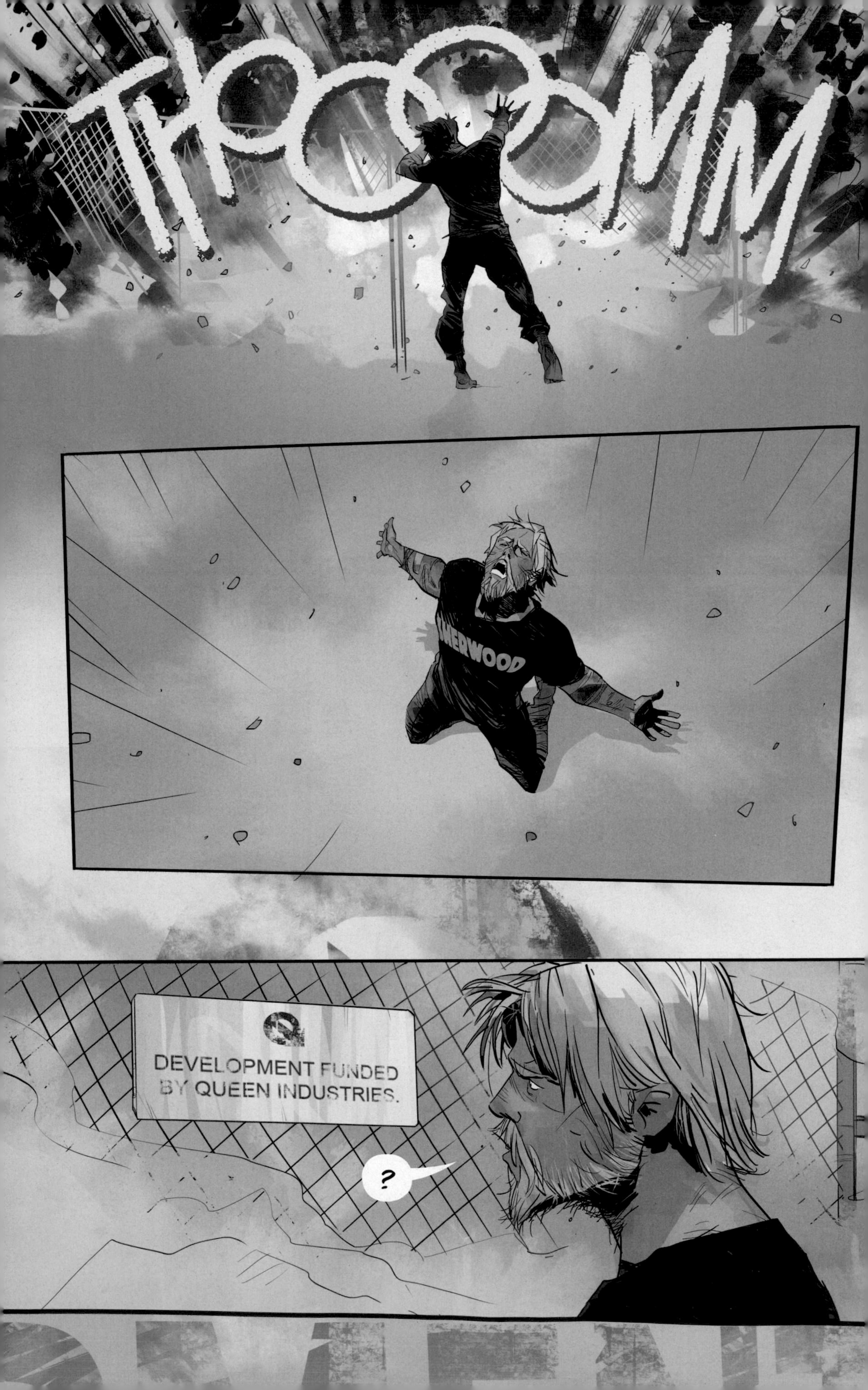

THOOOMM
SHERWOOD
DEVELOPMENT FUNDED BY QUEEN INDUSTRIES.
?

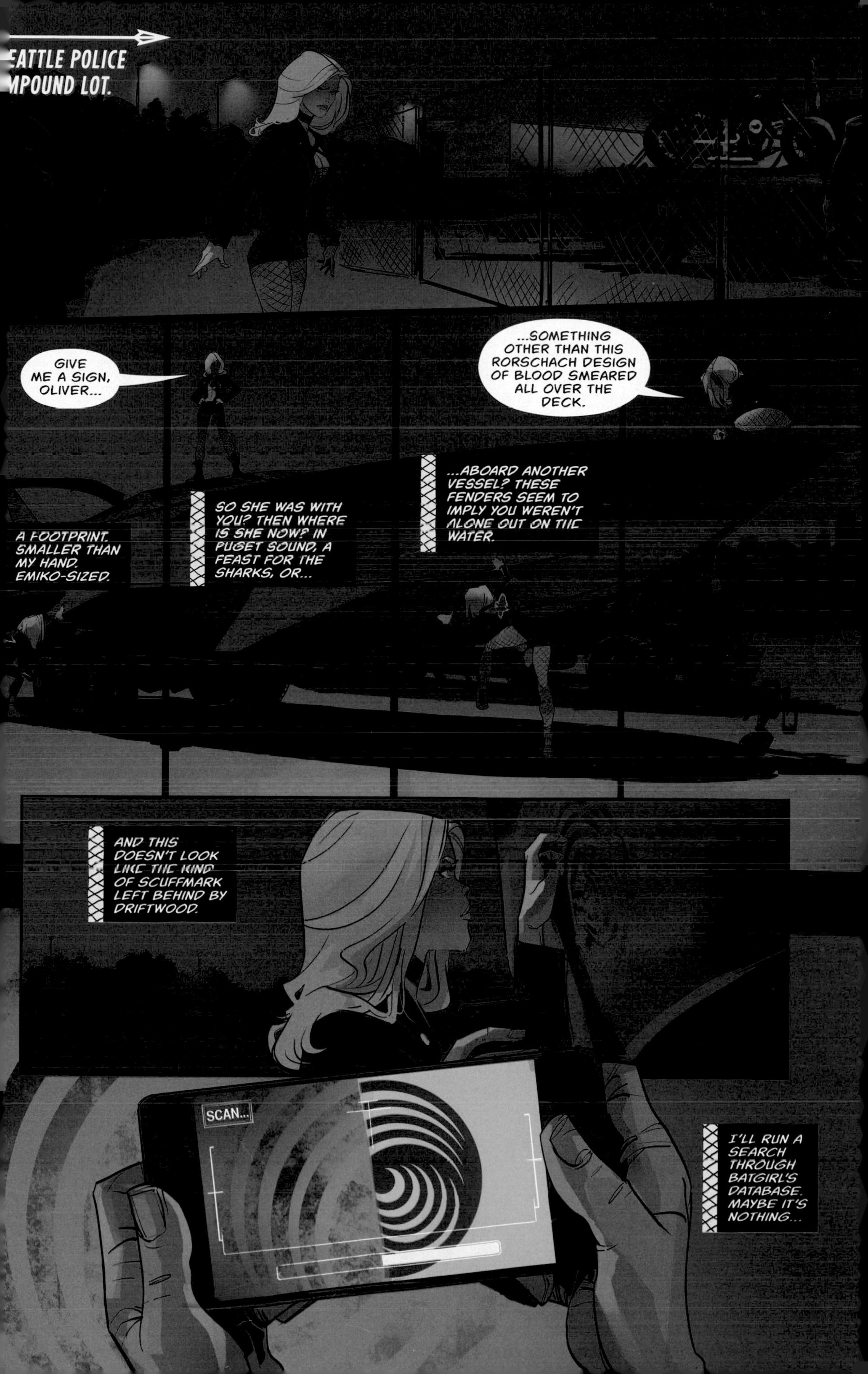

EATTLE POLICE MPOUND LOT.
GIVE ME A SIGN, OLIVER...
...SOMETHING OTHER THAN THIS RORSCHACH DESIGN OF BLOOD SMEARED ALL OVER THE DECK.
A FOOTPRINT. SMALLER THAN MY HAND. EMIKO-SIZED.
SO SHE WAS WITH YOU? THEN WHERE IS SHE NOW? IN PUGET SOUND, A FEAST FOR THE SHARKS, OR...
...ABOARD ANOTHER VESSEL? THESE FENDERS SEEM TO IMPLY YOU WEREN'T ALONE OUT ON THE WATER.
AND THIS DOESN'T LOOK LIKE THE KIND OF SCUFFMARK LEFT BEHIND BY DRIFTWOOD.
SCAN...
I'LL RUN A SEARCH THROUGH BATGIRL'S DATABASE. MAYBE IT'S NOTHING...

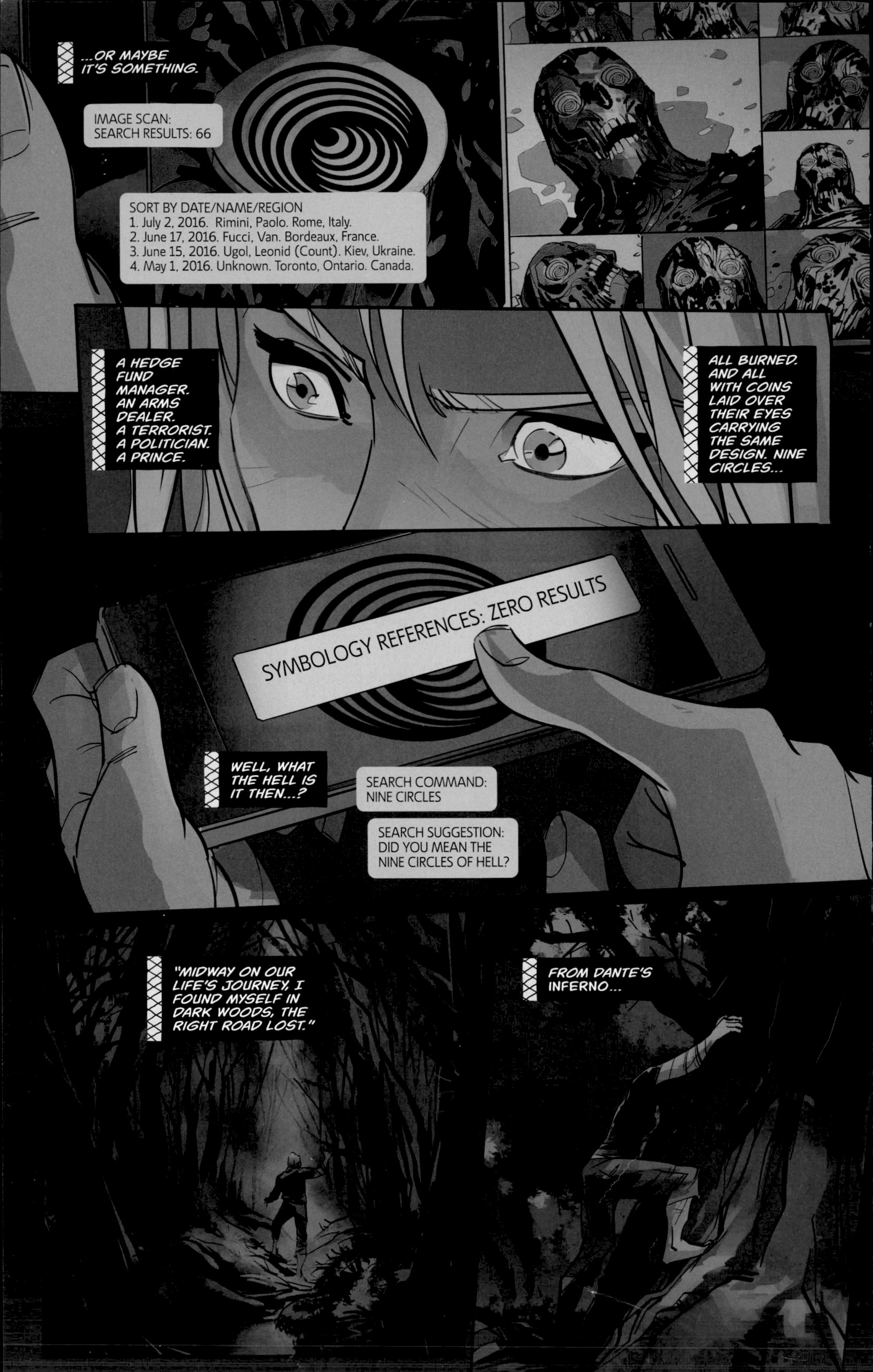
...OR MAYBE IT'S SOMETHING.
IMAGE SCAN:
SEARCH RESULTS: 66
SORT BY DATE/NAME/REGION
1. July 2, 2016. Rimini, Paolo. Rome, Italy.
2. June 17, 2016. Fucci, Van. Bordeaux, France.
3. June 15, 2016. Ugol, Leonid (Count). Kiev, Ukraine.
4. May 1, 2016. Unknown. Toronto, Ontario. Canada.
A HEDGE FUND MANAGER. AN ARMS DEALER. A TERRORIST. A POLITICIAN. A PRINCE.
ALL BURNED. AND ALL WITH COINS LAID OVER THEIR EYES CARRYING THE SAME DESIGN. NINE CIRCLES...
SYMBOLOGY REFERENCES: ZERO RESULTS
WELL, WHAT THE HELL IS IT THEN...?
SEARCH COMMAND:
NINE CIRCLES
SEARCH SUGGESTION:
DID YOU MEAN THE NINE CIRCLES OF HELL?
"MIDWAY ON OUR LIFE'S JOURNEY, I FOUND MYSELF IN DARK WOODS, THE RIGHT ROAD LOST."
FROM DANTE'S INFERNO...

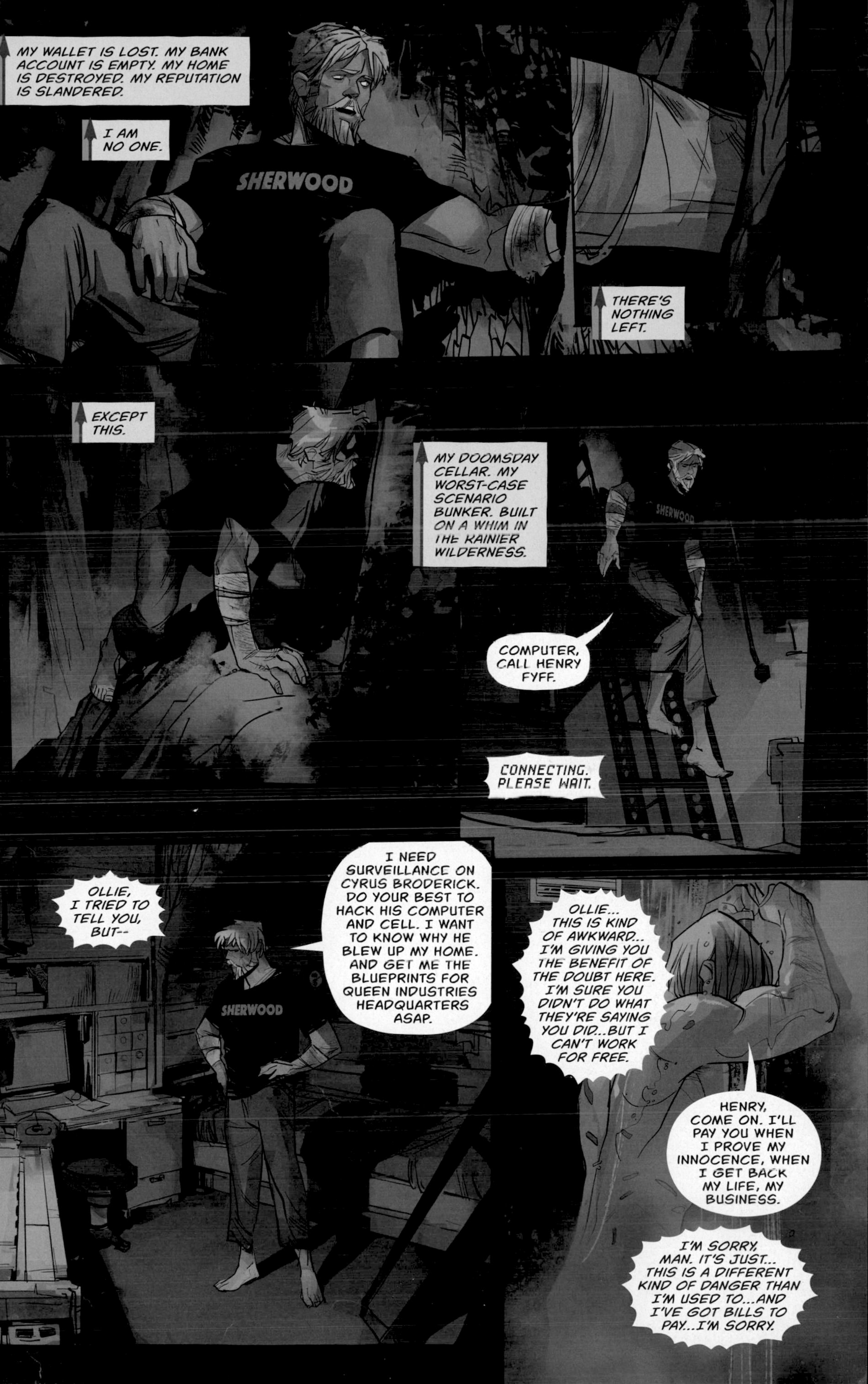
MY WALLET IS LOST. MY BANK ACCOUNT IS EMPTY. MY HOME IS DESTROYED. MY REPUTATION IS SLANDERED.
I AM NO ONE.
SHERWOOD
THERE'S NOTHING LEFT.
EXCEPT THIS.
MY DOOMSDAY CELLAR. MY WORST-CASE SCENARIO BUNKER. BUILT ON A WHIM IN THE RAINIER WILDERNESS.
SHERWOOD
COMPUTER, CALL HENRY FYFF.
CONNECTING. PLEASE WAIT.
OLLIE, I TRIED TO TELL YOU, BUT--
I NEED SURVEILLANCE ON CYRUS BRODERICK. DO YOUR BEST TO HACK HIS COMPUTER AND CELL. I WANT TO KNOW WHY HE BLEW UP MY HOME. AND GET ME THE BLUEPRINTS FOR QUEEN INDUSTRIES HEADQUARTERS ASAP.
SHERWOOD
OLLIE... THIS IS KIND OF AWKWARD... I'M GIVING YOU THE BENEFIT OF THE DOUBT HERE. I'M SURE YOU DIDN'T DO WHAT THEY'RE SAYING YOU DID...BUT I CAN'T WORK FOR FREE.
HENRY, COME ON. I'LL PAY YOU WHEN I PROVE MY INNOCENCE, WHEN I GET BACK MY LIFE, MY BUSINESS.
I'M SORRY, MAN. IT'S JUST... THIS IS A DIFFERENT KIND OF DANGER THAN I'M USED TO...AND I'VE GOT BILLS TO PAY...I'M SORRY.

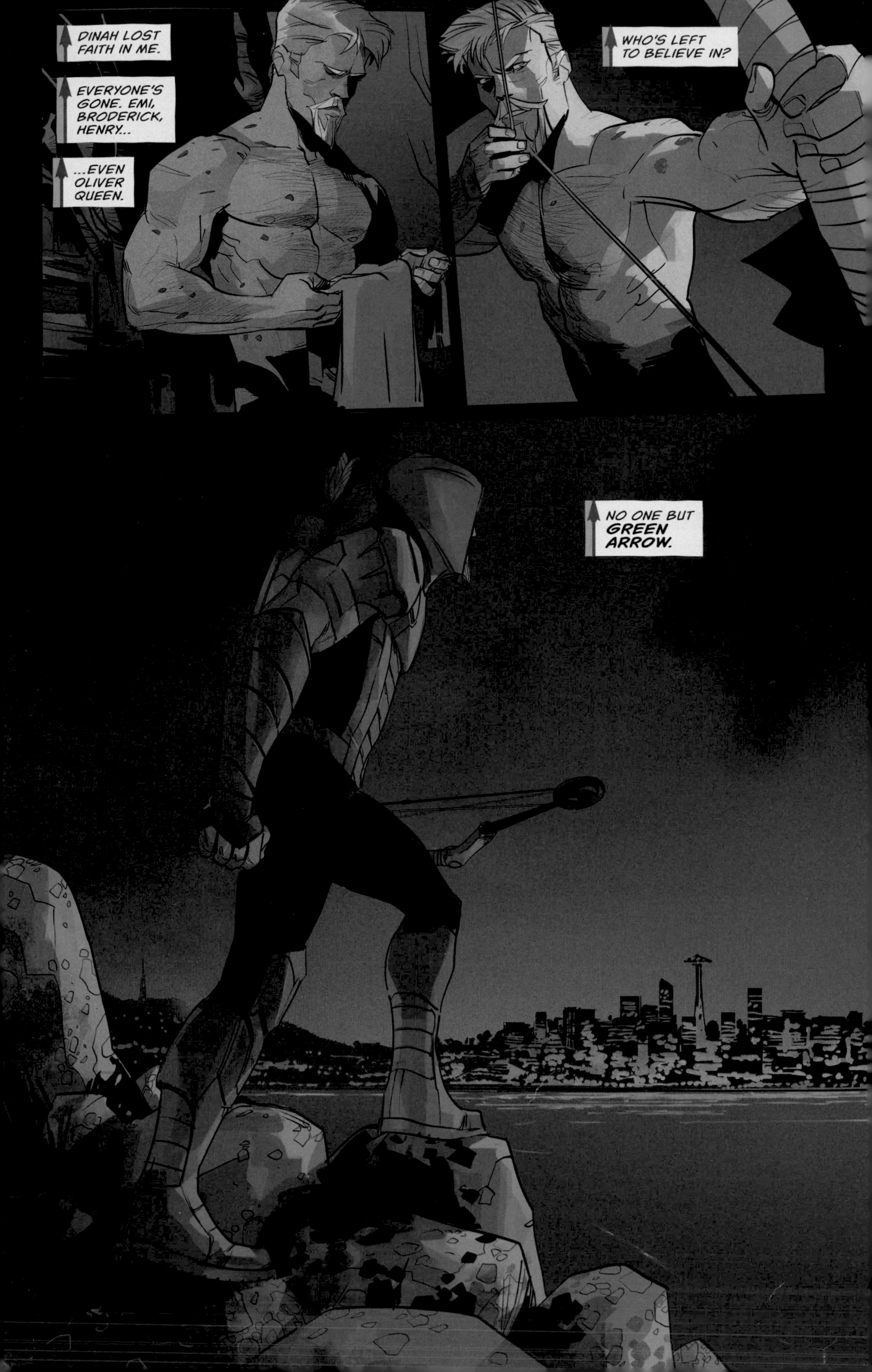
DINAH LOST FAITH IN ME.
EVERYONE'S GONE. EMI, BRODERICK, HENRY...
...EVEN OLIVER QUEEN.
WHO'S LEFT TO BELIEVE IN?
NO ONE BUT GREEN ARROW.

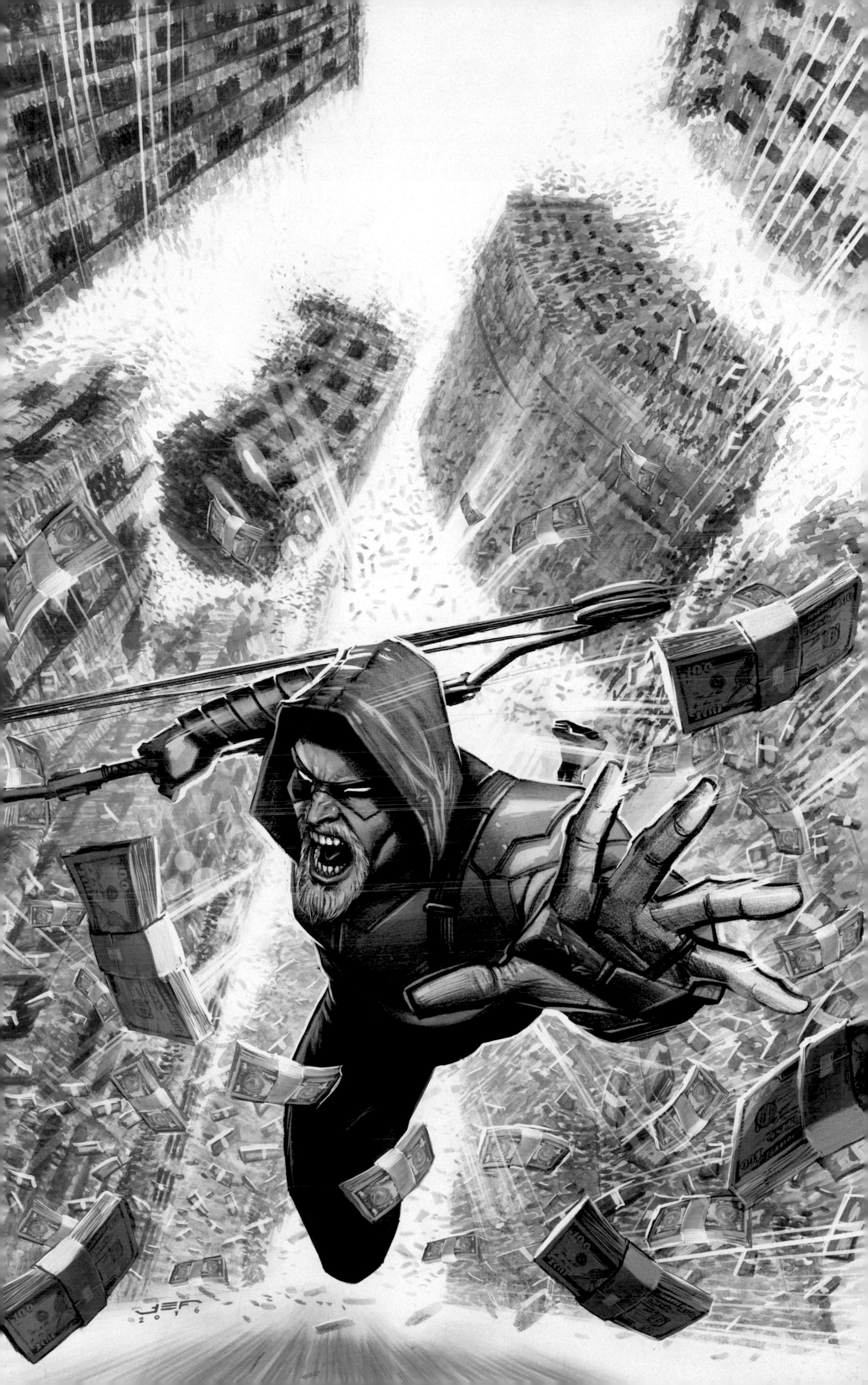

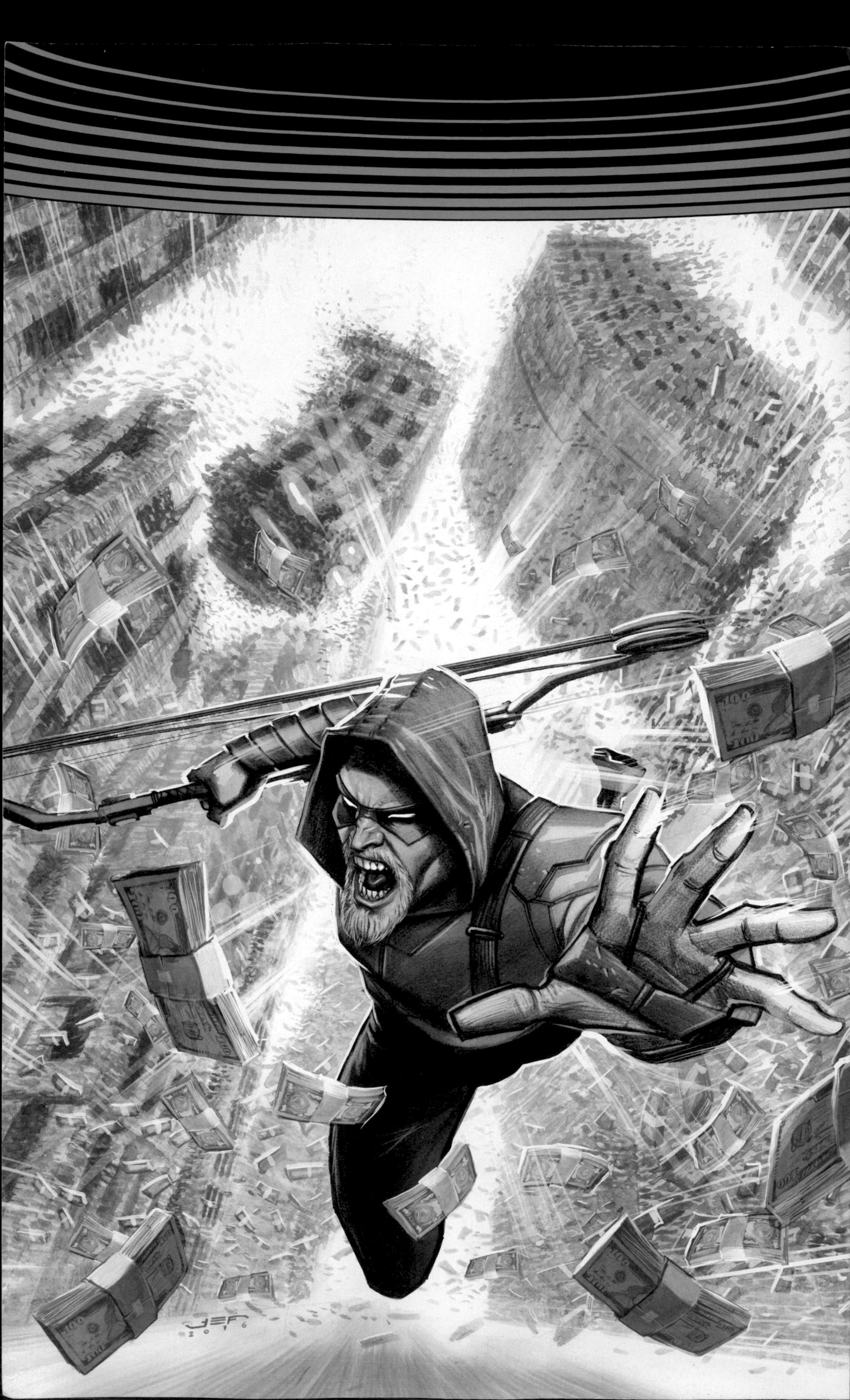

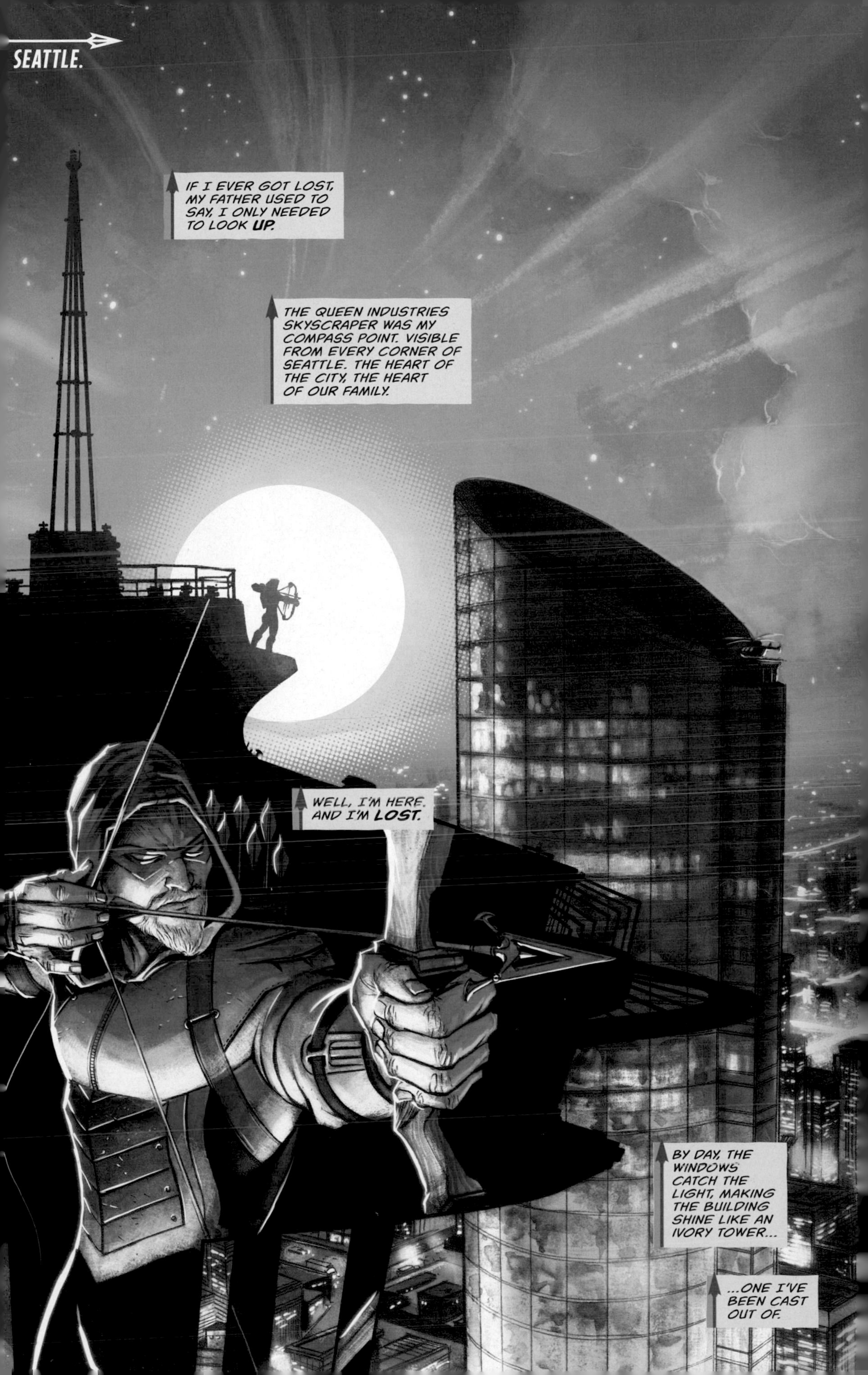

SEATTLE.
IF I EVER GOT LOST, MY FATHER USED TO SAY, I ONLY NEEDED TO LOOK UP.
THE QUEEN INDUSTRIES SKYSCRAPER WAS MY COMPASS POINT. VISIBLE FROM EVERY CORNER OF SEATTLE. THE HEART OF THE CITY, THE HEART OF OUR FAMILY.
WELL, I'M HERE. AND I'M LOST.
BY DAY, THE WINDOWS CATCH THE LIGHT, MAKING THE BUILDING SHINE LIKE AN IVORY TOWER...
...ONE I'VE BEEN CAST OUT OF.

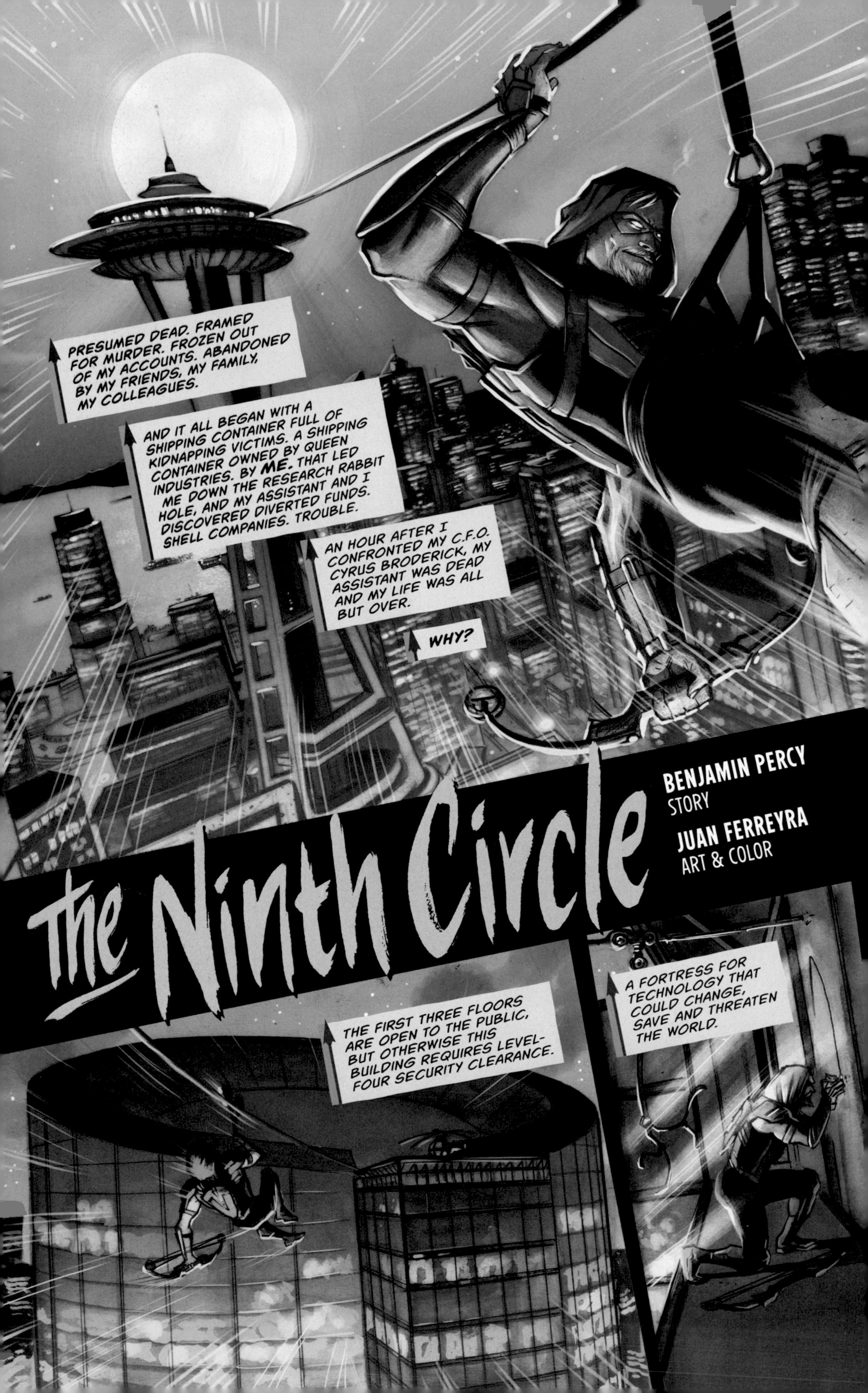
PRESUMED DEAD. FRAMED FOR MURDER. FROZEN OUT OF MY ACCOUNTS. ABANDONED BY MY FRIENDS, MY FAMILY, MY COLLEAGUES.
AND IT ALL BEGAN WITH A SHIPPING CONTAINER FULL OF KIDNAPPING VICTIMS. A SHIPPING CONTAINER OWNED BY QUEEN INDUSTRIES. BY ME. THAT LED ME DOWN THE RESEARCH RABBIT HOLE, AND MY ASSISTANT AND I DISCOVERED DIVERTED FUNDS. SHELL COMPANIES. TROUBLE.
AN HOUR AFTER I CONFRONTED MY C.F.O. CYRUS BRODERICK, MY ASSISTANT WAS DEAD AND MY LIFE WAS ALL BUT OVER.
WHY?
the Ninth Circle
BENJAMIN PERCY
STORY
JUAN FERREYRA
ART & COLOR
THE FIRST THREE FLOORS ARE OPEN TO THE PUBLIC, BUT OTHERWISE THIS BUILDING REQUIRES LEVEL-FOUR SECURITY CLEARANCE.
A FORTRESS FOR TECHNOLOGY THAT COULD CHANGE, SAVE AND THREATEN THE WORLD.

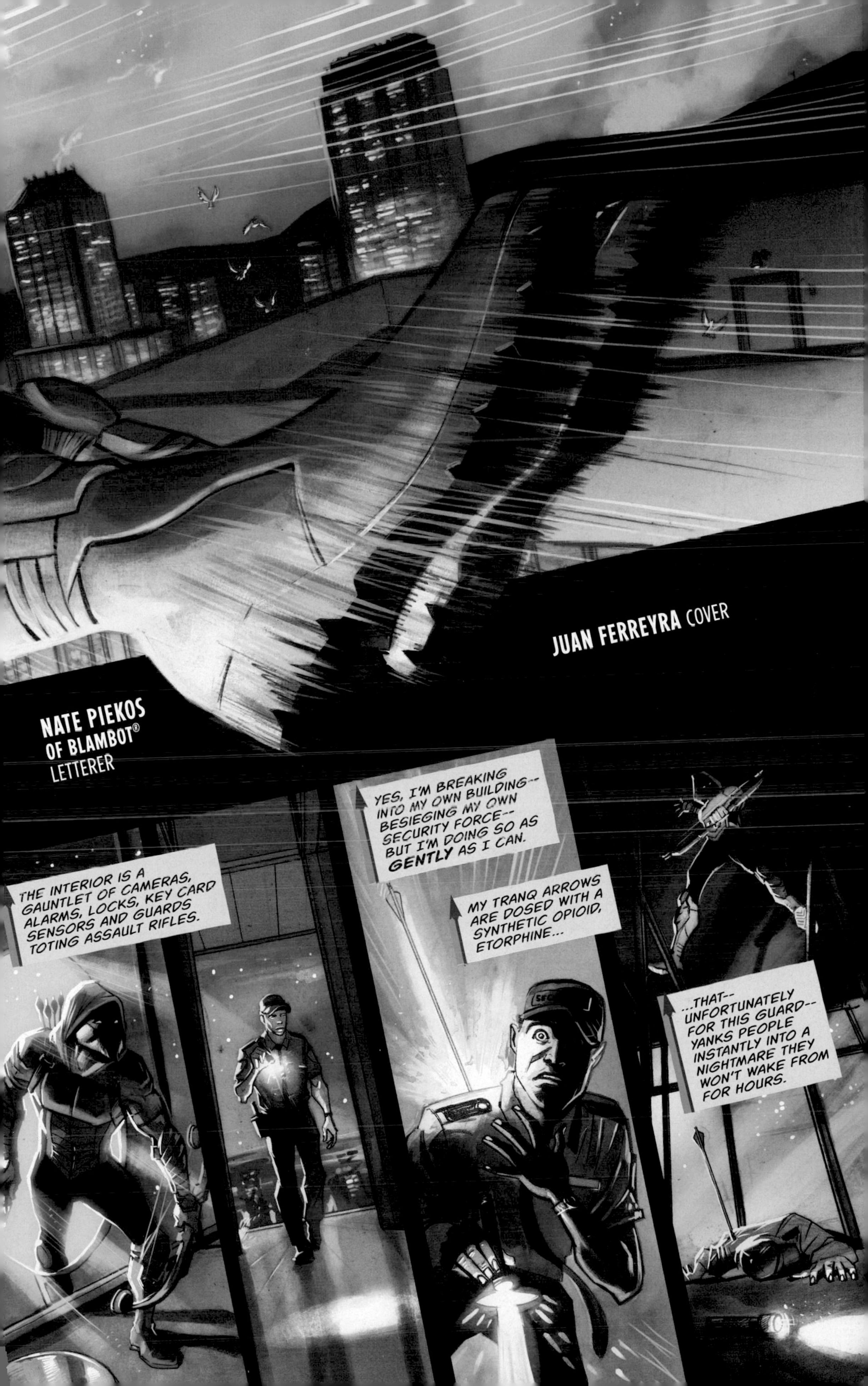
JUAN FERREYRA COVER
NATE PIEKOS OF BLAMBOT® LETTERER
THE INTERIOR IS A GAUNTLET OF CAMERAS, ALARMS, LOCKS, KEY CARD SENSORS AND GUARDS TOTING ASSAULT RIFLES.
YES, I'M BREAKING INTO MY OWN BUILDING-- BESIEGING MY OWN SECURITY FORCE-- BUT I'M DOING SO AS GENTLY AS I CAN.
MY TRANQ ARROWS ARE DOSED WITH A SYNTHETIC OPIOID, ETORPHINE...
...THAT-- UNFORTUNATELY FOR THIS GUARD-- YANKS PEOPLE INSTANTLY INTO A NIGHTMARE THEY WON'T WAKE FROM FOR HOURS.

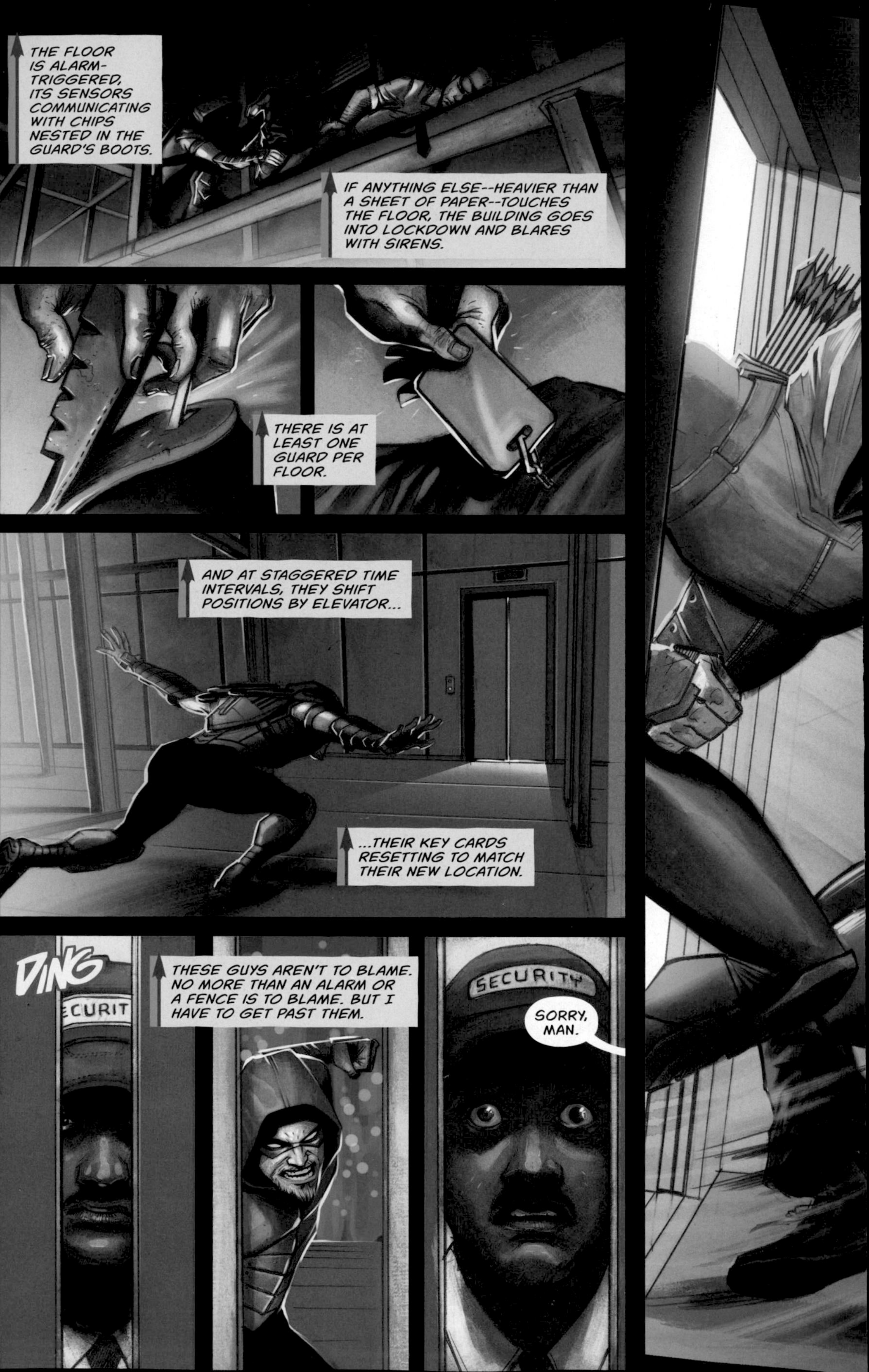
THE FLOOR IS ALARM-TRIGGERED, ITS SENSORS COMMUNICATING WITH CHIPS NESTED IN THE GUARD'S BOOTS.
IF ANYTHING ELSE--HEAVIER THAN A SHEET OF PAPER--TOUCHES THE FLOOR, THE BUILDING GOES INTO LOCKDOWN AND BLARES WITH SIRENS.
THERE IS AT LEAST ONE GUARD PER FLOOR.
AND AT STAGGERED TIME INTERVALS, THEY SHIFT POSITIONS BY ELEVATOR...
...THEIR KEY CARDS RESETTING TO MATCH THEIR NEW LOCATION.
DING
SECURIT
THESE GUYS AREN'T TO BLAME. NO MORE THAN AN ALARM OR A FENCE IS TO BLAME. BUT I HAVE TO GET PAST THEM.
SECURITY
SORRY, MAN.

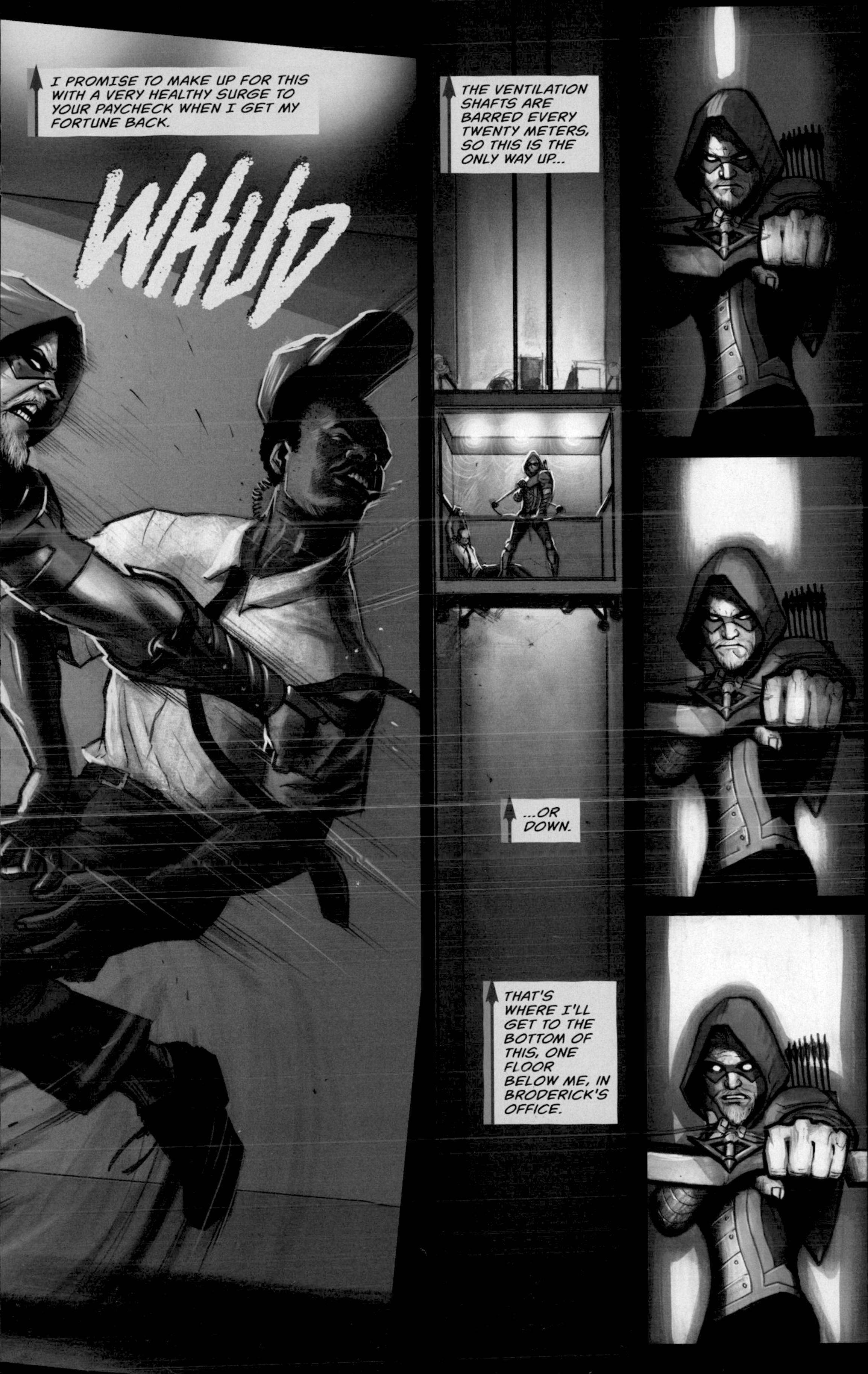
I PROMISE TO MAKE UP FOR THIS WITH A VERY HEALTHY SURGE TO YOUR PAYCHECK WHEN I GET MY FORTUNE BACK.
WHUD
THE VENTILATION SHAFTS ARE BARRED EVERY TWENTY METERS, SO THIS IS THE ONLY WAY UP...
...OR DOWN.
THAT'S WHERE I'LL GET TO THE BOTTOM OF THIS, ONE FLOOR BELOW ME, IN BRODERICK'S OFFICE.

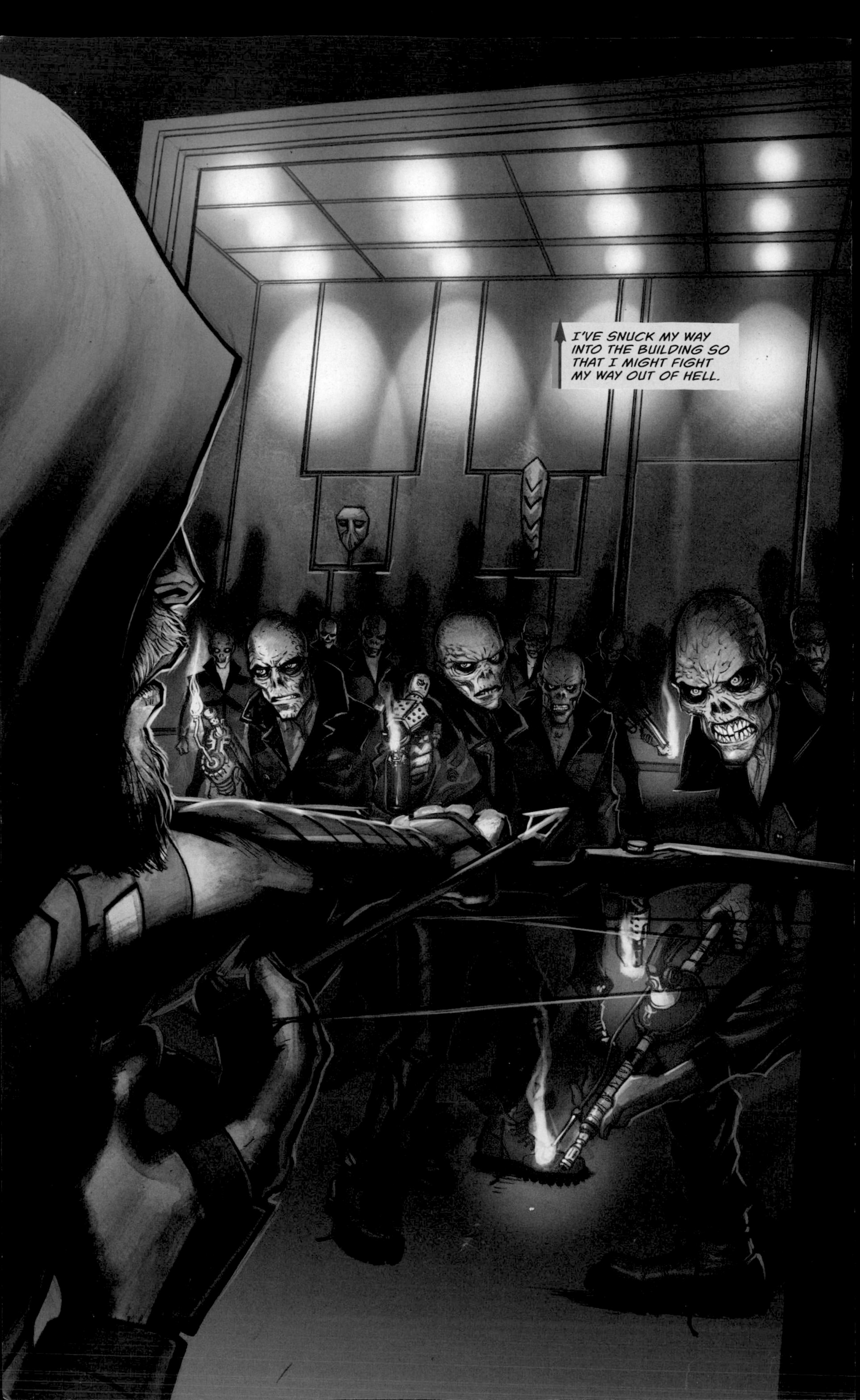
I'VE SNUCK MY WAY INTO THE BUILDING SO THAT I MIGHT FIGHT MY WAY OUT OF HELL.

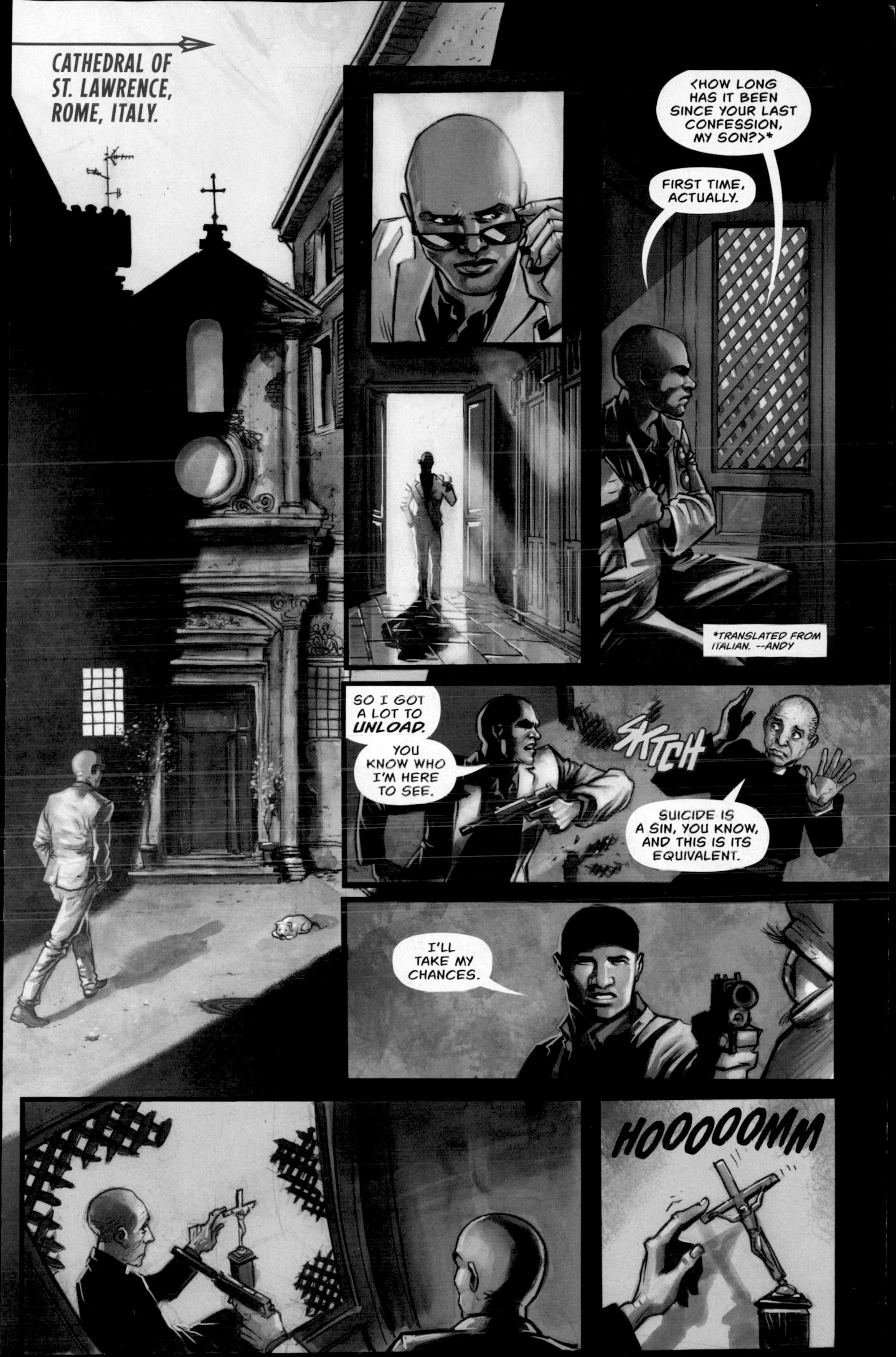
CATHEDRAL OF ST. LAWRENCE, ROME, ITALY.
<HOW LONG HAS IT BEEN SINCE YOUR LAST CONFESSION, MY SON?>*
FIRST TIME, ACTUALLY.
*TRANSLATED FROM ITALIAN. --ANDY
SO I GOT A LOT TO UNLOAD.
YOU KNOW WHO I'M HERE TO SEE.
SKTCH
SUICIDE IS A SIN, YOU KNOW, AND THIS IS ITS EQUIVALENT.
I'LL TAKE MY CHANCES.
HOOOOOMM

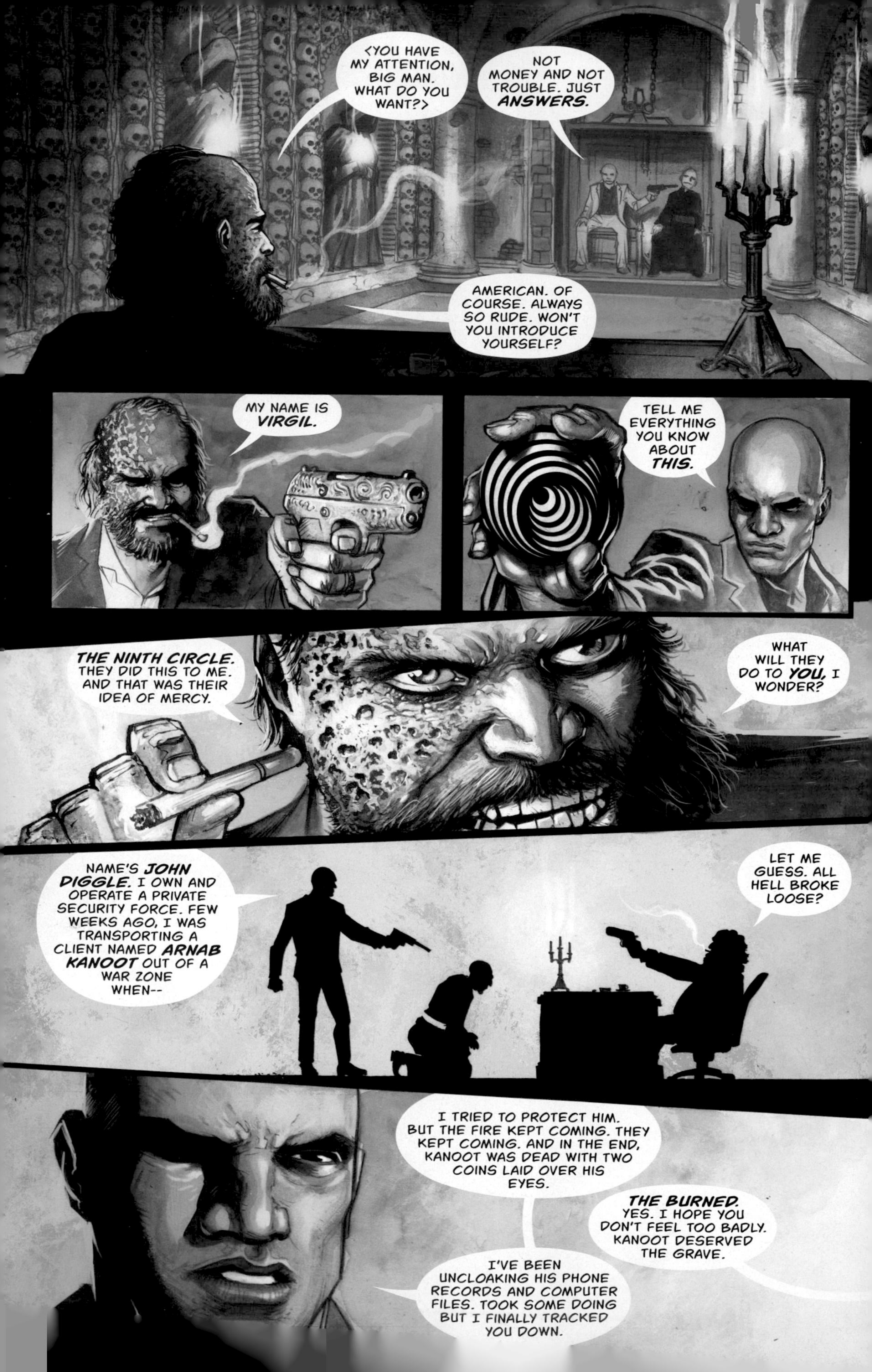
<YOU HAVE MY ATTENTION, BIG MAN. WHAT DO YOU WANT?>
NOT MONEY AND NOT TROUBLE. JUST ANSWERS.
AMERICAN. OF COURSE. ALWAYS SO RUDE. WON'T YOU INTRODUCE YOURSELF?
MY NAME IS VIRGIL.
TELL ME EVERYTHING YOU KNOW ABOUT THIS.
THE NINTH CIRCLE. THEY DID THIS TO ME. AND THAT WAS THEIR IDEA OF MERCY.
WHAT WILL THEY DO TO YOU, I WONDER?
NAME'S JOHN DIGGLE. I OWN AND OPERATE A PRIVATE SECURITY FORCE. FEW WEEKS AGO, I WAS TRANSPORTING A CLIENT NAMED ARNAB KANOOT OUT OF A WAR ZONE WHEN--
LET ME GUESS. ALL HELL BROKE LOOSE?
I TRIED TO PROTECT HIM. BUT THE FIRE KEPT COMING. THEY KEPT COMING. AND IN THE END, KANOOT WAS DEAD WITH TWO COINS LAID OVER HIS EYES.
THE BURNED. YES. I HOPE YOU DON'T FEEL TOO BADLY. KANOOT DESERVED THE GRAVE.
I'VE BEEN UNCLOAKING HIS PHONE RECORDS AND COMPUTER FILES. TOOK SOME DOING BUT I FINALLY TRACKED YOU DOWN.

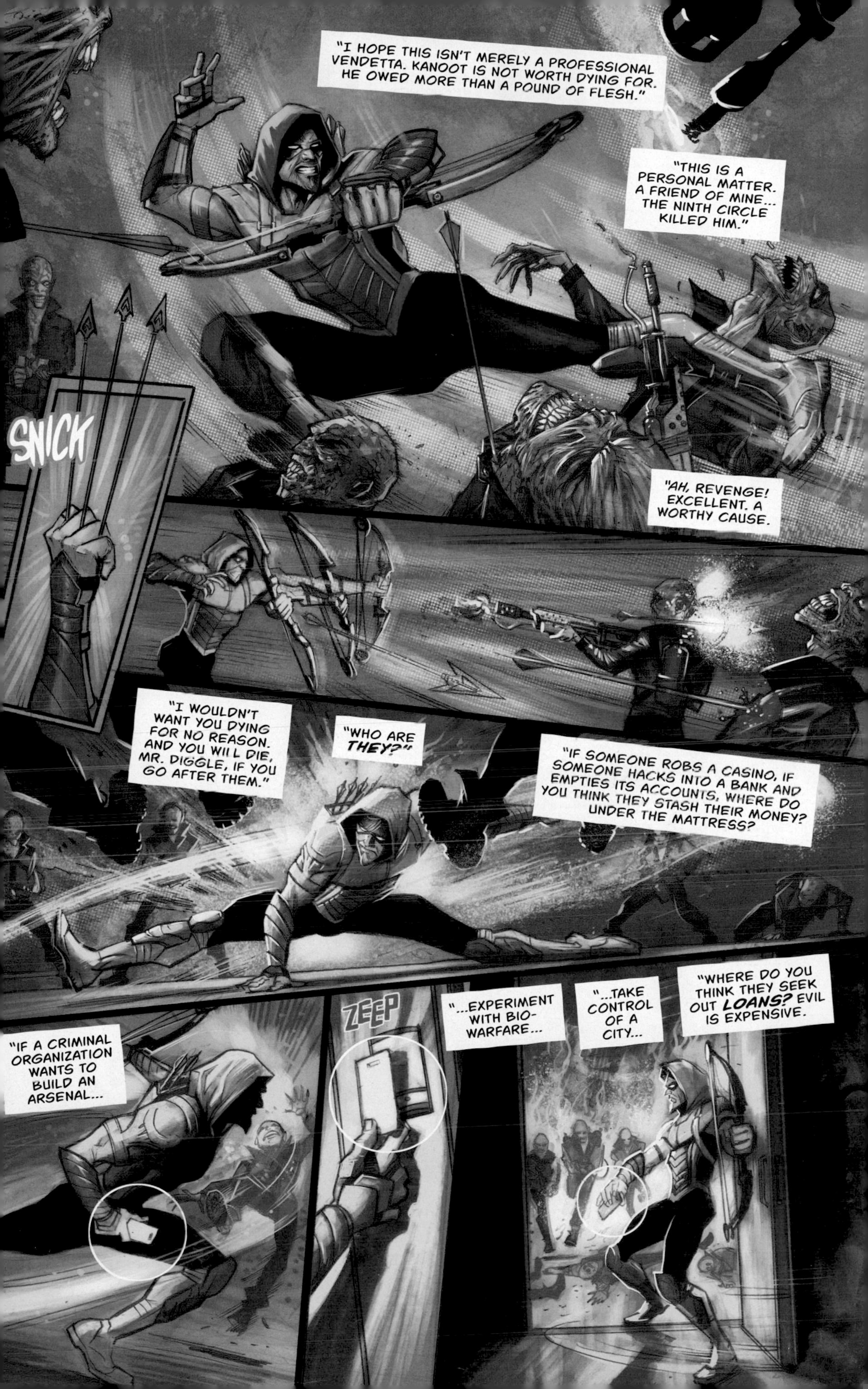
"I HOPE THIS ISN'T MERELY A PROFESSIONAL VENDETTA. KANOOT IS NOT WORTH DYING FOR. HE OWED MORE THAN A POUND OF FLESH."
"THIS IS A PERSONAL MATTER. A FRIEND OF MINE... THE NINTH CIRCLE KILLED HIM."
SNICK
"AH, REVENGE! EXCELLENT. A WORTHY CAUSE.
"I WOULDN'T WANT YOU DYING FOR NO REASON. AND YOU WILL DIE, MR. DIGGLE, IF YOU GO AFTER THEM."
"WHO ARE THEY?"
"IF SOMEONE ROBS A CASINO, IF SOMEONE HACKS INTO A BANK AND EMPTIES ITS ACCOUNTS, WHERE DO YOU THINK THEY STASH THEIR MONEY? UNDER THE MATTRESS?
"IF A CRIMINAL ORGANIZATION WANTS TO BUILD AN ARSENAL...
ZEEP
"...EXPERIMENT WITH BIO-WARFARE...
"...TAKE CONTROL OF A CITY...
"WHERE DO YOU THINK THEY SEEK OUT LOANS? EVIL IS EXPENSIVE.

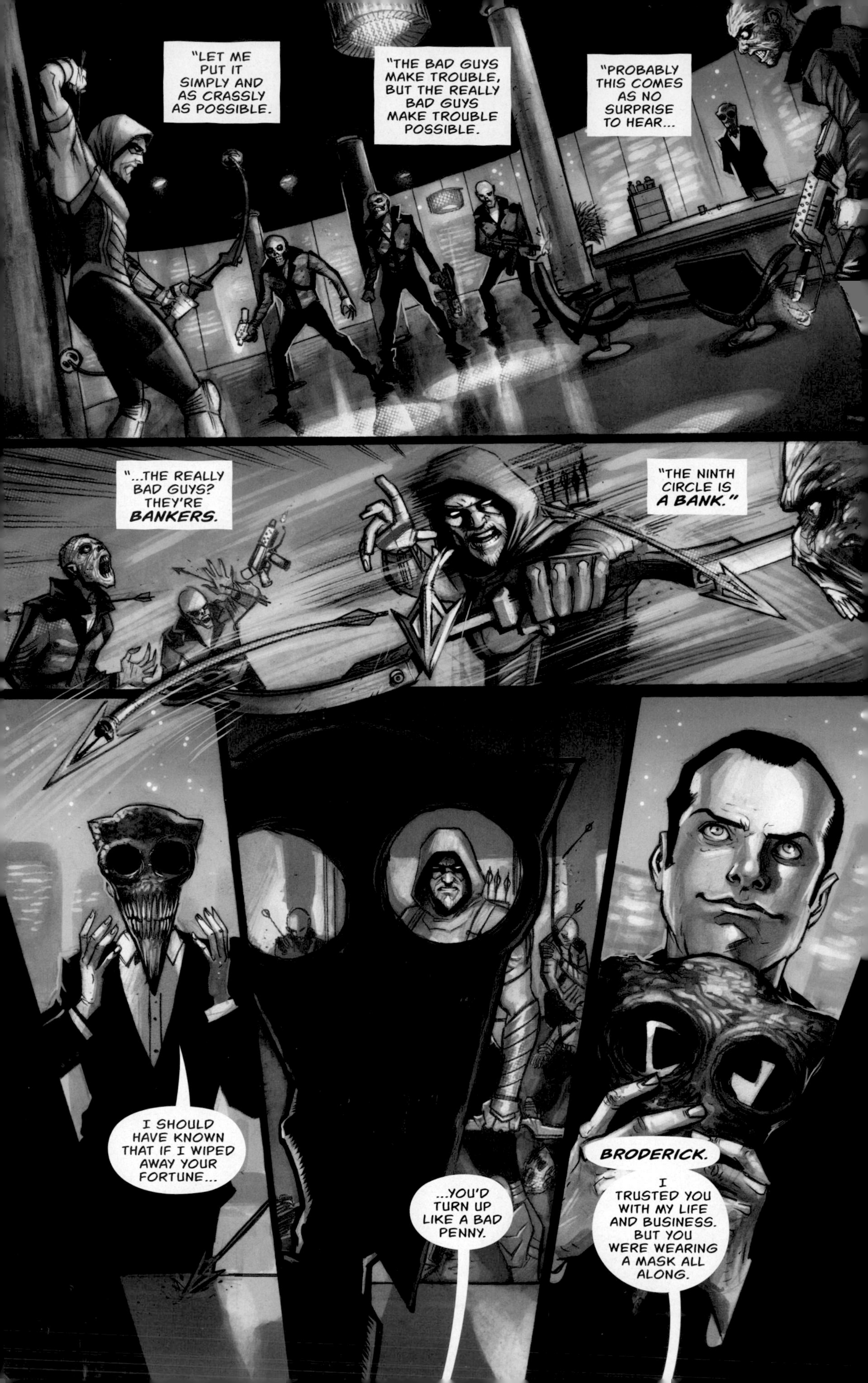
"LET ME PUT IT SIMPLY AND AS CRASSLY AS POSSIBLE.
"THE BAD GUYS MAKE TROUBLE, BUT THE REALLY BAD GUYS MAKE TROUBLE POSSIBLE.
"PROBABLY THIS COMES AS NO SURPRISE TO HEAR...
"...THE REALLY BAD GUYS? THEY'RE BANKERS.
"THE NINTH CIRCLE IS A BANK."
I SHOULD HAVE KNOWN THAT IF I WIPED AWAY YOUR FORTUNE...
...YOU'D TURN UP LIKE A BAD PENNY.
BRODERICK.
I TRUSTED YOU WITH MY LIFE AND BUSINESS. BUT YOU WERE WEARING A MASK ALL ALONG.

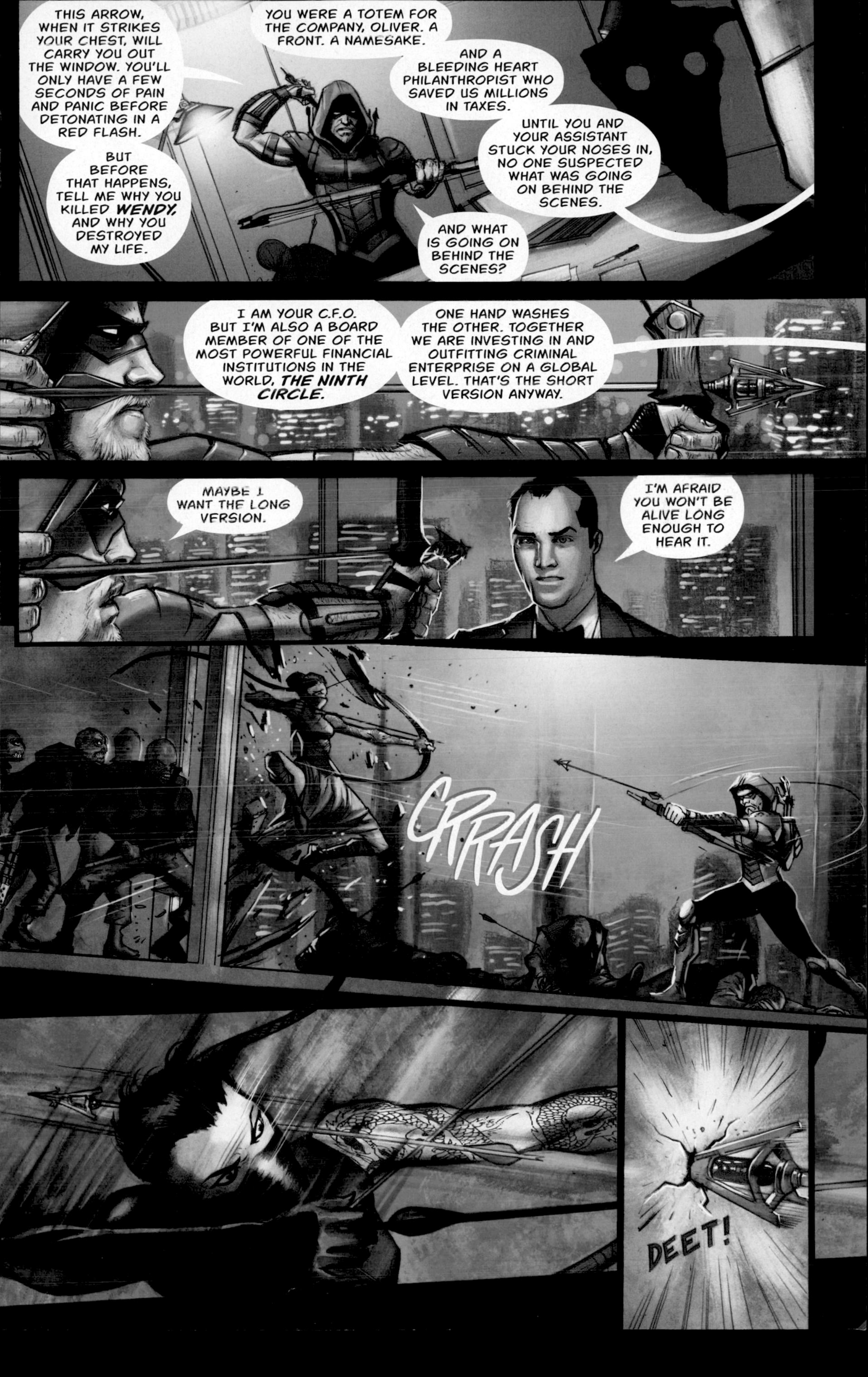

THIS ARROW, WHEN IT STRIKES YOUR CHEST, WILL CARRY YOU OUT THE WINDOW. YOU'LL ONLY HAVE A FEW SECONDS OF PAIN AND PANIC BEFORE DETONATING IN A RED FLASH.
BUT BEFORE THAT HAPPENS, TELL ME WHY YOU KILLED ***WENDY,*** AND WHY YOU DESTROYED MY LIFE.
YOU WERE A TOTEM FOR THE COMPANY, OLIVER. A FRONT. A NAMESAKE.
AND A BLEEDING HEART PHILANTHROPIST WHO SAVED US MILLIONS IN TAXES.
UNTIL YOU AND YOUR ASSISTANT STUCK YOUR NOSES IN, NO ONE SUSPECTED WHAT WAS GOING ON BEHIND THE SCENES.
AND WHAT IS GOING ON BEHIND THE SCENES?
I AM YOUR C.F.O. BUT I'M ALSO A BOARD MEMBER OF ONE OF THE MOST POWERFUL FINANCIAL INSTITUTIONS IN THE WORLD, ***THE NINTH CIRCLE.***
ONE HAND WASHES THE OTHER. TOGETHER WE ARE INVESTING IN AND OUTFITTING CRIMINAL ENTERPRISE ON A GLOBAL LEVEL. THAT'S THE SHORT VERSION ANYWAY.
MAYBE I WANT THE LONG VERSION.
I'M AFRAID YOU WON'T BE ALIVE LONG ENOUGH TO HEAR IT.
CRRASH
DEET!

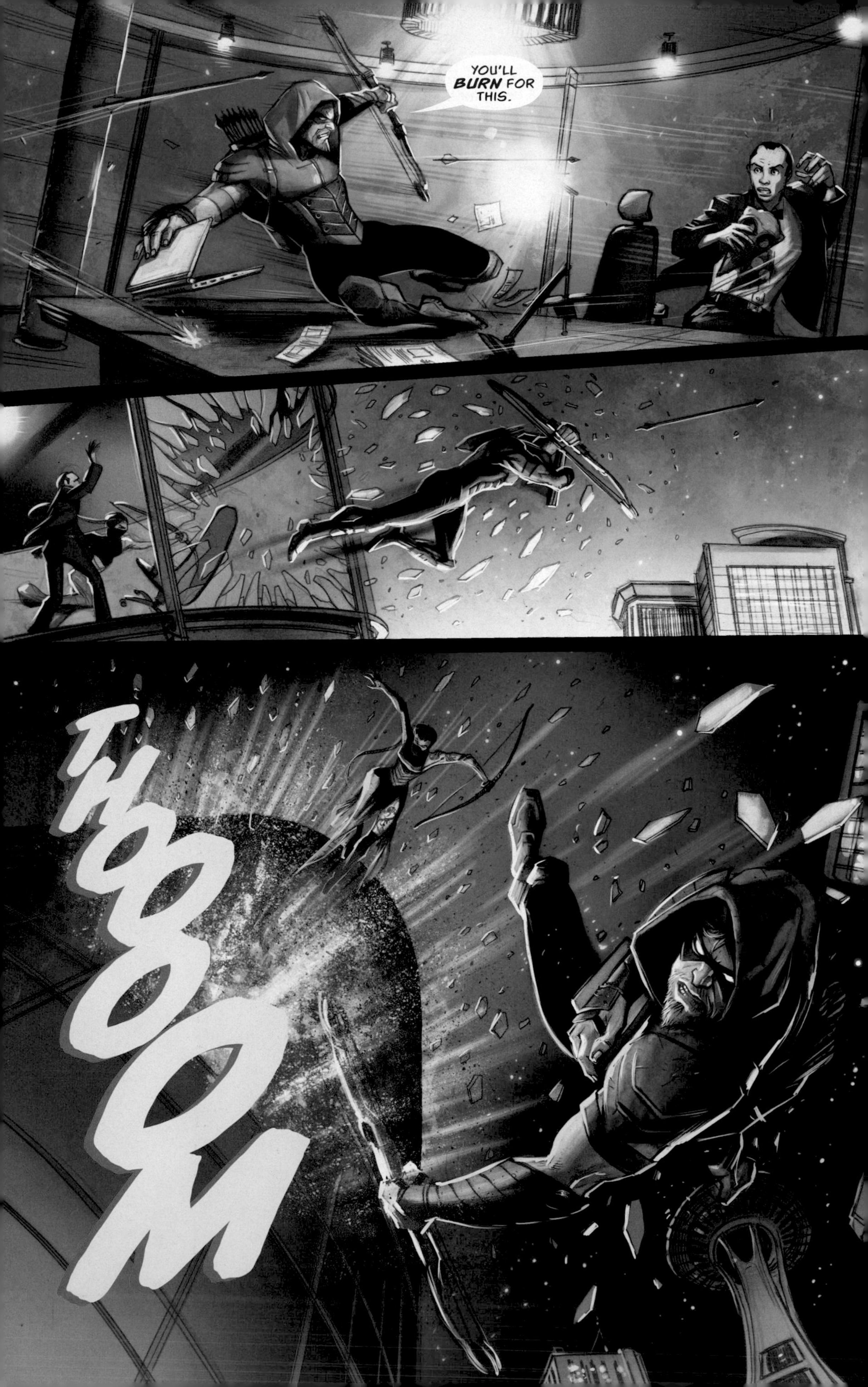
YOU'LL BURN FOR THIS.
THOOOM

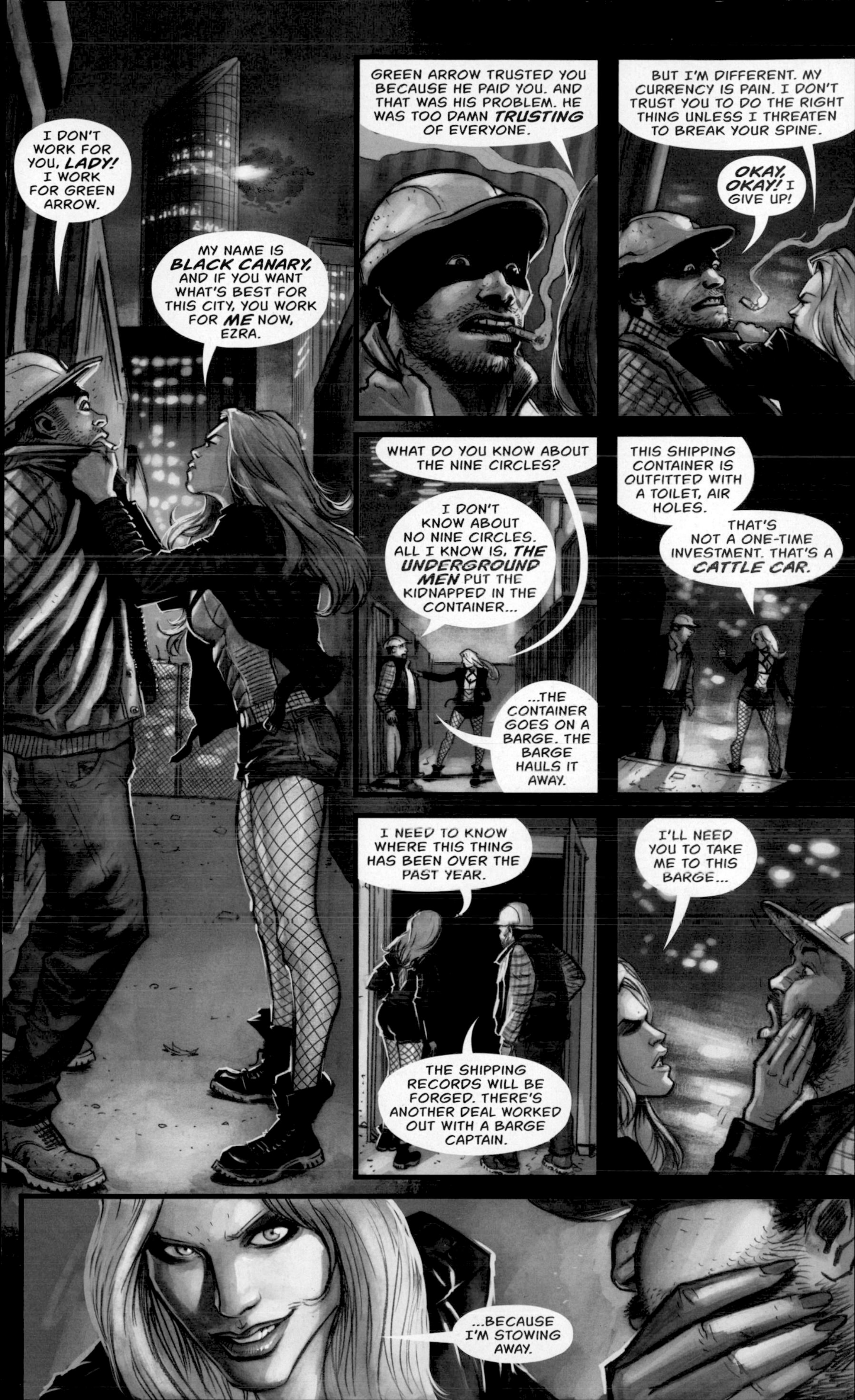
I DON'T WORK FOR YOU, LADY! I WORK FOR GREEN ARROW.
MY NAME IS BLACK CANARY. AND IF YOU WANT WHAT'S BEST FOR THIS CITY, YOU WORK FOR ME NOW, EZRA.
GREEN ARROW TRUSTED YOU BECAUSE HE PAID YOU. AND THAT WAS HIS PROBLEM. HE WAS TOO DAMN TRUSTING OF EVERYONE.
BUT I'M DIFFERENT. MY CURRENCY IS PAIN. I DON'T TRUST YOU TO DO THE RIGHT THING UNLESS I THREATEN TO BREAK YOUR SPINE.
OKAY, OKAY! I GIVE UP!
WHAT DO YOU KNOW ABOUT THE NINE CIRCLES?
I DON'T KNOW ABOUT NO NINE CIRCLES. ALL I KNOW IS, THE UNDERGROUND MEN PUT THE KIDNAPPED IN THE CONTAINER...
...THE CONTAINER GOES ON A BARGE. THE BARGE HAULS IT AWAY.
THIS SHIPPING CONTAINER IS OUTFITTED WITH A TOILET, AIR HOLES.
THAT'S NOT A ONE-TIME INVESTMENT. THAT'S A CATTLE CAR.
I NEED TO KNOW WHERE THIS THING HAS BEEN OVER THE PAST YEAR.
THE SHIPPING RECORDS WILL BE FORGED. THERE'S ANOTHER DEAL WORKED OUT WITH A BARGE CAPTAIN.
I'LL NEED YOU TO TAKE ME TO THIS BARGE...
...BECAUSE I'M STOWING AWAY.

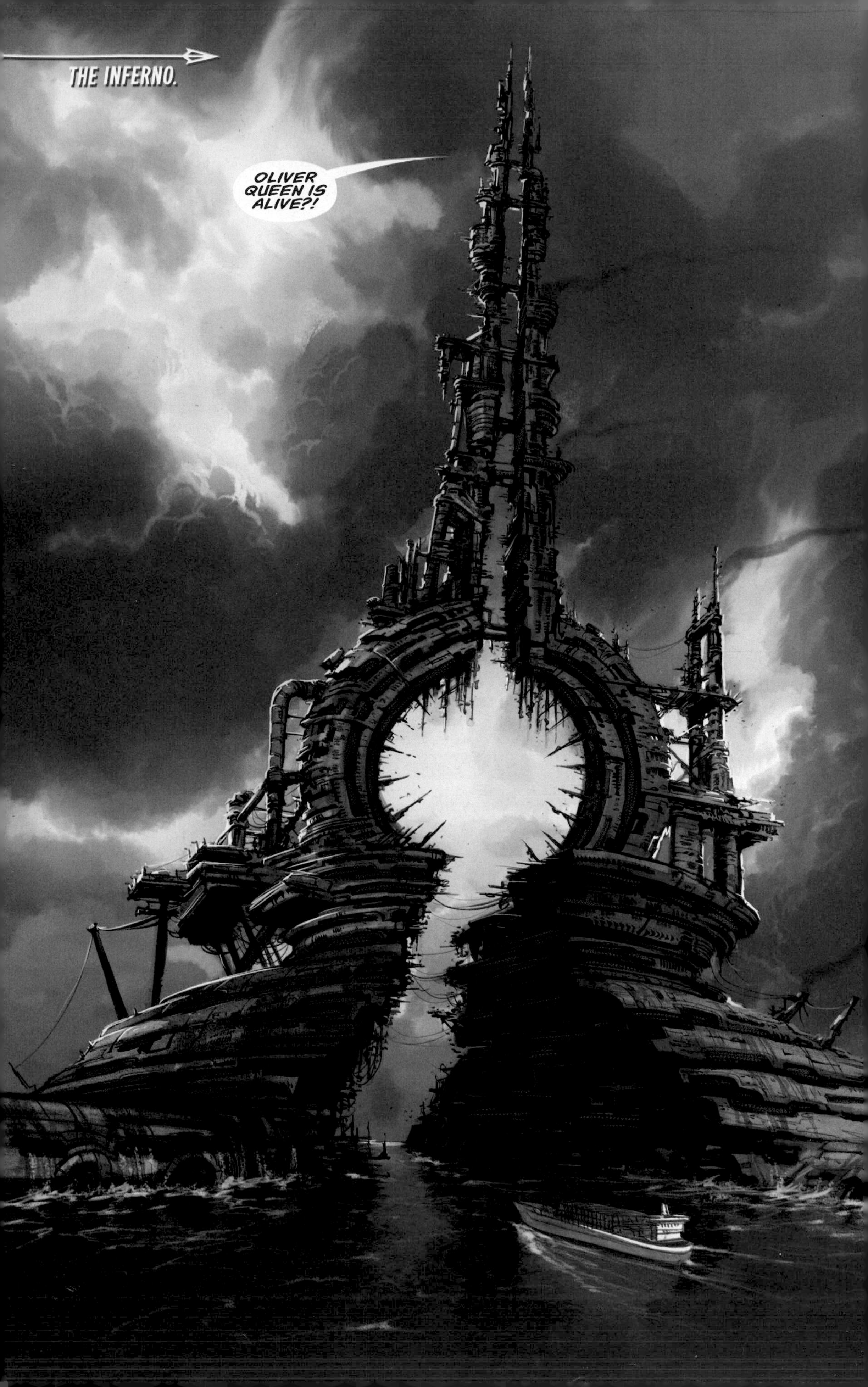
THE INFERNO.
OLIVER QUEEN IS ALIVE?!

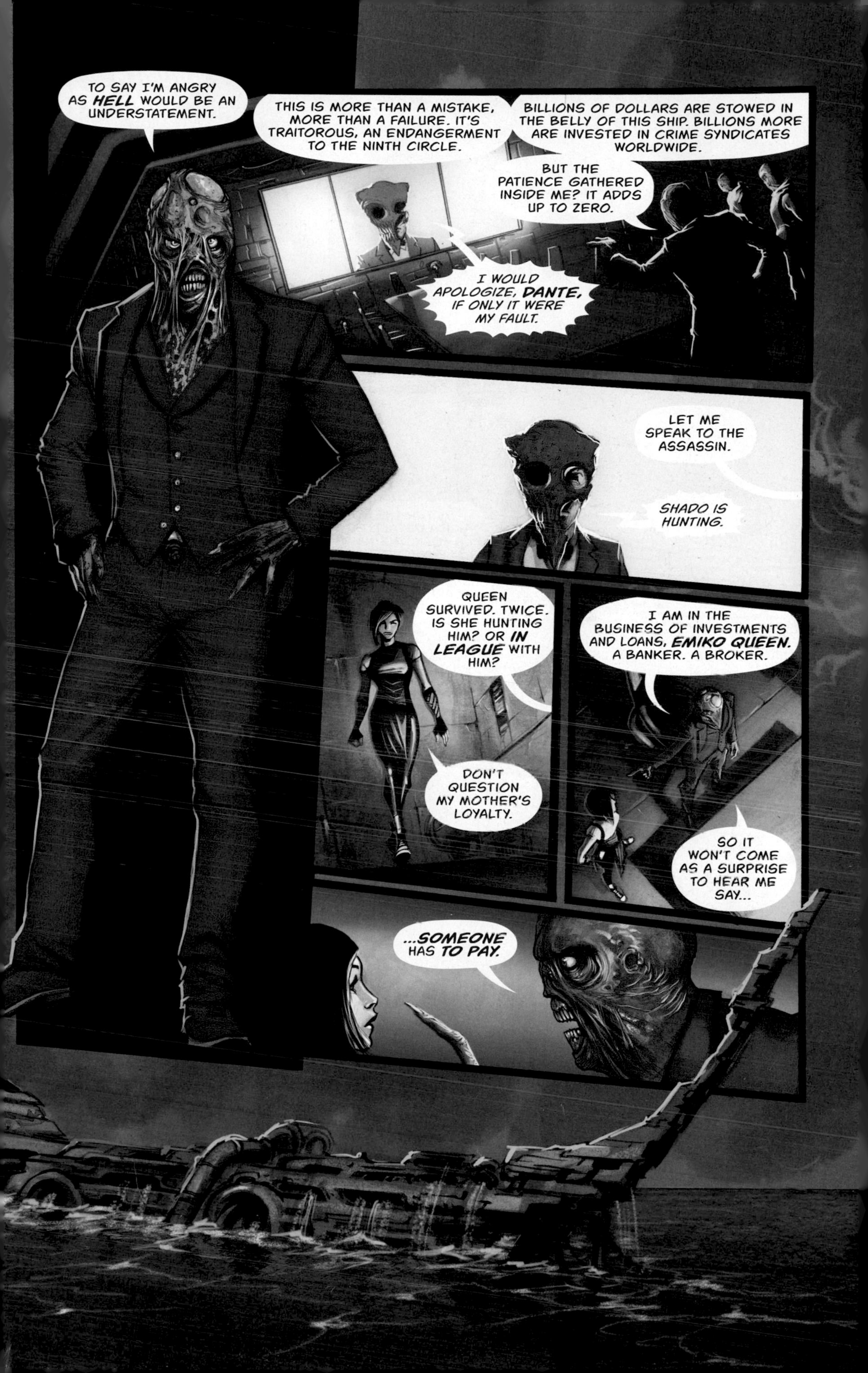
TO SAY I'M ANGRY AS HELL WOULD BE AN UNDERSTATEMENT.
THIS IS MORE THAN A MISTAKE, MORE THAN A FAILURE. IT'S TRAITOROUS, AN ENDANGERMENT TO THE NINTH CIRCLE.
BILLIONS OF DOLLARS ARE STOWED IN THE BELLY OF THIS SHIP. BILLIONS MORE ARE INVESTED IN CRIME SYNDICATES WORLDWIDE.
BUT THE PATIENCE GATHERED INSIDE ME? IT ADDS UP TO ZERO.
I WOULD APOLOGIZE, DANTE, IF ONLY IT WERE MY FAULT.
LET ME SPEAK TO THE ASSASSIN.
SHADO IS HUNTING.
QUEEN SURVIVED. TWICE. IS SHE HUNTING HIM? OR IN LEAGUE WITH HIM?
DON'T QUESTION MY MOTHER'S LOYALTY.
I AM IN THE BUSINESS OF INVESTMENTS AND LOANS, EMIKO QUEEN. A BANKER. A BROKER.
SO IT WON'T COME AS A SURPRISE TO HEAR ME SAY...
...SOMEONE HAS TO PAY.

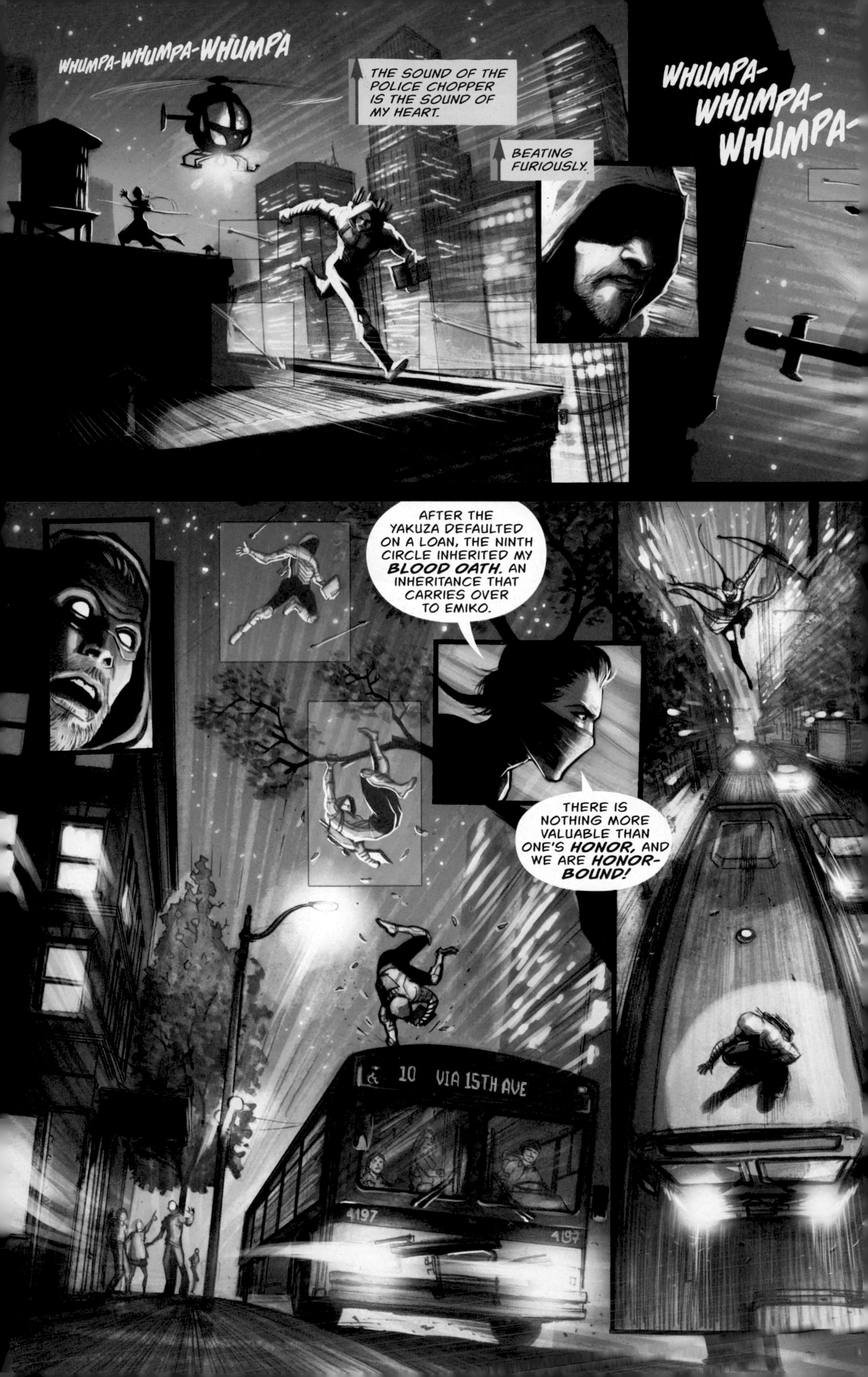

WHUMPA-WHUMPA-WHUMPA
THE SOUND OF THE POLICE CHOPPER IS THE SOUND OF MY HEART.
BEATING FURIOUSLY.
WHUMPA-WHUMPA-WHUMPA-
AFTER THE YAKUZA DEFAULTED ON A LOAN, THE NINTH CIRCLE INHERITED MY BLOOD OATH. AN INHERITANCE THAT CARRIES OVER TO EMIKO.
THERE IS NOTHING MORE VALUABLE THAN ONE'S HONOR, AND WE ARE HONOR-BOUND!
10 VIA 15TH AVE
4197
4197

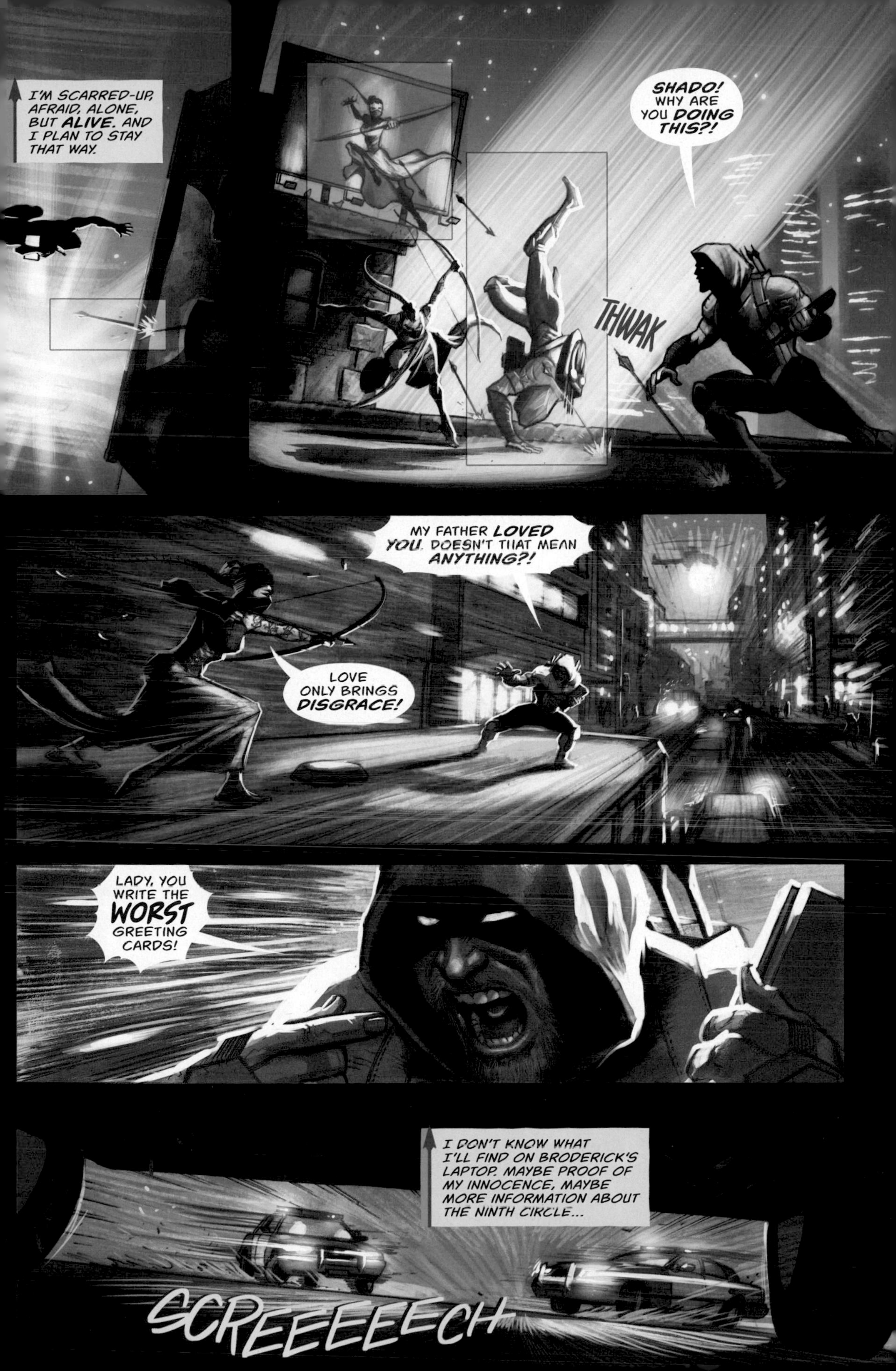
I'M SCARRED-UP, AFRAID, ALONE, BUT ALIVE. AND I PLAN TO STAY THAT WAY.
SHADO! WHY ARE YOU DOING THIS?!
THWAK
MY FATHER LOVED YOU. DOESN'T THAT MEAN ANYTHING?!
LOVE ONLY BRINGS DISGRACE!
LADY, YOU WRITE THE WORST GREETING CARDS!
I DON'T KNOW WHAT I'LL FIND ON BRODERICK'S LAPTOP. MAYBE PROOF OF MY INNOCENCE, MAYBE MORE INFORMATION ABOUT THE NINTH CIRCLE...
SCREEEEEECH

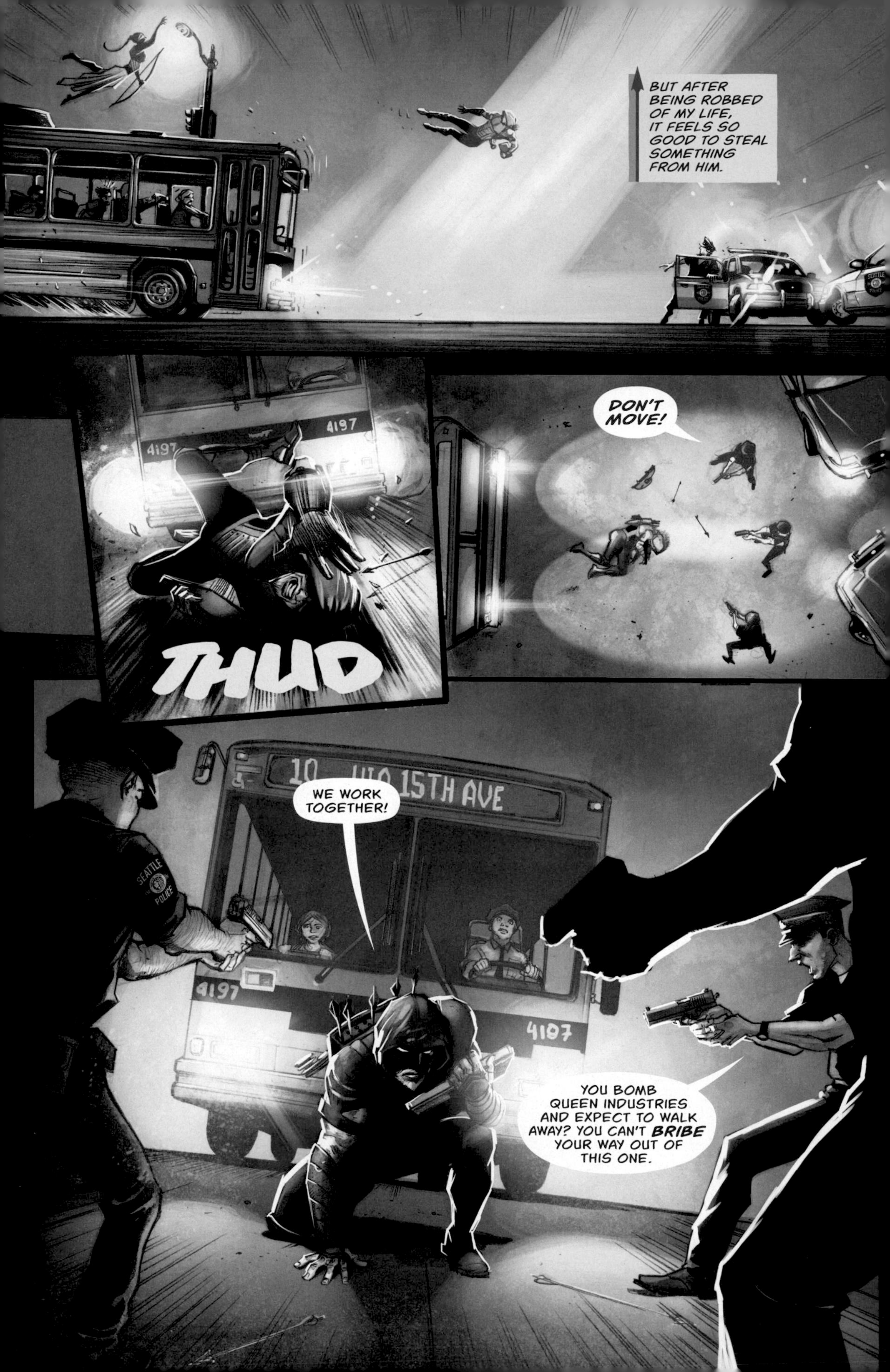
BUT AFTER BEING ROBBED OF MY LIFE, IT FEELS SO GOOD TO STEAL SOMETHING FROM HIM.
DON'T MOVE!
THUD
10 15TH AVE
WE WORK TOGETHER!
YOU BOMB QUEEN INDUSTRIES AND EXPECT TO WALK AWAY? YOU CAN'T BRIBE YOUR WAY OUT OF THIS ONE.

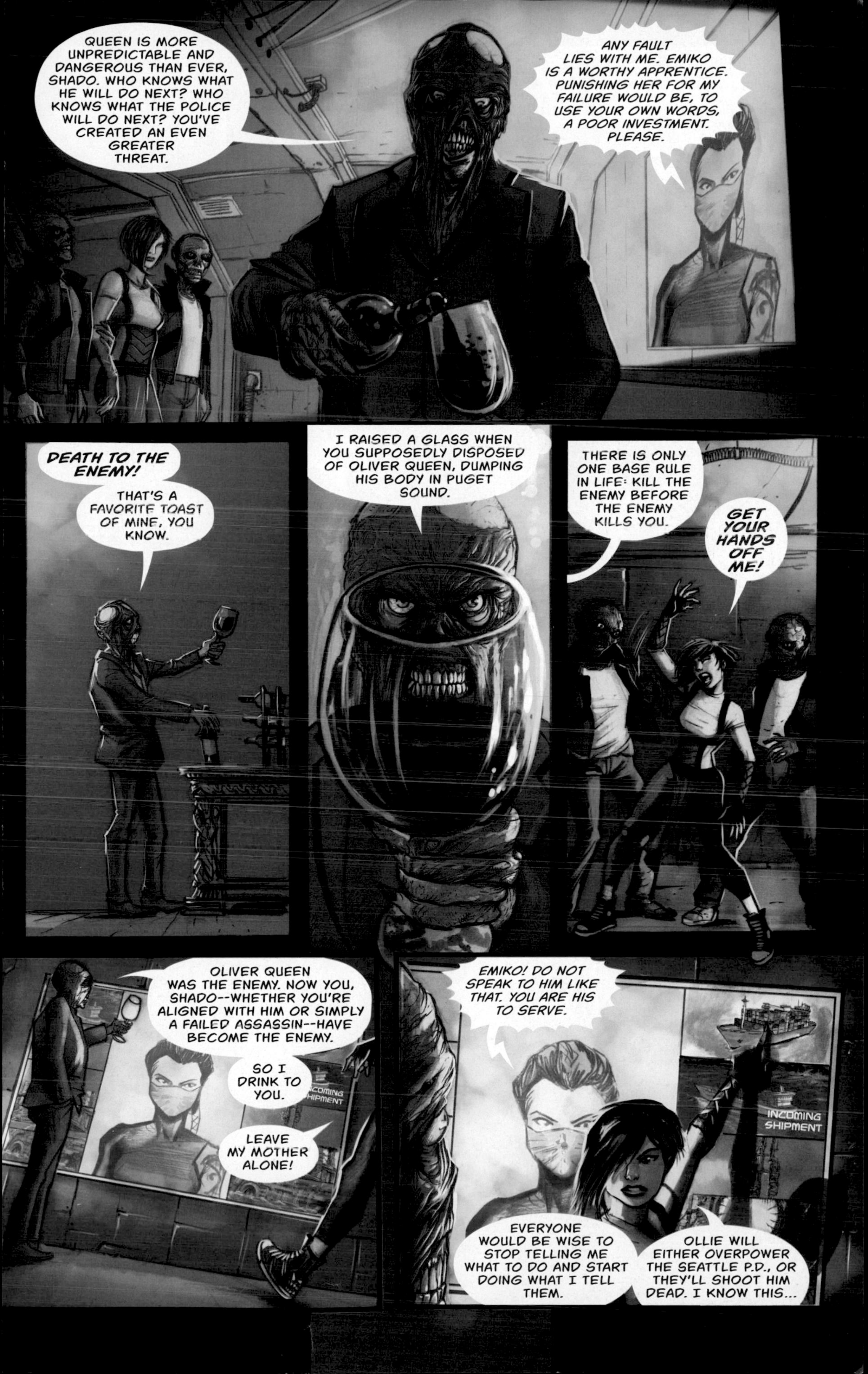
QUEEN IS MORE UNPREDICTABLE AND DANGEROUS THAN EVER, SHADO. WHO KNOWS WHAT HE WILL DO NEXT? WHO KNOWS WHAT THE POLICE WILL DO NEXT? YOU'VE CREATED AN EVEN GREATER THREAT.
ANY FAULT LIES WITH ME. EMIKO IS A WORTHY APPRENTICE. PUNISHING HER FOR MY FAILURE WOULD BE, TO USE YOUR OWN WORDS, A POOR INVESTMENT. PLEASE.
DEATH TO THE ENEMY!
THAT'S A FAVORITE TOAST OF MINE, YOU KNOW.
I RAISED A GLASS WHEN YOU SUPPOSEDLY DISPOSED OF OLIVER QUEEN, DUMPING HIS BODY IN PUGET SOUND.
THERE IS ONLY ONE BASE RULE IN LIFE: KILL THE ENEMY BEFORE THE ENEMY KILLS YOU.
GET YOUR HANDS OFF ME!
OLIVER QUEEN WAS THE ENEMY. NOW YOU, SHADO--WHETHER YOU'RE ALIGNED WITH HIM OR SIMPLY A FAILED ASSASSIN--HAVE BECOME THE ENEMY.
SO I DRINK TO YOU.
LEAVE MY MOTHER ALONE!
EMIKO! DO NOT SPEAK TO HIM LIKE THAT. YOU ARE HIS TO SERVE.
INCOMING SHIPMENT
EVERYONE WOULD BE WISE TO STOP TELLING ME WHAT TO DO AND START DOING WHAT I TELL THEM.
OLLIE WILL EITHER OVERPOWER THE SEATTLE P.D., OR THEY'LL SHOOT HIM DEAD. I KNOW THIS...

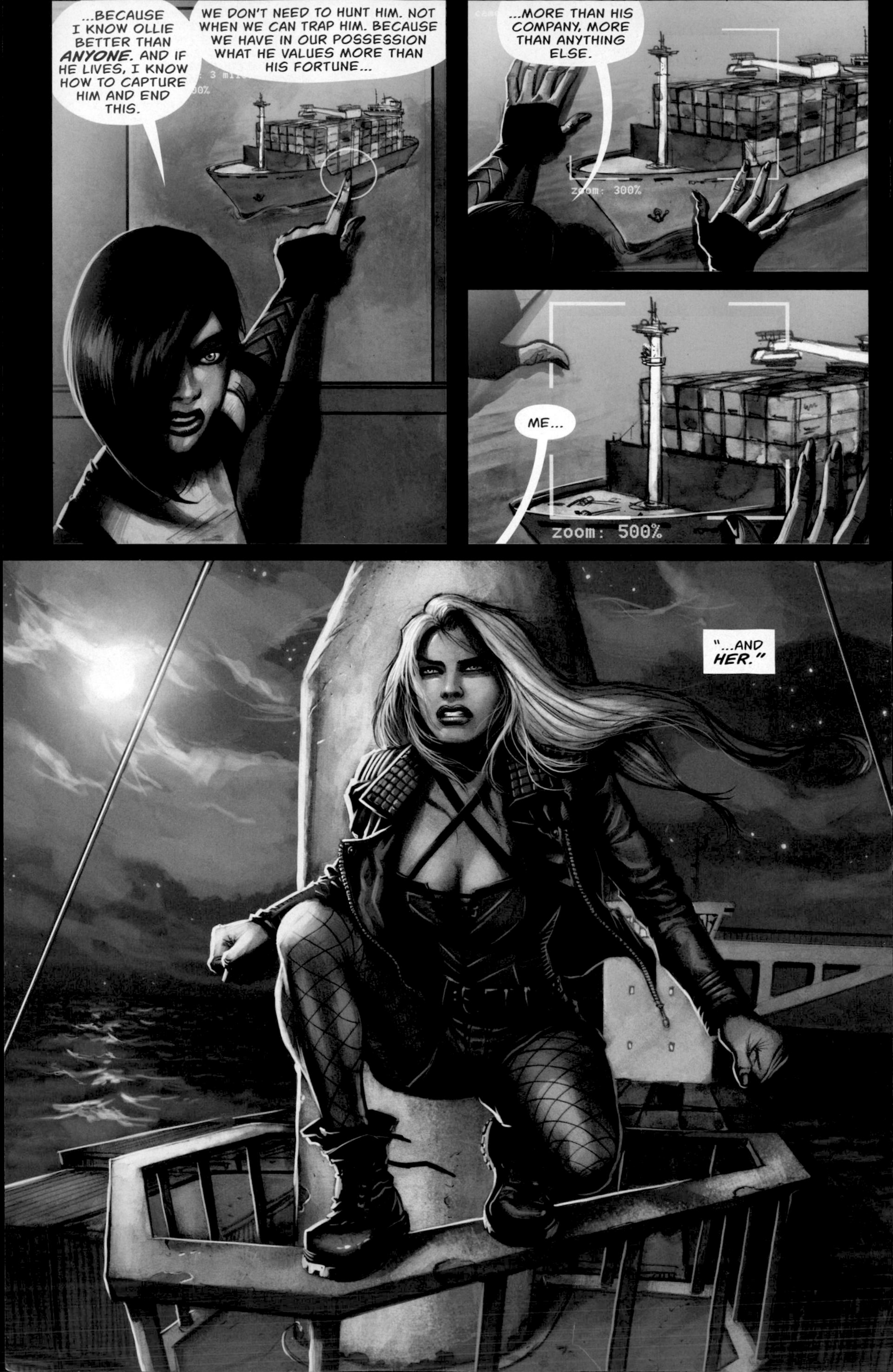
...BECAUSE I KNOW OLLIE BETTER THAN ***ANYONE.*** AND IF HE LIVES, I KNOW HOW TO CAPTURE HIM AND END THIS.
WE DON'T NEED TO HUNT HIM. NOT WHEN WE CAN TRAP HIM. BECAUSE WE HAVE IN OUR POSSESSION WHAT HE VALUES MORE THAN HIS FORTUNE...
...MORE THAN HIS COMPANY, MORE THAN ANYTHING ELSE.
zoom: 300%
ME...
zoom: 500%
"...AND ***HER.***"

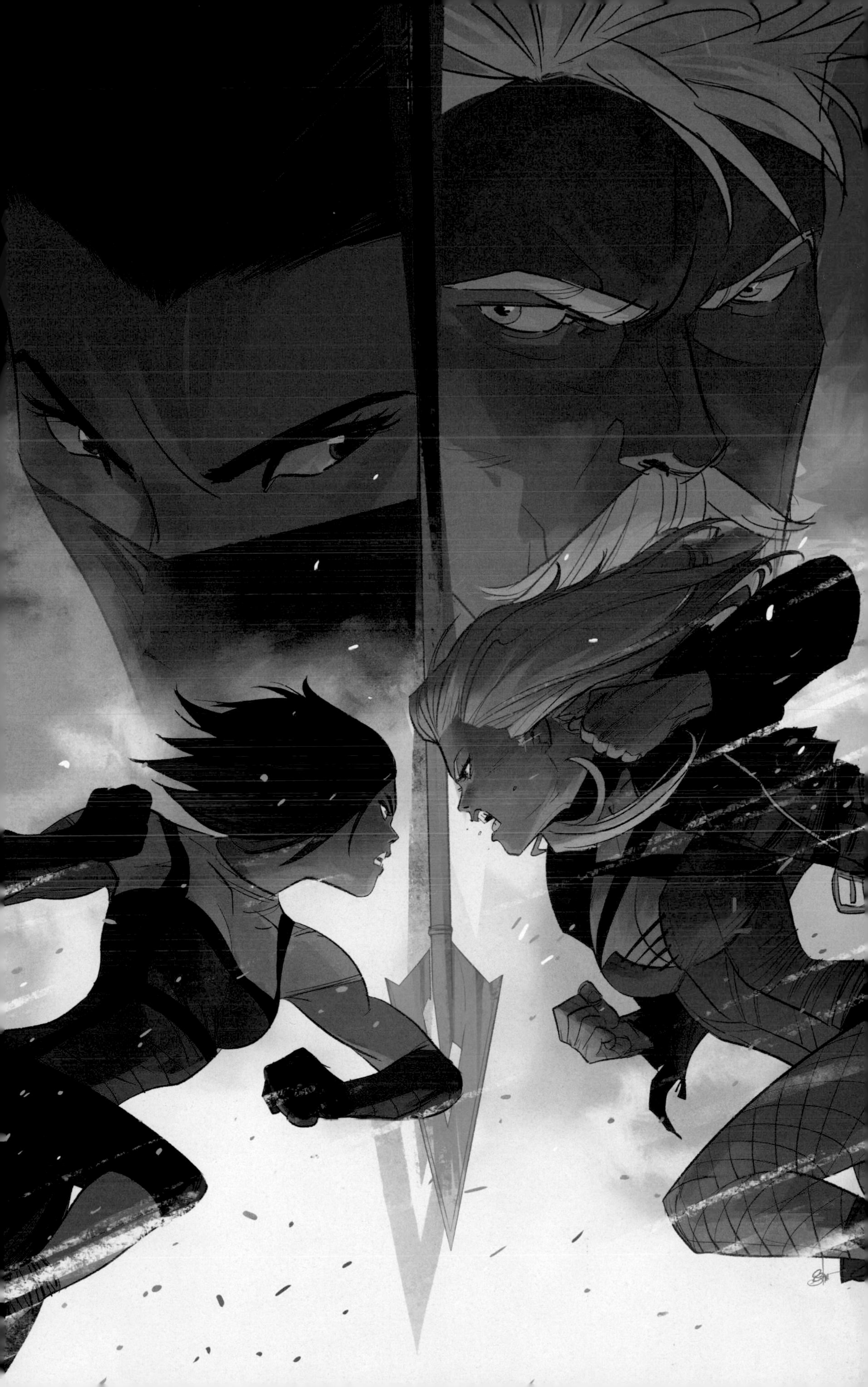

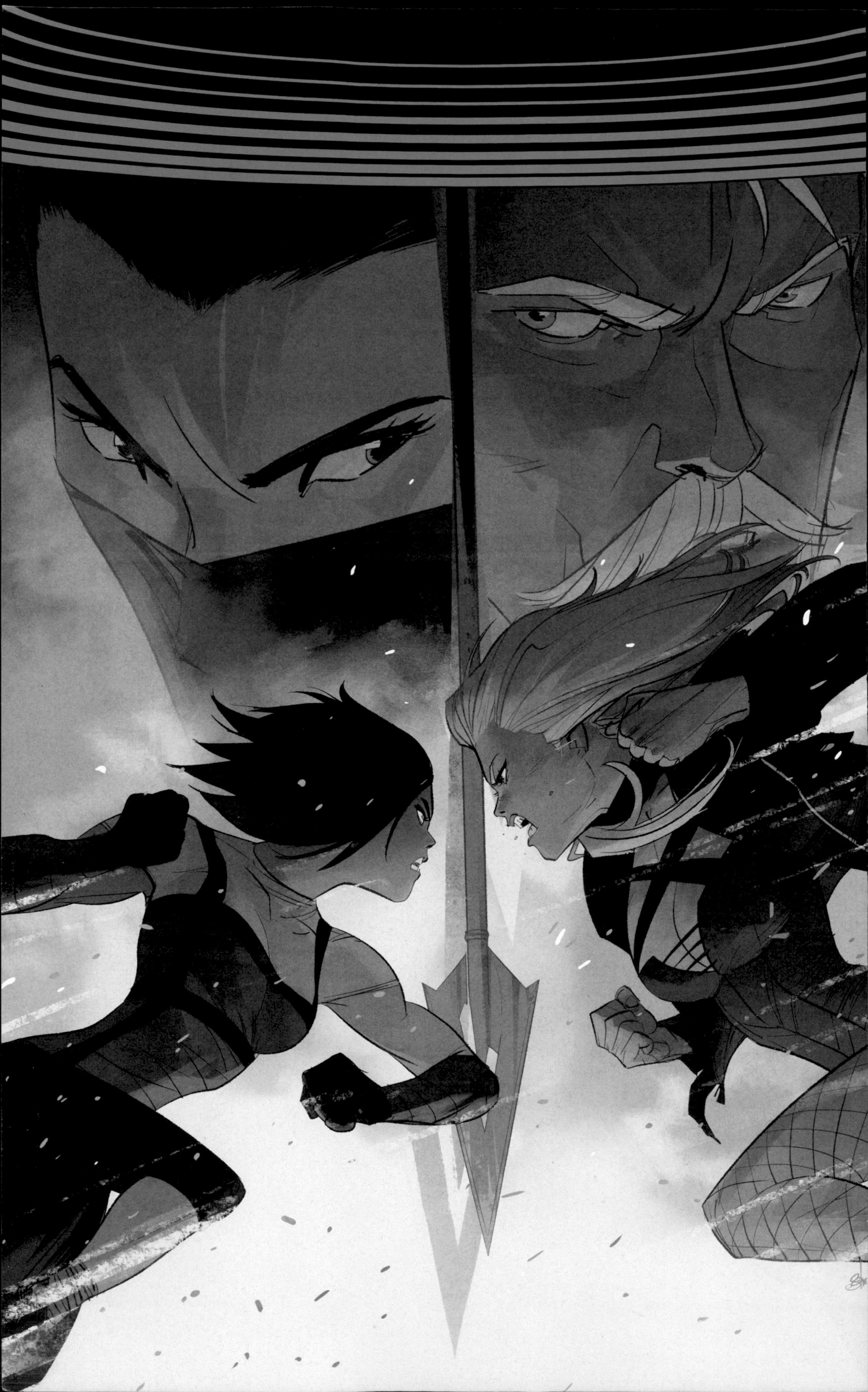

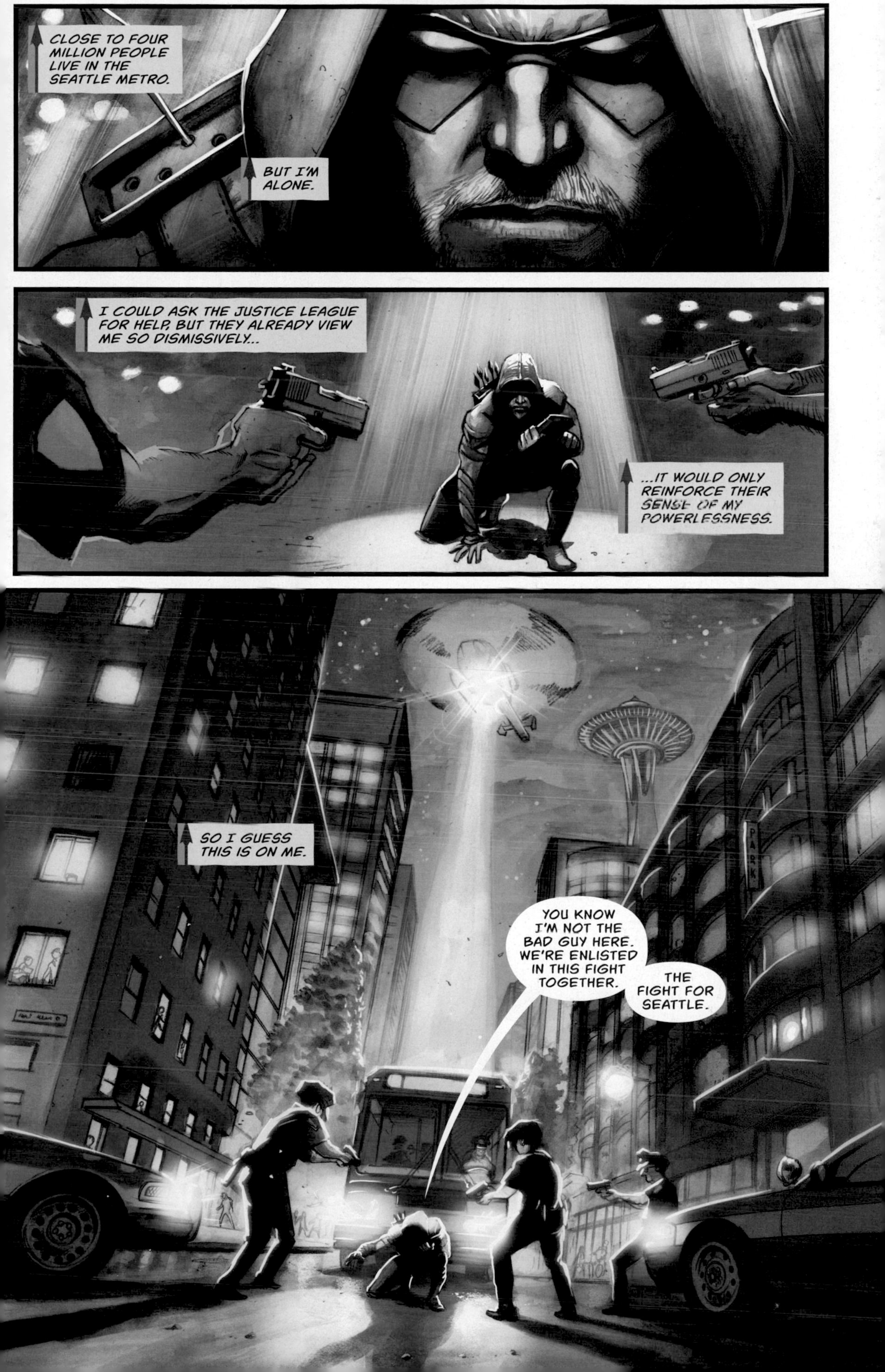
CLOSE TO FOUR MILLION PEOPLE LIVE IN THE SEATTLE METRO.
BUT I'M ALONE.
I COULD ASK THE JUSTICE LEAGUE FOR HELP, BUT THEY ALREADY VIEW ME SO DISMISSIVELY...
...IT WOULD ONLY REINFORCE THEIR SENSE OF MY POWERLESSNESS.
SO I GUESS THIS IS ON ME.
YOU KNOW I'M NOT THE BAD GUY HERE. WE'RE ENLISTED IN THIS FIGHT TOGETHER.
THE FIGHT FOR SEATTLE.
PARK

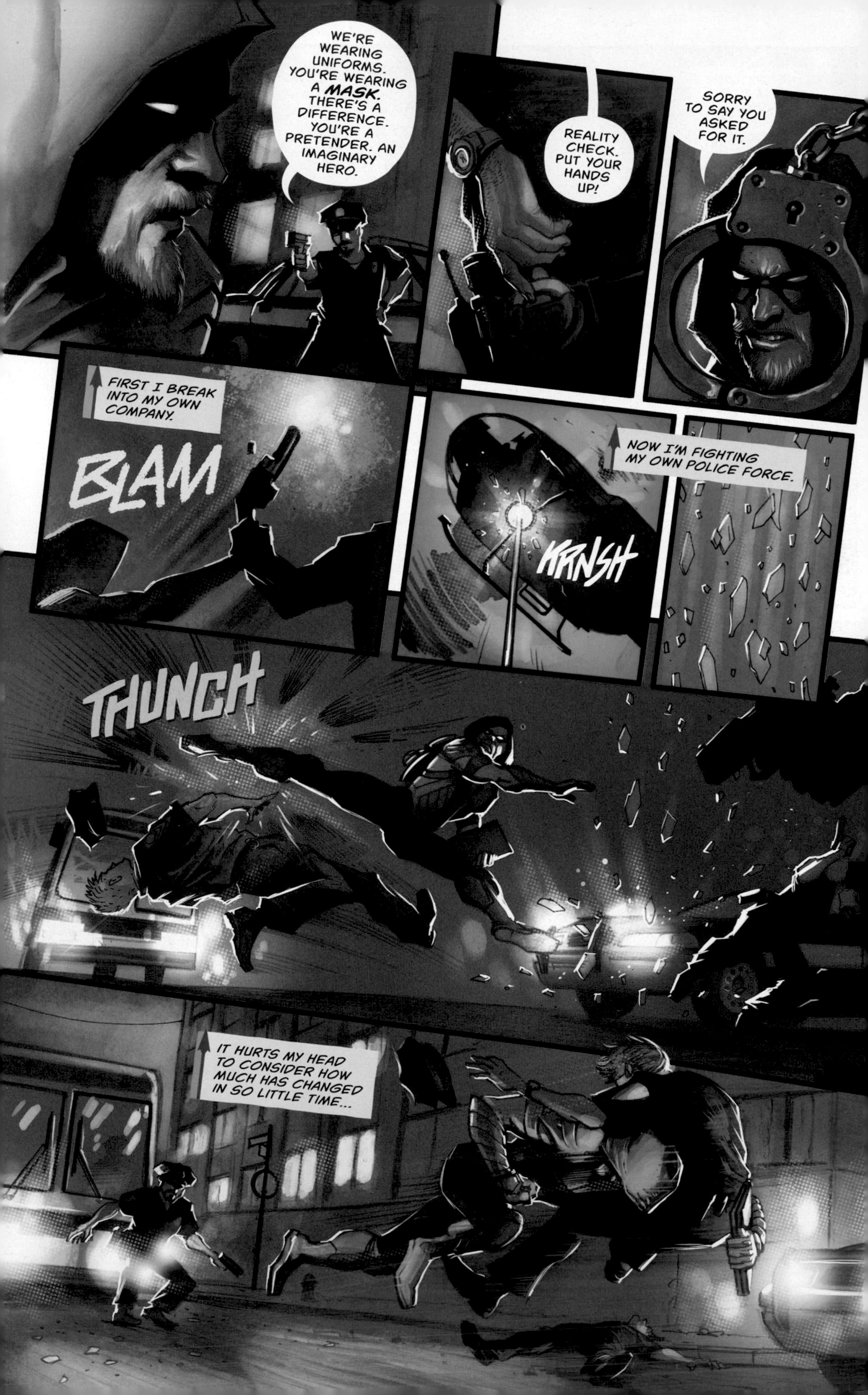
WE'RE WEARING UNIFORMS. YOU'RE WEARING A MASK. THERE'S A DIFFERENCE. YOU'RE A PRETENDER. AN IMAGINARY HERO.
REALITY CHECK. PUT YOUR HANDS UP!
SORRY TO SAY YOU ASKED FOR IT.
FIRST I BREAK INTO MY OWN COMPANY.
BLAM
NOW I'M FIGHTING MY OWN POLICE FORCE.
KRNSH
THUNCH
IT HURTS MY HEAD TO CONSIDER HOW MUCH HAS CHANGED IN SO LITTLE TIME...

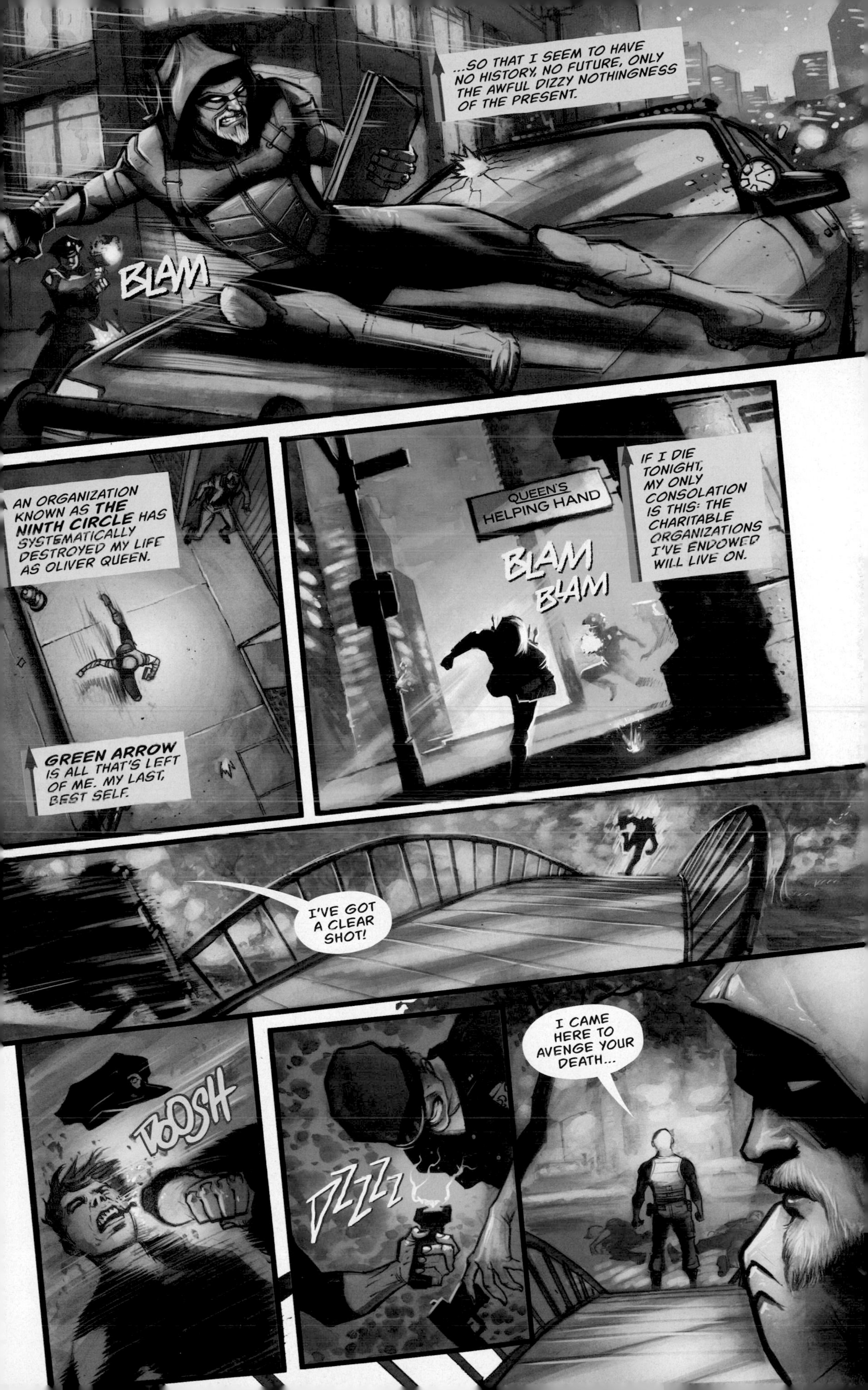
...SO THAT I SEEM TO HAVE NO HISTORY, NO FUTURE, ONLY THE AWFUL DIZZY NOTHINGNESS OF THE PRESENT.
BLAM
AN ORGANIZATION KNOWN AS THE NINTH CIRCLE HAS SYSTEMATICALLY DESTROYED MY LIFE AS OLIVER QUEEN.
GREEN ARROW IS ALL THAT'S LEFT OF ME. MY LAST, BEST SELF.
QUEEN'S HELPING HAND
BLAM
BLAM
IF I DIE TONIGHT, MY ONLY CONSOLATION IS THIS: THE CHARITABLE ORGANIZATIONS I'VE ENDOWED WILL LIVE ON.
I'VE GOT A CLEAR SHOT!
TOOSH
DZZZZ
I CAME HERE TO AVENGE YOUR DEATH...

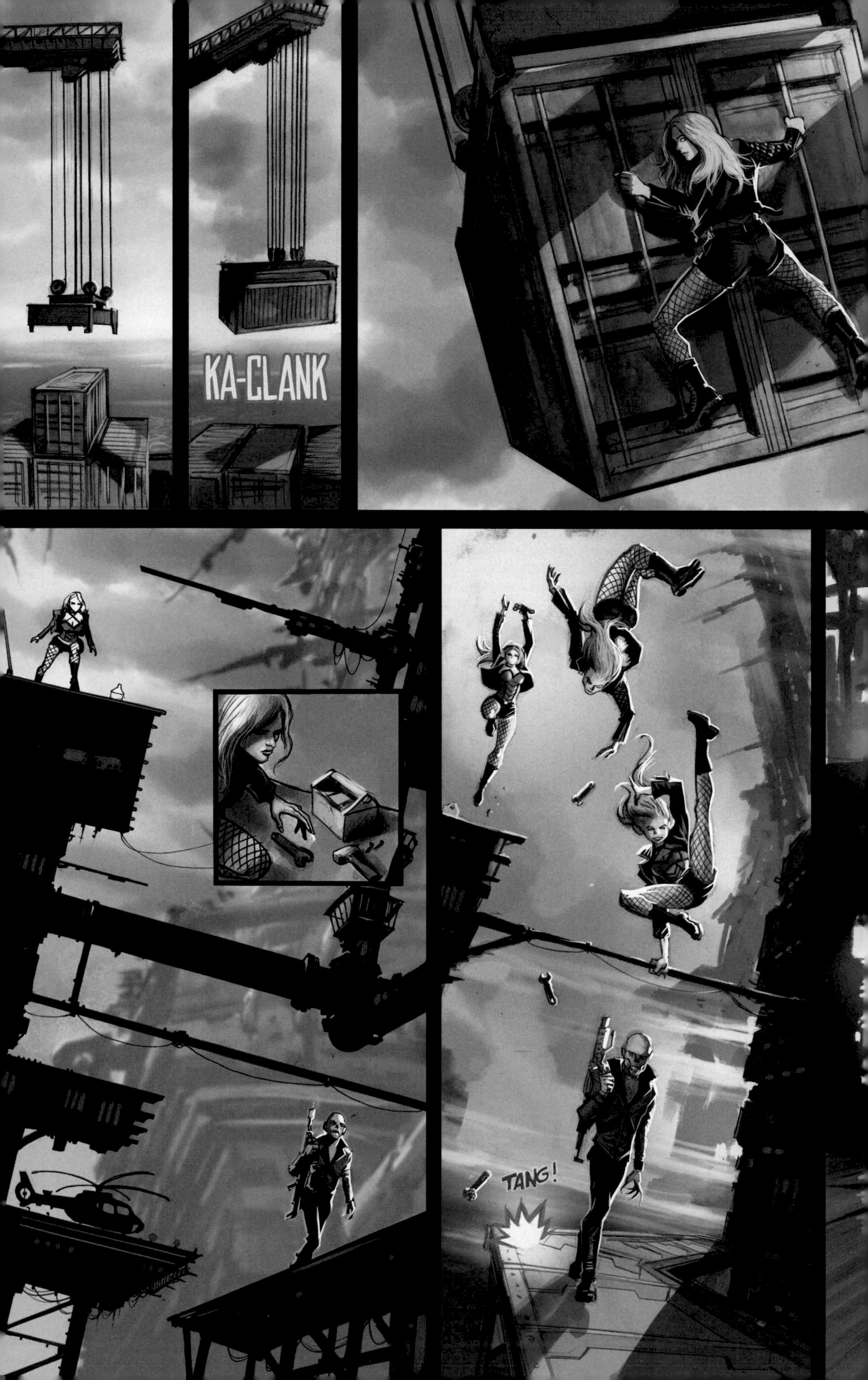
KA-CLANK
TANG!

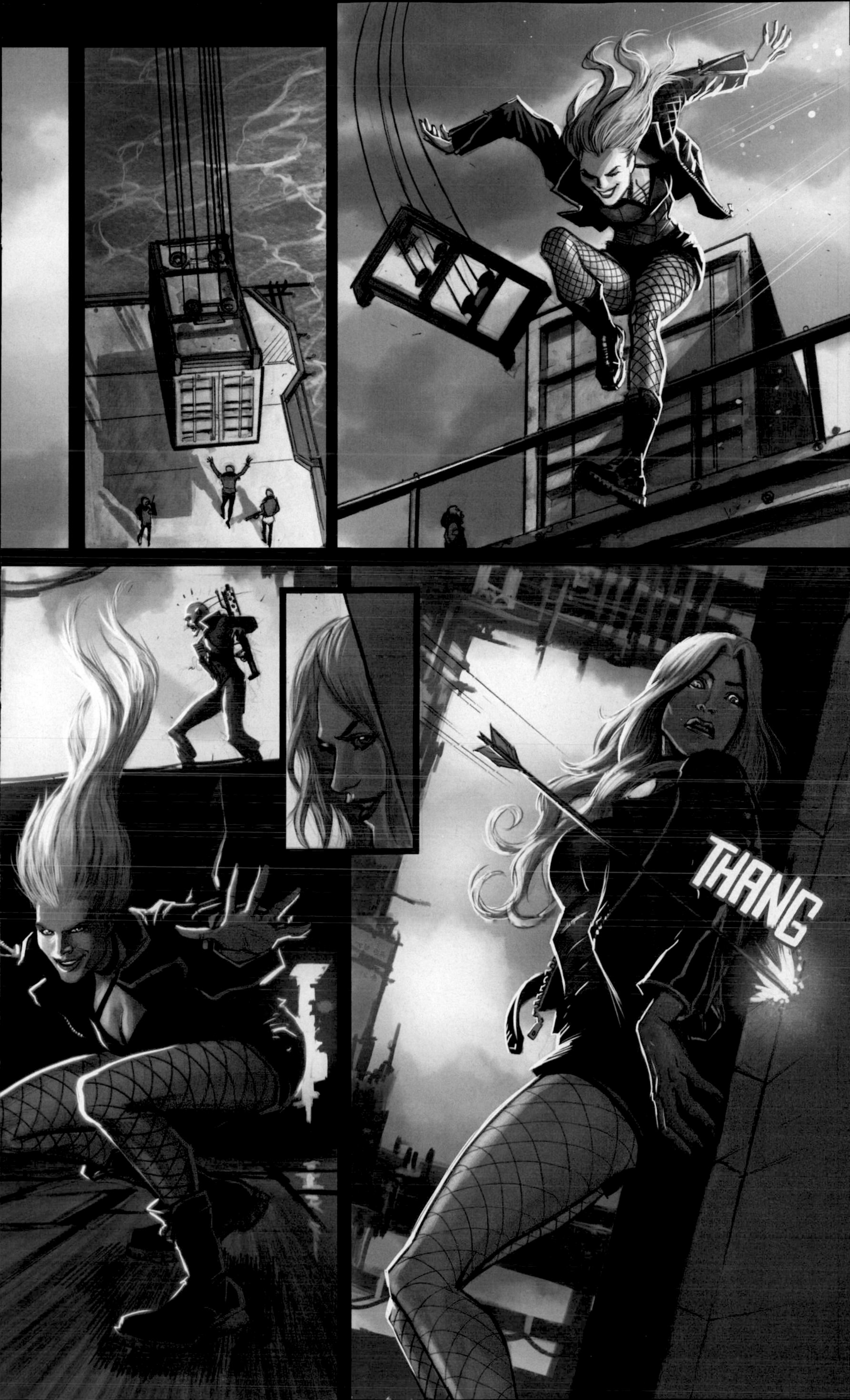
THANG

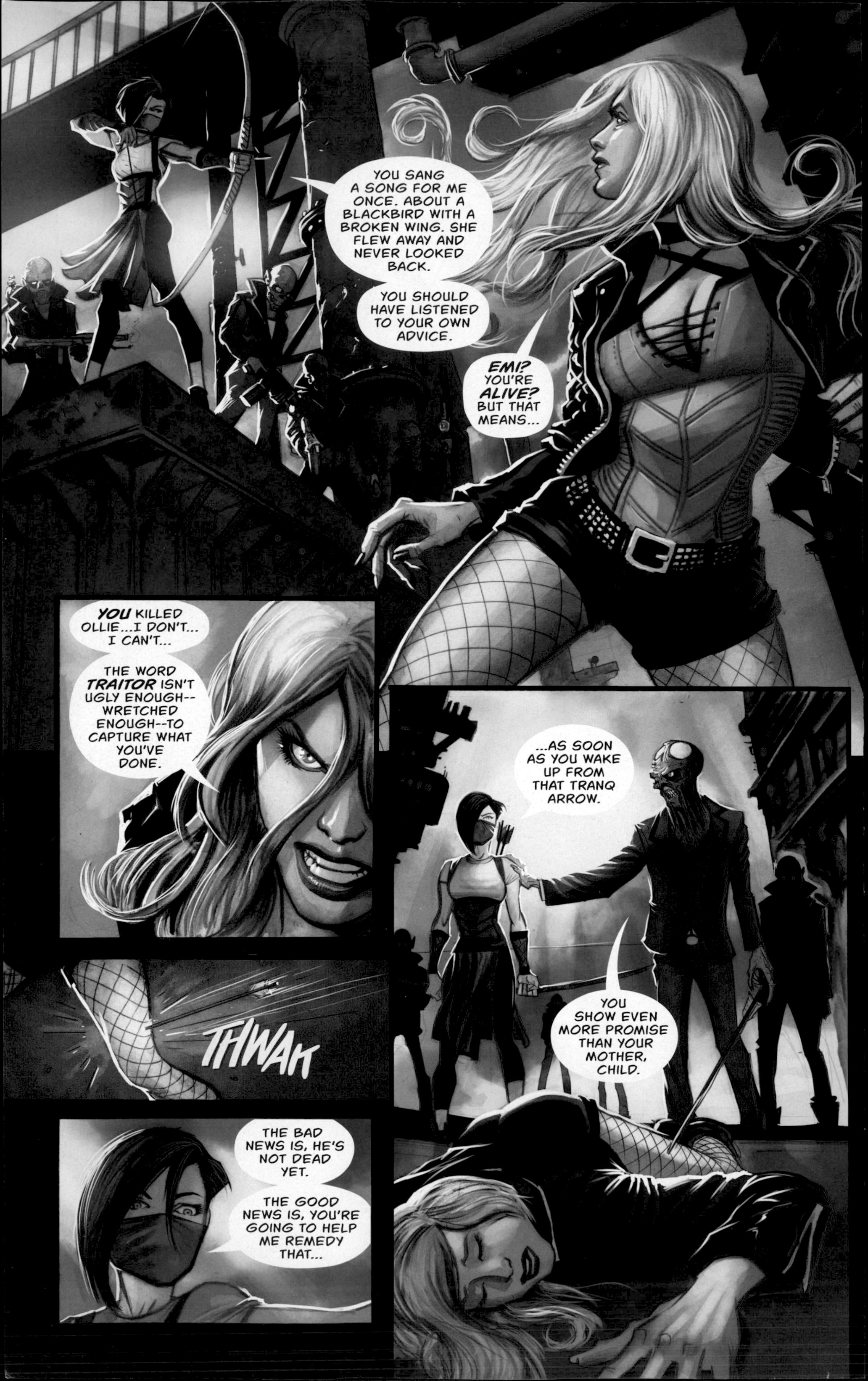
YOU SANG A SONG FOR ME ONCE. ABOUT A BLACKBIRD WITH A BROKEN WING. SHE FLEW AWAY AND NEVER LOOKED BACK.
YOU SHOULD HAVE LISTENED TO YOUR OWN ADVICE.
EMI? YOU'RE ALIVE? BUT THAT MEANS...
YOU KILLED OLLIE...I DON'T... I CAN'T...
THE WORD TRAITOR ISN'T UGLY ENOUGH--WRETCHED ENOUGH--TO CAPTURE WHAT YOU'VE DONE.
THWAK
THE BAD NEWS IS, HE'S NOT DEAD YET.
THE GOOD NEWS IS, YOU'RE GOING TO HELP ME REMEDY THAT...
...AS SOON AS YOU WAKE UP FROM THAT TRANQ ARROW.
YOU SHOW EVEN MORE PROMISE THAN YOUR MOTHER, CHILD.

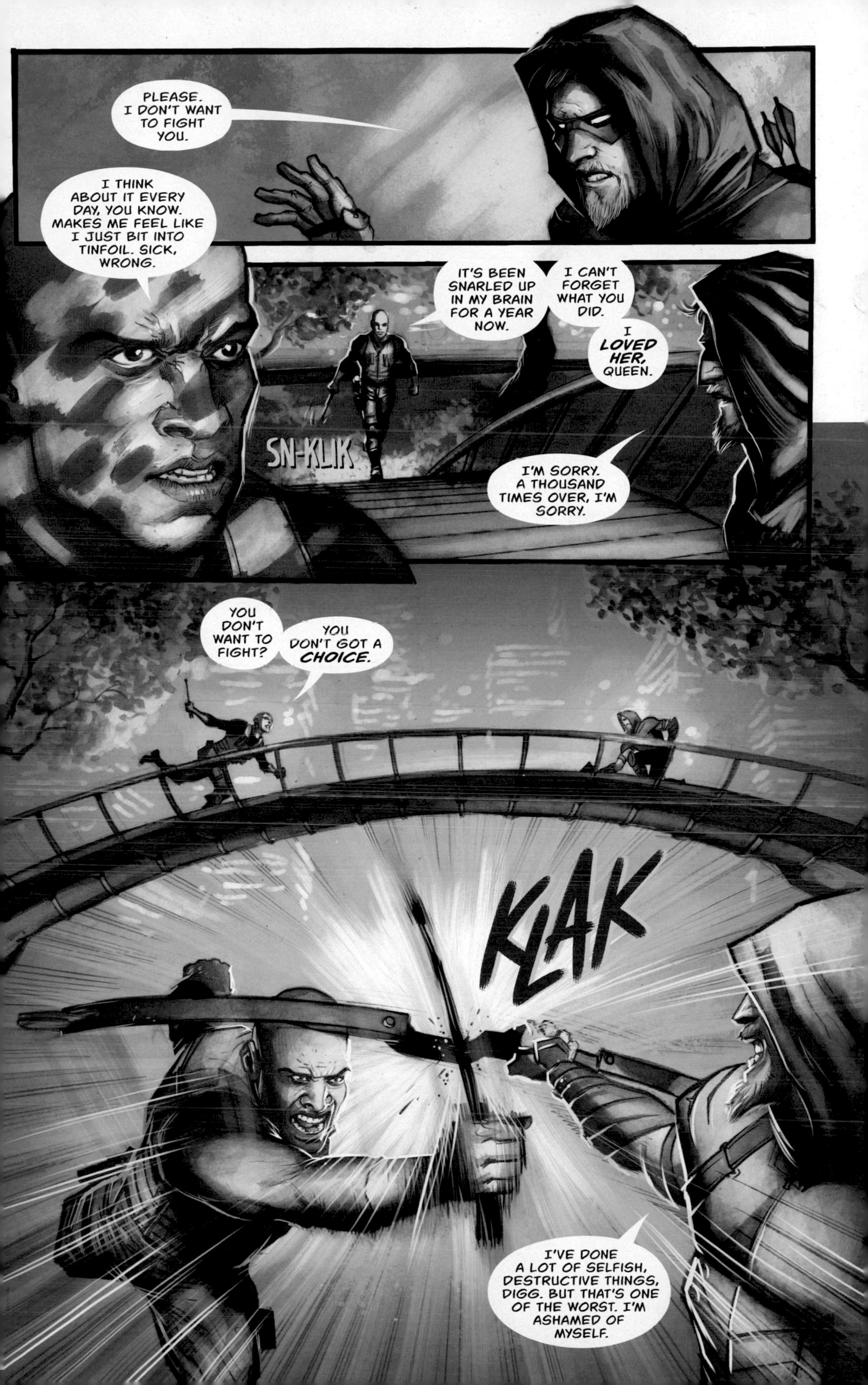
PLEASE. I DON'T WANT TO FIGHT YOU.
I THINK ABOUT IT EVERY DAY, YOU KNOW. MAKES ME FEEL LIKE I JUST BIT INTO TINFOIL. SICK, WRONG.
IT'S BEEN SNARLED UP IN MY BRAIN FOR A YEAR NOW.
I CAN'T FORGET WHAT YOU DID.
I LOVED HER, QUEEN.
SN-KLIK
I'M SORRY. A THOUSAND TIMES OVER, I'M SORRY.
YOU DON'T WANT TO FIGHT?
YOU DON'T GOT A CHOICE.
KLAK
I'VE DONE A LOT OF SELFISH, DESTRUCTIVE THINGS, DIGG. BUT THAT'S ONE OF THE WORST. I'M ASHAMED OF MYSELF.

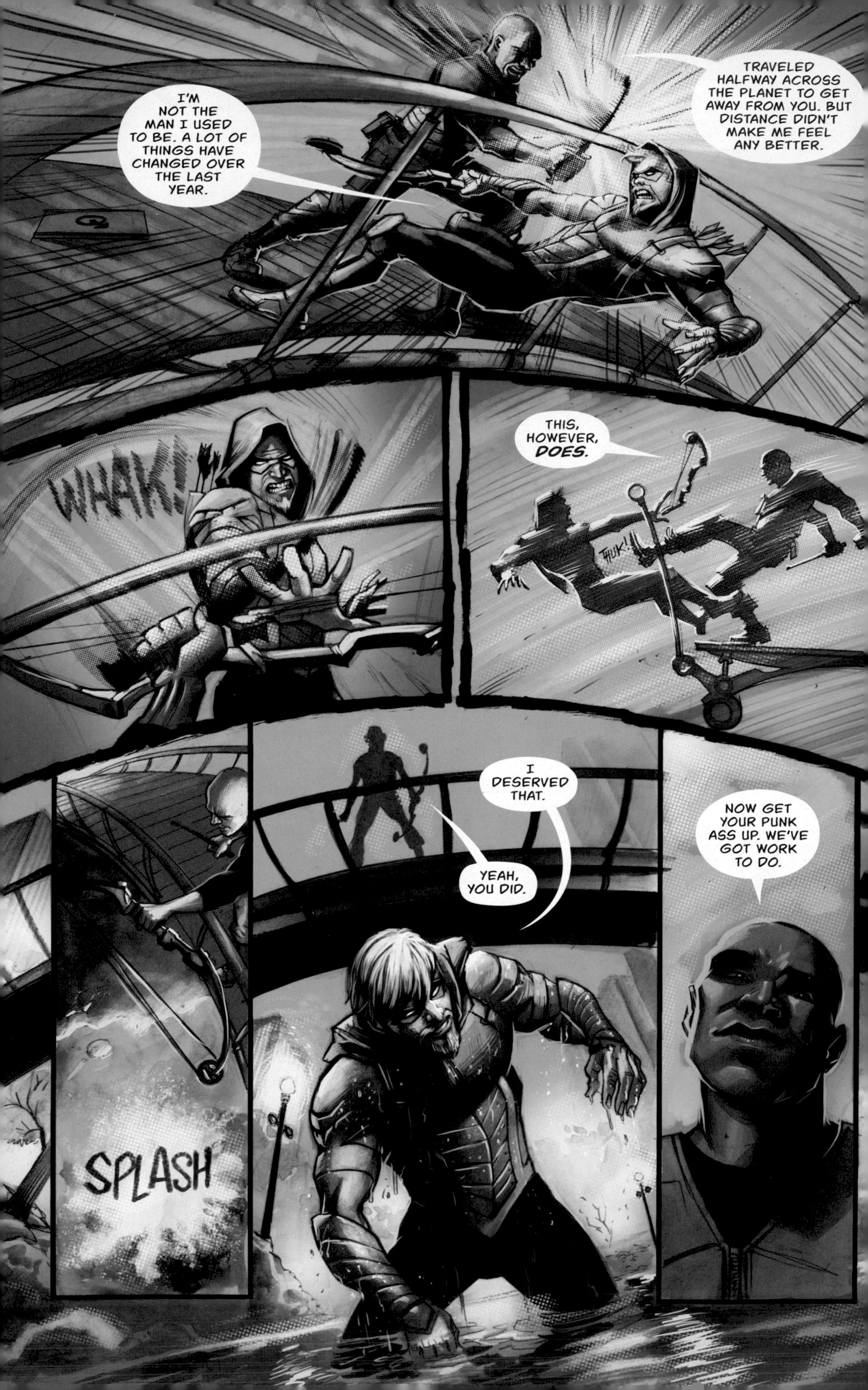
I'M NOT THE MAN I USED TO BE. A LOT OF THINGS HAVE CHANGED OVER THE LAST YEAR.
TRAVELED HALFWAY ACROSS THE PLANET TO GET AWAY FROM YOU. BUT DISTANCE DIDN'T MAKE ME FEEL ANY BETTER.
WHAK!
THIS, HOWEVER, DOES.
THUK!
SPLASH
I DESERVED THAT.
YEAH, YOU DID.
NOW GET YOUR PUNK ASS UP. WE'VE GOT WORK TO DO.

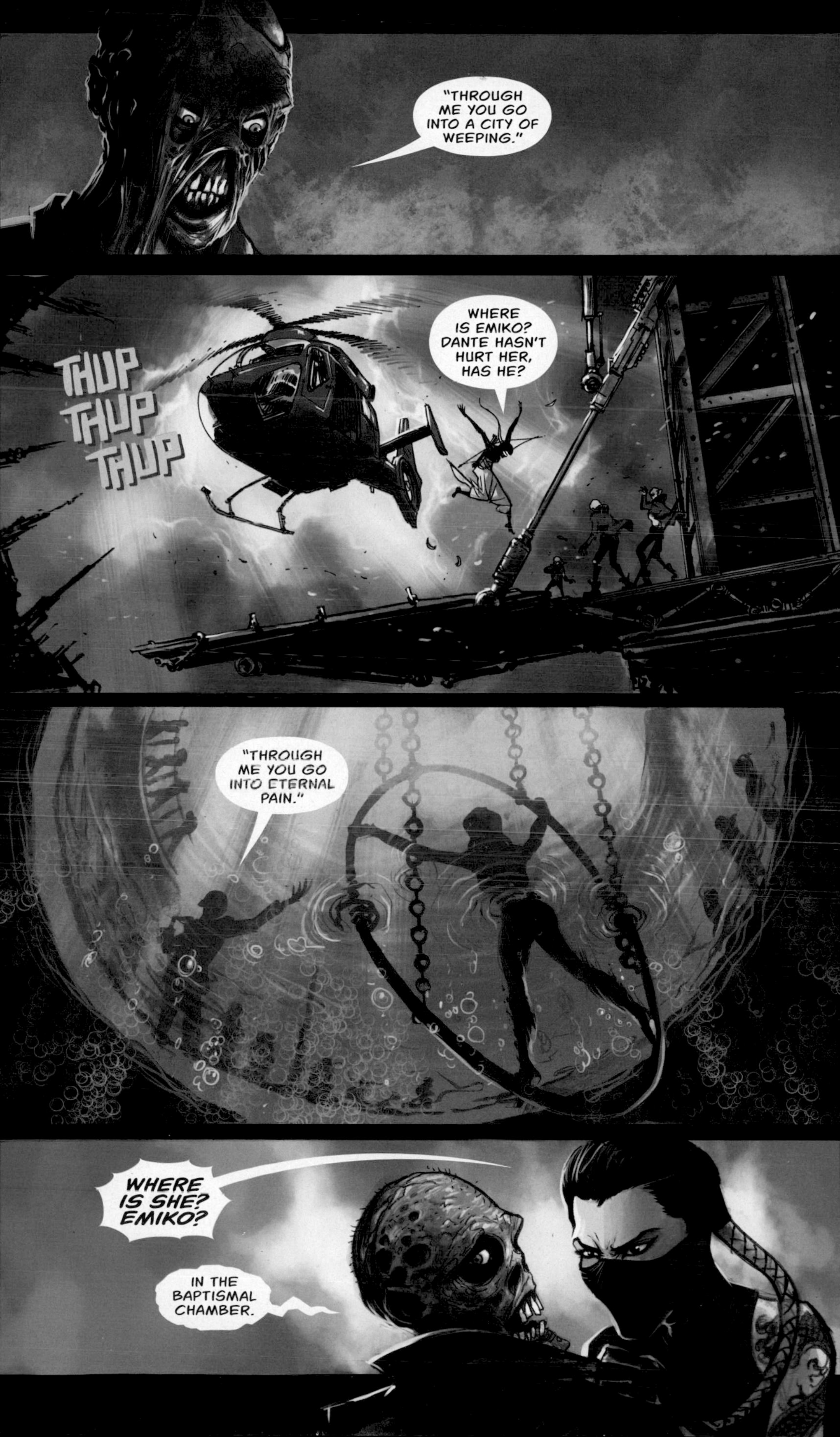
"THROUGH ME YOU GO INTO A CITY OF WEEPING."
THUP THUP THUP
WHERE IS EMIKO? DANTE HASN'T HURT HER, HAS HE?
"THROUGH ME YOU GO INTO ETERNAL PAIN."
WHERE IS SHE? EMIKO?
IN THE BAPTISMAL CHAMBER.

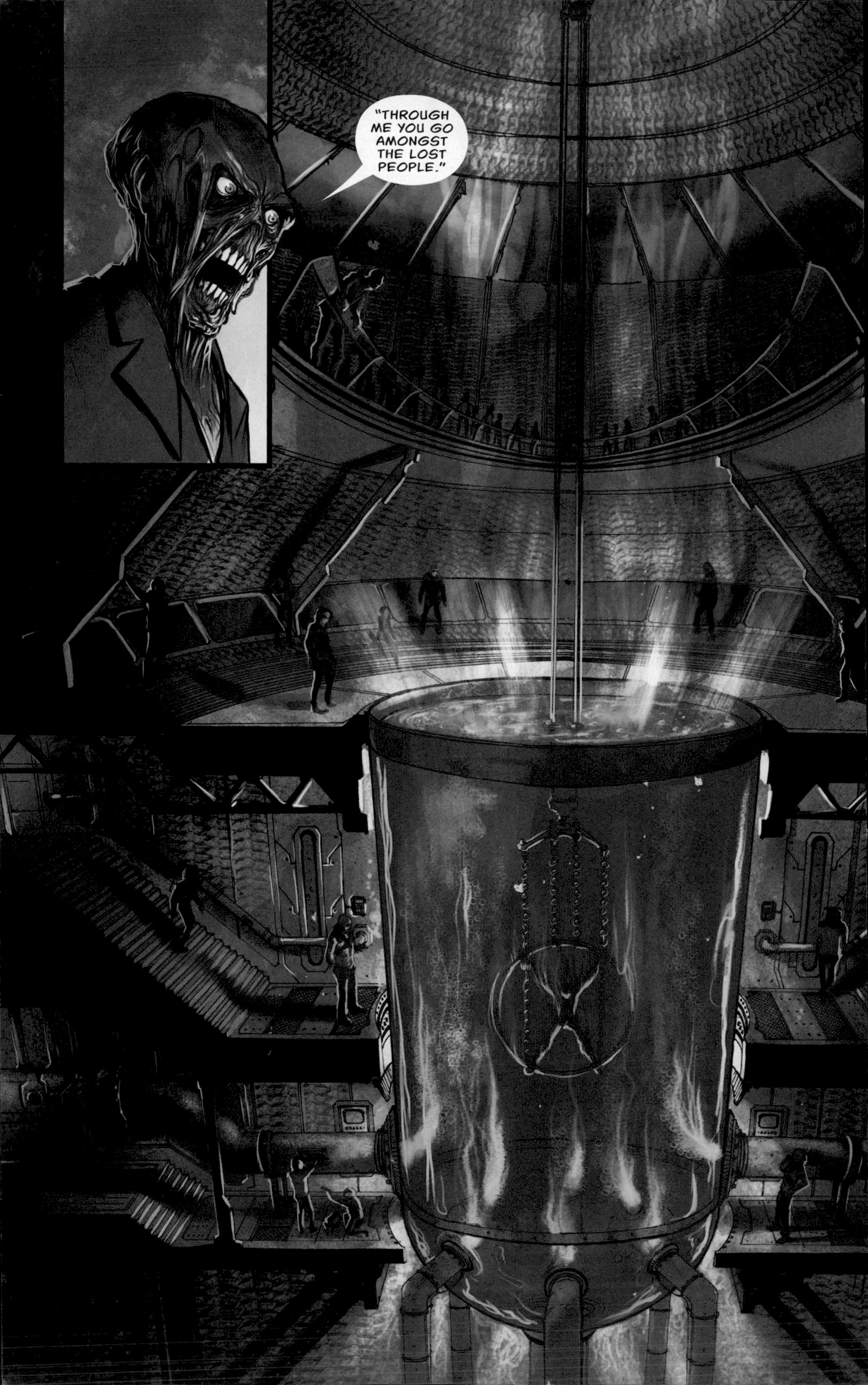
"THROUGH ME YOU GO AMONGST THE LOST PEOPLE."

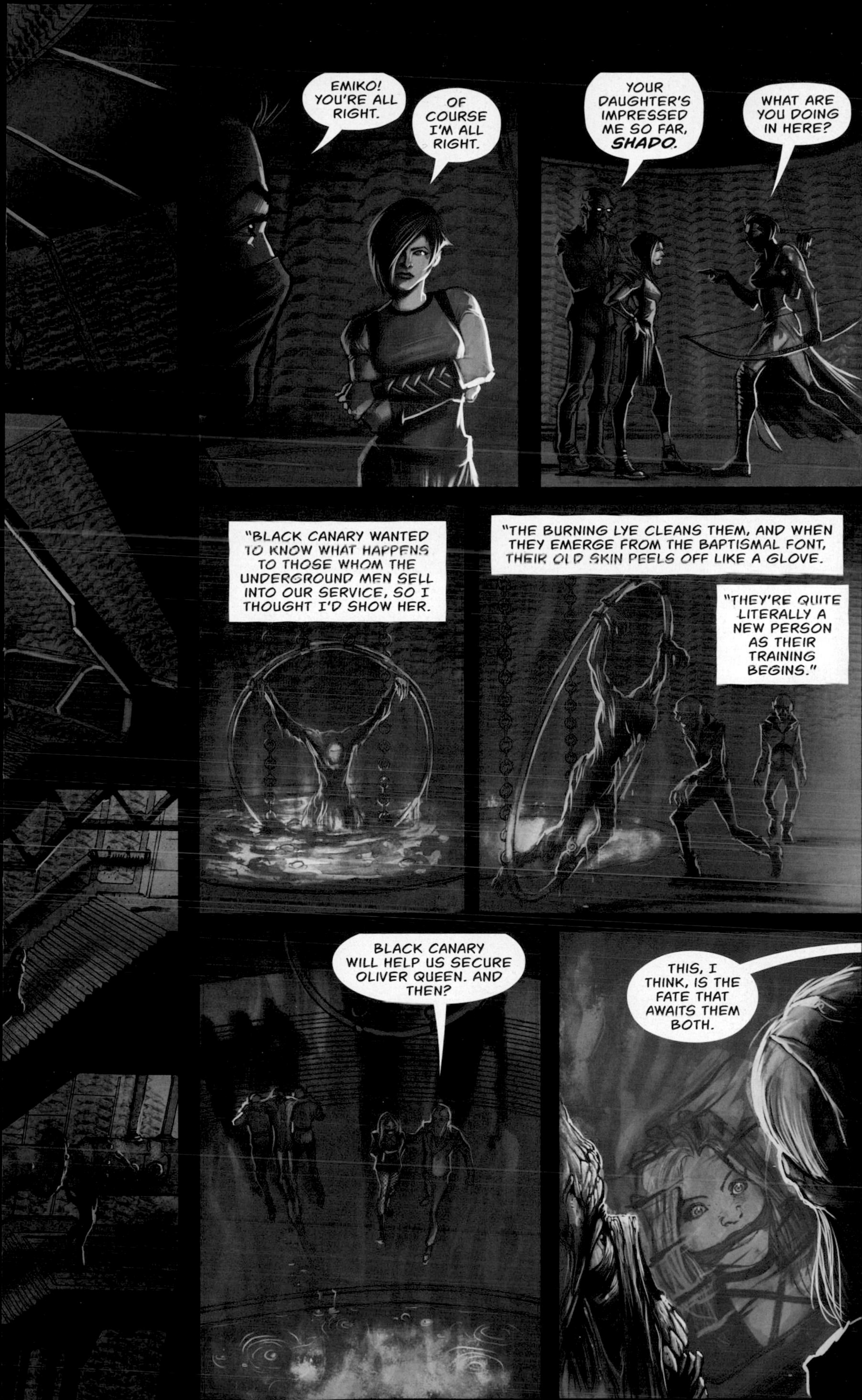
EMIKO! YOU'RE ALL RIGHT.
OF COURSE I'M ALL RIGHT.
YOUR DAUGHTER'S IMPRESSED ME SO FAR, SHADO.
WHAT ARE YOU DOING IN HERE?
"BLACK CANARY WANTED TO KNOW WHAT HAPPENS TO THOSE WHOM THE UNDERGROUND MEN SELL INTO OUR SERVICE, SO I THOUGHT I'D SHOW HER.
"THE BURNING LYE CLEANS THEM, AND WHEN THEY EMERGE FROM THE BAPTISMAL FONT, THEIR OLD SKIN PEELS OFF LIKE A GLOVE.
"THEY'RE QUITE LITERALLY A NEW PERSON AS THEIR TRAINING BEGINS."
BLACK CANARY WILL HELP US SECURE OLIVER QUEEN. AND THEN?
THIS, I THINK, IS THE FATE THAT AWAITS THEM BOTH.

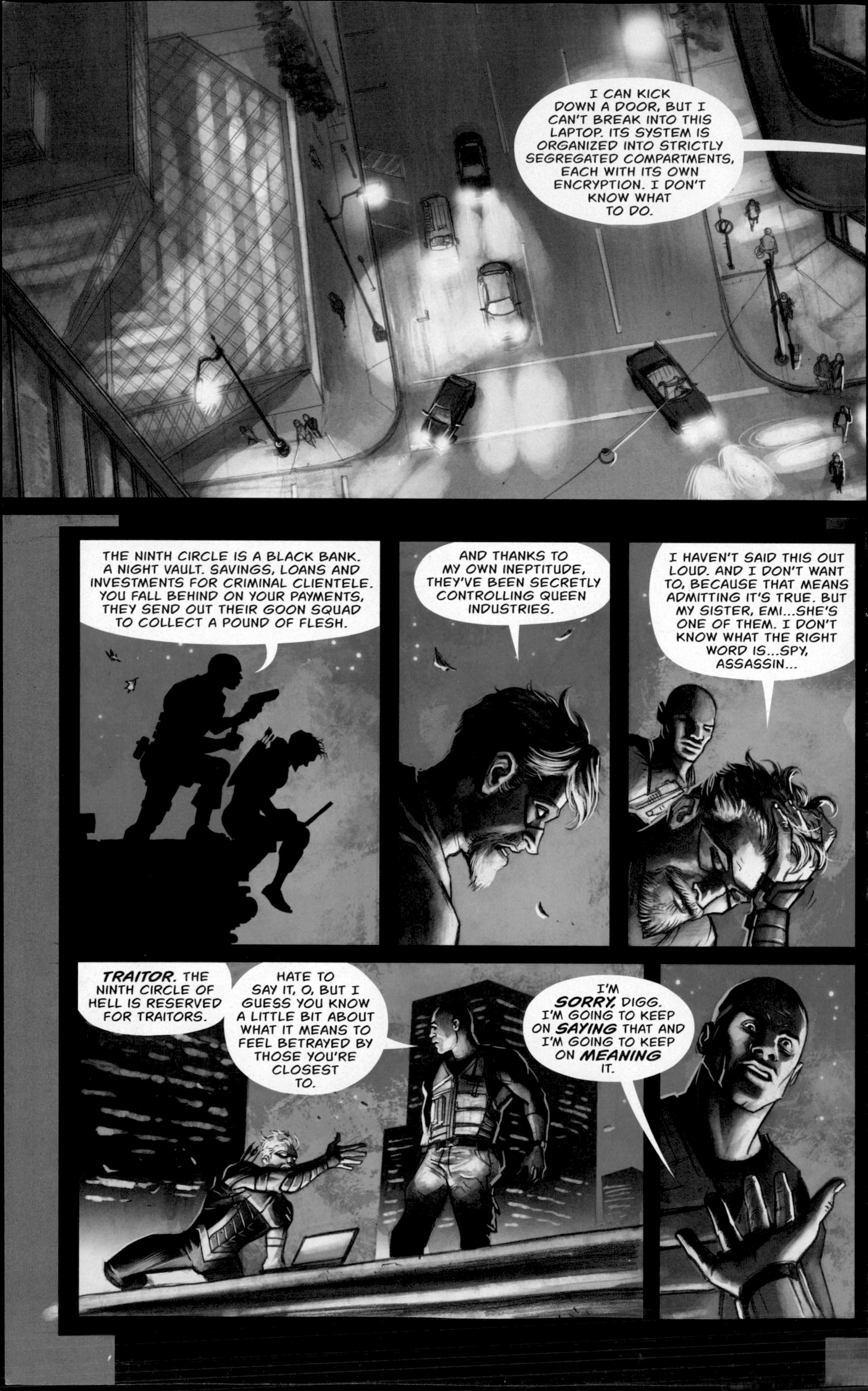
I CAN KICK DOWN A DOOR, BUT I CAN'T BREAK INTO THIS LAPTOP. ITS SYSTEM IS ORGANIZED INTO STRICTLY SEGREGATED COMPARTMENTS, EACH WITH ITS OWN ENCRYPTION. I DON'T KNOW WHAT TO DO.
THE NINTH CIRCLE IS A BLACK BANK. A NIGHT VAULT. SAVINGS, LOANS AND INVESTMENTS FOR CRIMINAL CLIENTELE. YOU FALL BEHIND ON YOUR PAYMENTS, THEY SEND OUT THEIR GOON SQUAD TO COLLECT A POUND OF FLESH.
AND THANKS TO MY OWN INEPTITUDE, THEY'VE BEEN SECRETLY CONTROLLING QUEEN INDUSTRIES.
I HAVEN'T SAID THIS OUT LOUD. AND I DON'T WANT TO, BECAUSE THAT MEANS ADMITTING IT'S TRUE. BUT MY SISTER, EMI...SHE'S ONE OF THEM. I DON'T KNOW WHAT THE RIGHT WORD IS...SPY, ASSASSIN...
TRAITOR. THE NINTH CIRCLE OF HELL IS RESERVED FOR TRAITORS.
HATE TO SAY IT, O, BUT I GUESS YOU KNOW A LITTLE BIT ABOUT WHAT IT MEANS TO FEEL BETRAYED BY THOSE YOU'RE CLOSEST TO.
I'M SORRY, DIGG. I'M GOING TO KEEP ON SAYING THAT AND I'M GOING TO KEEP ON MEANING IT.

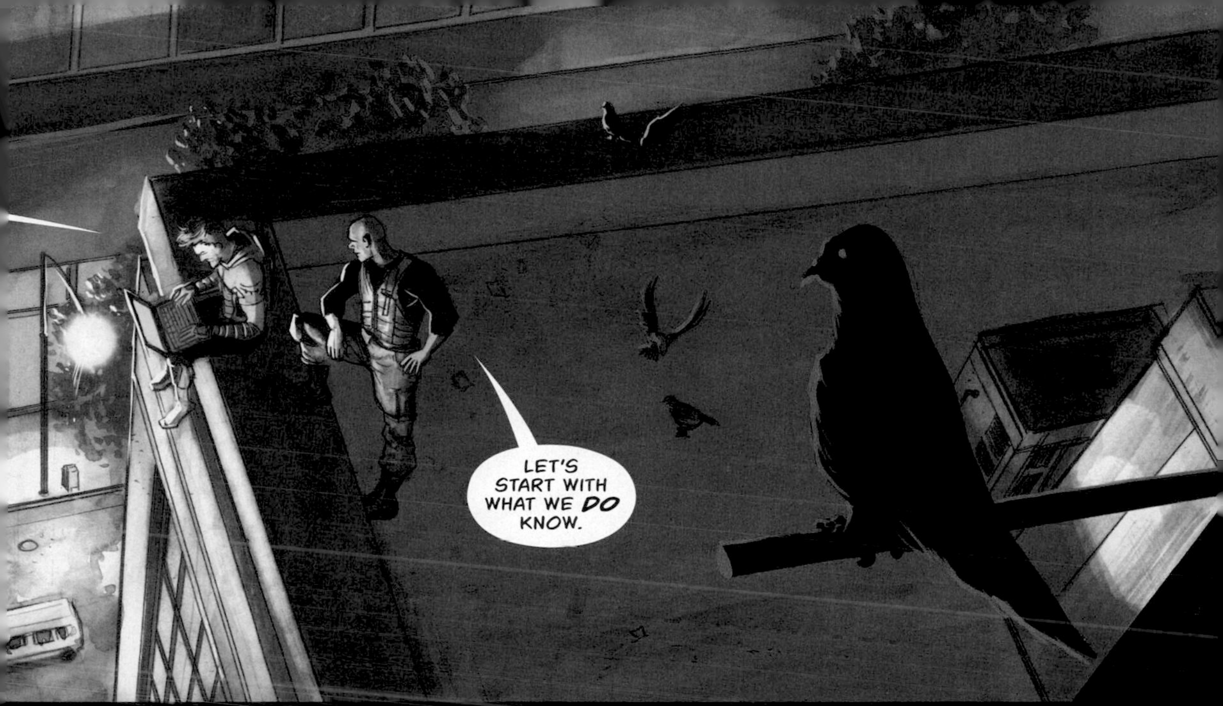
LET'S START WITH WHAT WE DO KNOW.
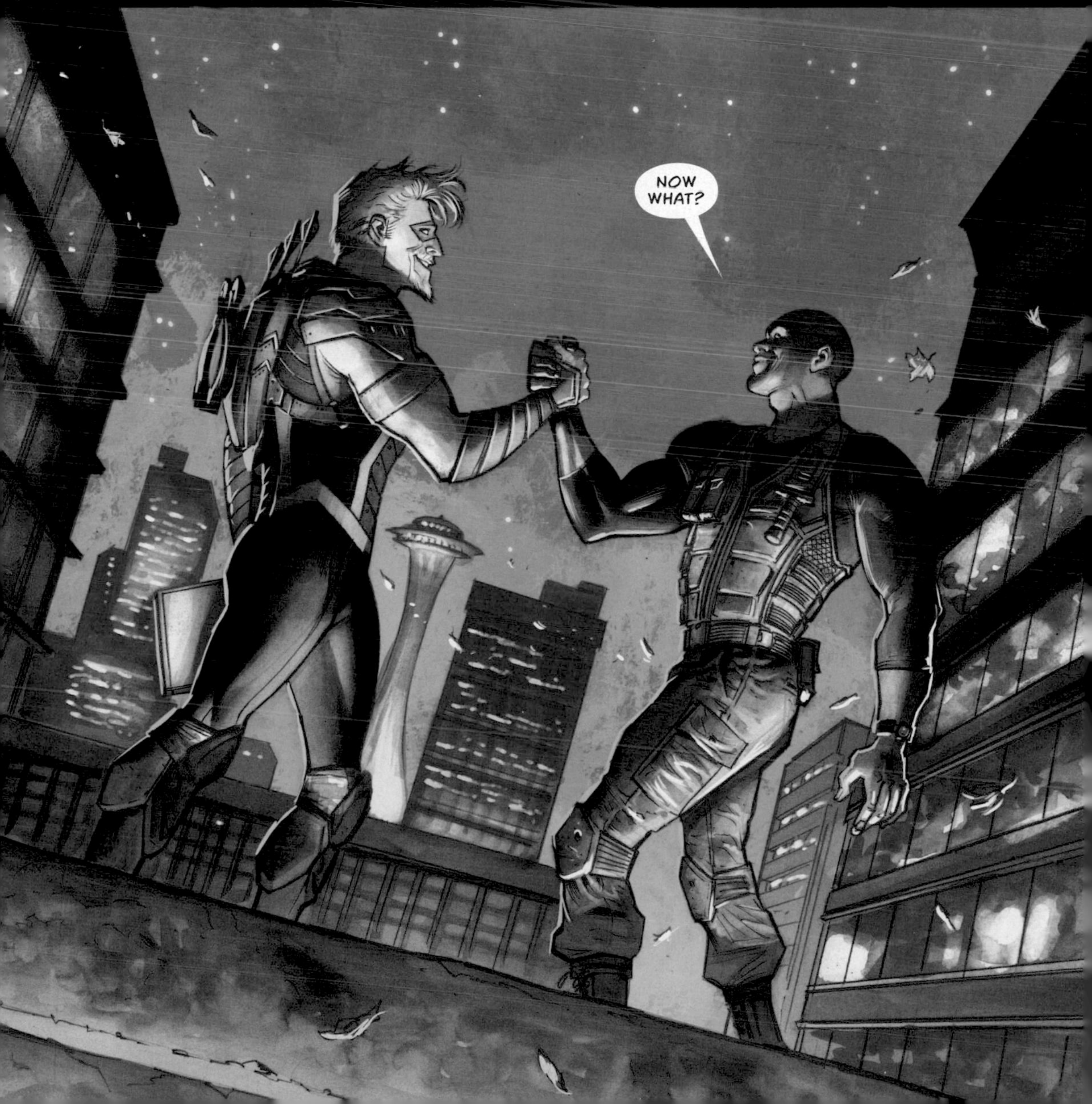
NOW WHAT?

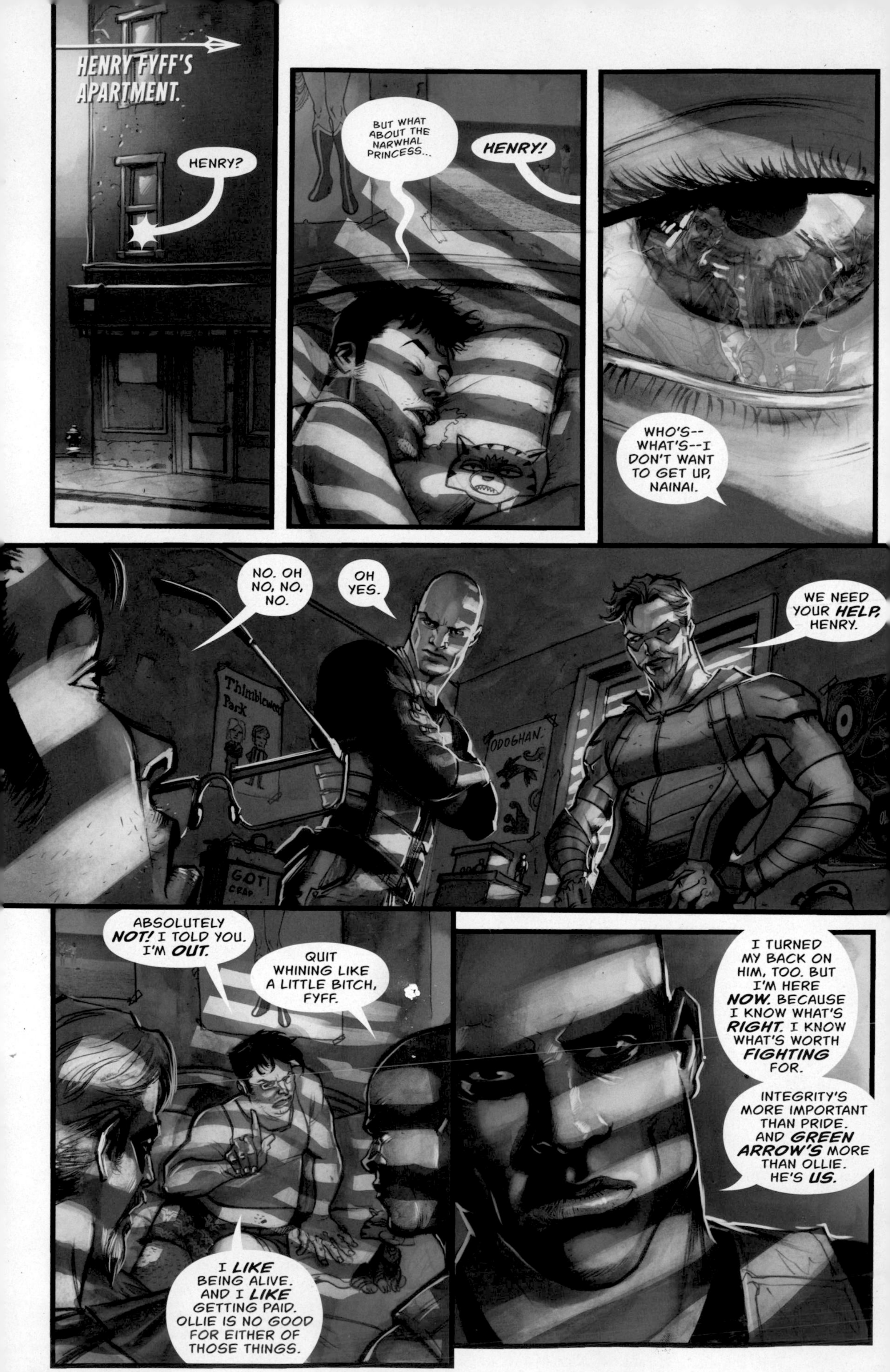
HENRY FYFF'S APARTMENT.
HENRY?
BUT WHAT ABOUT THE NARWHAL PRINCESS...
HENRY!
WHO'S-- WHAT'S--I DON'T WANT TO GET UP, NAINAI.
NO. OH NO, NO, NO.
OH YES.
WE NEED YOUR HELP, HENRY.
Thimbleweed Park
ODOGHAN
GOT CRAP
ABSOLUTELY NOT! I TOLD YOU. I'M OUT.
QUIT WHINING LIKE A LITTLE BITCH, FYFF.
I LIKE BEING ALIVE. AND I LIKE GETTING PAID. OLLIE IS NO GOOD FOR EITHER OF THOSE THINGS.
I TURNED MY BACK ON HIM, TOO. BUT I'M HERE NOW. BECAUSE I KNOW WHAT'S RIGHT. I KNOW WHAT'S WORTH FIGHTING FOR.
INTEGRITY'S MORE IMPORTANT THAN PRIDE. AND GREEN ARROW'S MORE THAN OLLIE. HE'S US.

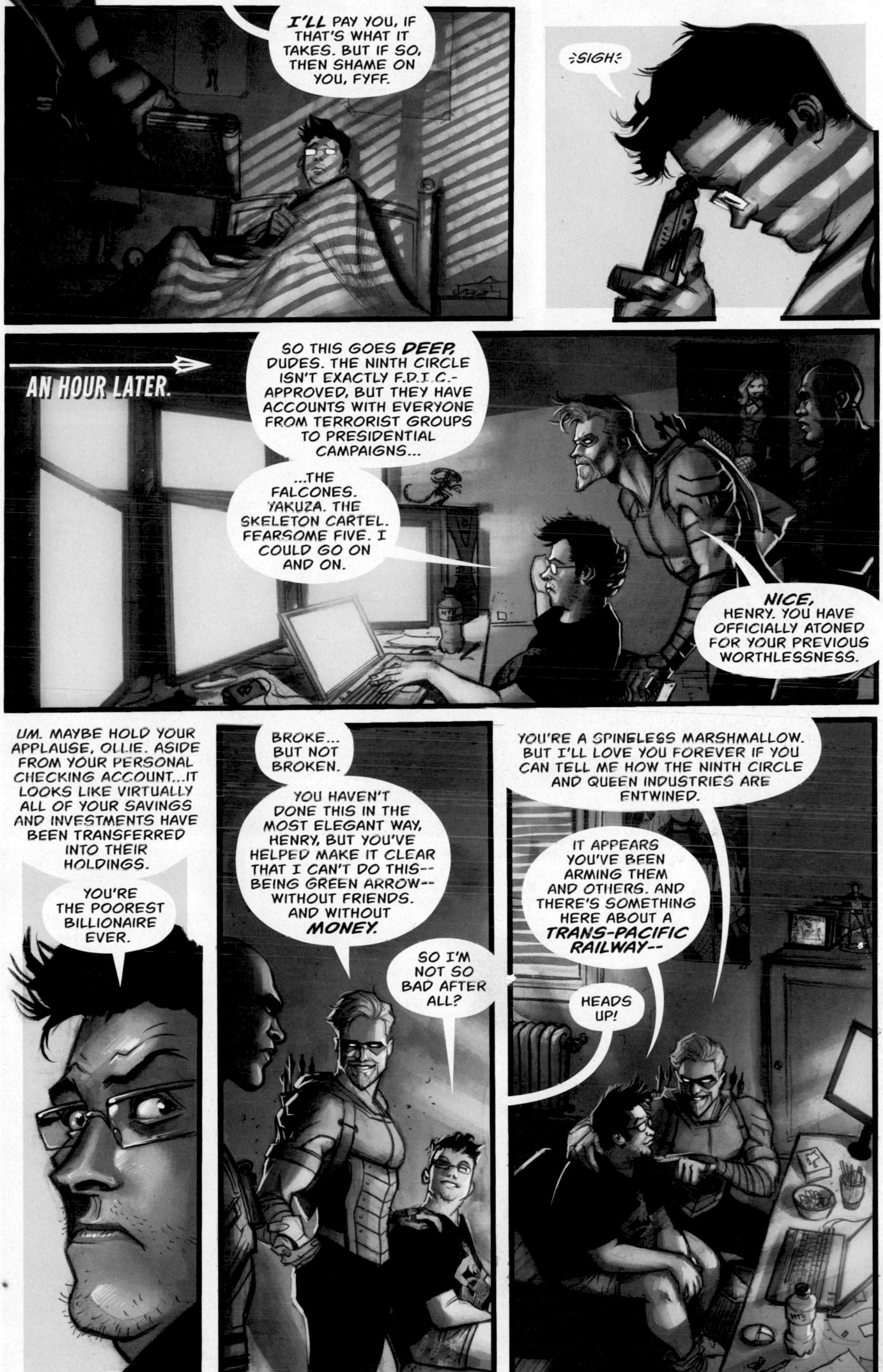
I'LL PAY YOU, IF THAT'S WHAT IT TAKES. BUT IF SO, THEN SHAME ON YOU, FYFF.
SIGH
AN HOUR LATER.
SO THIS GOES DEEP, DUDES. THE NINTH CIRCLE ISN'T EXACTLY F.D.I.C.-APPROVED, BUT THEY HAVE ACCOUNTS WITH EVERYONE FROM TERRORIST GROUPS TO PRESIDENTIAL CAMPAIGNS...
...THE FALCONES. YAKUZA. THE SKELETON CARTEL. FEARSOME FIVE. I COULD GO ON AND ON.
NICE, HENRY. YOU HAVE OFFICIALLY ATONED FOR YOUR PREVIOUS WORTHLESSNESS.
UM. MAYBE HOLD YOUR APPLAUSE, OLLIE. ASIDE FROM YOUR PERSONAL CHECKING ACCOUNT...IT LOOKS LIKE VIRTUALLY ALL OF YOUR SAVINGS AND INVESTMENTS HAVE BEEN TRANSFERRED INTO THEIR HOLDINGS.
YOU'RE THE POOREST BILLIONAIRE EVER.
BROKE... BUT NOT BROKEN.
YOU HAVEN'T DONE THIS IN THE MOST ELEGANT WAY, HENRY, BUT YOU'VE HELPED MAKE IT CLEAR THAT I CAN'T DO THIS--BEING GREEN ARROW--WITHOUT FRIENDS. AND WITHOUT MONEY.
SO I'M NOT SO BAD AFTER ALL?
YOU'RE A SPINELESS MARSHMALLOW. BUT I'LL LOVE YOU FOREVER IF YOU CAN TELL ME HOW THE NINTH CIRCLE AND QUEEN INDUSTRIES ARE ENTWINED.
IT APPEARS YOU'VE BEEN ARMING THEM AND OTHERS. AND THERE'S SOMETHING HERE ABOUT A TRANS-PACIFIC RAILWAY--
HEADS UP!

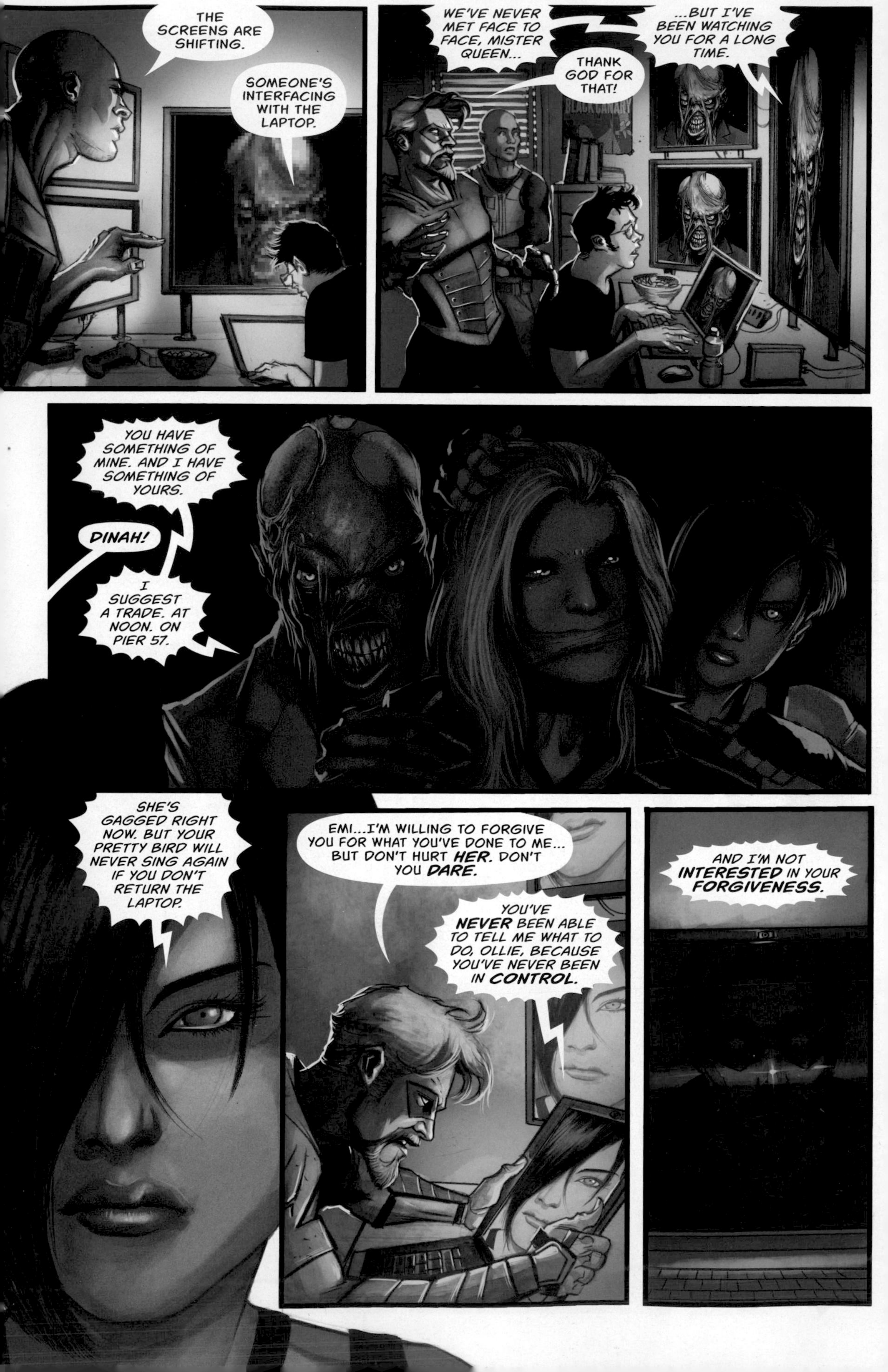
THE SCREENS ARE SHIFTING.
SOMEONE'S INTERFACING WITH THE LAPTOP.
WE'VE NEVER MET FACE TO FACE, MISTER QUEEN...
THANK GOD FOR THAT!
...BUT I'VE BEEN WATCHING YOU FOR A LONG TIME.
BLACK CANARY
YOU HAVE SOMETHING OF MINE. AND I HAVE SOMETHING OF YOURS.
DINAH!
I SUGGEST A TRADE. AT NOON. ON PIER 57.
SHE'S GAGGED RIGHT NOW. BUT YOUR PRETTY BIRD WILL NEVER SING AGAIN IF YOU DON'T RETURN THE LAPTOP.
EMI...I'M WILLING TO FORGIVE YOU FOR WHAT YOU'VE DONE TO ME... BUT DON'T HURT HER. DON'T YOU DARE.
YOU'VE NEVER BEEN ABLE TO TELL ME WHAT TO DO, OLLIE, BECAUSE YOU'VE NEVER BEEN IN CONTROL.
AND I'M NOT INTERESTED IN YOUR FORGIVENESS.

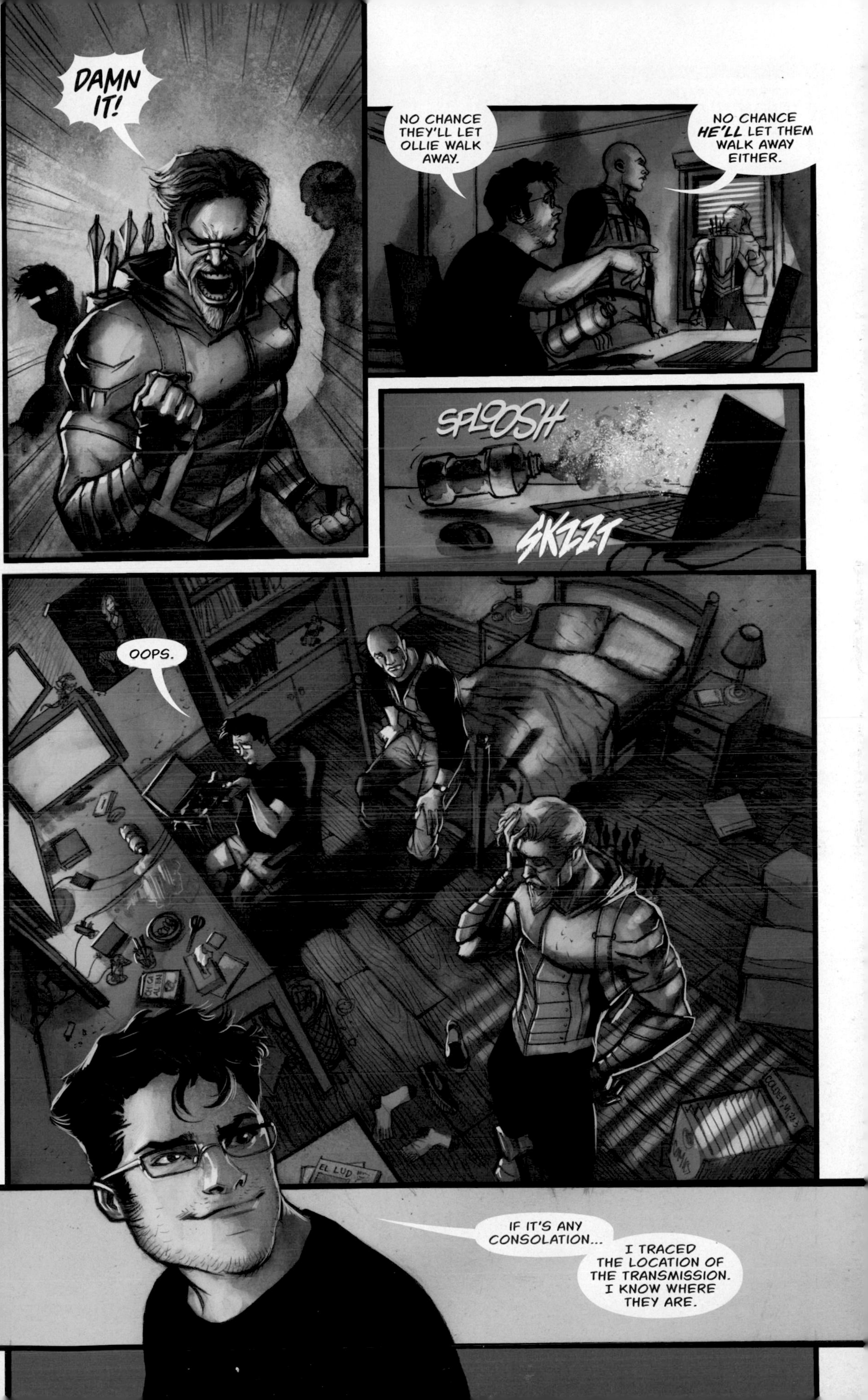
DAMN IT!
NO CHANCE THEY'LL LET OLLIE WALK AWAY.
NO CHANCE **HE'LL** LET THEM WALK AWAY EITHER.
SPLOOSH
SKZZT
OOPS.
IF IT'S ANY CONSOLATION...
I TRACED THE LOCATION OF THE TRANSMISSION. I KNOW WHERE THEY ARE.

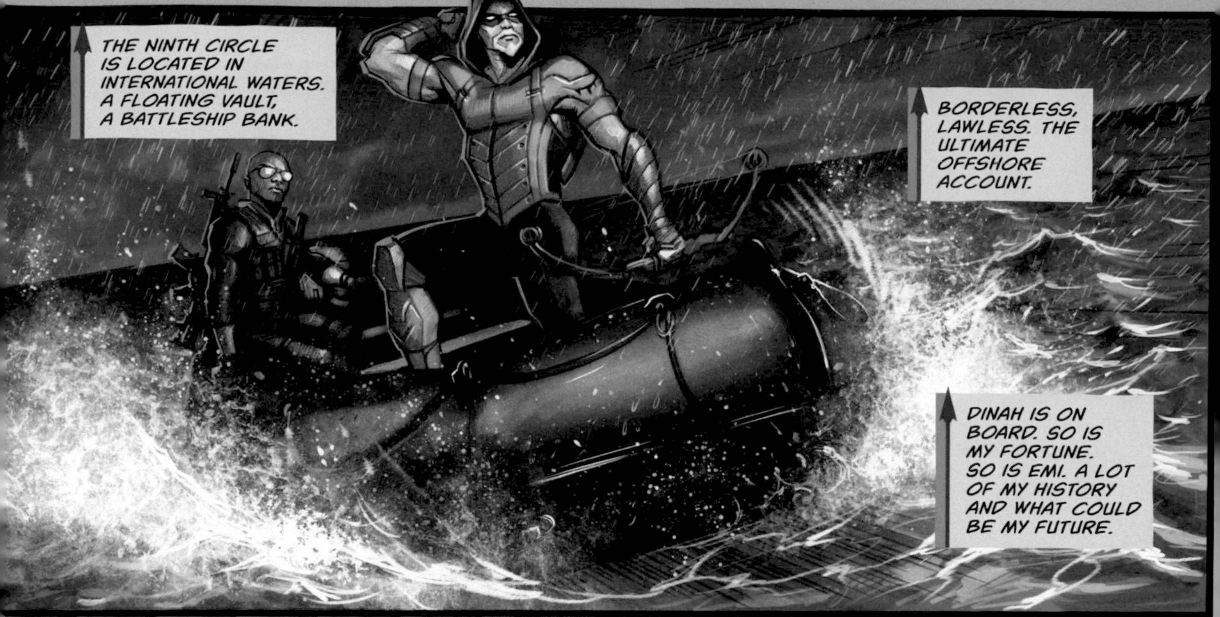
THE NINTH CIRCLE IS LOCATED IN INTERNATIONAL WATERS. A FLOATING VAULT, A BATTLESHIP BANK.
BORDERLESS, LAWLESS. THE ULTIMATE OFFSHORE ACCOUNT.
DINAH IS ON BOARD. SO IS MY FORTUNE. SO IS EMI. A LOT OF MY HISTORY AND WHAT COULD BE MY FUTURE.
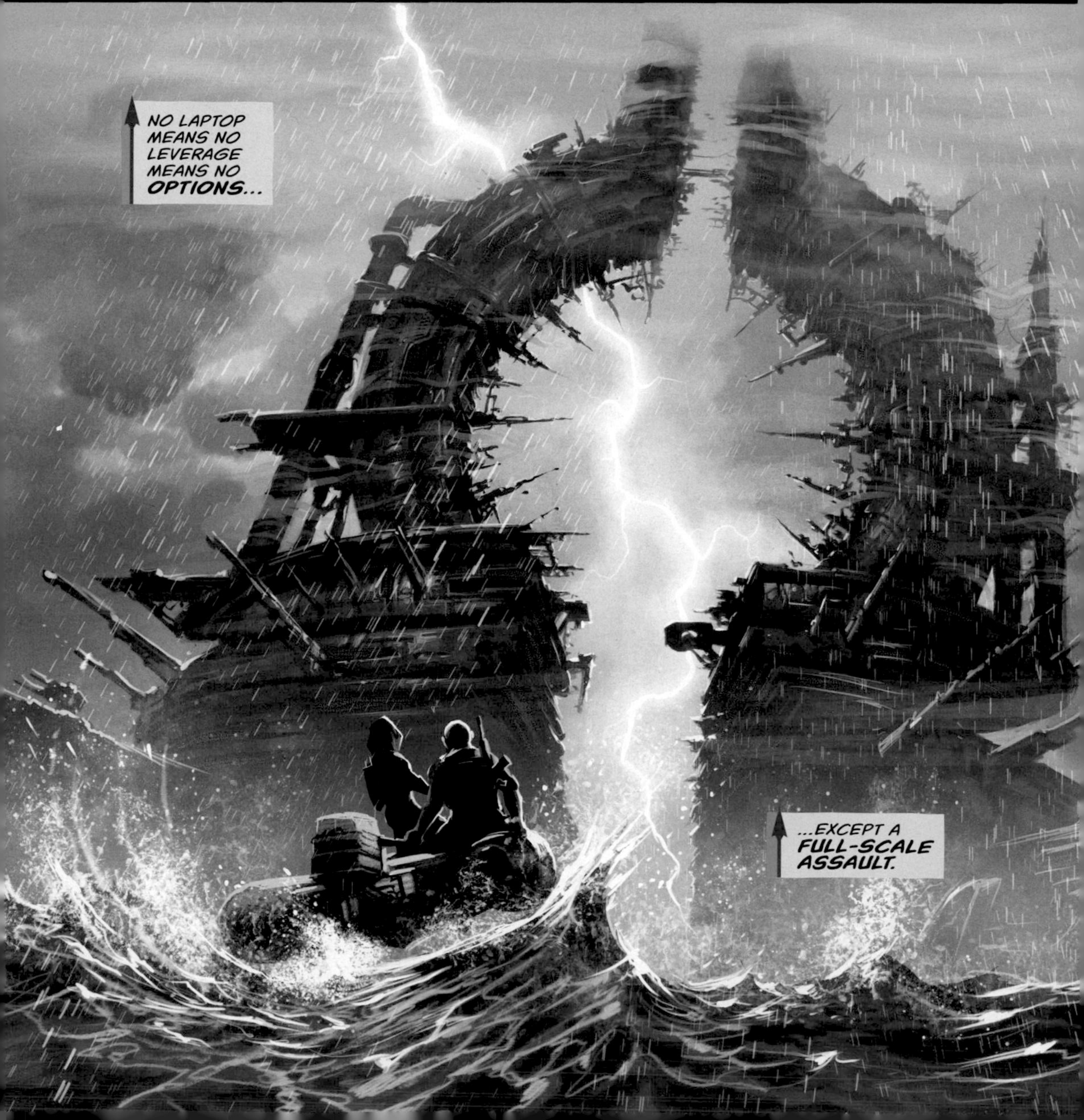
NO LAPTOP MEANS NO LEVERAGE MEANS NO OPTIONS...
...EXCEPT A FULL-SCALE ASSAULT.

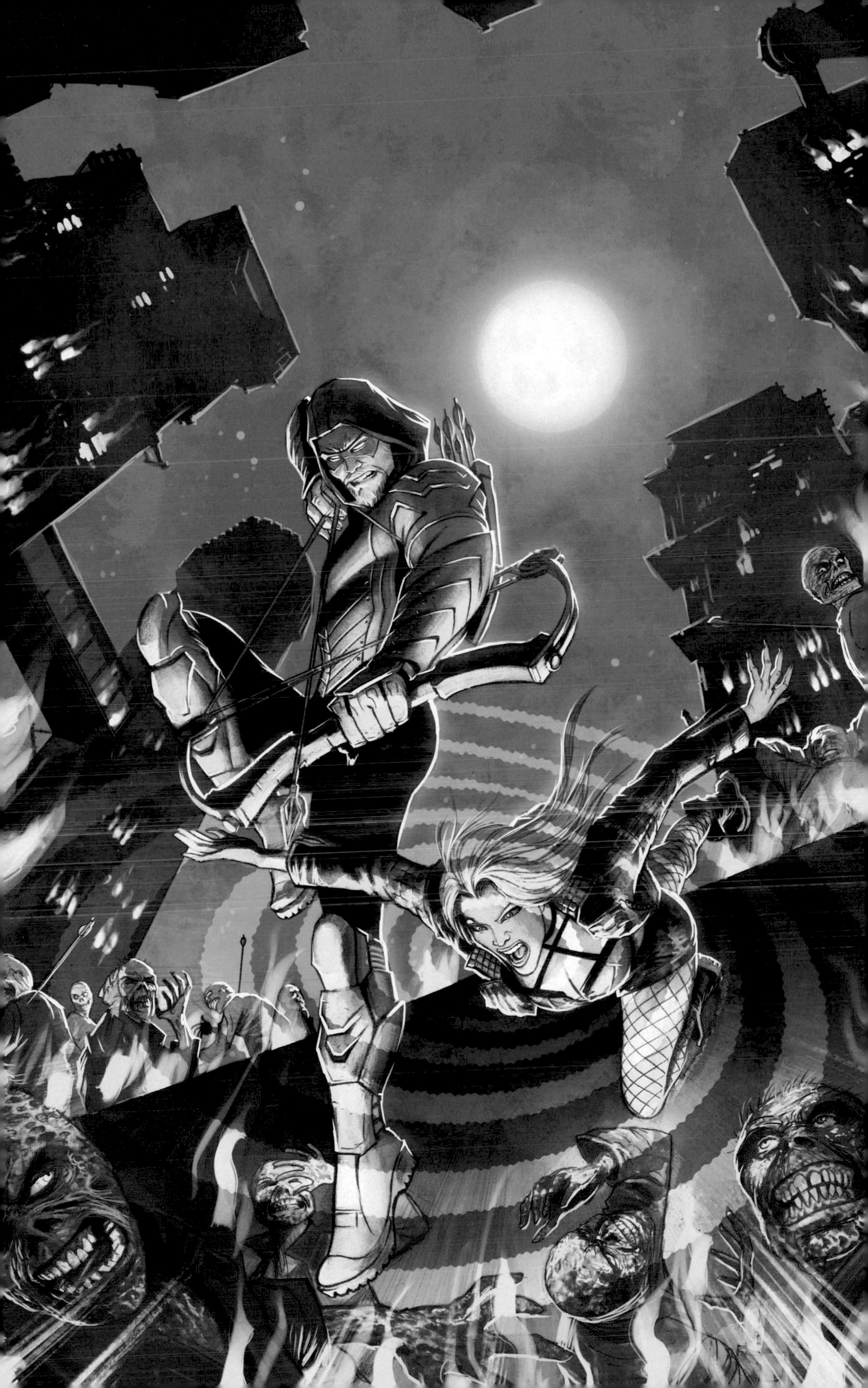

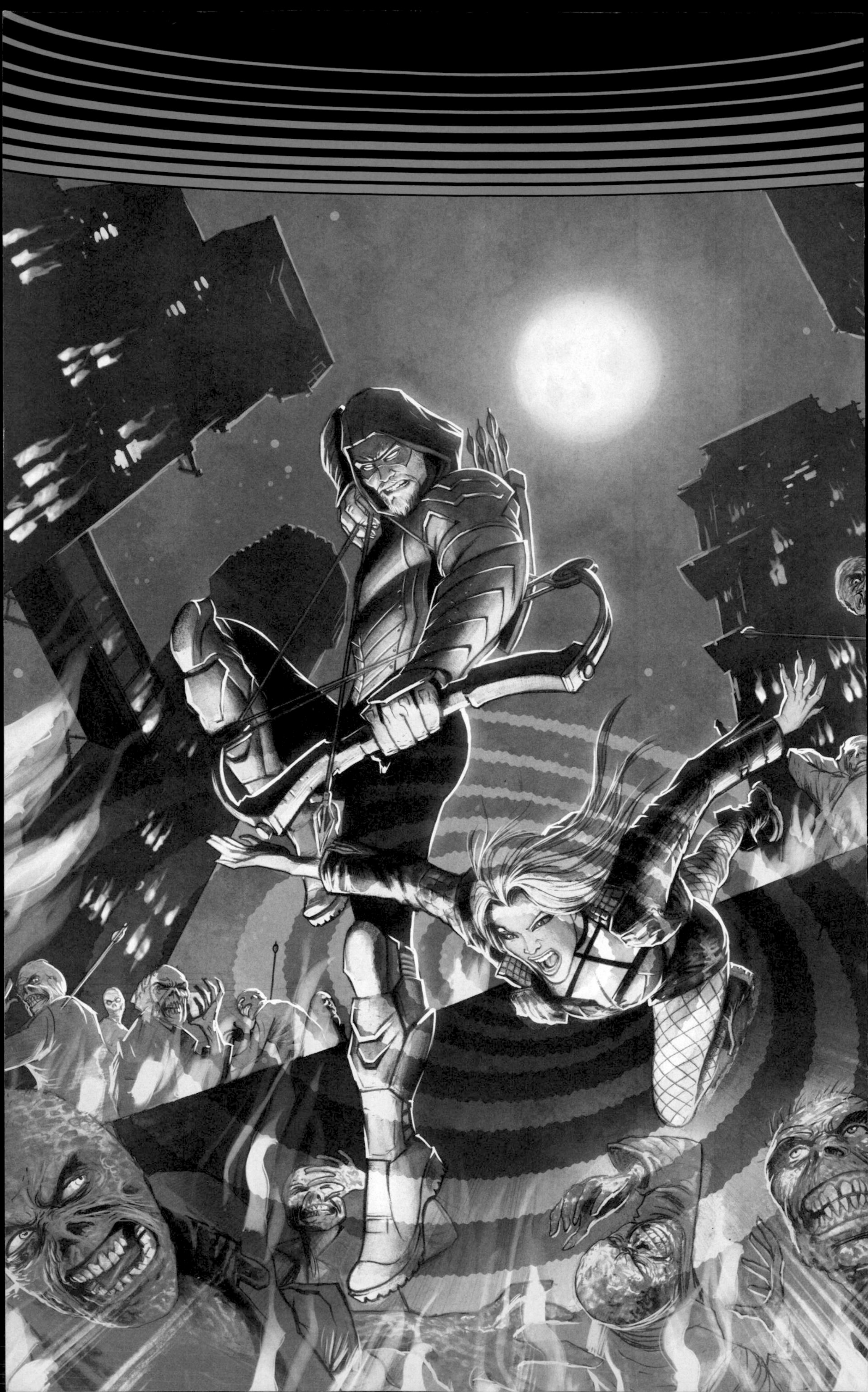

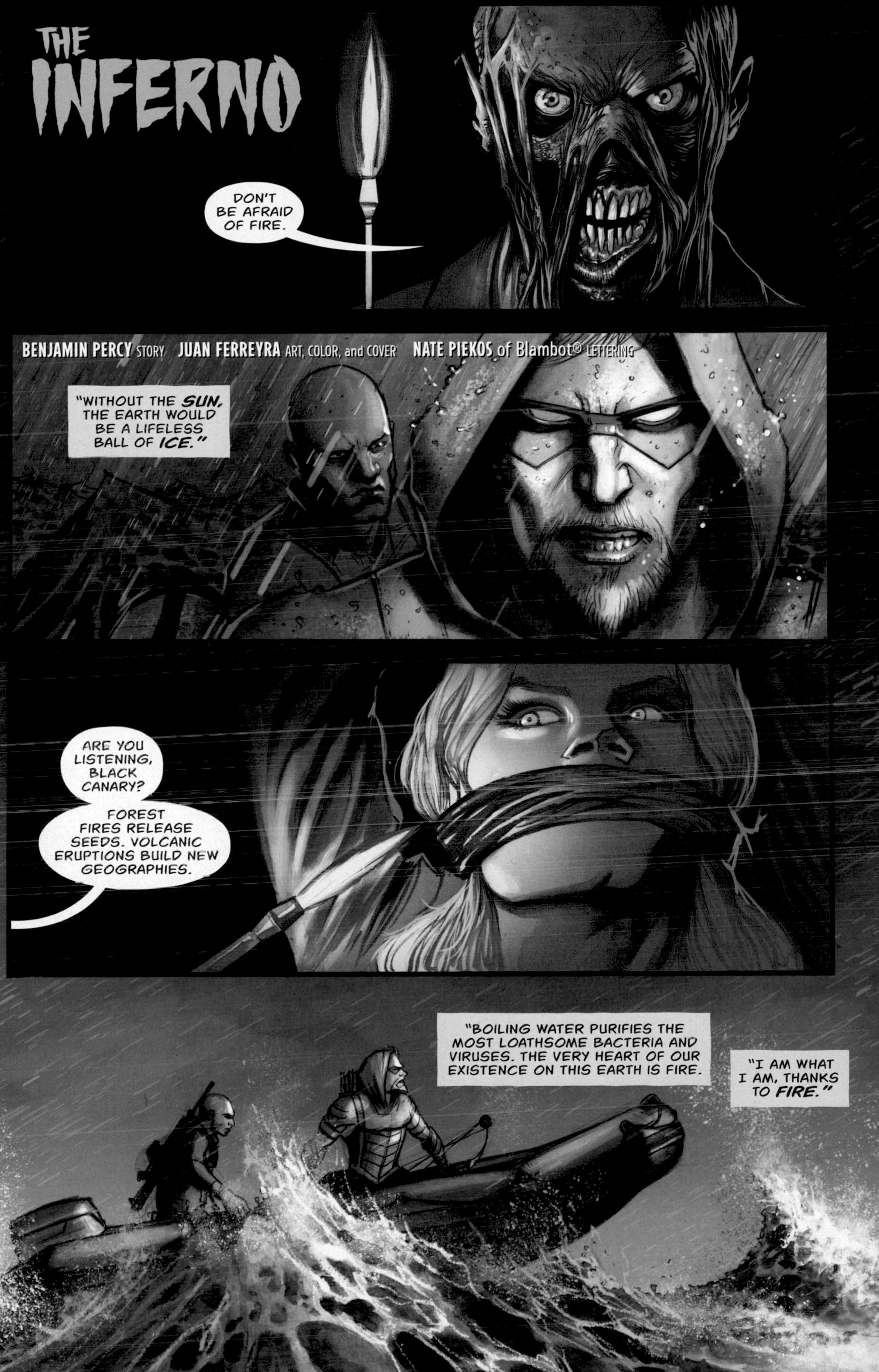
THE INFERNO
DON'T BE AFRAID OF FIRE.
BENJAMIN PERCY STORY JUAN FERREYRA ART, COLOR, and COVER NATE PIEKOS of Blambot® LETTERING
"WITHOUT THE SUN, THE EARTH WOULD BE A LIFELESS BALL OF ICE."
ARE YOU LISTENING, BLACK CANARY?
FOREST FIRES RELEASE SEEDS. VOLCANIC ERUPTIONS BUILD NEW GEOGRAPHIES.
"BOILING WATER PURIFIES THE MOST LOATHSOME BACTERIA AND VIRUSES. THE VERY HEART OF OUR EXISTENCE ON THIS EARTH IS FIRE.
"I AM WHAT I AM, THANKS TO FIRE."

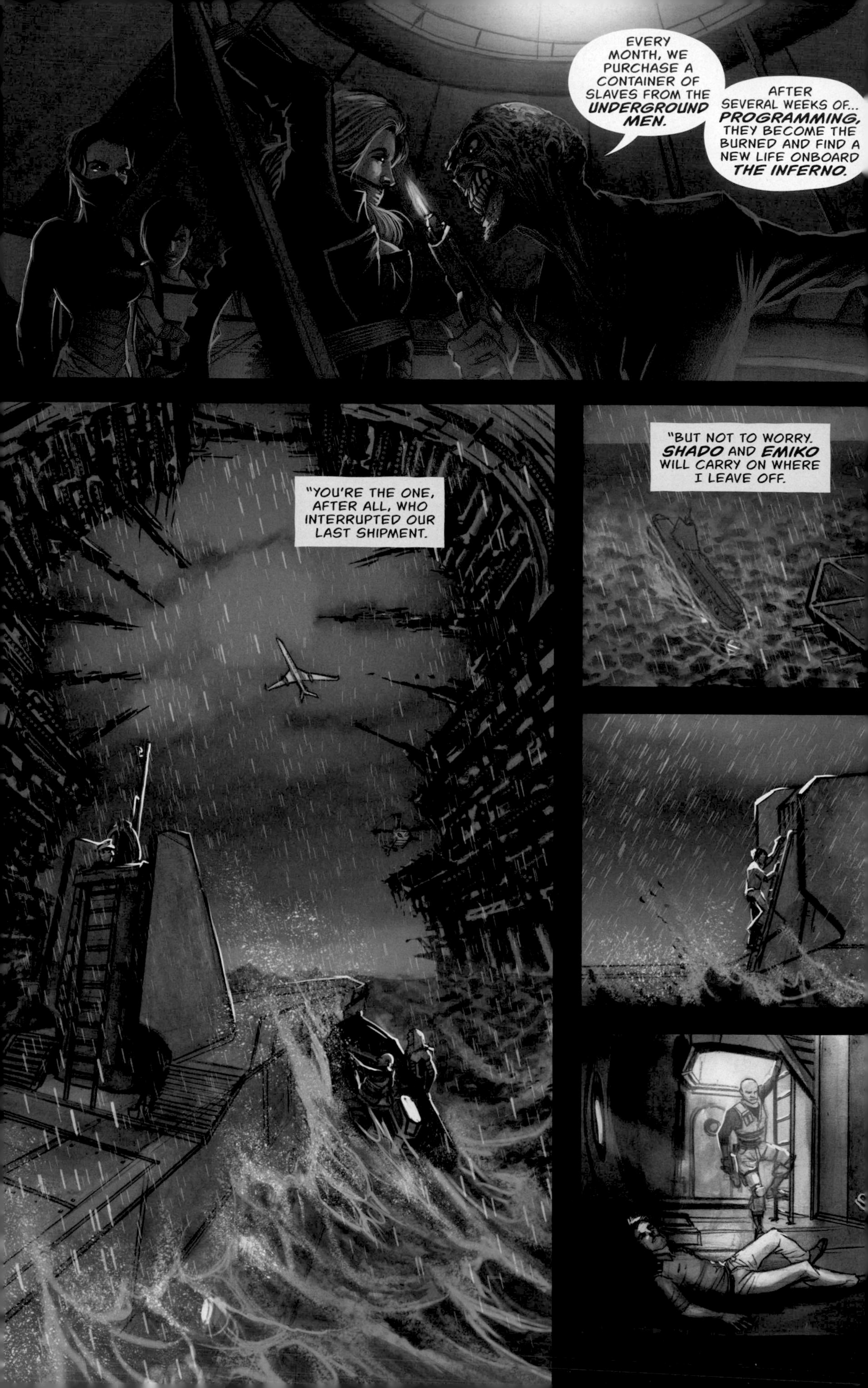
EVERY MONTH, WE PURCHASE A CONTAINER OF SLAVES FROM THE UNDERGROUND MEN.
AFTER SEVERAL WEEKS OF... PROGRAMMING, THEY BECOME THE BURNED AND FIND A NEW LIFE ONBOARD THE INFERNO.
"YOU'RE THE ONE, AFTER ALL, WHO INTERRUPTED OUR LAST SHIPMENT.
"BUT NOT TO WORRY. SHADO AND EMIKO WILL CARRY ON WHERE I LEAVE OFF.

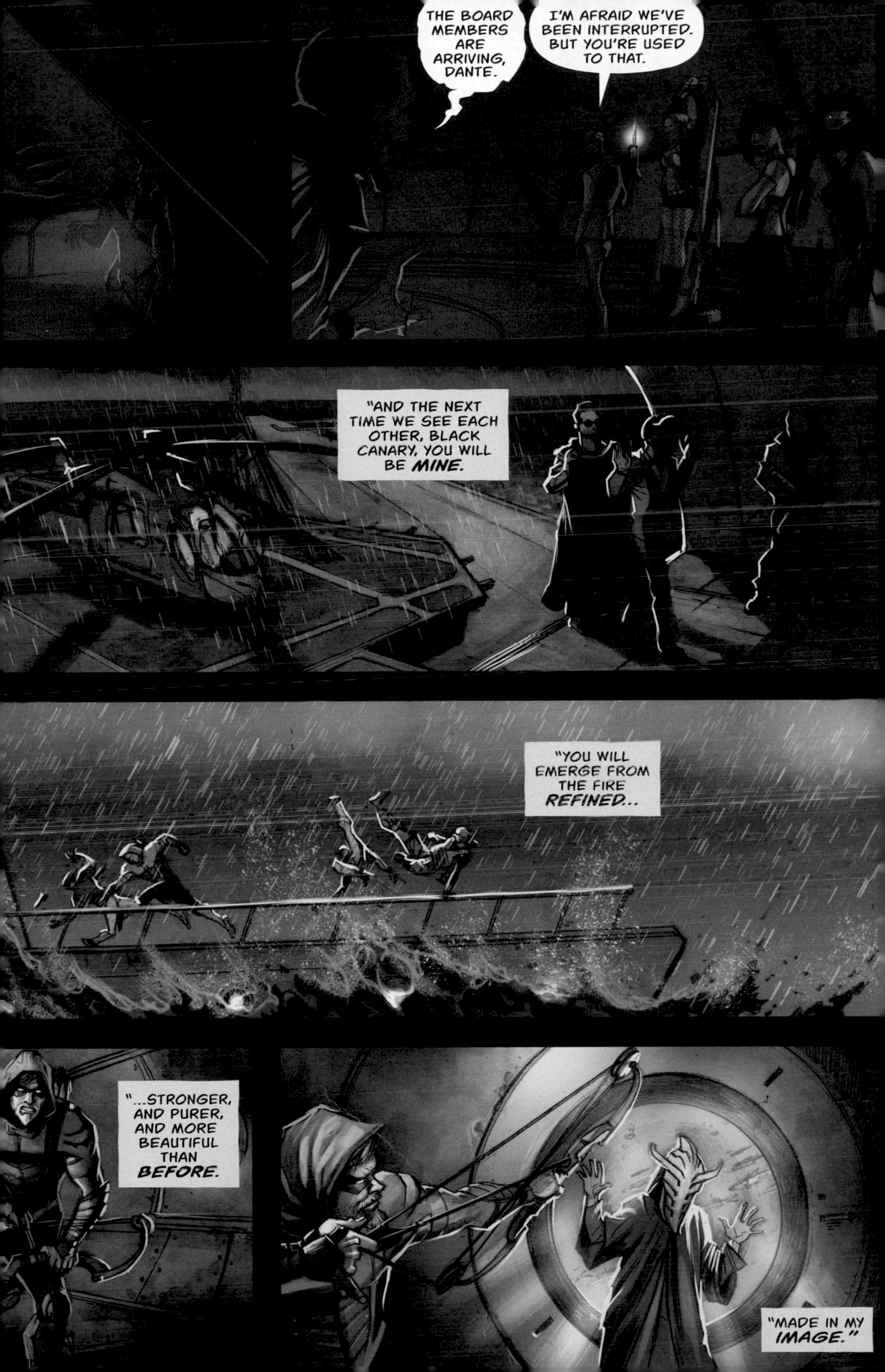
THE BOARD MEMBERS ARE ARRIVING, DANTE.
I'M AFRAID WE'VE BEEN INTERRUPTED. BUT YOU'RE USED TO THAT.
"AND THE NEXT TIME WE SEE EACH OTHER, BLACK CANARY, YOU WILL BE *MINE.*
"YOU WILL EMERGE FROM THE FIRE *REFINED...*
"...STRONGER, AND PURER, AND MORE BEAUTIFUL THAN *BEFORE.*
"MADE IN MY *IMAGE.*"

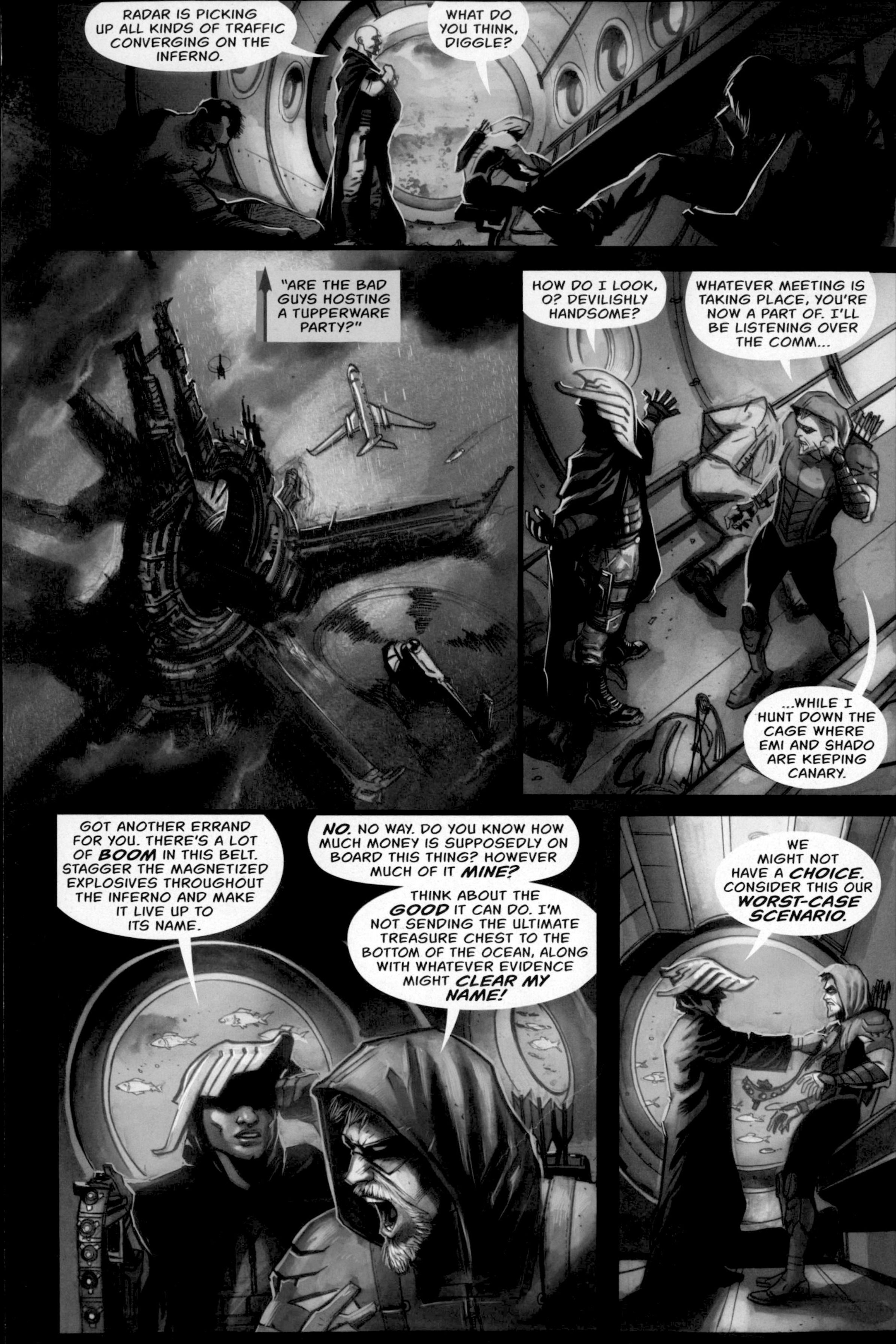
RADAR IS PICKING UP ALL KINDS OF TRAFFIC CONVERGING ON THE INFERNO.
WHAT DO YOU THINK, DIGGLE?
"ARE THE BAD GUYS HOSTING A TUPPERWARE PARTY?"
HOW DO I LOOK, O? DEVILISHLY HANDSOME?
WHATEVER MEETING IS TAKING PLACE, YOU'RE NOW A PART OF. I'LL BE LISTENING OVER THE COMM...
...WHILE I HUNT DOWN THE CAGE WHERE EMI AND SHADO ARE KEEPING CANARY.
GOT ANOTHER ERRAND FOR YOU. THERE'S A LOT OF BOOM IN THIS BELT. STAGGER THE MAGNETIZED EXPLOSIVES THROUGHOUT THE INFERNO AND MAKE IT LIVE UP TO ITS NAME.
NO. NO WAY. DO YOU KNOW HOW MUCH MONEY IS SUPPOSEDLY ON BOARD THIS THING? HOWEVER MUCH OF IT MINE?
THINK ABOUT THE GOOD IT CAN DO. I'M NOT SENDING THE ULTIMATE TREASURE CHEST TO THE BOTTOM OF THE OCEAN, ALONG WITH WHATEVER EVIDENCE MIGHT CLEAR MY NAME!
WE MIGHT NOT HAVE A CHOICE. CONSIDER THIS OUR WORST-CASE SCENARIO.

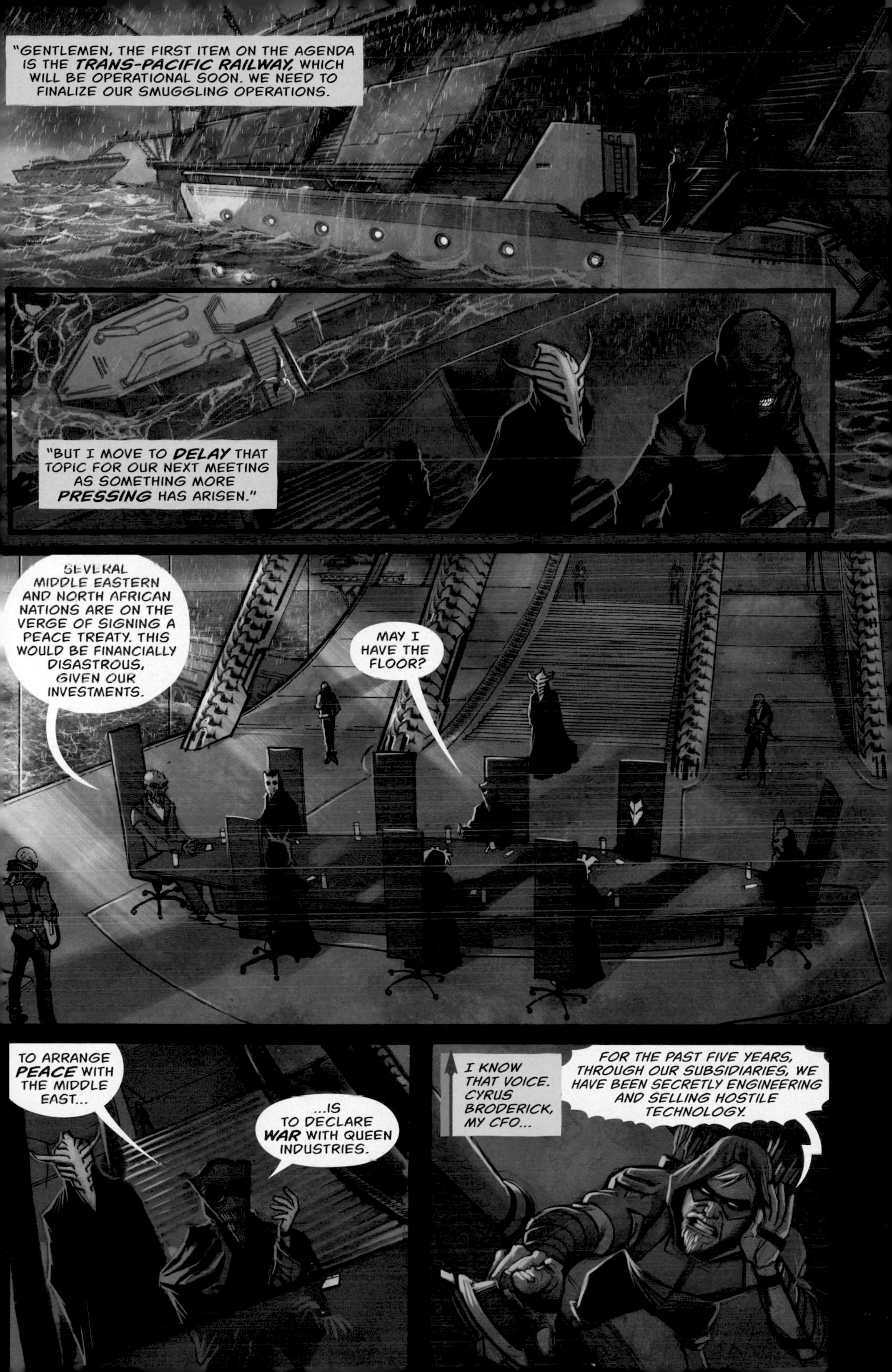
"GENTLEMEN, THE FIRST ITEM ON THE AGENDA IS THE TRANS-PACIFIC RAILWAY, WHICH WILL BE OPERATIONAL SOON. WE NEED TO FINALIZE OUR SMUGGLING OPERATIONS.
"BUT I MOVE TO DELAY THAT TOPIC FOR OUR NEXT MEETING AS SOMETHING MORE PRESSING HAS ARISEN."
SEVERAL MIDDLE EASTERN AND NORTH AFRICAN NATIONS ARE ON THE VERGE OF SIGNING A PEACE TREATY. THIS WOULD BE FINANCIALLY DISASTROUS, GIVEN OUR INVESTMENTS.
MAY I HAVE THE FLOOR?
TO ARRANGE PEACE WITH THE MIDDLE EAST...
...IS TO DECLARE WAR WITH QUEEN INDUSTRIES.
I KNOW THAT VOICE. CYRUS BRODERICK, MY CFO...
FOR THE PAST FIVE YEARS, THROUGH OUR SUBSIDIARIES, WE HAVE BEEN SECRETLY ENGINEERING AND SELLING HOSTILE TECHNOLOGY.

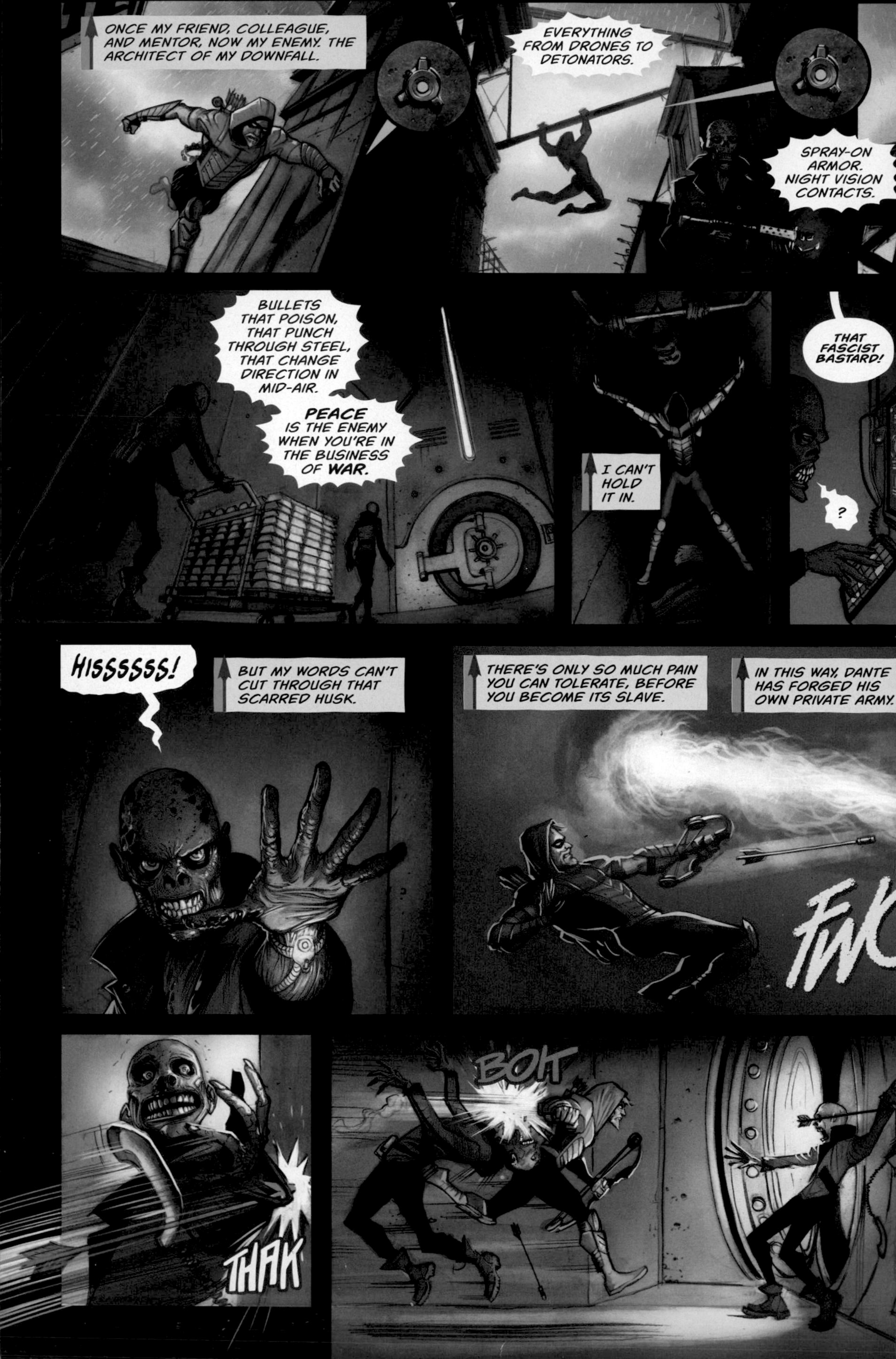
ONCE MY FRIEND, COLLEAGUE, AND MENTOR, NOW MY ENEMY. THE ARCHITECT OF MY DOWNFALL.
EVERYTHING FROM DRONES TO DETONATORS.
SPRAY-ON ARMOR. NIGHT VISION CONTACTS.
BULLETS THAT POISON, THAT PUNCH THROUGH STEEL, THAT CHANGE DIRECTION IN MID-AIR.
PEACE IS THE ENEMY WHEN YOU'RE IN THE BUSINESS OF WAR.
I CAN'T HOLD IT IN.
THAT FASCIST BASTARD!
?
HISSSSSS!
BUT MY WORDS CAN'T CUT THROUGH THAT SCARRED HUSK.
THERE'S ONLY SO MUCH PAIN YOU CAN TOLERATE, BEFORE YOU BECOME ITS SLAVE.
IN THIS WAY, DANTE HAS FORGED HIS OWN PRIVATE ARMY.
FWC
THAK
BOK

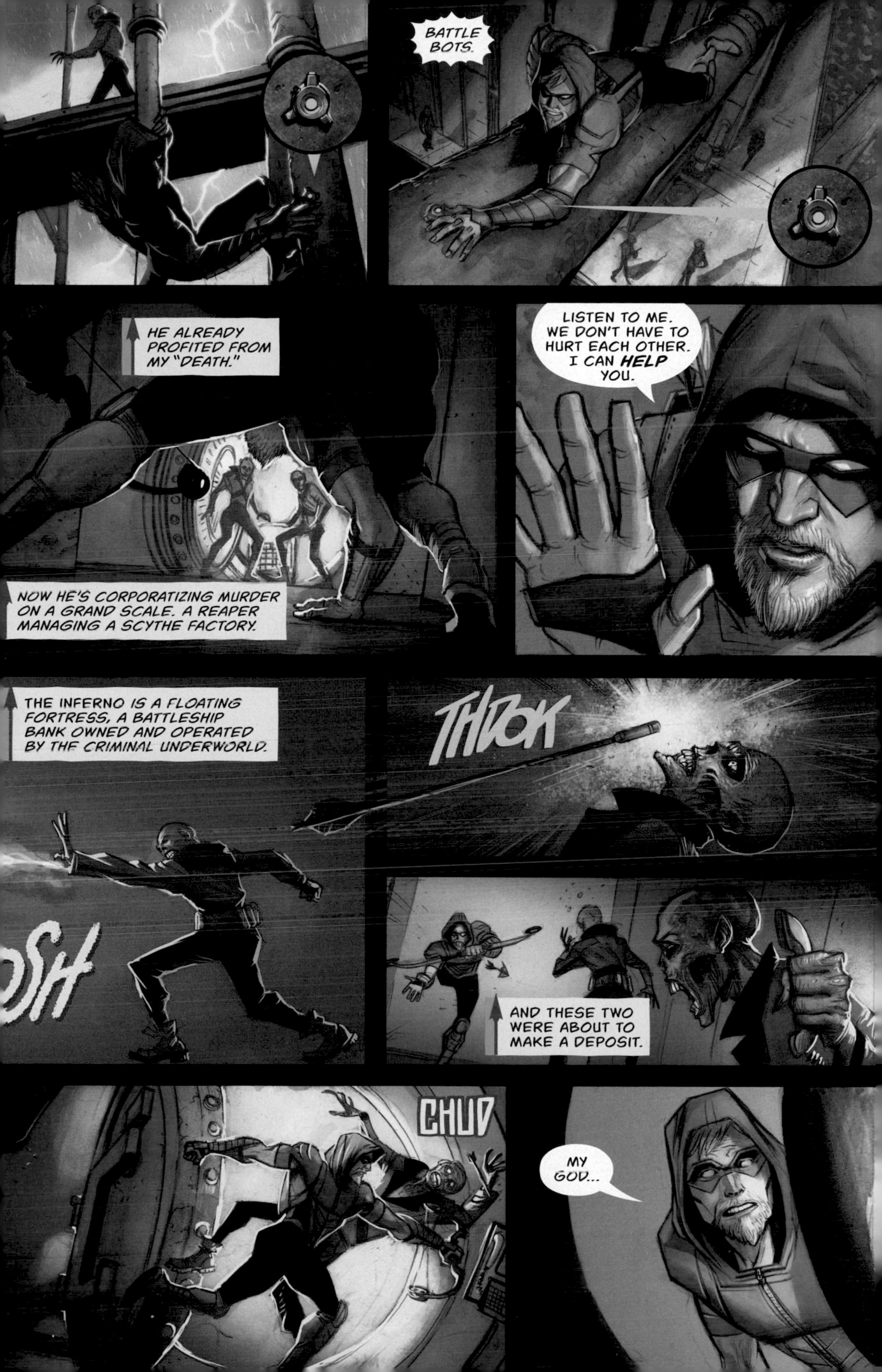
BATTLE BOTS.
HE ALREADY PROFITED FROM MY "DEATH."
NOW HE'S CORPORATIZING MURDER ON A GRAND SCALE. A REAPER MANAGING A SCYTHE FACTORY.
LISTEN TO ME. WE DON'T HAVE TO HURT EACH OTHER. I CAN HELP YOU.
THE INFERNO IS A FLOATING FORTRESS, A BATTLESHIP BANK OWNED AND OPERATED BY THE CRIMINAL UNDERWORLD.
THDOK
AND THESE TWO WERE ABOUT TO MAKE A DEPOSIT.
CHUD
MY GOD...

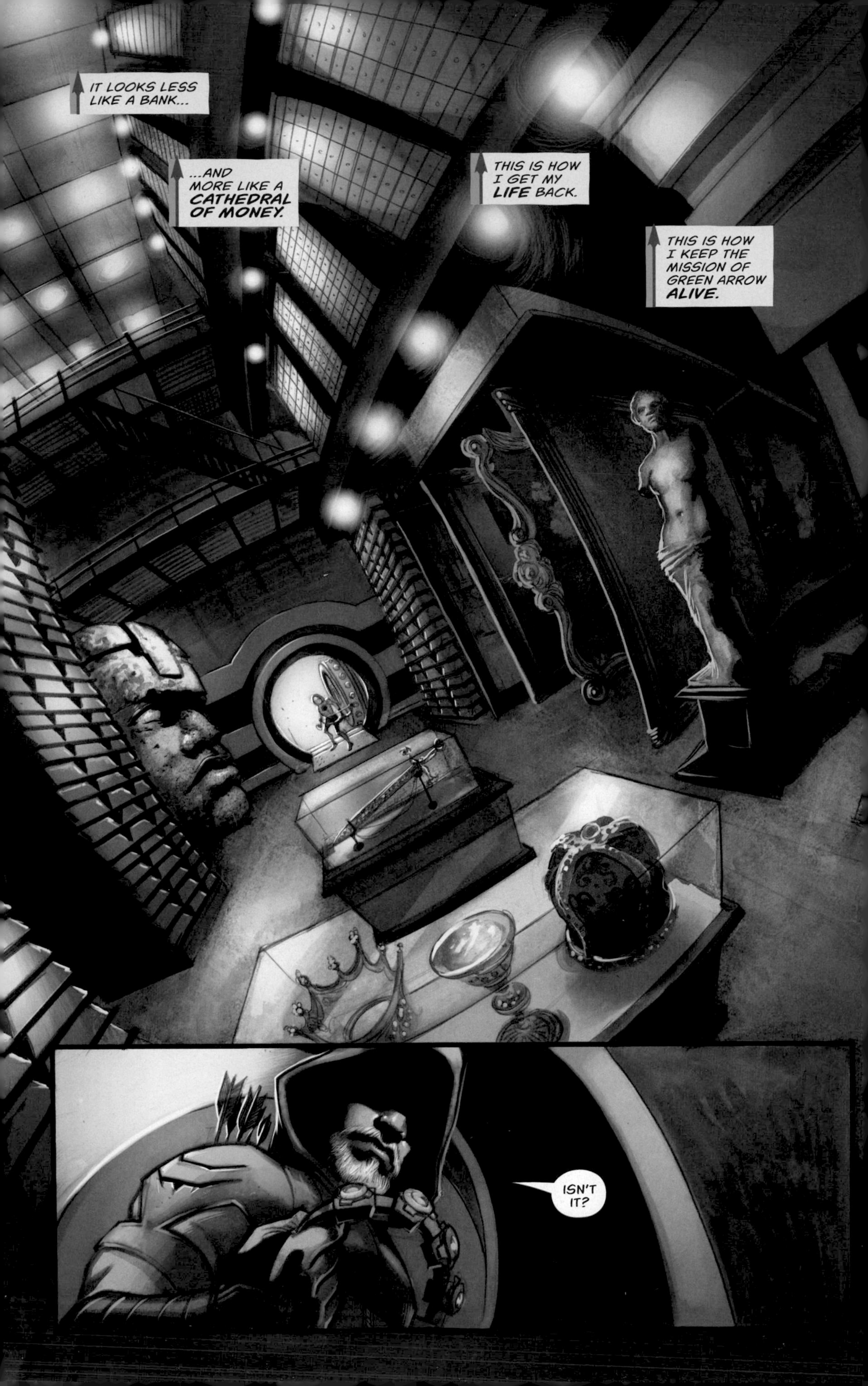
IT LOOKS LESS LIKE A BANK...
...AND MORE LIKE A **CATHEDRAL OF MONEY.**
THIS IS HOW I GET MY **LIFE** BACK.
THIS IS HOW I KEEP THE MISSION OF GREEN ARROW **ALIVE.**
ISN'T IT?

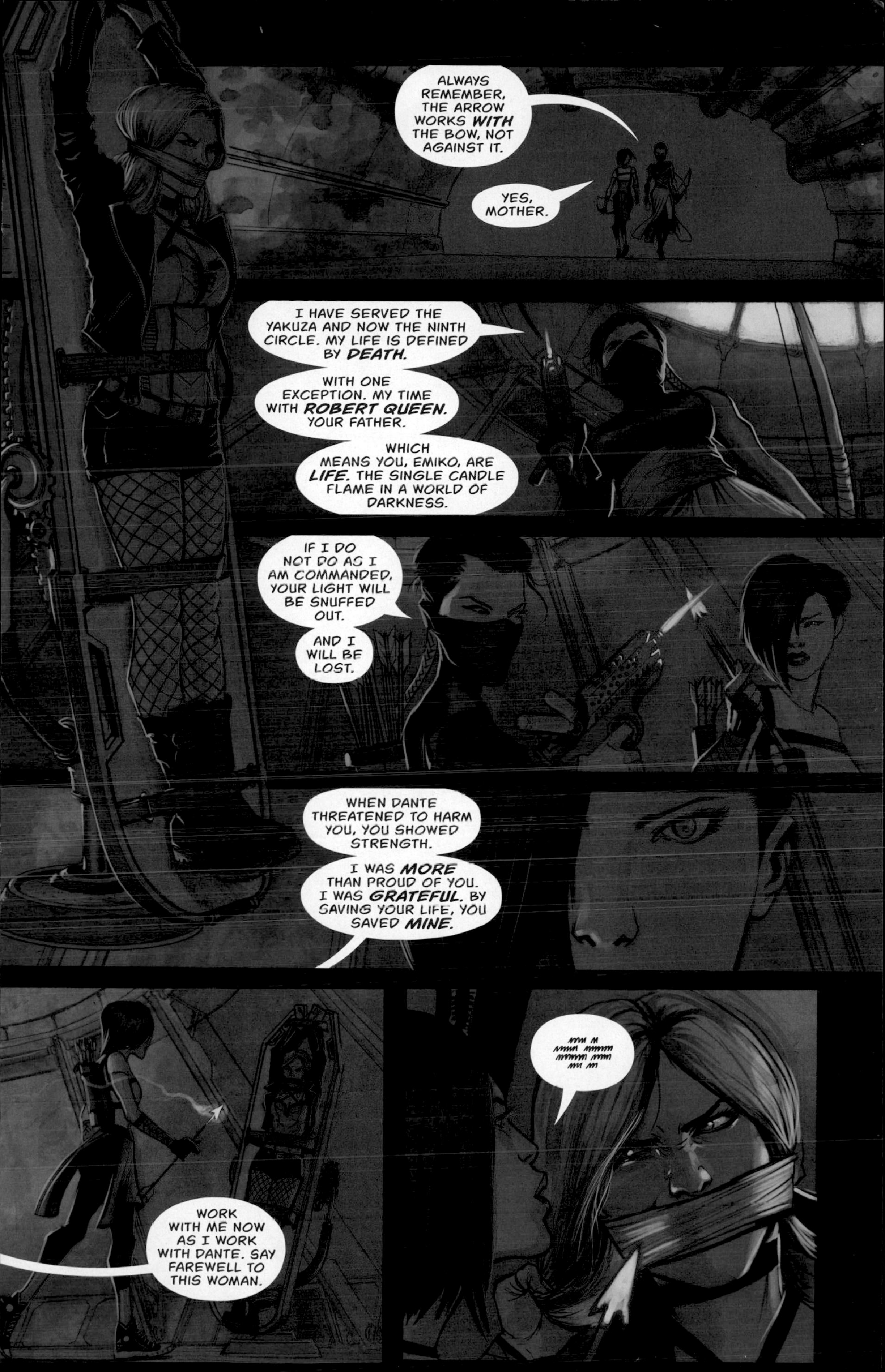
ALWAYS REMEMBER, THE ARROW WORKS WITH THE BOW, NOT AGAINST IT.
YES, MOTHER.
I HAVE SERVED THE YAKUZA AND NOW THE NINTH CIRCLE. MY LIFE IS DEFINED BY DEATH.
WITH ONE EXCEPTION. MY TIME WITH ROBERT QUEEN. YOUR FATHER.
WHICH MEANS YOU, EMIKO, ARE LIFE. THE SINGLE CANDLE FLAME IN A WORLD OF DARKNESS.
IF I DO NOT DO AS I AM COMMANDED, YOUR LIGHT WILL BE SNUFFED OUT.
AND I WILL BE LOST.
WHEN DANTE THREATENED TO HARM YOU, YOU SHOWED STRENGTH.
I WAS MORE THAN PROUD OF YOU. I WAS GRATEFUL. BY SAVING YOUR LIFE, YOU SAVED MINE.
WORK WITH ME NOW AS I WORK WITH DANTE. SAY FAREWELL TO THIS WOMAN.

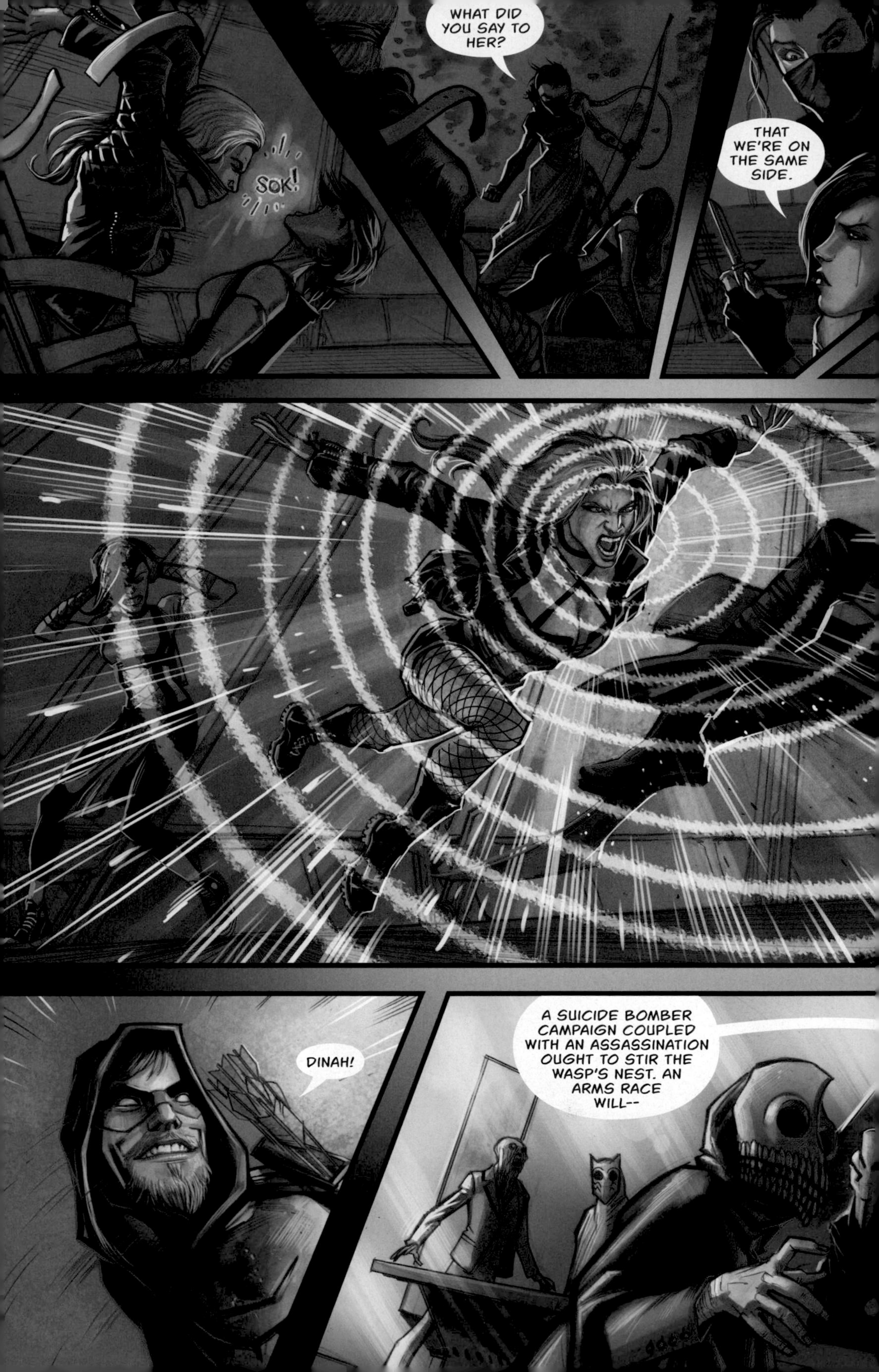
SOK!
WHAT DID YOU SAY TO HER?
THAT WE'RE ON THE SAME SIDE.
DINAH!
A SUICIDE BOMBER CAMPAIGN COUPLED WITH AN ASSASSINATION OUGHT TO STIR THE WASP'S NEST. AN ARMS RACE WILL--

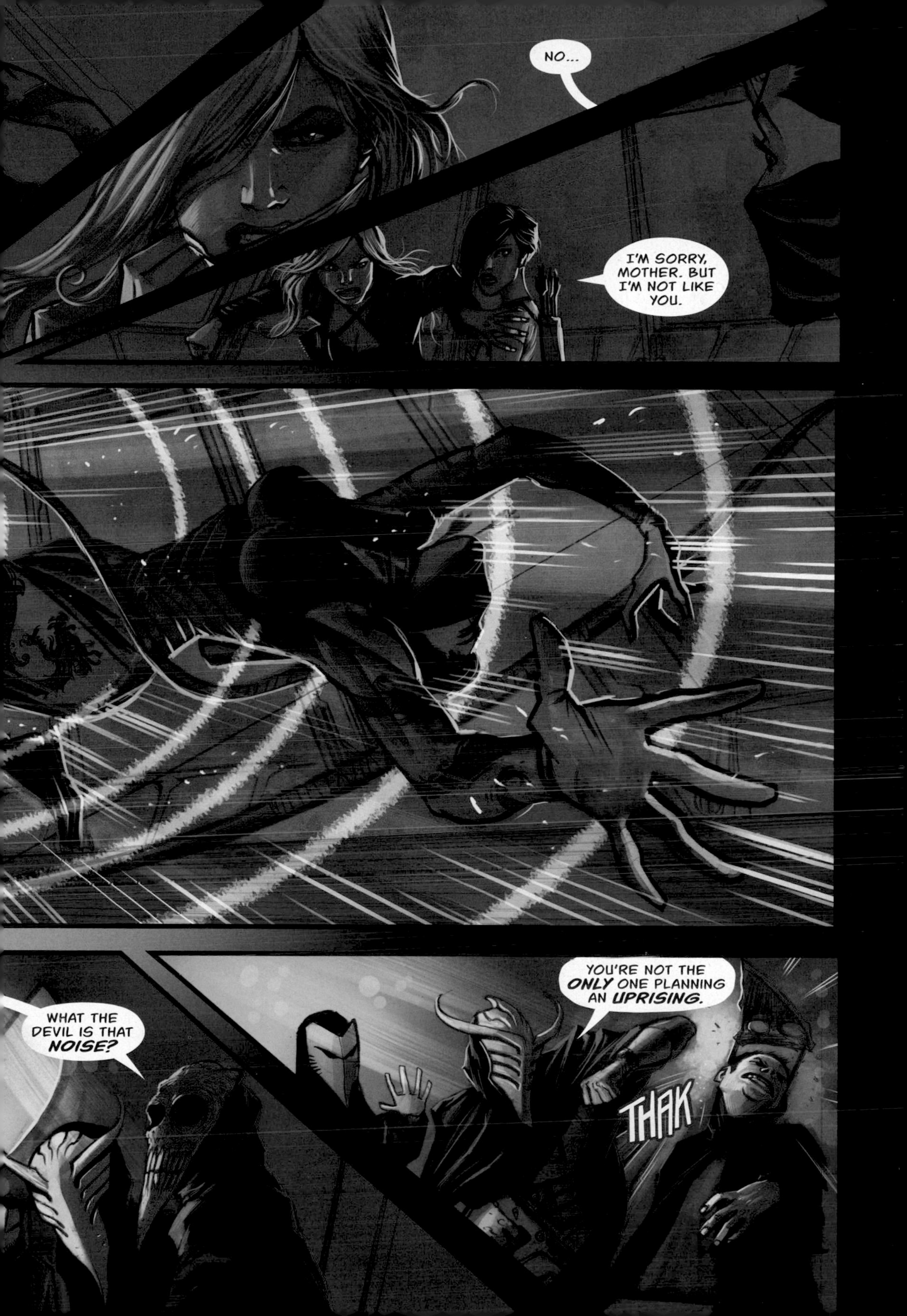
NO...
I'M SORRY, MOTHER. BUT I'M NOT LIKE YOU.
WHAT THE DEVIL IS THAT NOISE?
YOU'RE NOT THE ONLY ONE PLANNING AN UPRISING.
THAK

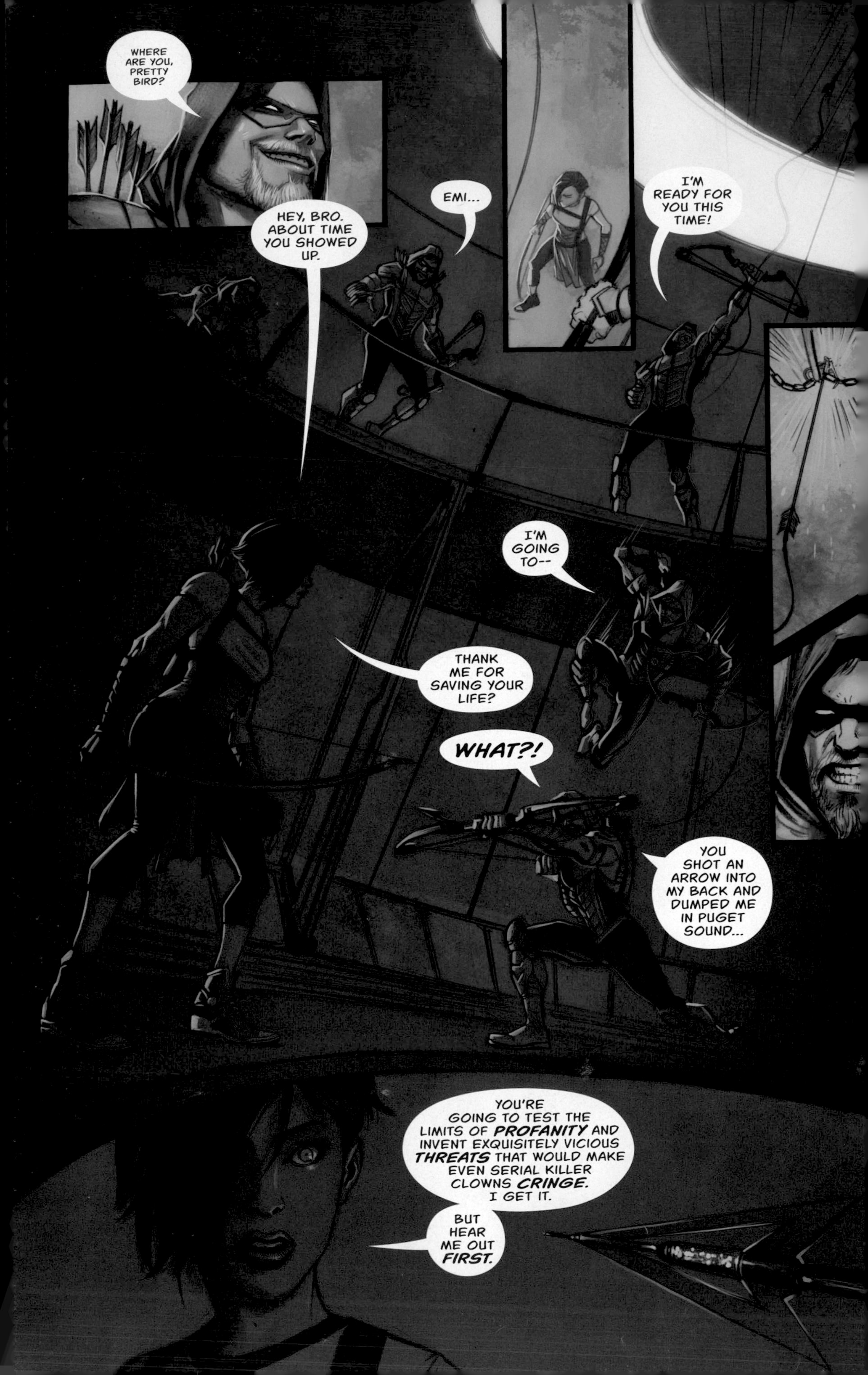
WHERE ARE YOU, PRETTY BIRD?
EMI...
HEY, BRO. ABOUT TIME YOU SHOWED UP.
I'M READY FOR YOU THIS TIME!
I'M GOING TO--
THANK ME FOR SAVING YOUR LIFE?
WHAT?!
YOU SHOT AN ARROW INTO MY BACK AND DUMPED ME IN PUGET SOUND...
YOU'RE GOING TO TEST THE LIMITS OF PROFANITY AND INVENT EXQUISITELY VICIOUS THREATS THAT WOULD MAKE EVEN SERIAL KILLER CLOWNS CRINGE. I GET IT.
BUT HEAR ME OUT FIRST.

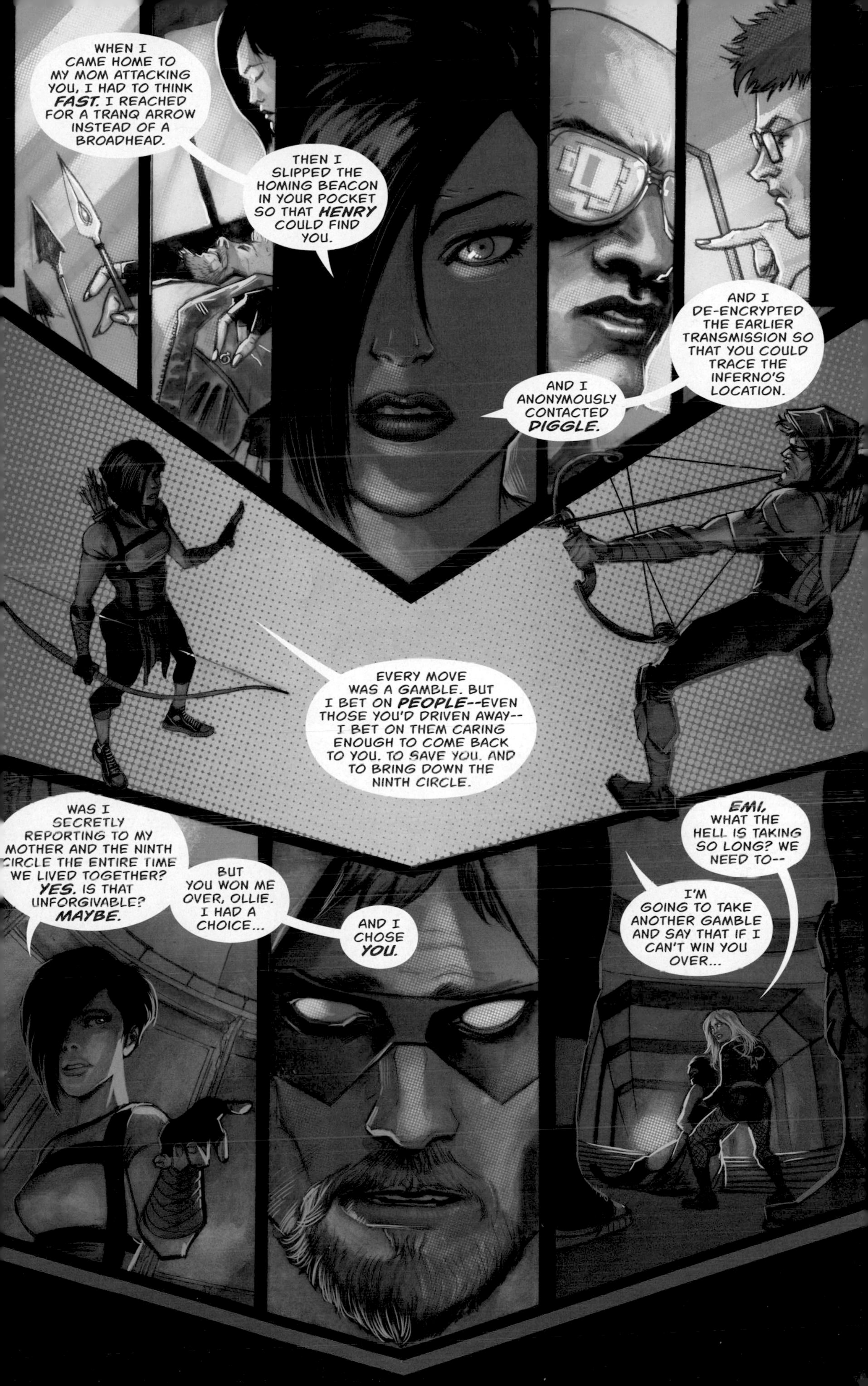
WHEN I CAME HOME TO MY MOM ATTACKING YOU, I HAD TO THINK FAST. I REACHED FOR A TRANQ ARROW INSTEAD OF A BROADHEAD.
THEN I SLIPPED THE HOMING BEACON IN YOUR POCKET SO THAT HENRY COULD FIND YOU.
AND I DE-ENCRYPTED THE EARLIER TRANSMISSION SO THAT YOU COULD TRACE THE INFERNO'S LOCATION.
AND I ANONYMOUSLY CONTACTED DIGGLE.
EVERY MOVE WAS A GAMBLE. BUT I BET ON PEOPLE--EVEN THOSE YOU'D DRIVEN AWAY--I BET ON THEM CARING ENOUGH TO COME BACK TO YOU. TO SAVE YOU. AND TO BRING DOWN THE NINTH CIRCLE.
WAS I SECRETLY REPORTING TO MY MOTHER AND THE NINTH CIRCLE THE ENTIRE TIME WE LIVED TOGETHER? YES. IS THAT UNFORGIVABLE? MAYBE.
BUT YOU WON ME OVER, OLLIE. I HAD A CHOICE...
AND I CHOSE YOU.
EMI, WHAT THE HELL IS TAKING SO LONG? WE NEED TO--
I'M GOING TO TAKE ANOTHER GAMBLE AND SAY THAT IF I CAN'T WIN YOU OVER...

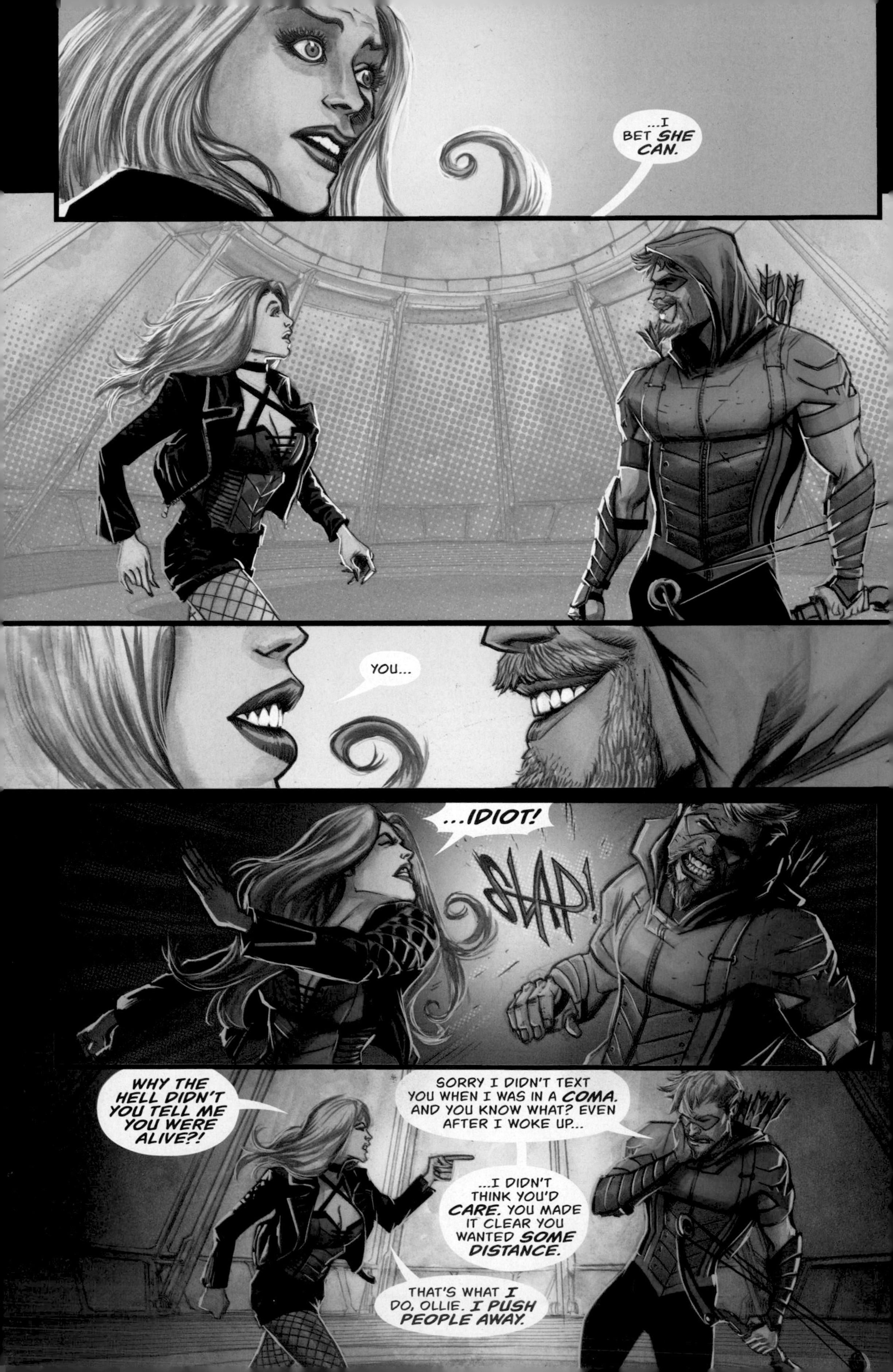
...I BET SHE CAN.
YOU...
...IDIOT!
SLAP!
WHY THE HELL DIDN'T YOU TELL ME YOU WERE ALIVE?!
SORRY I DIDN'T TEXT YOU WHEN I WAS IN A COMA. AND YOU KNOW WHAT? EVEN AFTER I WOKE UP...
...I DIDN'T THINK YOU'D CARE. YOU MADE IT CLEAR YOU WANTED SOME DISTANCE.
THAT'S WHAT I DO, OLLIE. I PUSH PEOPLE AWAY.

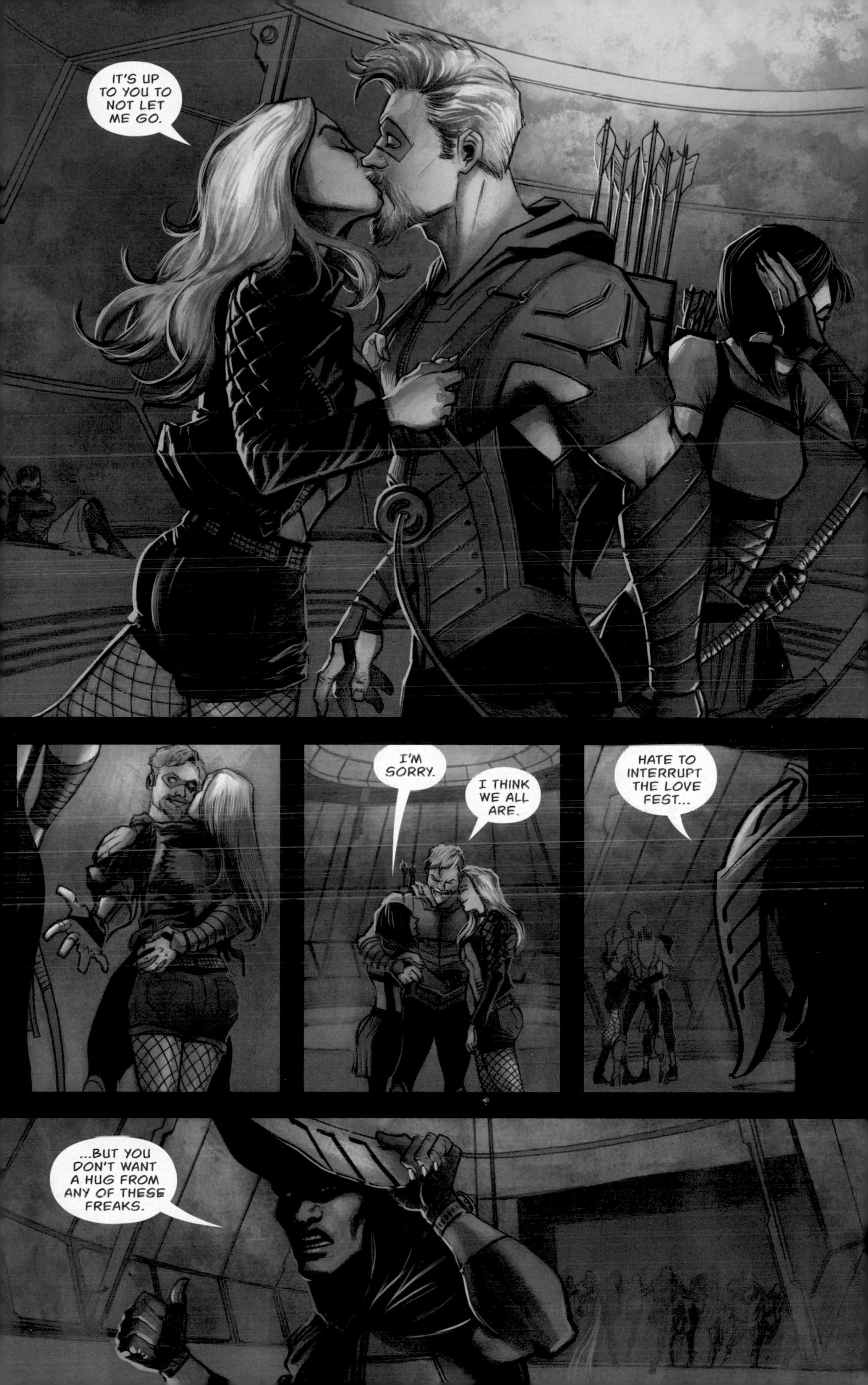
IT'S UP TO YOU TO NOT LET ME GO.
I'M SORRY.
I THINK WE ALL ARE.
HATE TO INTERRUPT THE LOVE FEST...
...BUT YOU DON'T WANT A HUG FROM ANY OF THESE FREAKS.

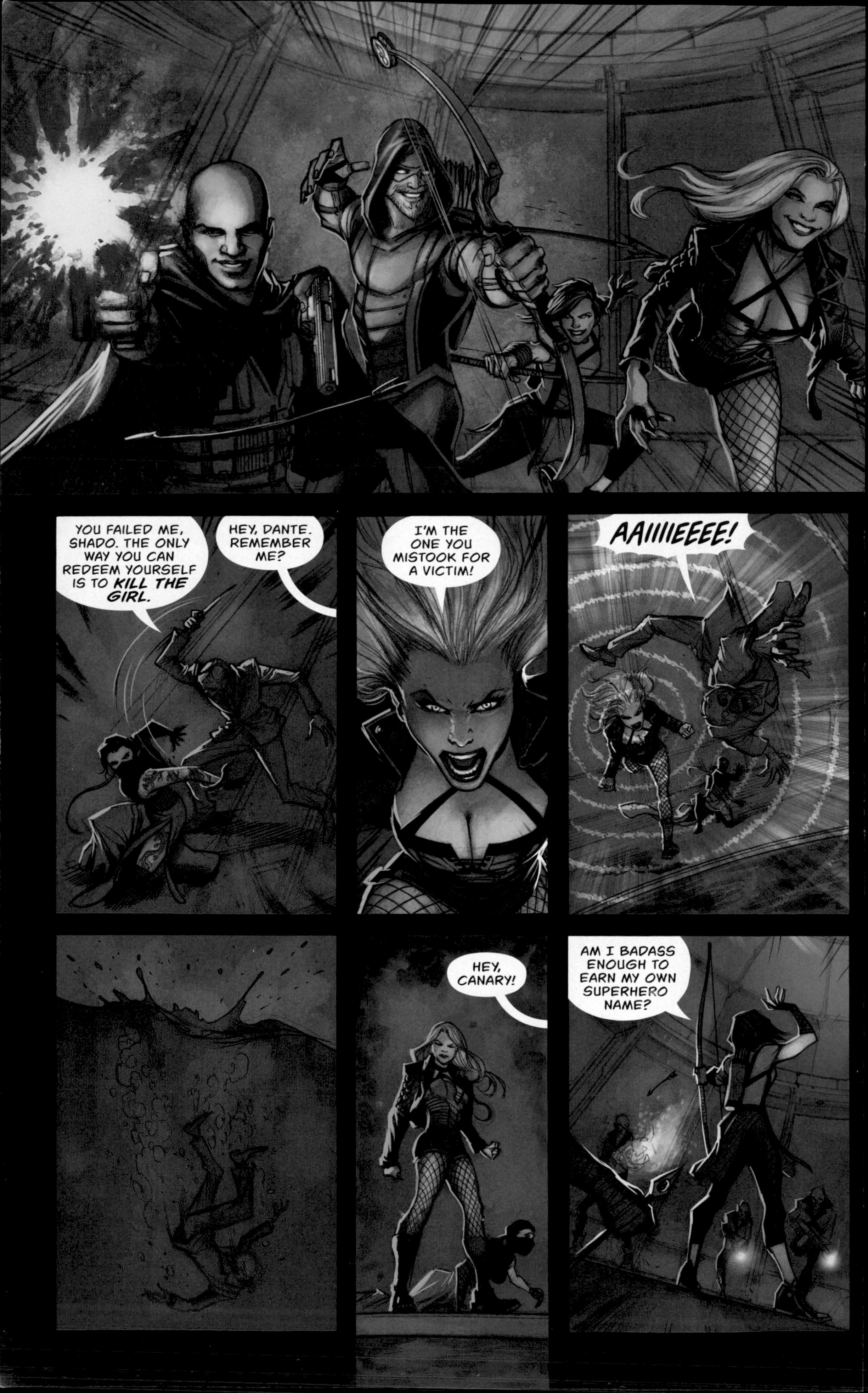

YOU FAILED ME, SHADO. THE ONLY WAY YOU CAN REDEEM YOURSELF IS TO **KILL THE GIRL.**
HEY, DANTE. REMEMBER ME?
I'M THE ONE YOU MISTOOK FOR A VICTIM!
AAIIIIEEEE!
HEY, CANARY!
AM I BADASS ENOUGH TO EARN MY OWN SUPERHERO NAME?

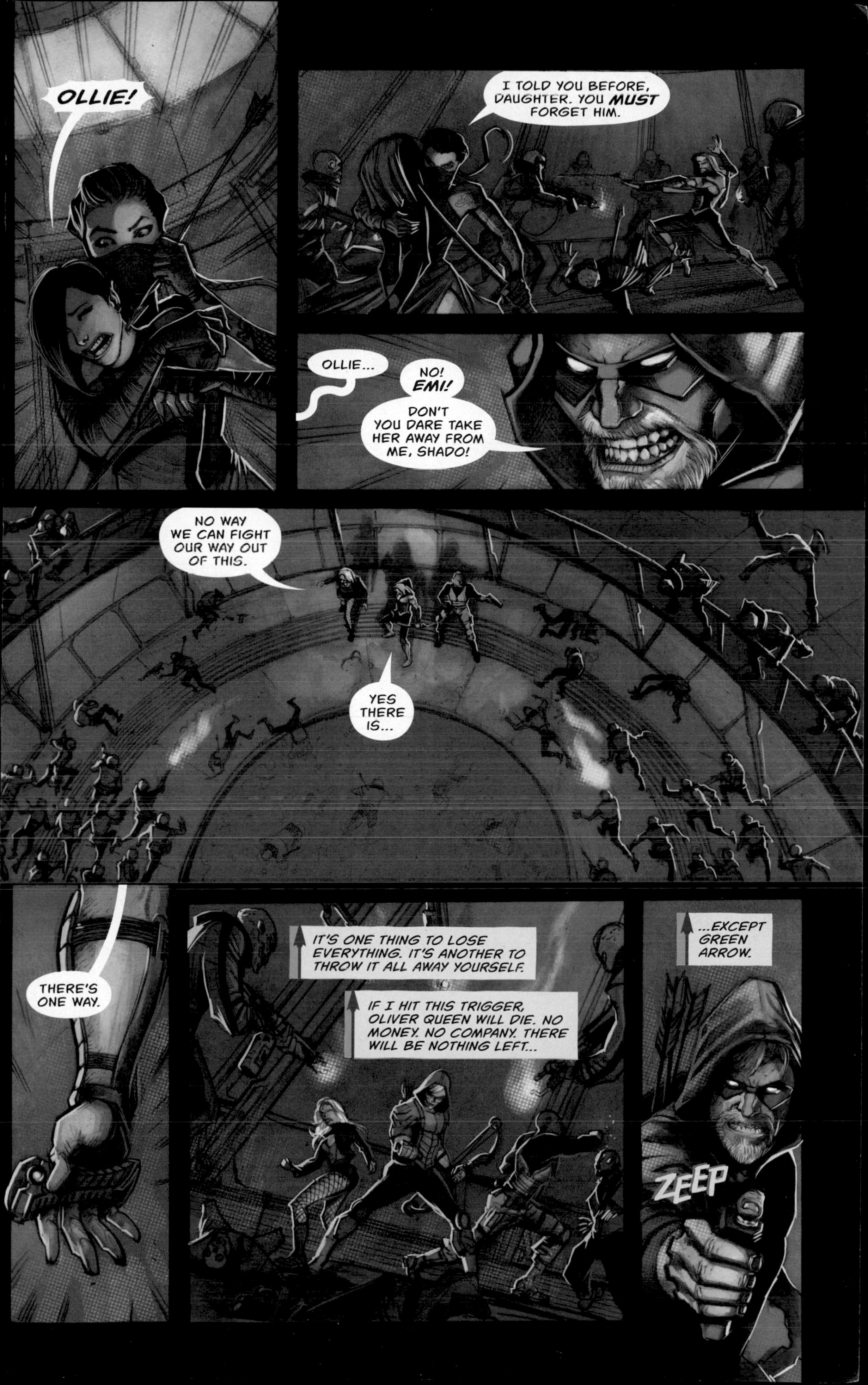
OLLIE!
I TOLD YOU BEFORE, DAUGHTER. YOU MUST FORGET HIM.
OLLIE...
NO! EMI!
DON'T YOU DARE TAKE HER AWAY FROM ME, SHADO!
NO WAY WE CAN FIGHT OUR WAY OUT OF THIS.
YES THERE IS...
THERE'S ONE WAY.
IT'S ONE THING TO LOSE EVERYTHING. IT'S ANOTHER TO THROW IT ALL AWAY YOURSELF.
IF I HIT THIS TRIGGER, OLIVER QUEEN WILL DIE. NO MONEY. NO COMPANY. THERE WILL BE NOTHING LEFT...
...EXCEPT GREEN ARROW.
ZEEP

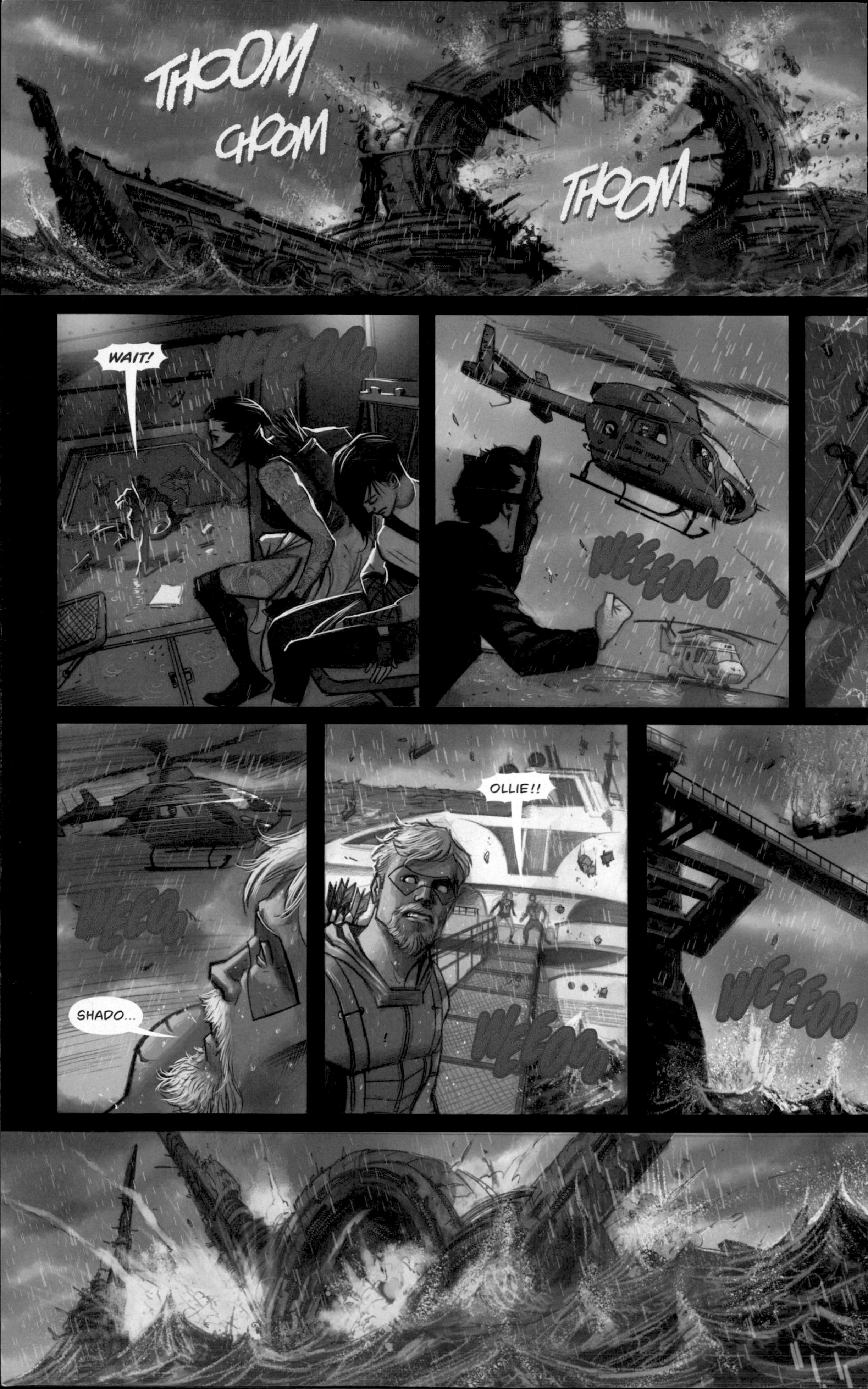

THOOM
CHOOM
THOOM
WAIT!
WEEEOOO
WEEEOOO
WEEEOO
SHADO...
OLLIE!!
WEEEOO
WEEEOO

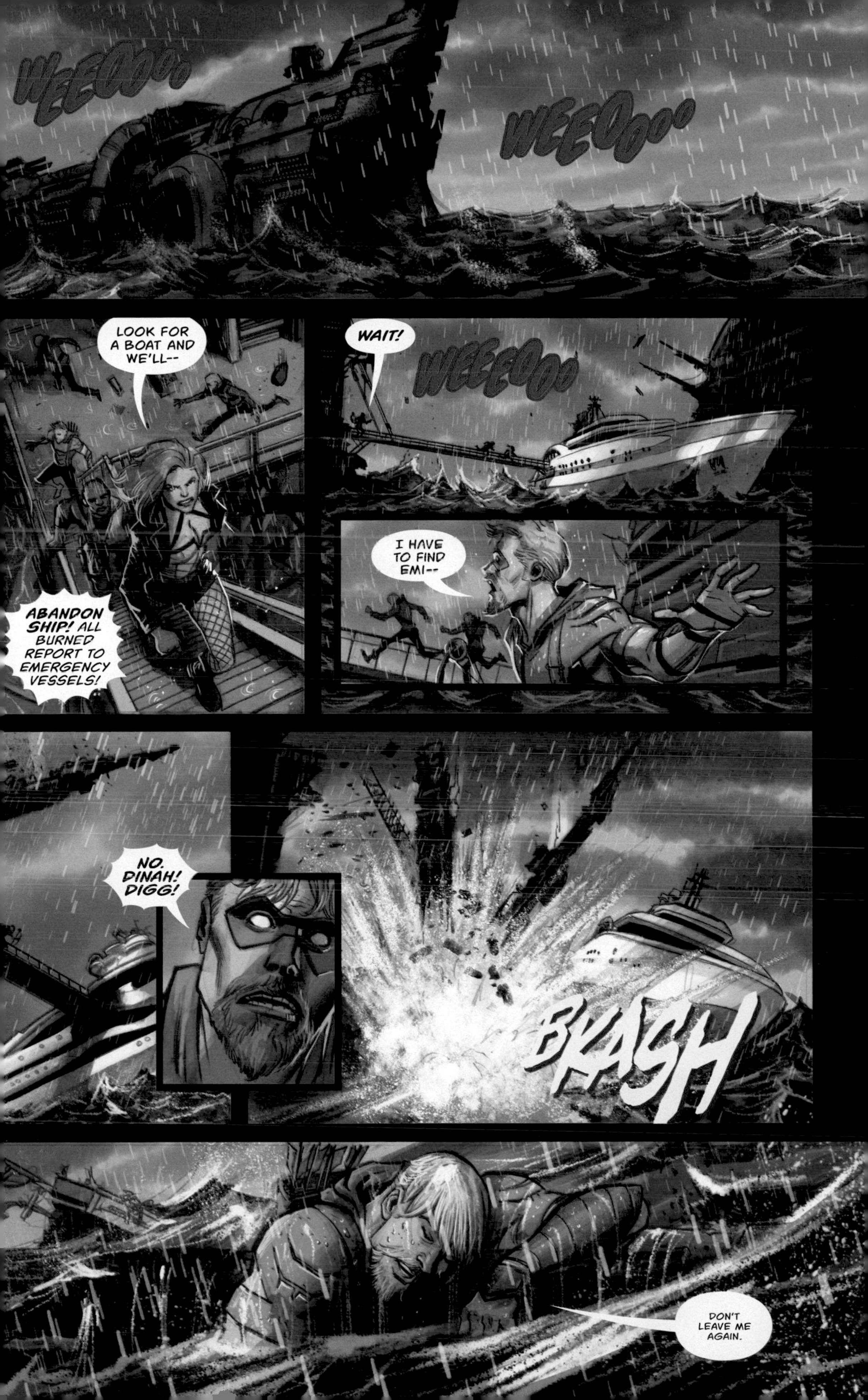
WEEOooo
WEEOooo
LOOK FOR A BOAT AND WE'LL--
WAIT!
WEEEOooo
ABANDON SHIP! ALL BURNED REPORT TO EMERGENCY VESSELS!
I HAVE TO FIND EMI--
NO. DINAH! DIGG!
BKASH
DON'T LEAVE ME AGAIN.

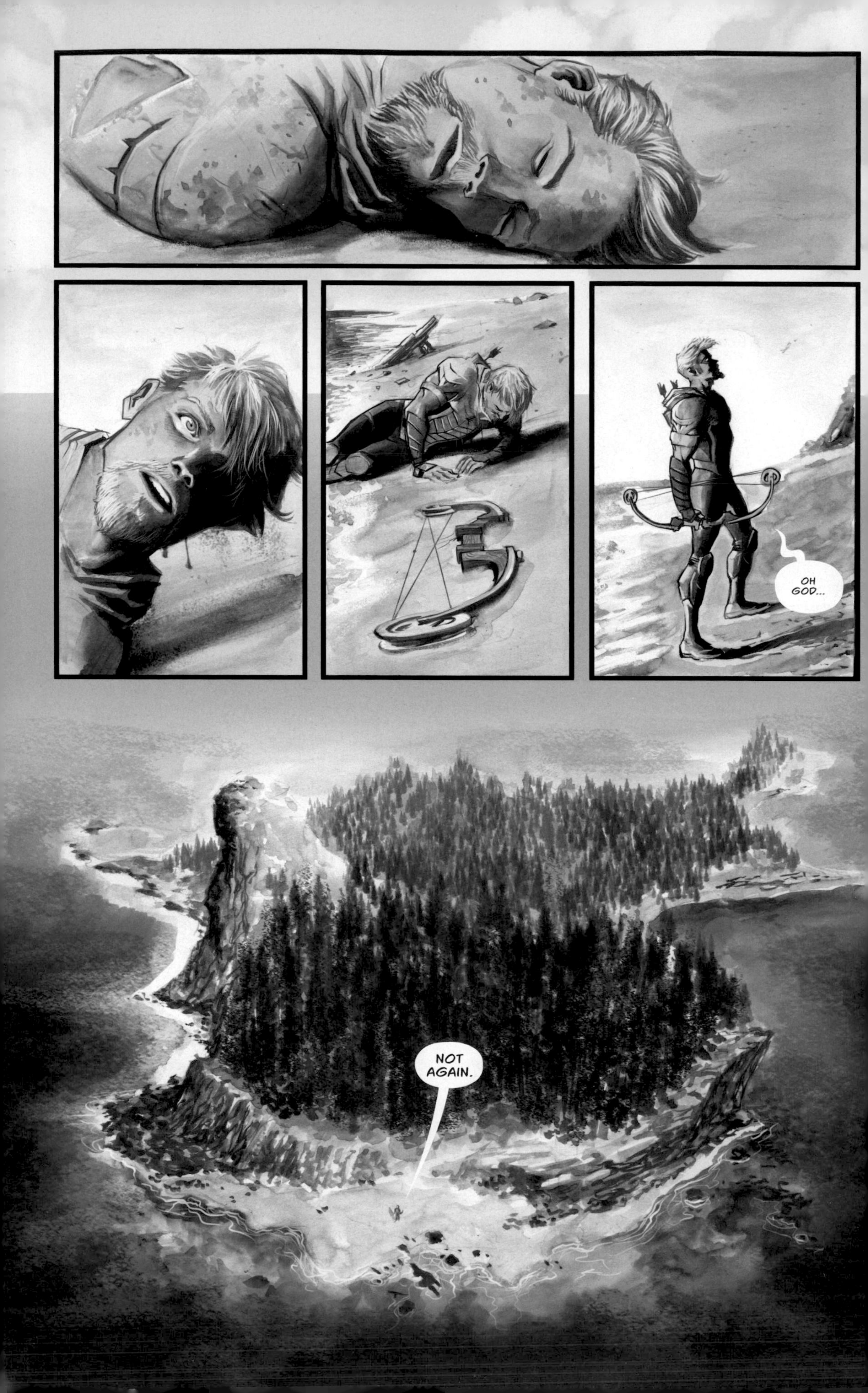
OH GOD...
NOT AGAIN.

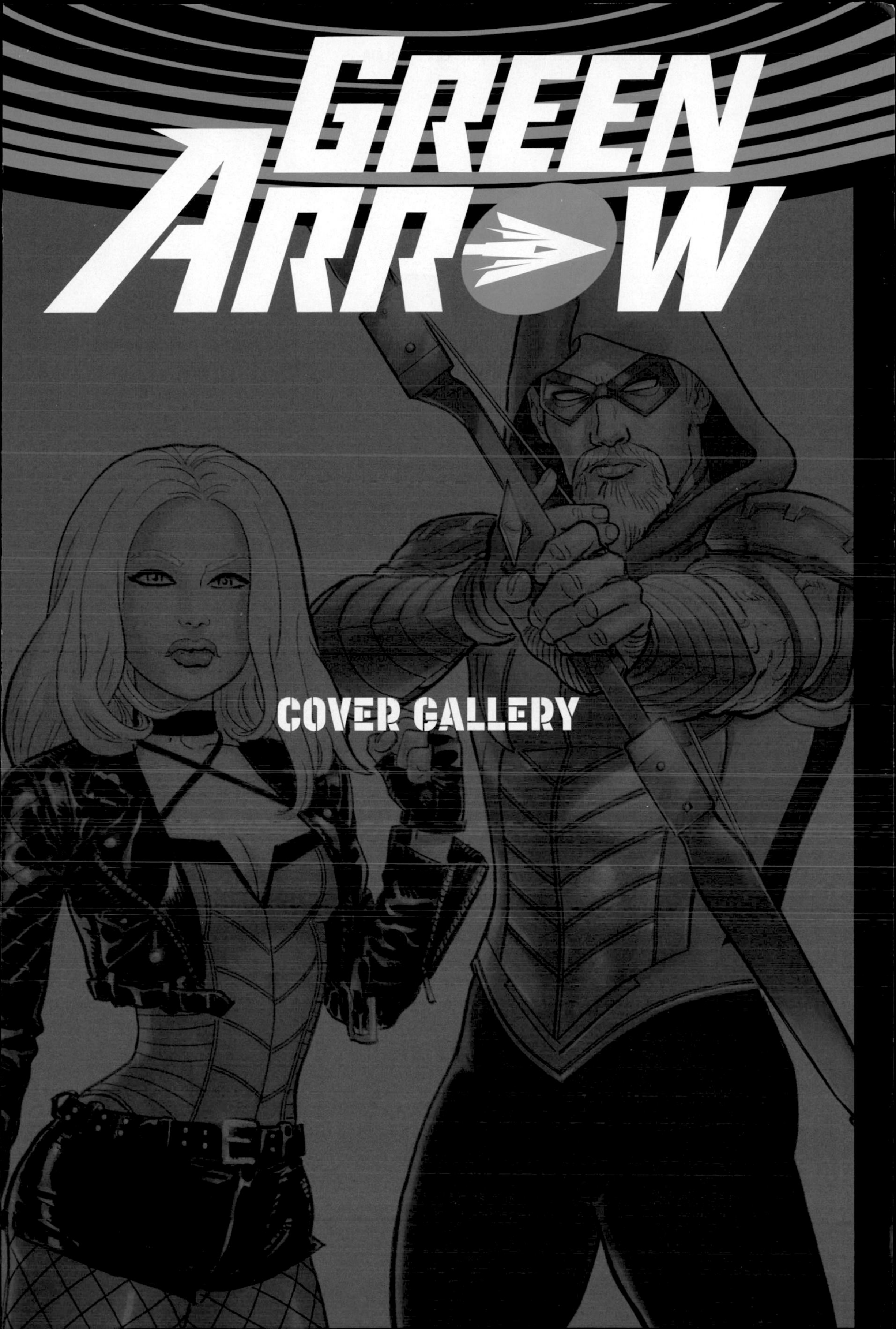
GREEN ARROW

COVER GALLERY

GREEN ARROW: REBIRTH #1 Variant by STEVE SKROCE with ALEX SINCLAIR

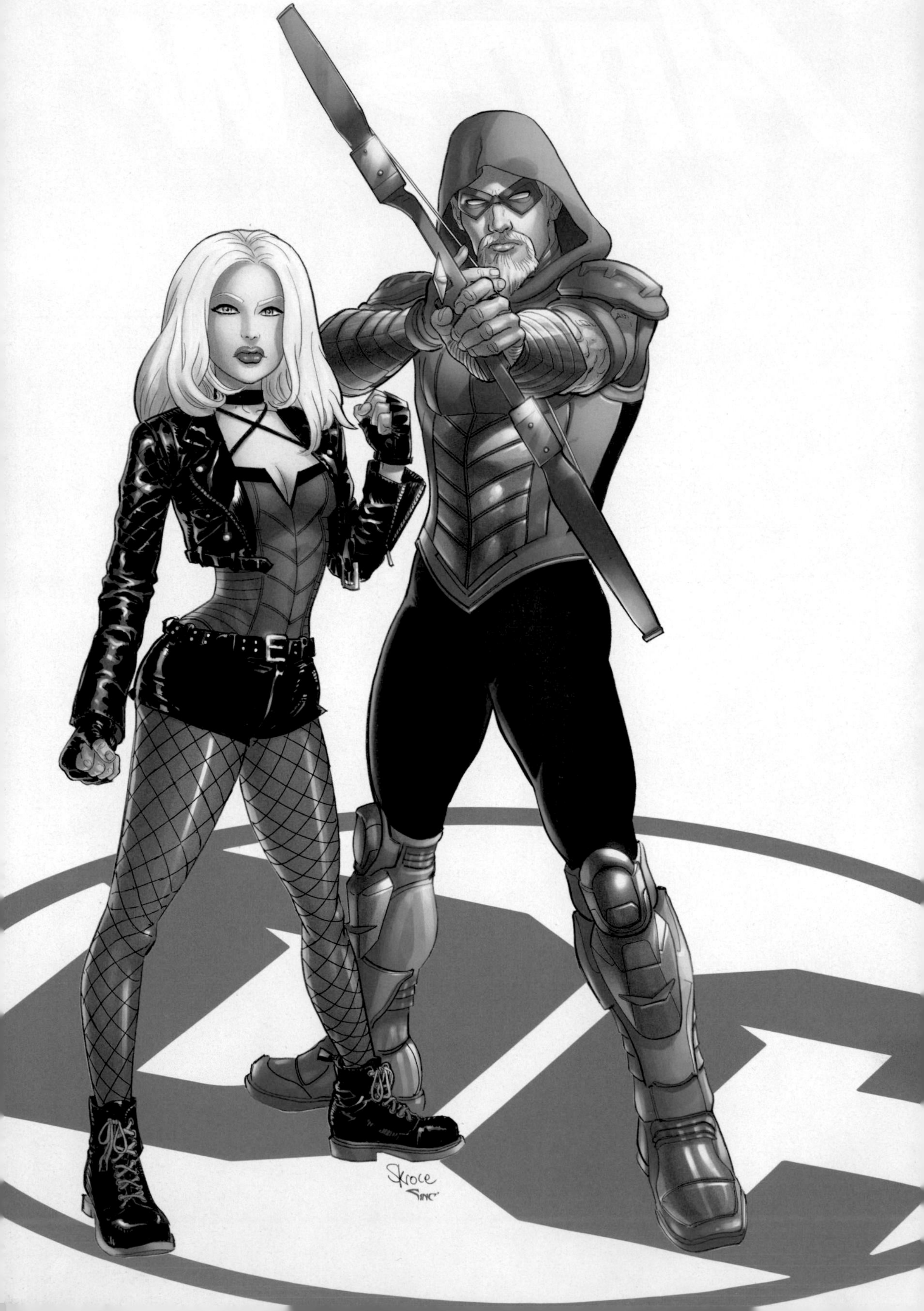

GREEN ARROW #1 Variant by NEAL ADAMS and KEVIN NOWLAN with DAVE McCAIG

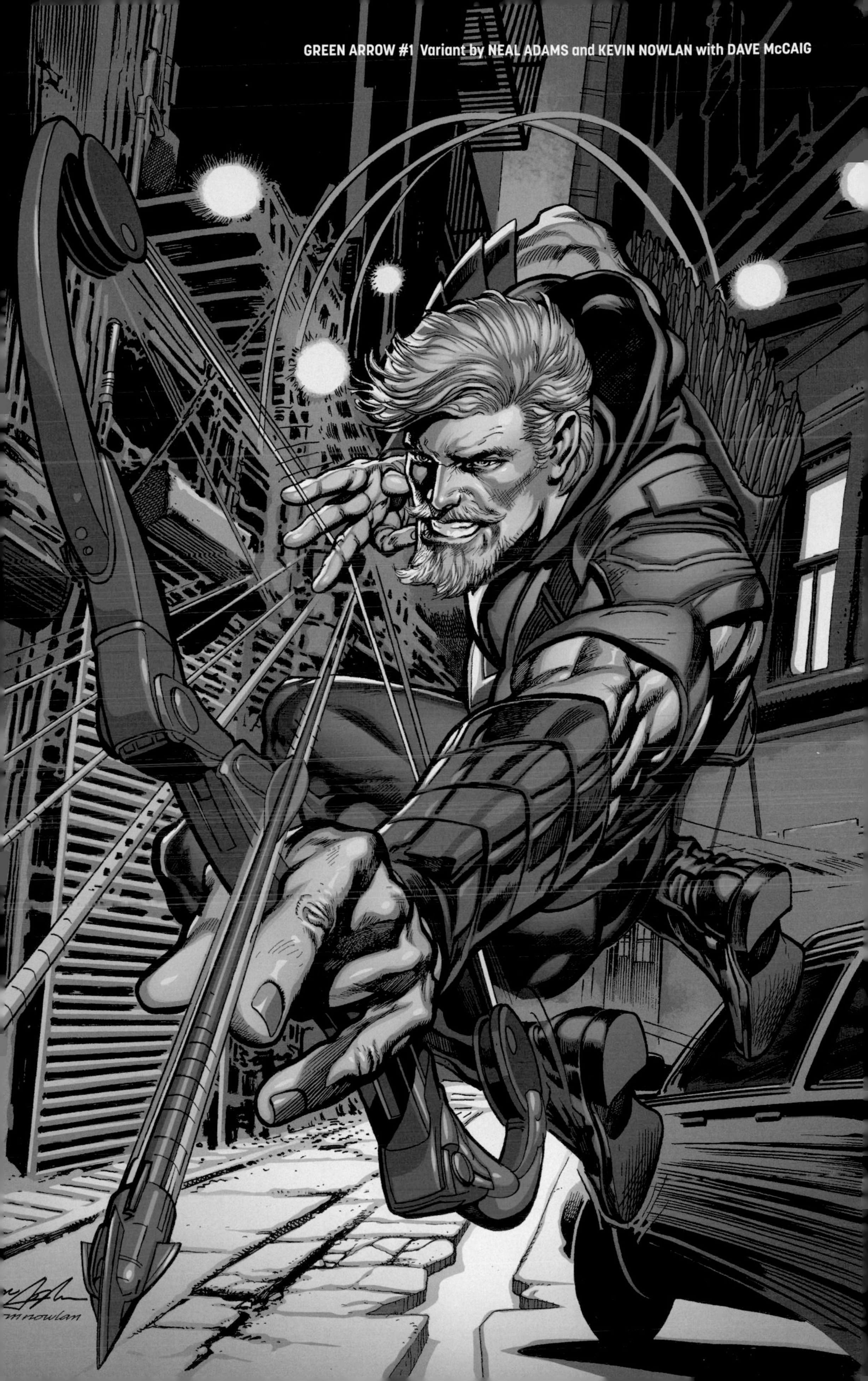
nowlan

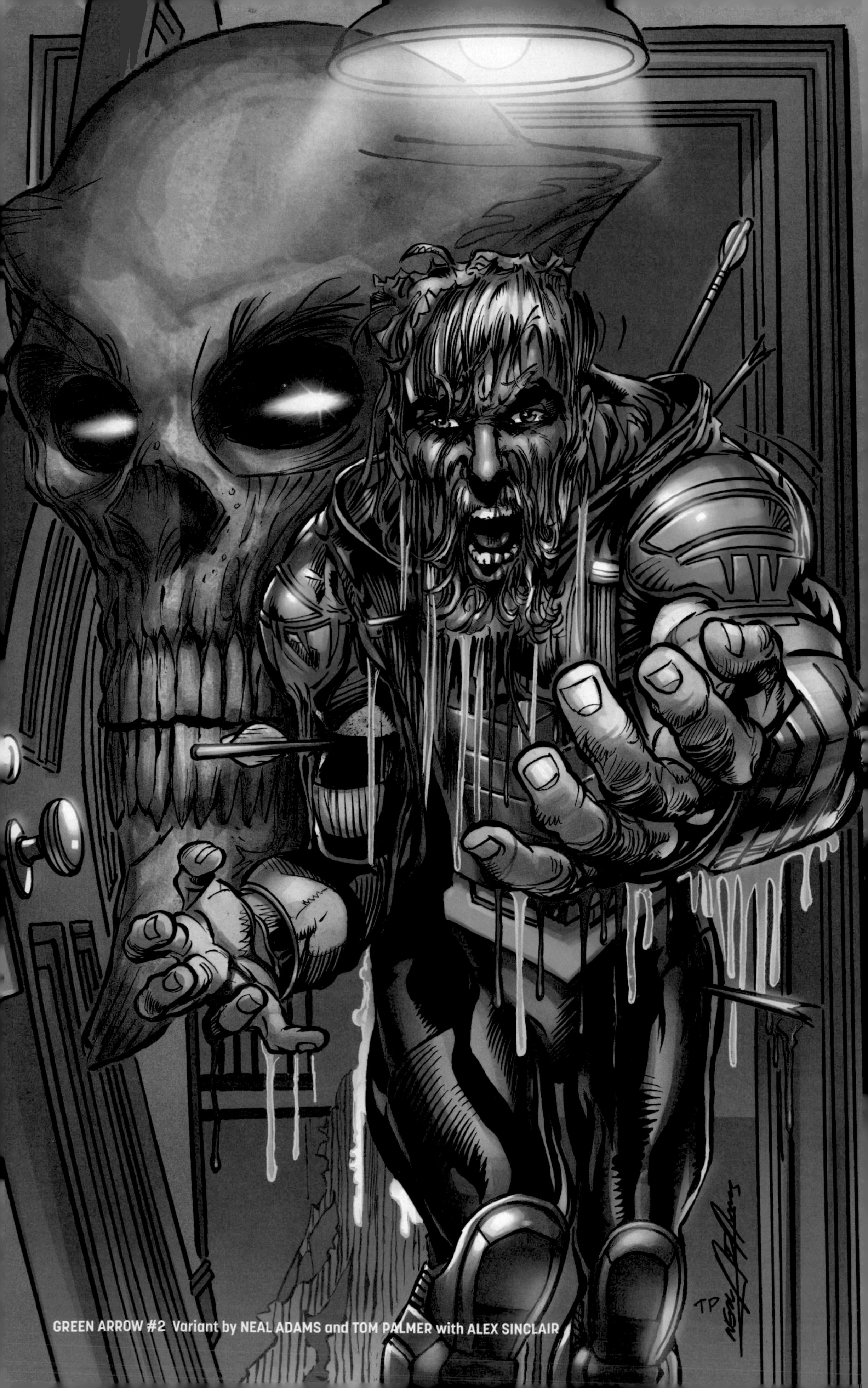

GREEN ARROW #2 Variant by NEAL ADAMS and TOM PALMER with ALEX SINCLAIR

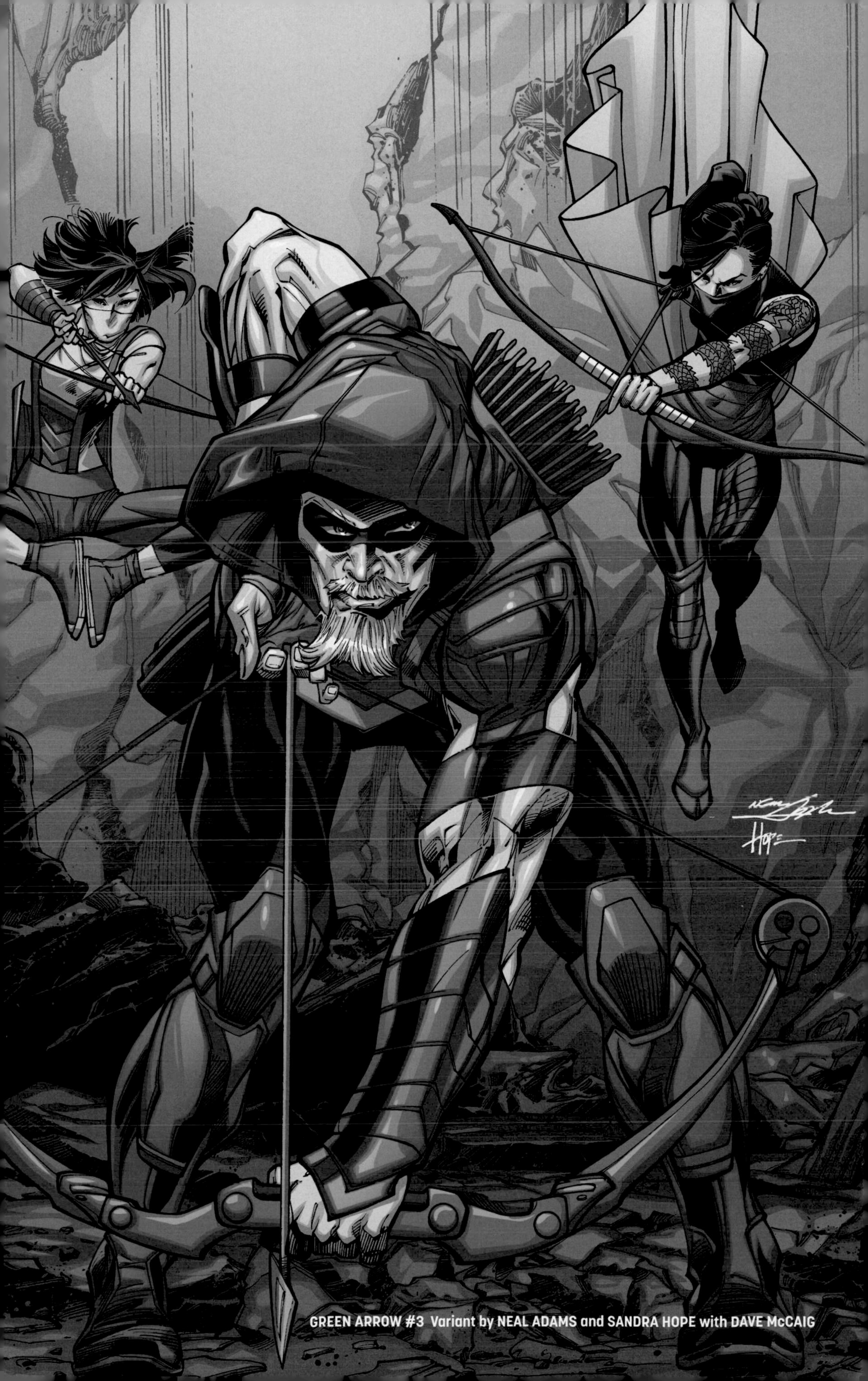
Hope
GREEN ARROW #3 Variant by NEAL ADAMS and SANDRA HOPE with DAVE McCAIG

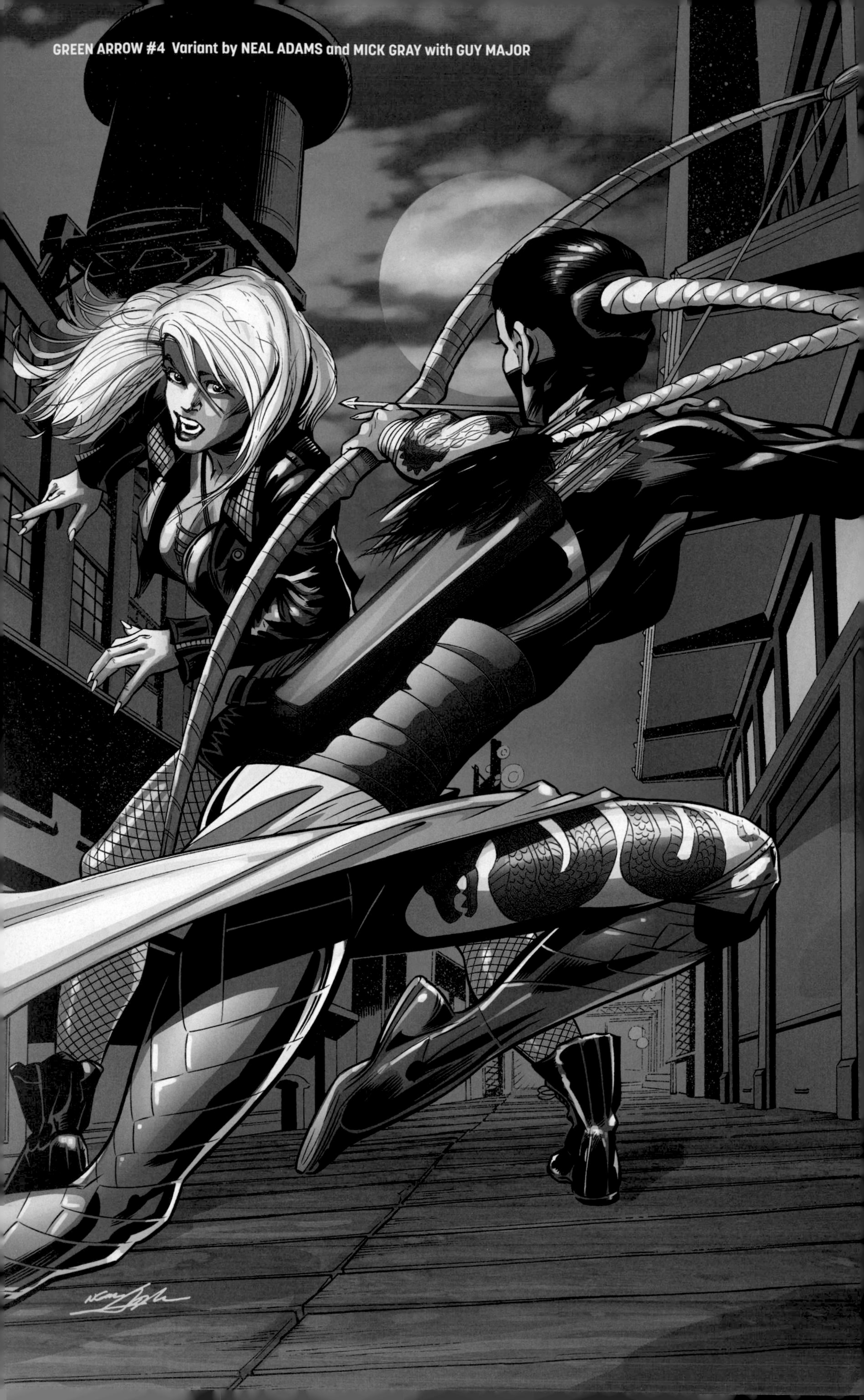

GREEN ARROW #4 Variant by NEAL ADAMS and MICK GRAY with GUY MAJOR

GREEN ARROW #5 Variant by NEAL ADAMS and BILL SIENKIEWICZ with JEROMY COX

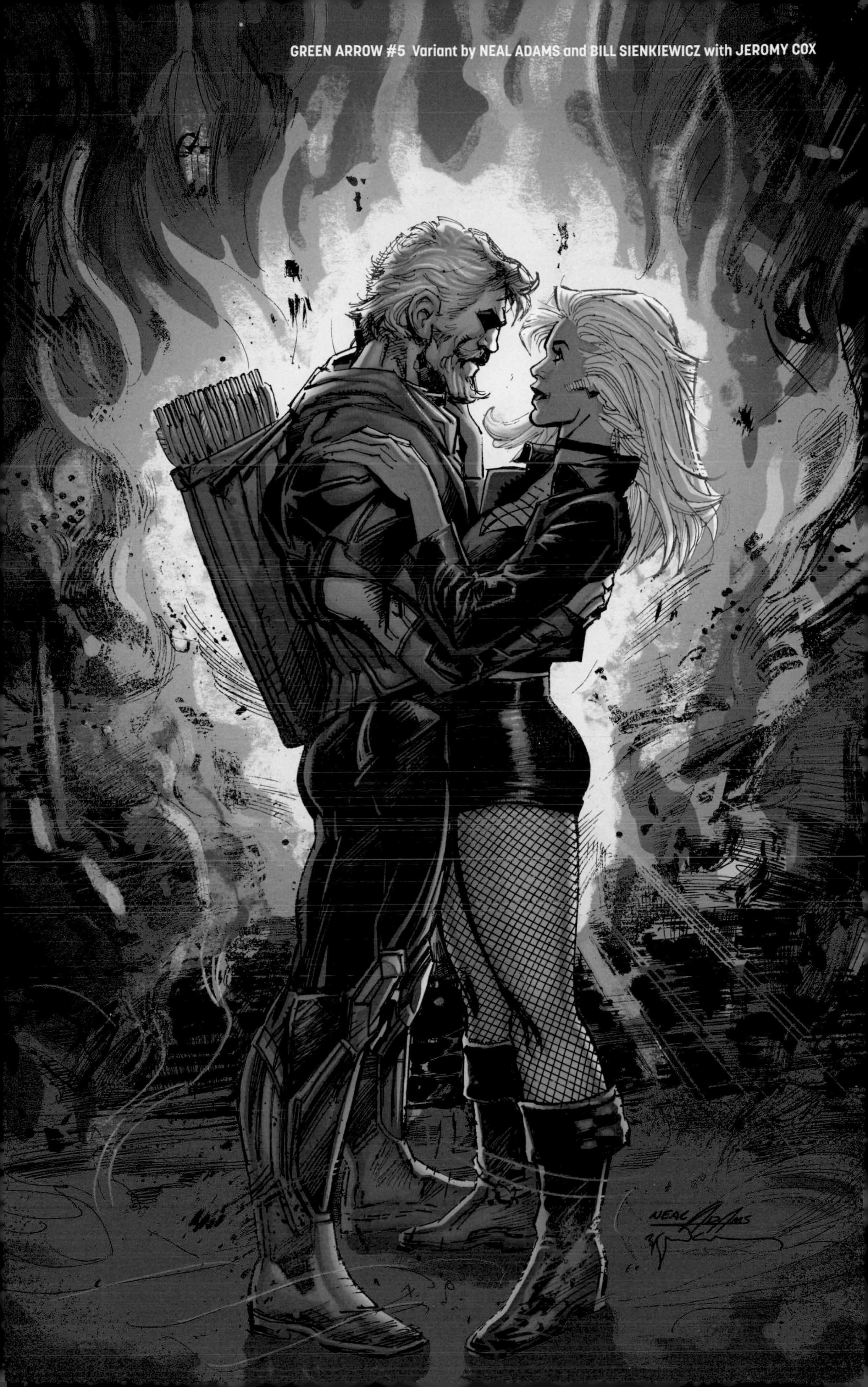

CHARACTER SKETCHES
By OTTO SCHMIDT

GREEN ARROW

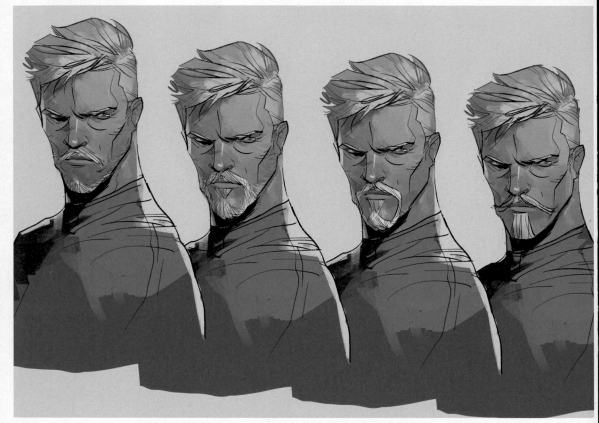

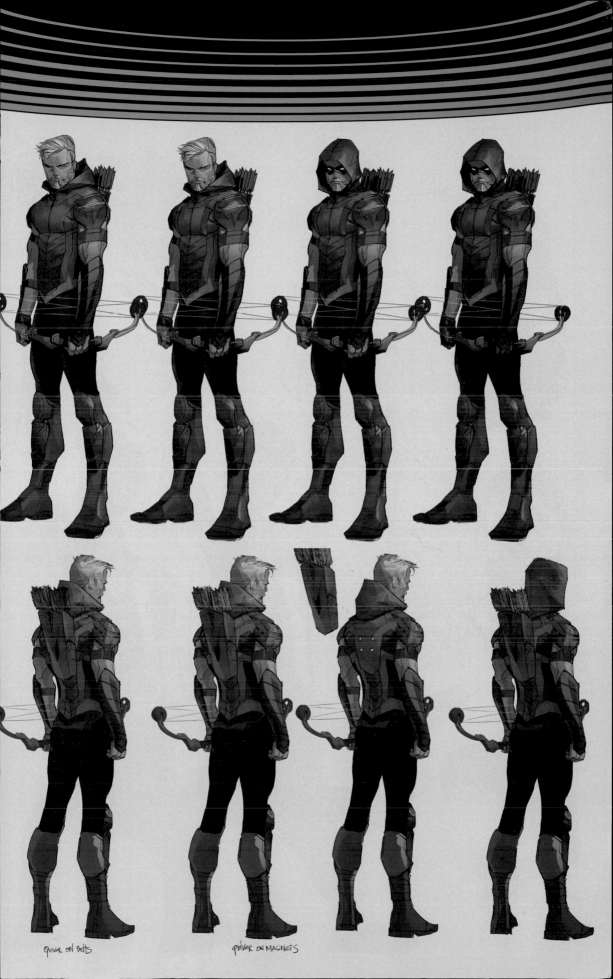

QUIVER ON BELTS

QUIVER ON MAGNETS

EMIKO

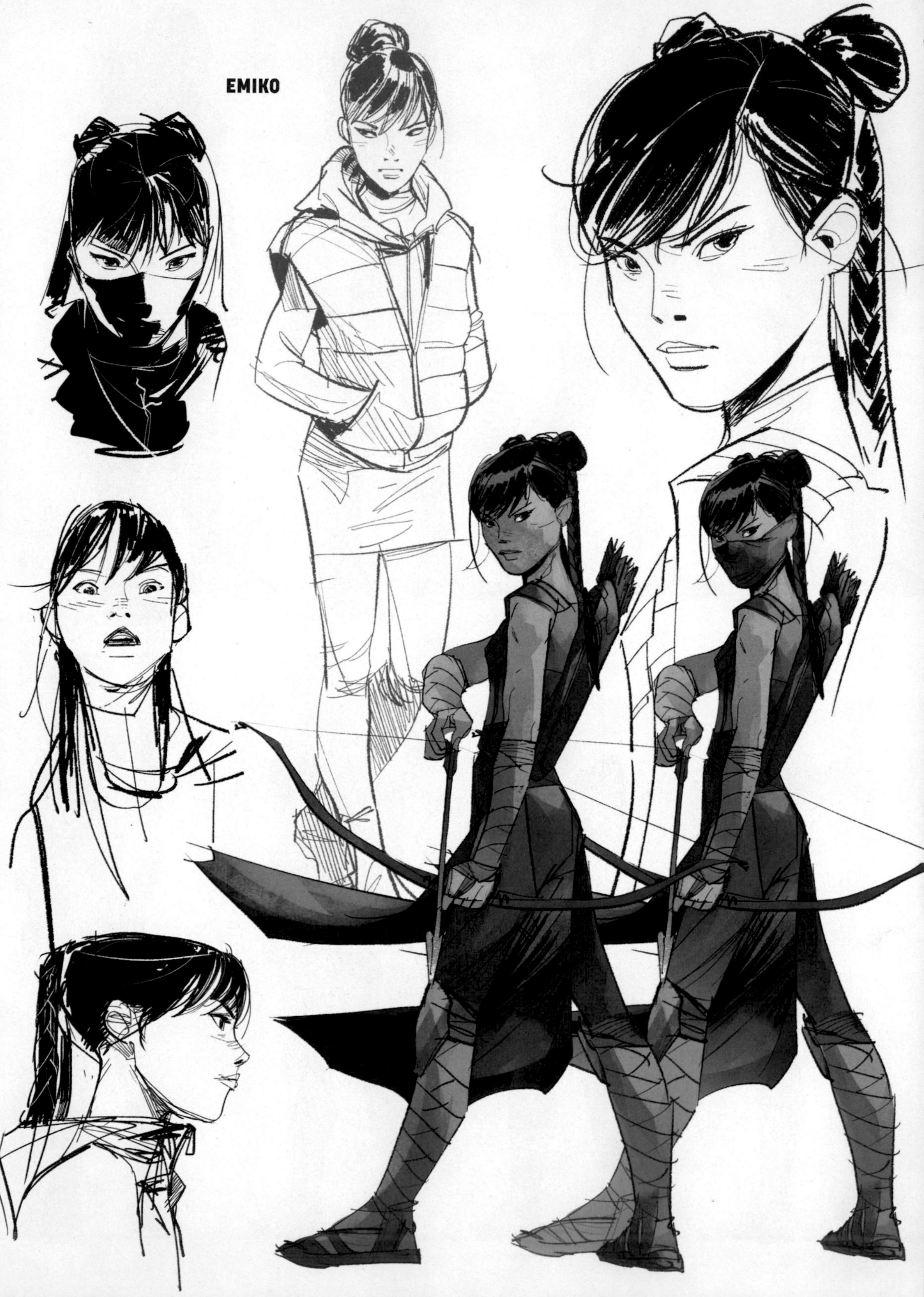

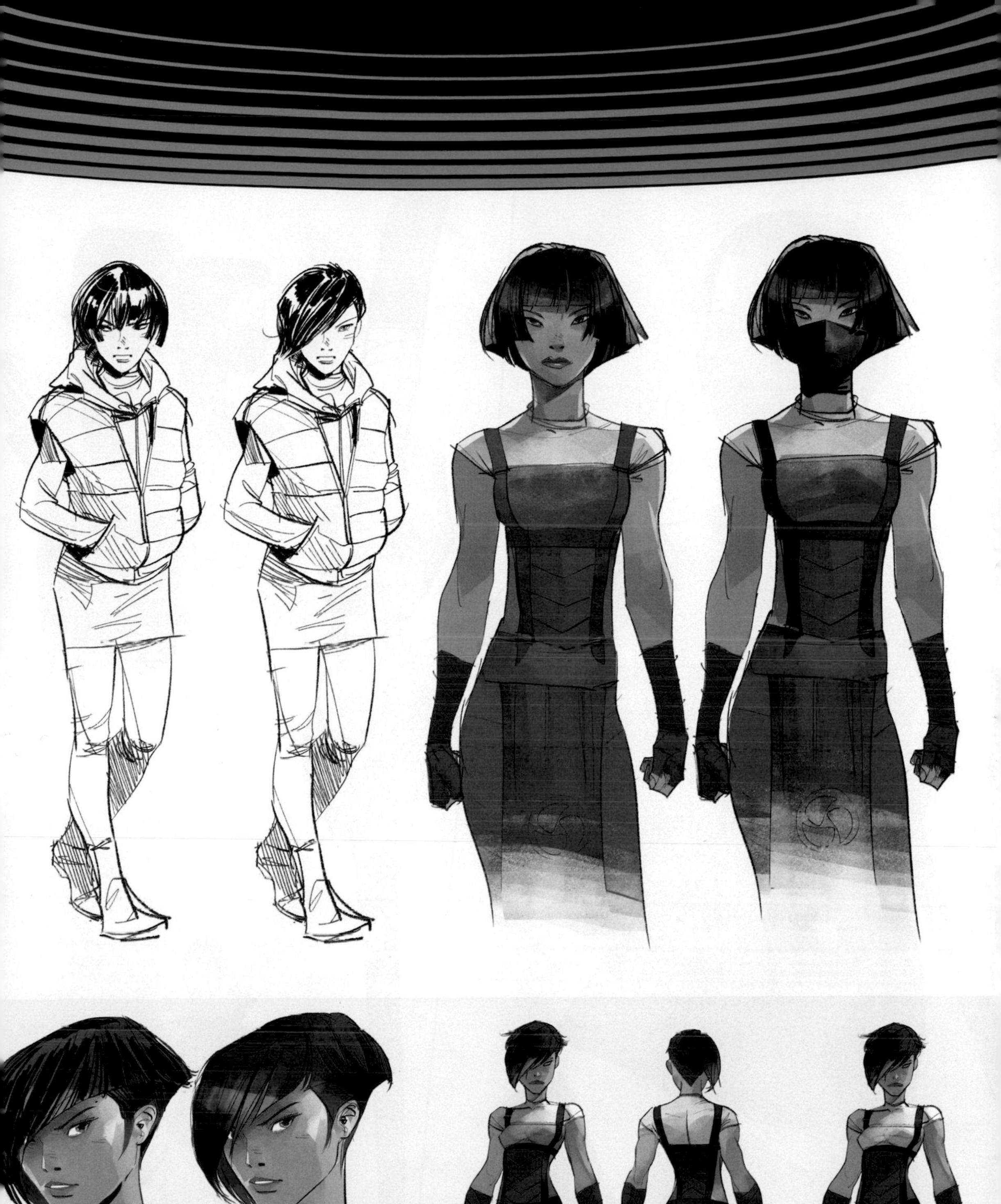

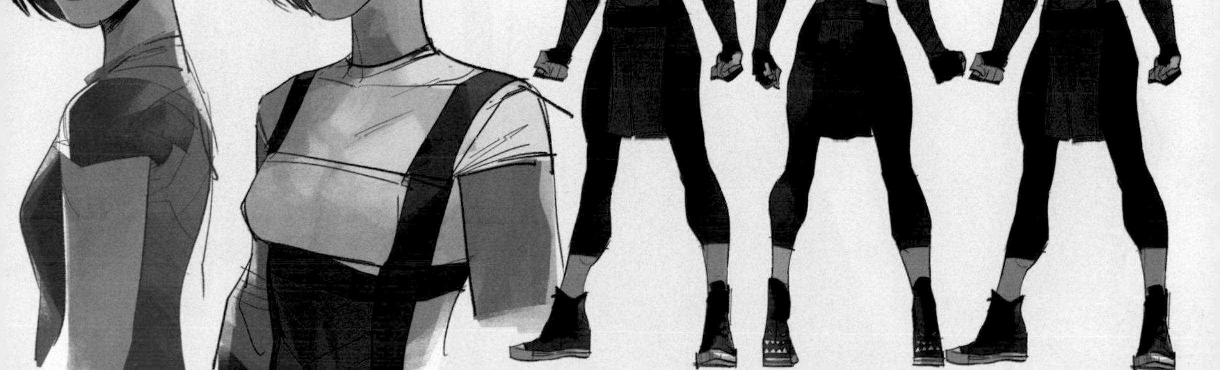

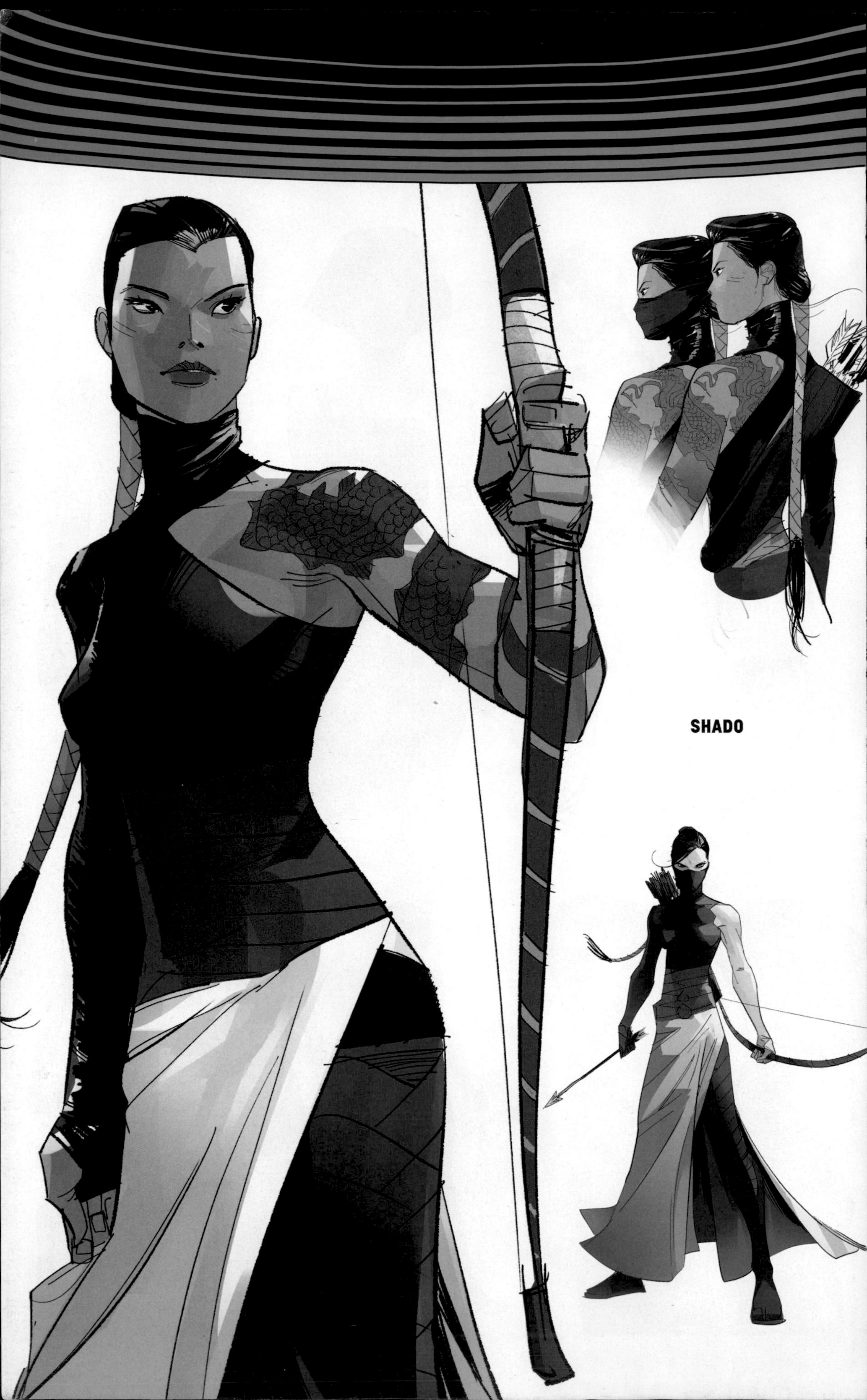

SHADO

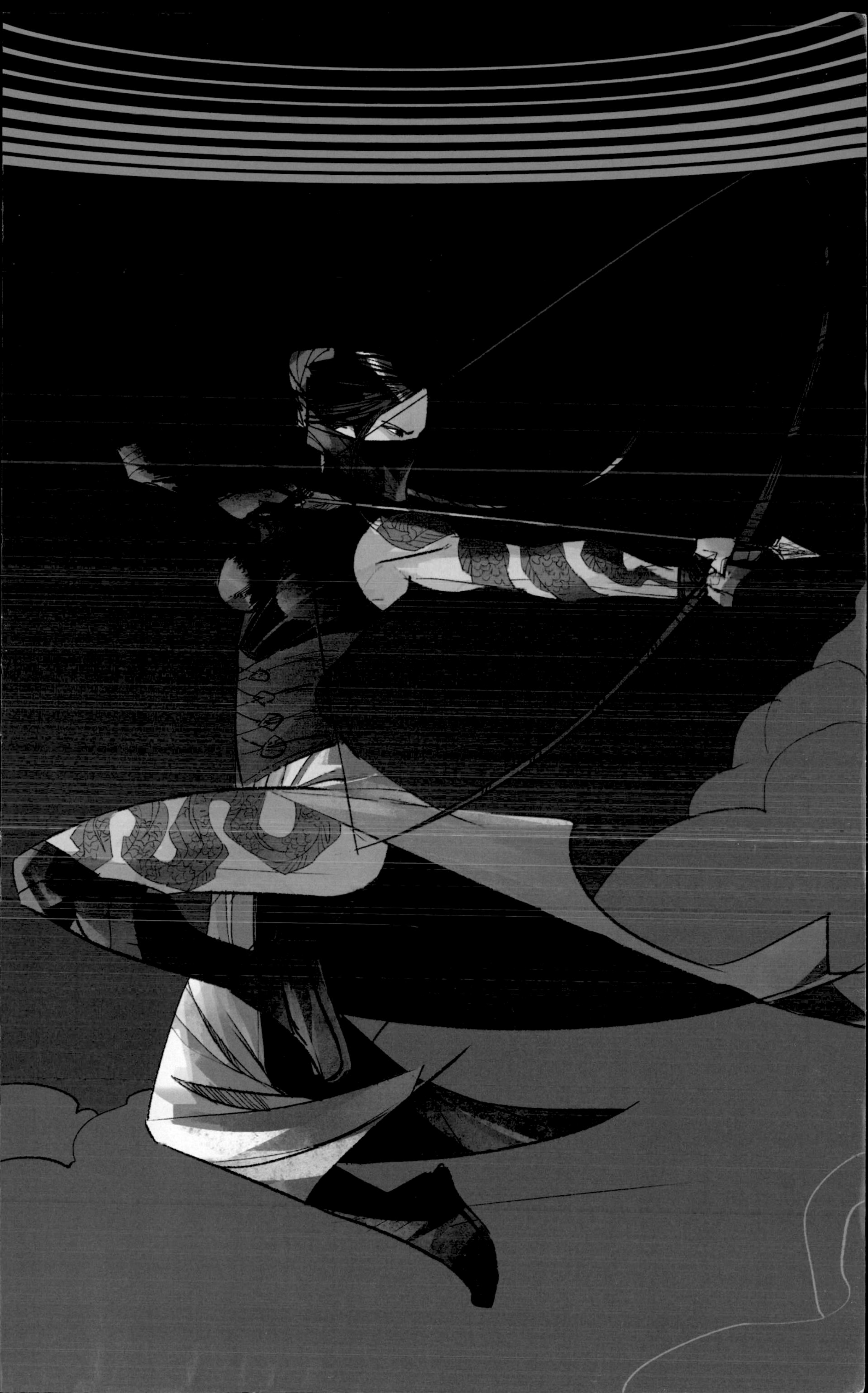

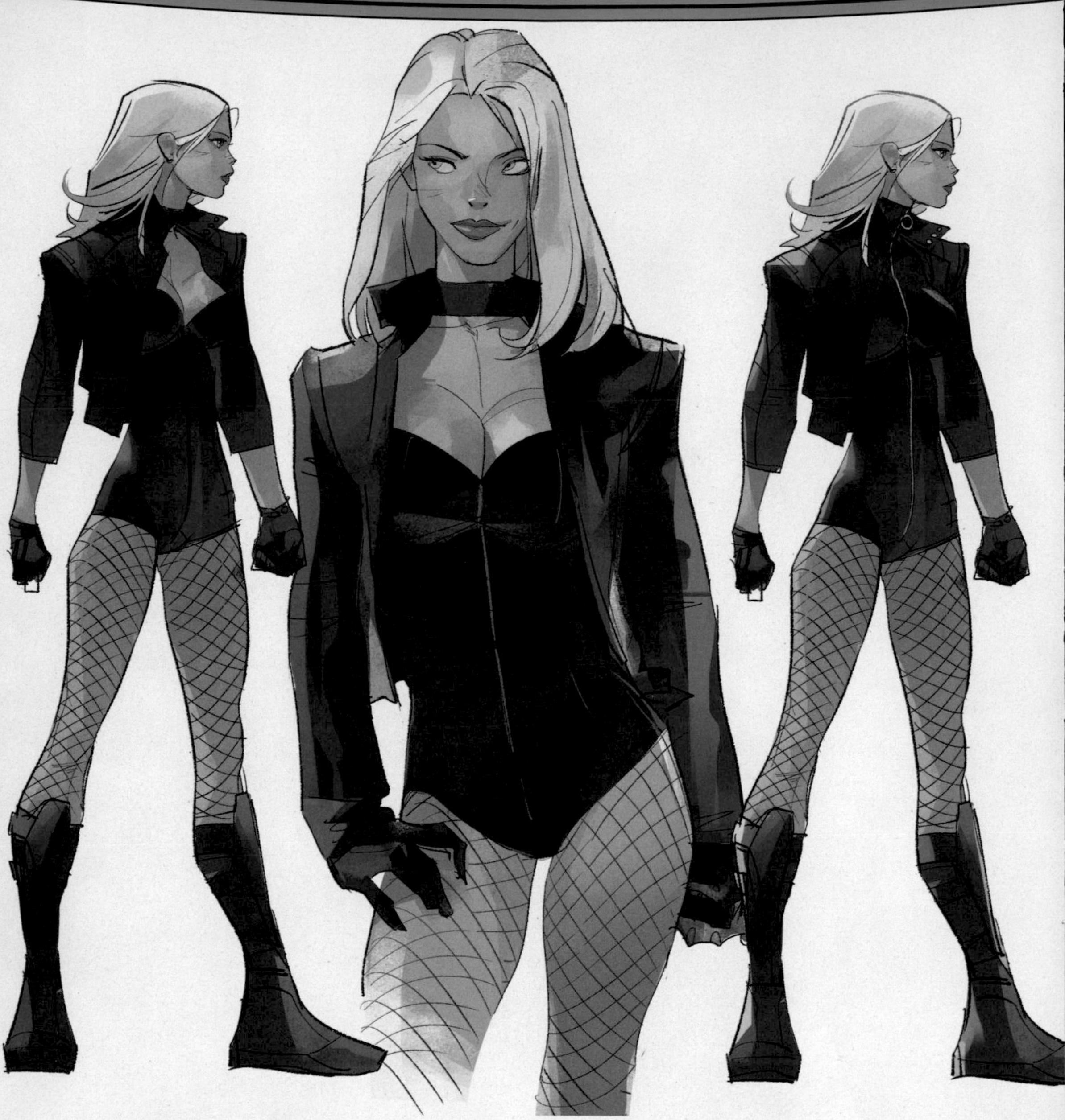

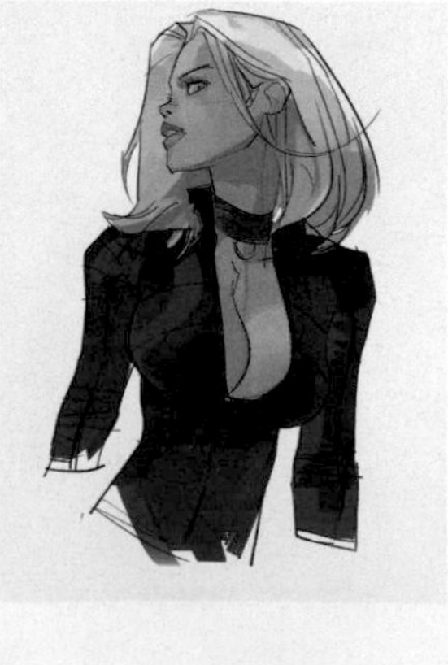

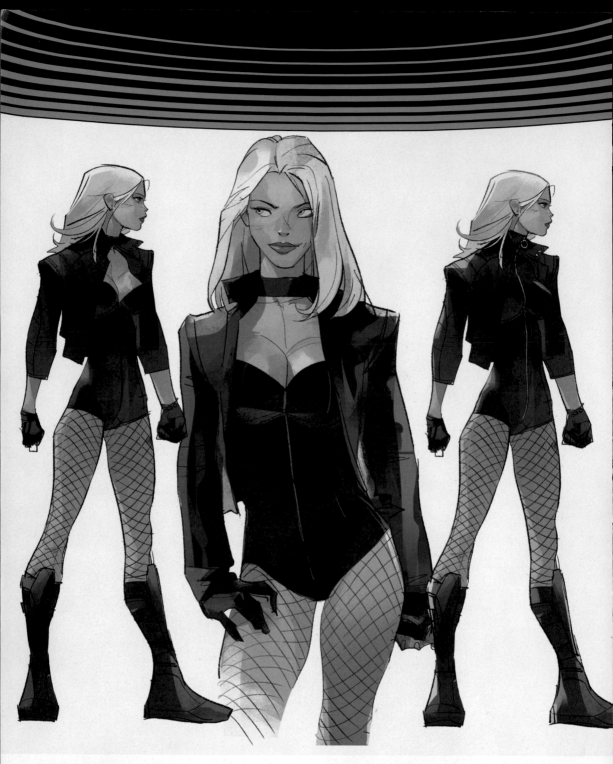

BLACK CANARY

COVER SKETCHES
By JUAN FERREYRA

GREEN ARROW #2

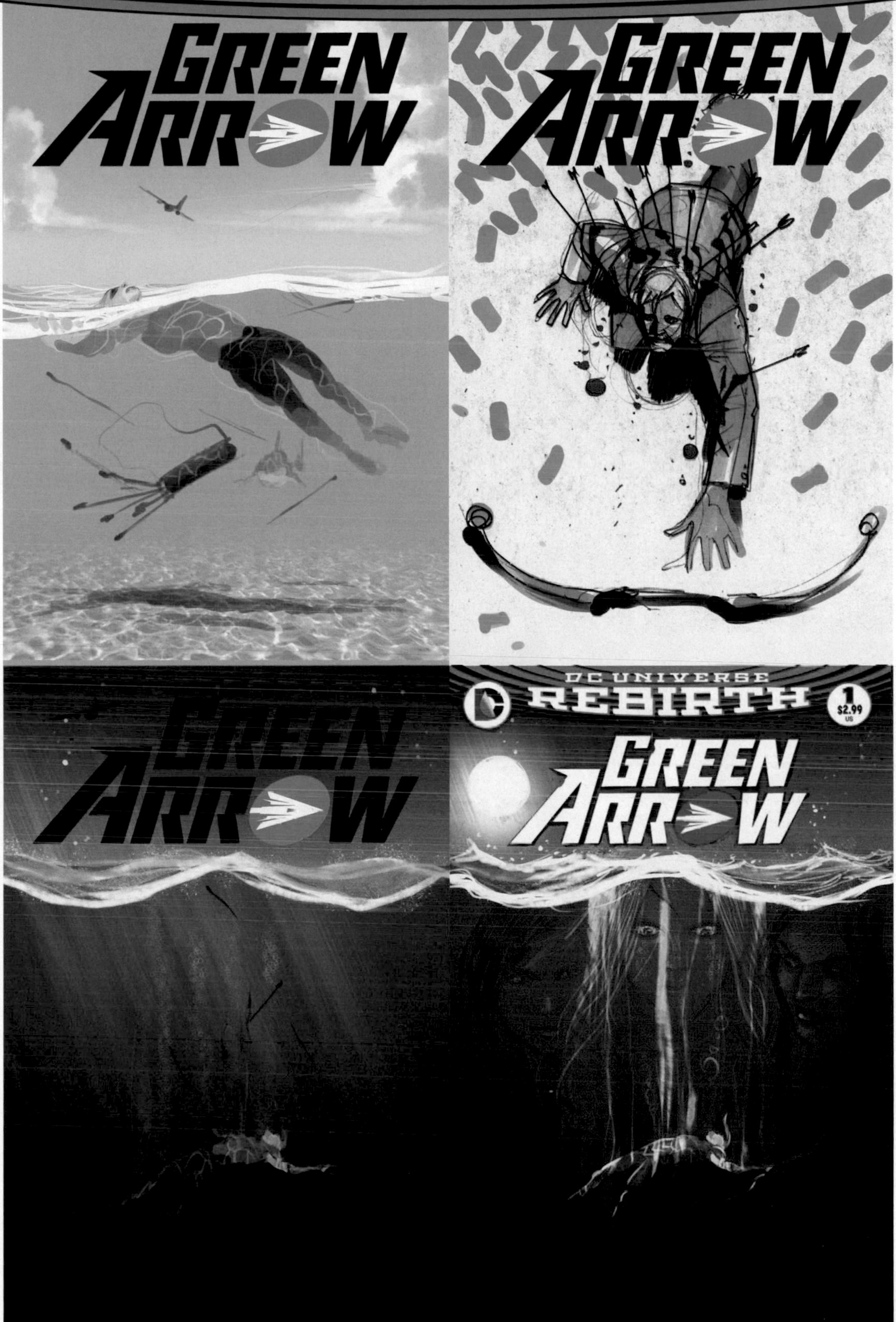
GREEN ARROW
GREEN ARROW
GREEN ARROW
DC UNIVERSE
REBIRTH
1
$2.99
US
GREEN ARROW

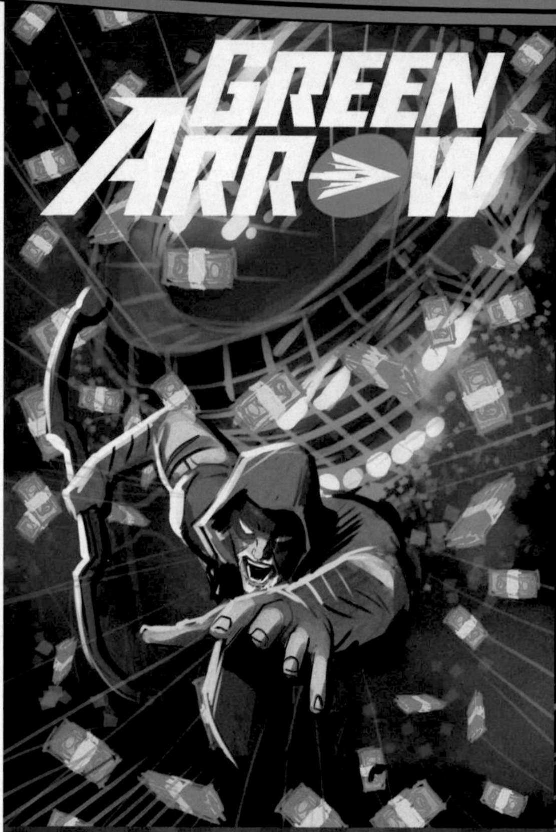
GREEN
ARROW

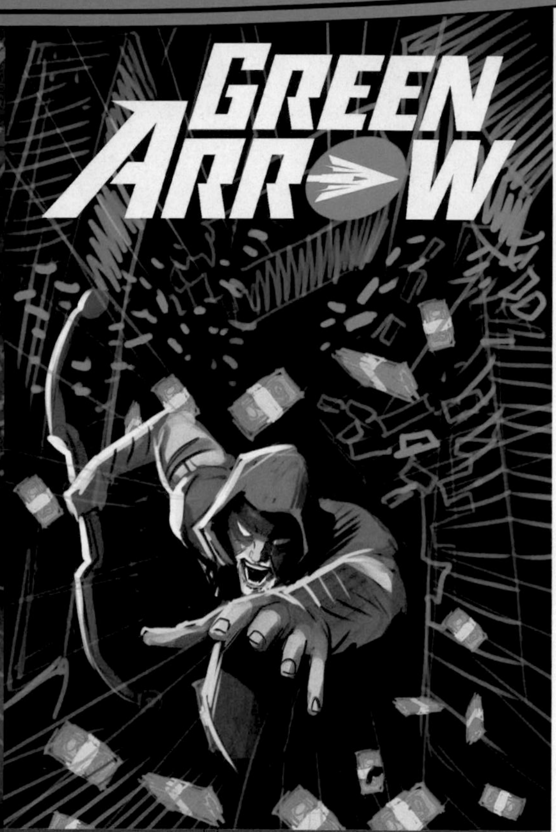
GREEN
ARROW

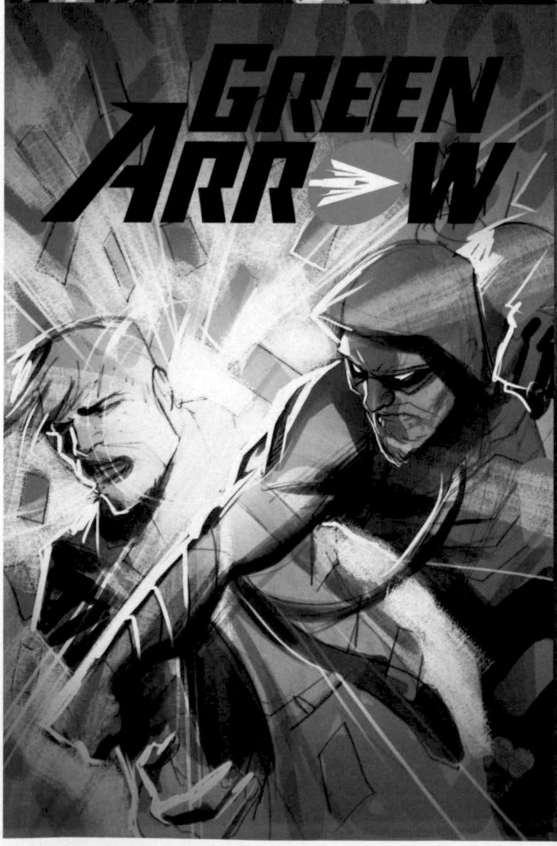
GREEN
ARROW

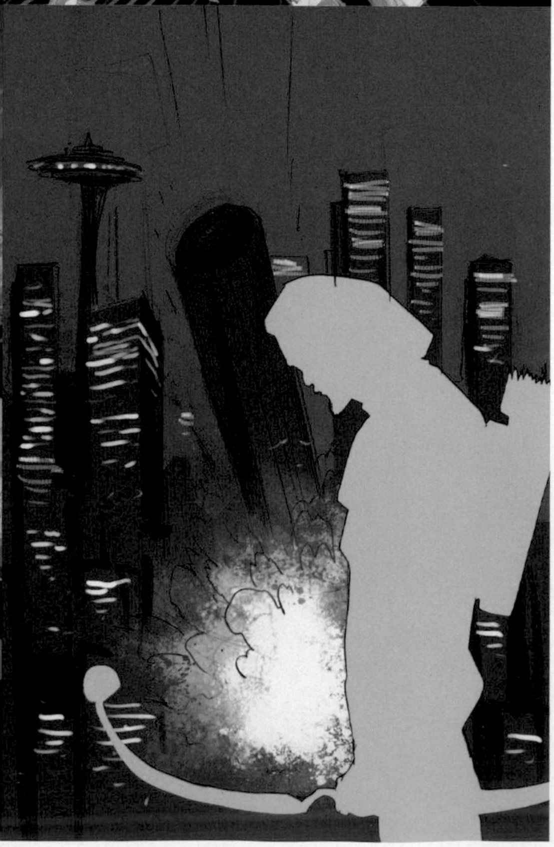

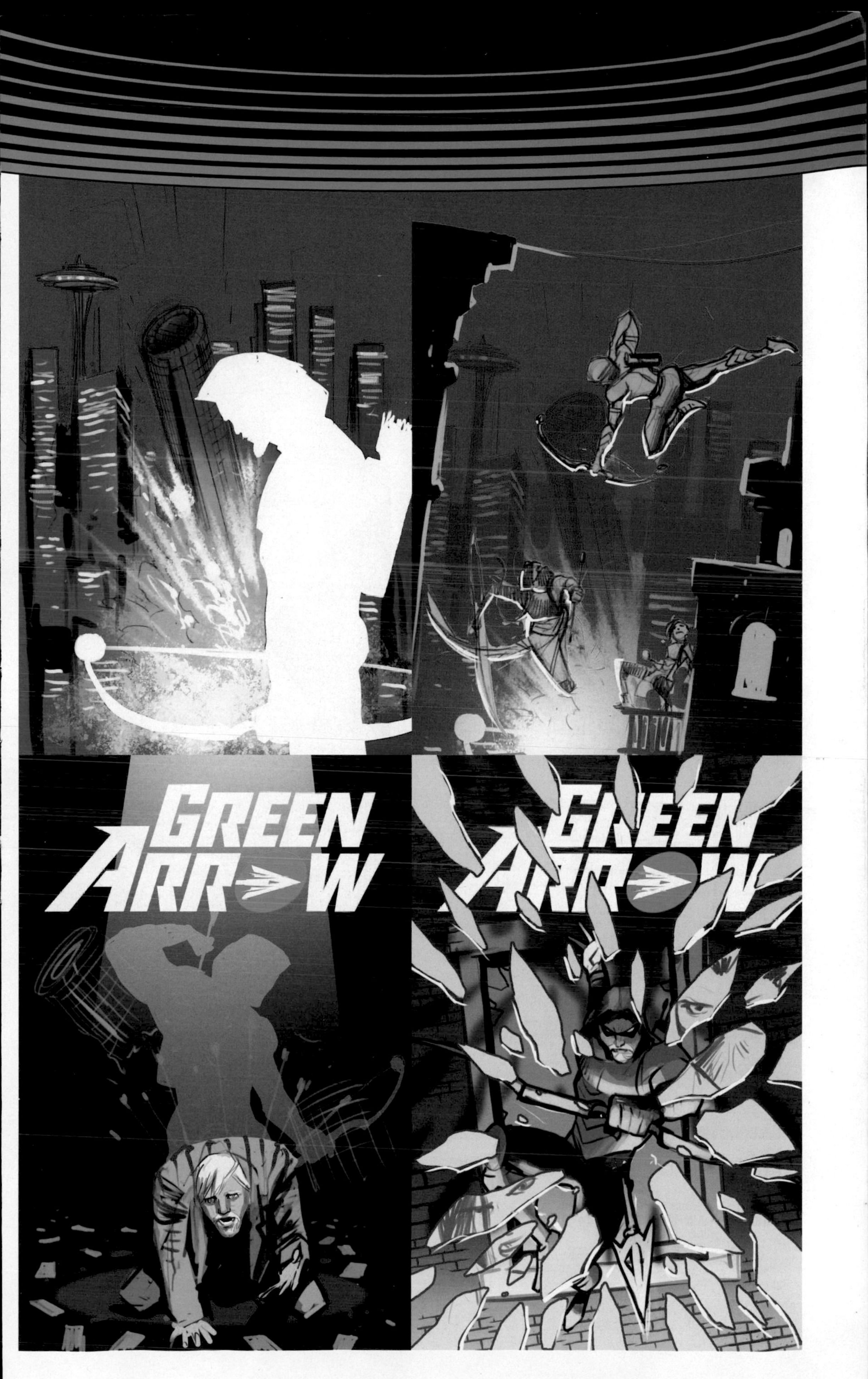
GREEN ARROW
GREEN ARROW

GREEN ARROW #1 Rough Layout
By OTTO SCHMIDT

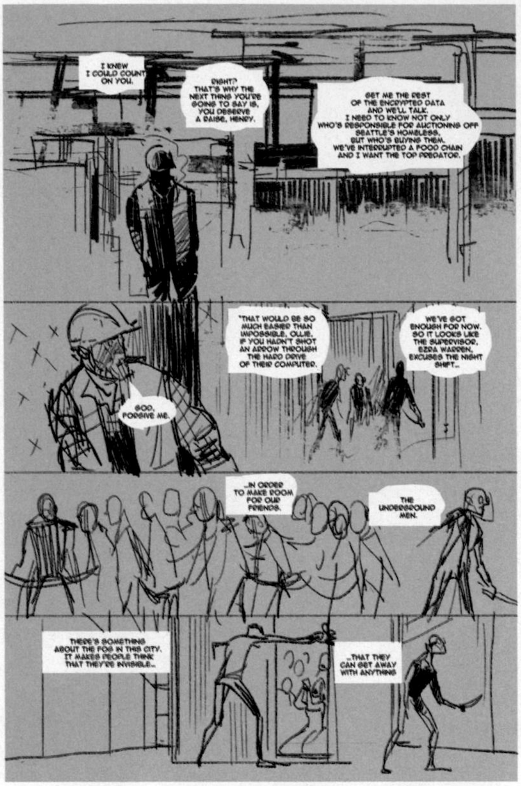
I KNEW I COULD COUNT ON YOU.
RIGHT? THAT'S WHY THE NEXT THING YOU'RE GOING TO SAY IS, YOU DESERVE A RAISE, HENRY.
GET ME THE REST OF THE ENCRYPTED DATA AND WE'LL TALK. I NEED TO KNOW NOT ONLY WHO'S RESPONSIBLE FOR AUCTIONING OFF SEATTLE'S HOMELESS, BUT WHO'S BUYING THEM. WE'VE INTERRUPTED A FOOD CHAIN AND I WANT THE TOP PREDATOR.
"THAT WOULD BE SO MUCH EASIER THAN IMPOSSIBLE, OLLIE, IF YOU HADN'T SHOT AN ARROW THROUGH THE HARD DRIVE OF THEIR COMPUTER.
WE'VE GOT ENOUGH FOR NOW. SO IT LOOKS LIKE THE SUPERVISOR, EZRA WARREN, EXCUSES THE NIGHT SHIFT...
GOD, FORGIVE ME.
...IN ORDER TO MAKE ROOM FOR OUR FRIENDS.
THE UNDERGROUND MEN.
THERE'S SOMETHING ABOUT THE FOG IN THIS CITY. IT MAKES PEOPLE THINK THAT THEY'RE INVISIBLE...
...THAT THEY CAN GET AWAY WITH ANYTHING

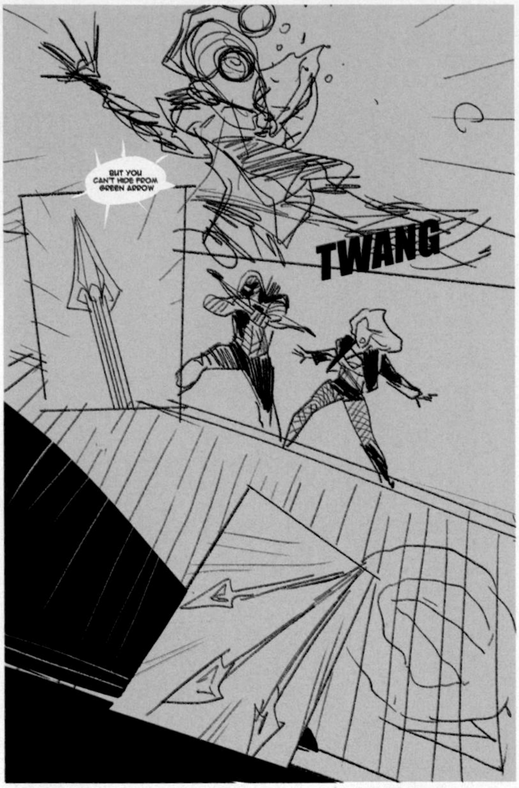
BUT YOU CAN'T HIDE FROM GREEN ARROW
TWANG

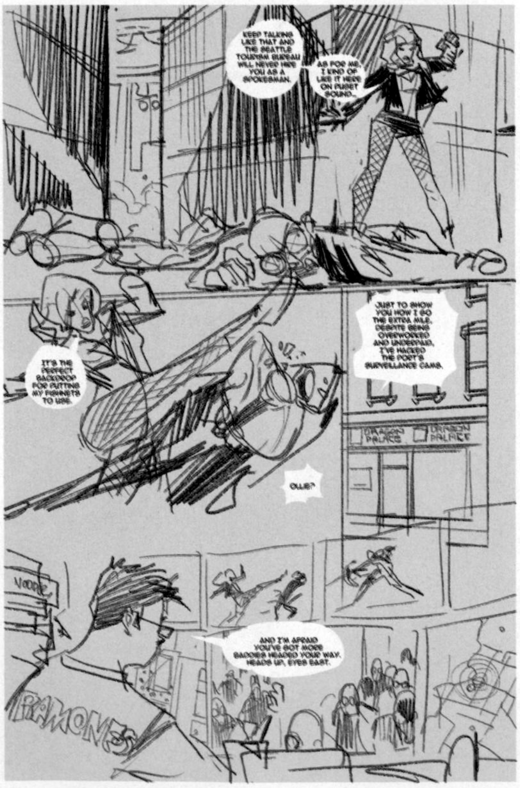
KEEP TALKING LIKE THAT AND THE SEATTLE TOURISM BUREAU WILL NEVER HIRE YOU AS A SPOKESMAN.
AS FOR ME, I KIND OF LIKE IT HERE ON PUGET SOUND...
IT'S THE PERFECT BACKDROP FOR PUTTING MY FISHNETS TO USE.
JUST TO SHOW YOU HOW I GO THE EXTRA MILE, DESPITE BEING OVERWORKED AND UNDERPAID, I'VE HACKED THE PORT'S SURVEILLANCE CAMS.
DRAGON PALACE
DRAGON PALACE
OLLIE?
AND I'M AFRAID YOU'VE GOT MORE BADDIES HEADED YOUR WAY. HEADS UP, EYES EAST.
RAMONES

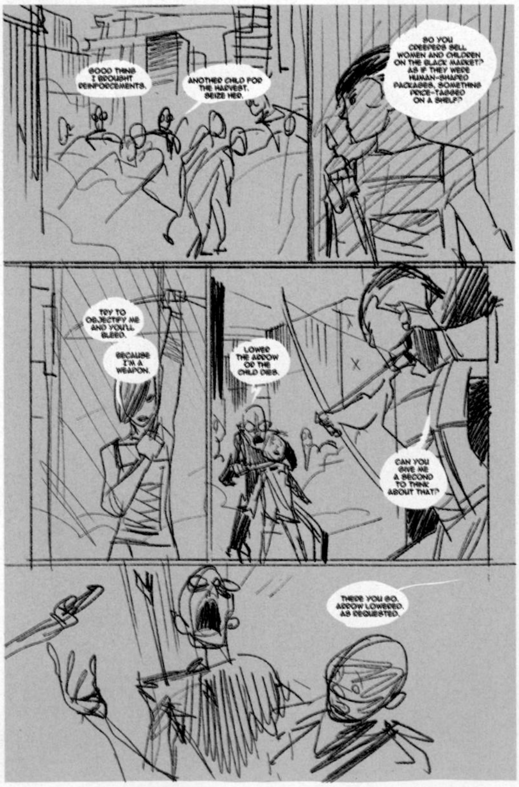
GOOD THING I BROUGHT REINFORCEMENTS.
ANOTHER CHILD FOR THE HARVEST. SEIZE HER.
SO YOU CREEPERS SELL WOMEN AND CHILDREN ON THE BLACK MARKET? AS IF THEY WERE HUMAN-SHAPED PACKAGES, SOMETHING PRICE-TAGGED ON A SHELF?
TRY TO OBJECTIFY ME AND YOU'LL BLEED.
BECAUSE I'M A WEAPON.
LOWER THE ARROW OR THE CHILD DIES.
CAN YOU GIVE ME A SECOND TO THINK ABOUT THAT?
THERE YOU GO. ARROW LOWERED. AS REQUESTED.

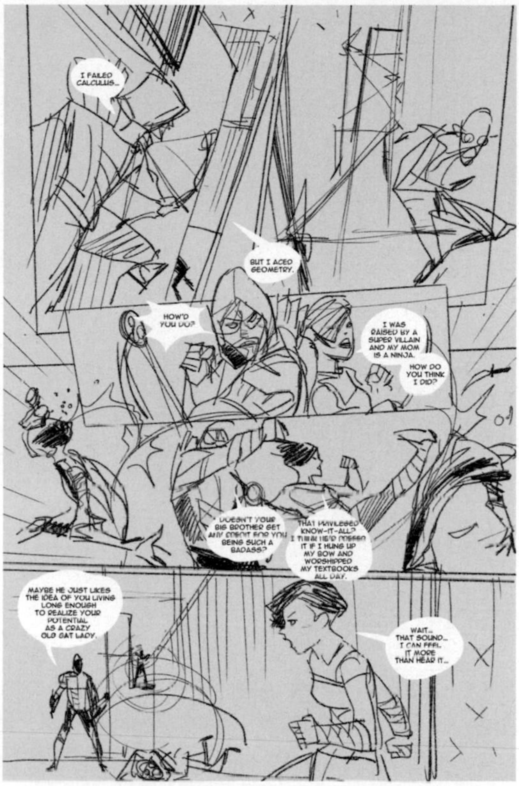
I FAILED CALCULUS...
BUT I ACED GEOMETRY.
HOW'D YOU DO?
I WAS RAISED BY A SUPER VILLAIN AND MY MOM IS A NINJA.
HOW DO YOU THINK I DID?
DOESN'T YOUR BIG BROTHER GET ANY CREDIT FOR YOU BEING SUCH A BADASS?
THAT PRIVILEGED KNOW-IT-ALL? I THINK HE'D PREFER IT IF I HUNG UP MY BOW AND WORSHIPPED MY TEXTBOOKS ALL DAY.
MAYBE HE JUST LIKES THE IDEA OF YOU LIVING LONG ENOUGH TO REALIZE YOUR POTENTIAL AS A CRAZY OLD CAT LADY.
WAIT... THAT SOUND... I CAN FEEL IT MORE THAN HEAR IT...

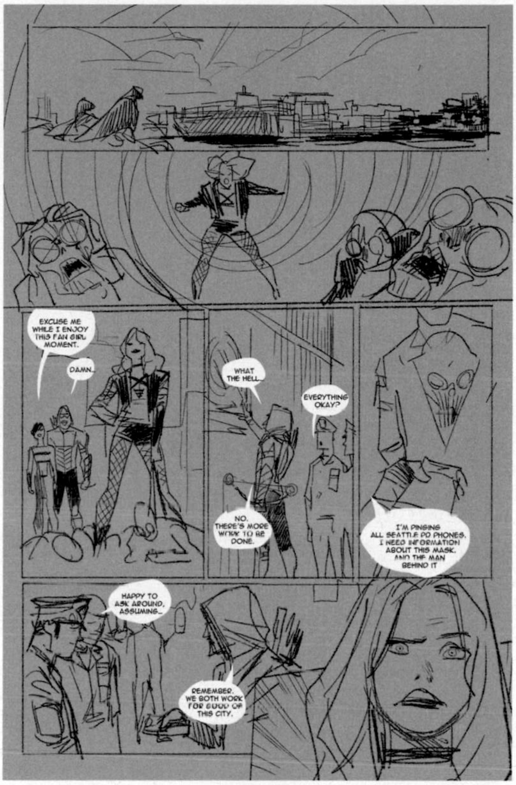
EXCUSE ME WHILE I ENJOY THIS FAN GIRL MOMENT.
DAMN...
WHAT THE HELL...
EVERYTHING OKAY?
NO. THERE'S MORE WORK TO BE DONE.
I'M PINGING ALL SEATTLE PD PHONES. I NEED INFORMATION ABOUT THIS MASK. AND THE MAN BEHIND IT
HAPPY TO ASK AROUND, ASSUMING...
REMEMBER. WE BOTH WORK FOR GOOD OF THIS CITY.

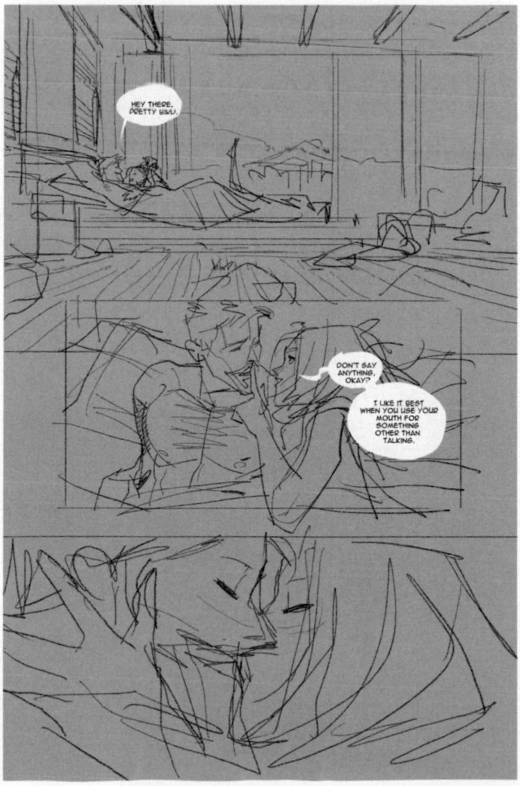
HEY THERE, PRETTY BIRD.
DON'T SAY ANYTHING, OKAY?
I LIKE IT BEST WHEN YOU USE YOUR MOUTH FOR SOMETHING OTHER THAN TALKING.

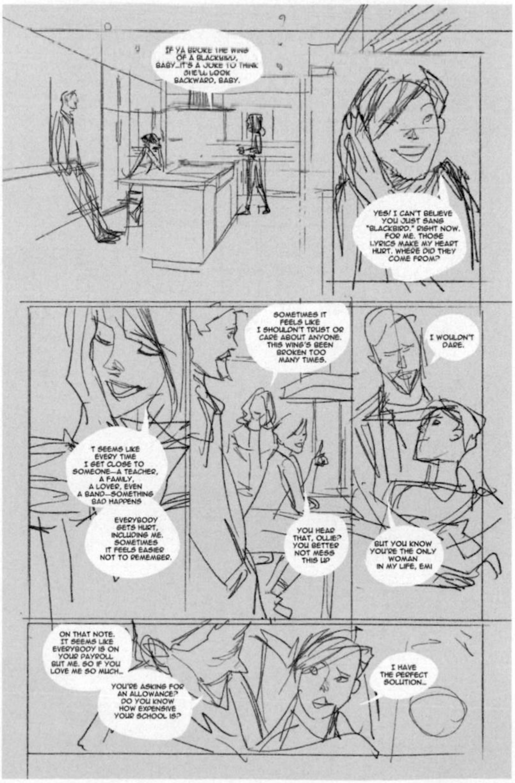
IF YA BROKE THE WING OF A BLACKBIRD, BABY...IT'S A JOKE TO THINK SHE'LL LOOK BACKWARD, BABY.
YES! I CAN'T BELIEVE YOU JUST SANG "BLACKBIRD," RIGHT NOW. FOR ME. THOSE LYRICS MAKE MY HEART HURT. WHERE DID THEY COME FROM?
T SEEMS LIKE EVERY TIME I GET CLOSE TO SOMEONE—A TEACHER, A FAMILY, A LOVER, EVEN A BAND—SOMETHING BAD HAPPENS
EVERYBODY GETS HURT, INCLUDING ME. SOMETIMES IT FEELS EASIER NOT TO REMEMBER.
SOMETIMES IT FEELS LIKE I SHOULDN'T TRUST OR CARE ABOUT ANYONE. THIS WING'S BEEN BROKEN TOO MANY TIMES.
YOU HEAR THAT, OLLIE? YOU BETTER NOT MESS THIS UP
I WOULDN'T DARE.
BUT YOU KNOW YOU'RE THE ONLY WOMAN IN MY LIFE, EMI
ON THAT NOTE. IT SEEMS LIKE EVERYBODY IS ON YOUR PAYROLL BUT ME. SO IF YOU LOVE ME SO MUCH...
YOU'RE ASKING FOR AN ALLOWANCE? DO YOU KNOW HOW EXPENSIVE YOUR SCHOOL IS?
I HAVE THE PERFECT SOLUTION...

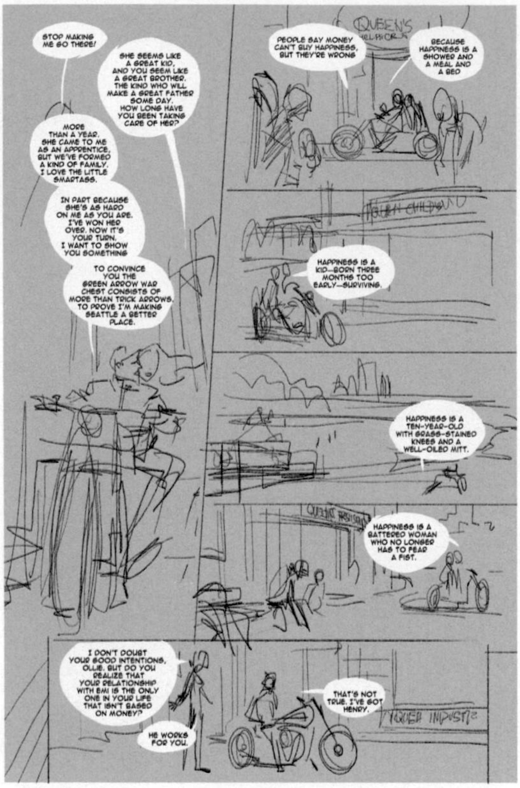
STOP MAKING ME GO THERE!
SHE SEEMS LIKE A GREAT KID, AND YOU SEEM LIKE A GREAT BROTHER. THE KIND WHO WILL MAKE A GREAT FATHER SOME DAY. HOW LONG HAVE YOU BEEN TAKING CARE OF HER?
MORE THAN A YEAR. SHE CAME TO ME AS AN APPRENTICE, BUT WE'VE FORMED A KIND OF FAMILY. I LOVE THE LITTLE SMARTASS.
IN PART BECAUSE SHE'S AS HARD ON ME AS YOU ARE. I'VE WON HER OVER. NOW IT'S YOUR TURN. I WANT TO SHOW YOU SOMETHING
TO CONVINCE YOU THE GREEN ARROW WAR CHEST CONSISTS OF MORE THAN TRICK ARROWS. TO PROVE I'M MAKING SEATTLE A BETTER PLACE.
PEOPLE SAY MONEY CAN'T BUY HAPPINESS, BUT THEY'RE WRONG
BECAUSE HAPPINESS IS A SHOWER AND A MEAL AND A BED
HAPPINESS IS A KID—BORN THREE MONTHS TOO EARLY—SURVIVING.
HAPPINESS IS A TEN-YEAR-OLD WITH GRASS-STAINED KNEES AND A WELL-OILED MITT.
HAPPINESS IS A BATTERED WOMAN WHO NO LONGER HAS TO FEAR A FIST.
I DON'T DOUBT YOUR GOOD INTENTIONS, OLLIE. BUT DO YOU REALIZE THAT YOUR RELATIONSHIP WITH EMI IS THE ONLY ONE IN YOUR LIFE THAT ISN'T BASED ON MONEY?
THAT'S NOT TRUE. I'VE GOT HENRY.
HE WORKS FOR YOU.

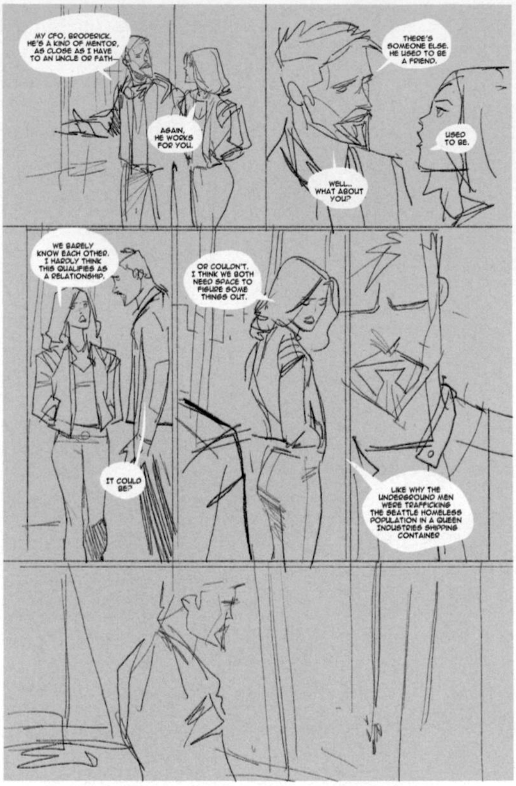
MY CFO, BRODERICK. HE'S A KIND OF MENTOR, AS CLOSE AS I HAVE TO AN UNCLE OR FATH—
AGAIN, HE WORKS FOR YOU.
THERE'S SOMEONE ELSE. HE USED TO BE A FRIEND.
USED TO BE.
WELL... WHAT ABOUT YOU?
WE BARELY KNOW EACH OTHER. I HARDLY THINK THIS QUALIFIES AS A RELATIONSHIP.
IT COULD BE?
OR COULDN'T. I THINK WE BOTH NEED SPACE TO FIGURE SOME THINGS OUT.
LIKE WHY THE UNDERGROUND MEN WERE TRAFFICKING THE SEATTLE HOMELESS POPULATION IN A QUEEN INDUSTRIES SHIPPING CONTAINER

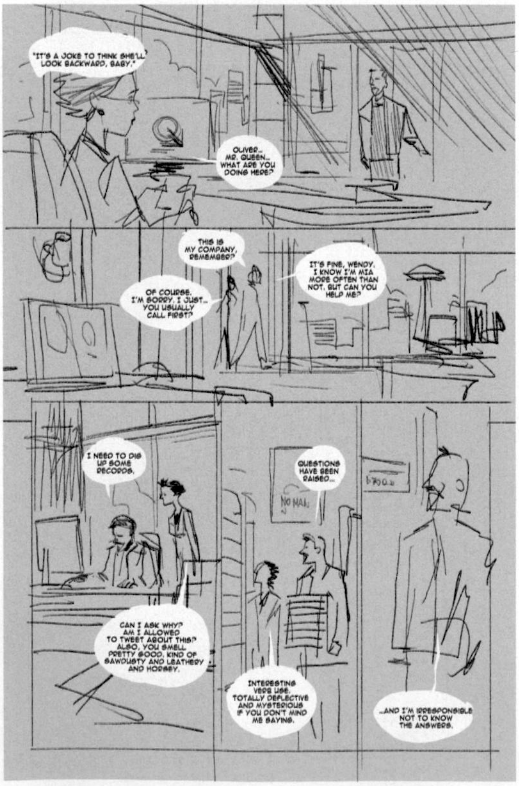
"IT'S A JOKE TO THINK SHE'LL LOOK BACKWARD, BABY."
OLIVER... MR. QUEEN... WHAT ARE YOU DOING HERE?
THIS IS MY COMPANY, REMEMBER?
OF COURSE. I'M SORRY. I JUST... YOU USUALLY CALL FIRST?
IT'S FINE, WENDY. I KNOW I'M MIA MORE OFTEN THAN NOT. BUT CAN YOU HELP ME?
I NEED TO DIG UP SOME RECORDS.
CAN I ASK WHY? AM I ALLOWED TO TWEET ABOUT THIS? ALSO, YOU SMELL PRETTY GOOD. KIND OF SAWDUSTY AND LEATHERY AND HORSEY.
QUESTIONS HAVE BEEN RAISED...
INTERESTING VERB USE. TOTALLY DEFLECTIVE AND MYSTERIOUS IF YOU DON'T MIND ME SAYING.
...AND I'M IRRESPONSIBLE NOT TO KNOW THE ANSWERS.

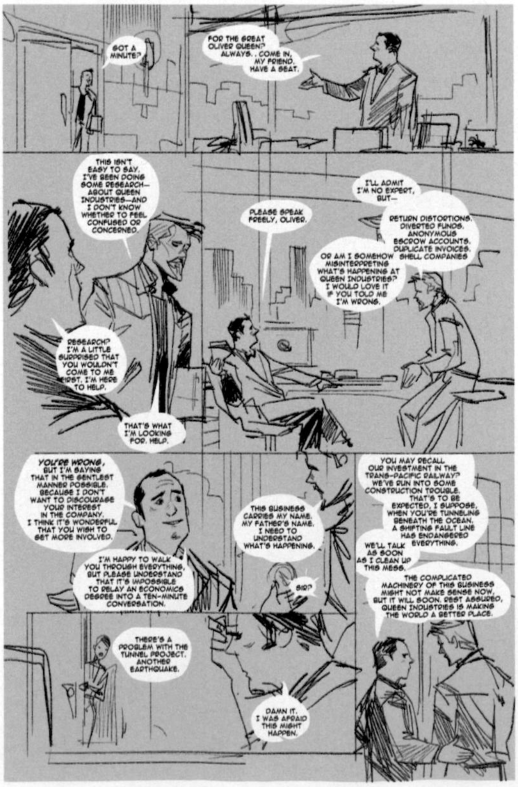
GOT A MINUTE?
FOR THE GREAT OLIVER QUEEN? ALWAYS. . COME IN, MY FRIEND. HAVE A SEAT.
THIS ISN'T EASY TO SAY. I'VE BEEN DOING SOME RESEARCH—ABOUT QUEEN INDUSTRIES—AND I DON'T KNOW WHETHER TO FEEL CONFUSED OR CONCERNED.
PLEASE SPEAK FREELY, OLIVER.
I'LL ADMIT I'M NO EXPERT, BUT—
RETURN DISTORTIONS. DIVERTED FUNDS. ANONYMOUS ESCROW ACCOUNTS. DUPLICATE INVOICES. SHELL COMPANIES
OR AM I SOMEHOW MISINTERPRETING WHAT'S HAPPENING AT QUEEN INDUSTRIES? I WOULD LOVE IT IF YOU TOLD ME I'M WRONG.
RESEARCH? I'M A LITTLE SURPRISED THAT YOU WOULDN'T COME TO ME FIRST. I'M HERE TO HELP.
THAT'S WHAT I'M LOOKING FOR. HELP.
YOU'RE WRONG, BUT I'M SAYING THAT IN THE GENTLEST MANNER POSSIBLE. BECAUSE I DON'T WANT TO DISCOURAGE YOUR INTEREST IN THE COMPANY. I THINK IT'S WONDERFUL THAT YOU WISH TO GET MORE INVOLVED.
I'M HAPPY TO WALK YOU THROUGH EVERYTHING, BUT PLEASE UNDERSTAND THAT IT'S IMPOSSIBLE TO RELAY AN ECONOMICS DEGREE INTO A TEN-MINUTE CONVERSATION.
THIS BUSINESS CARRIES MY NAME. MY FATHER'S NAME. I NEED TO UNDERSTAND WHAT'S HAPPENING.
SIR?
YOU MAY RECALL OUR INVESTMENT IN THE TRANS-PACIFIC RAILWAY? WE'VE RUN INTO SOME CONSTRUCTION TROUBLE.
THAT'S TO BE EXPECTED, I SUPPOSE, WHEN YOU'RE TUNNELING BENEATH THE OCEAN. A SHIFTING FAULT LINE HAS ENDANGERED EVERYTHING.
WE'LL TALK AS SOON AS I CLEAN UP THIS MESS.
THE COMPLICATED MACHINERY OF THIS BUSINESS MIGHT NOT MAKE SENSE NOW, BUT IT WILL SOON. REST ASSURED, QUEEN INDUSTRIES IS MAKING THE WORLD A BETTER PLACE.
THERE'S A PROBLEM WITH THE TUNNEL PROJECT. ANOTHER EARTHQUAKE.
DAMN IT. I WAS AFRAID THIS MIGHT HAPPEN.

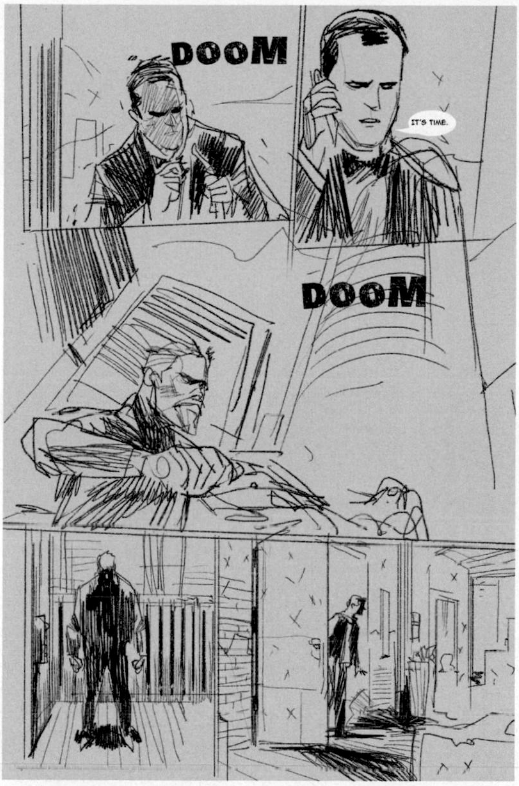
DOOM
IT'S TIME.
DOOM

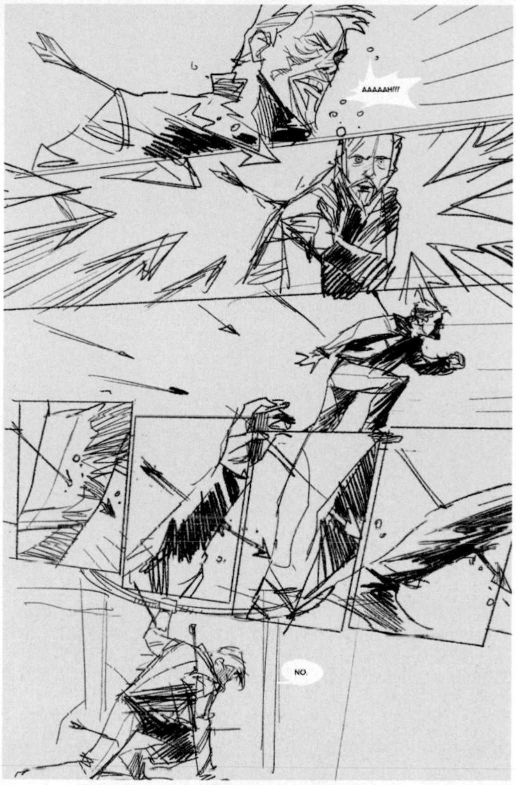
AAAAAH!!!
NO.

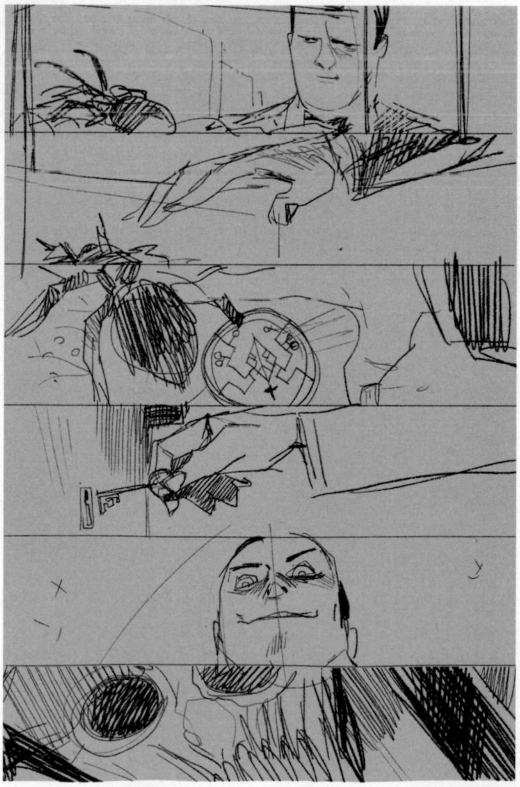

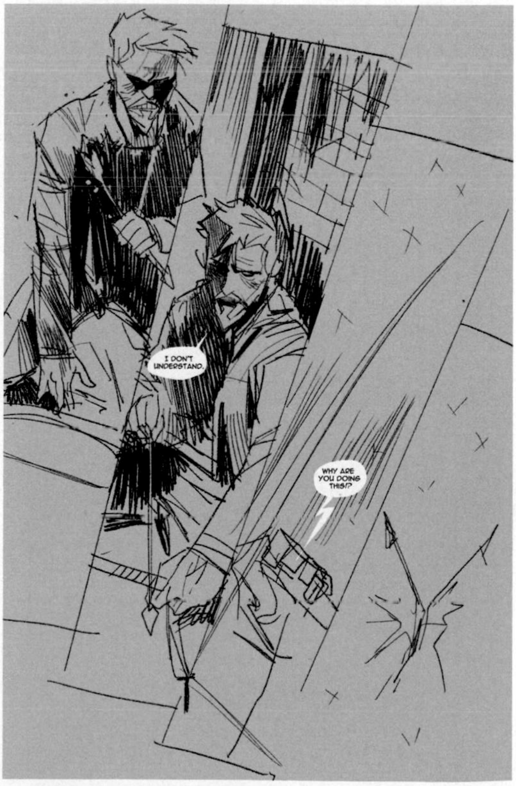
I DON'T UNDERSTAND.
WHY ARE YOU DOING THIS!?

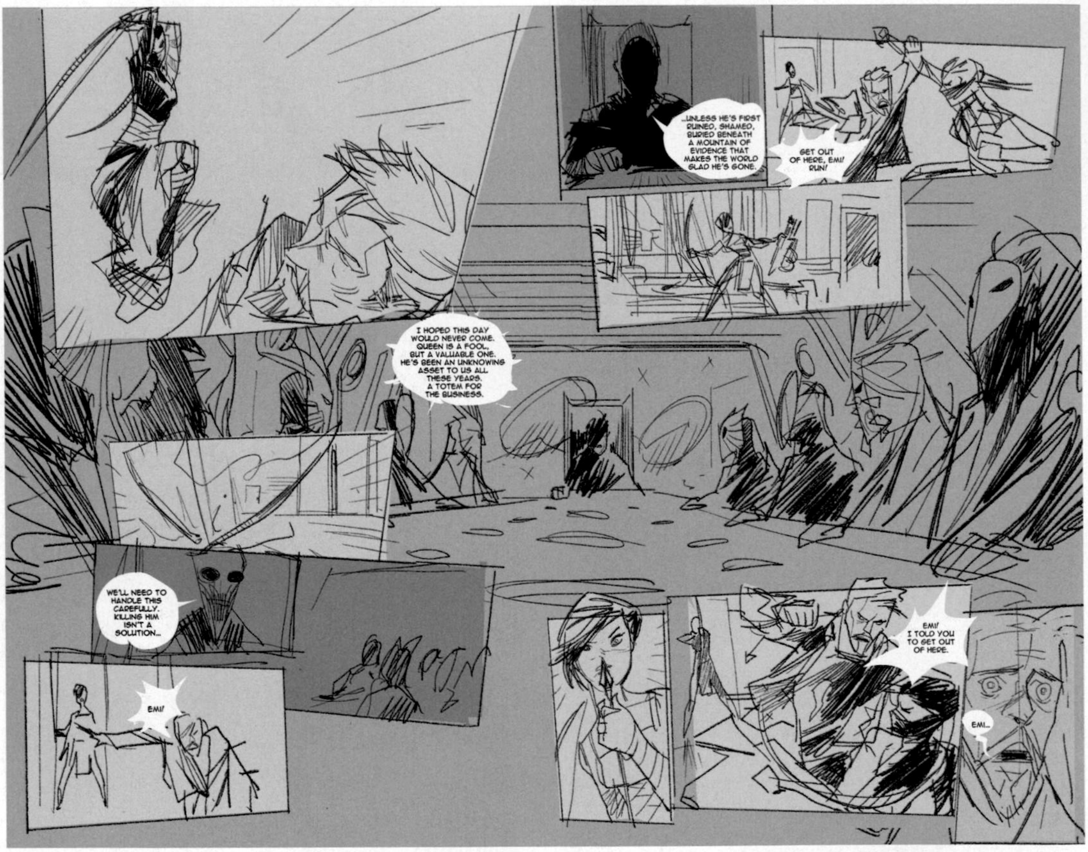
...UNLESS HE'S FIRST RUINED, SHAMED, BURIED BENEATH A MOUNTAIN OF EVIDENCE THAT MAKES THE WORLD GLAD HE'S GONE.
GET OUT OF HERE, EMI! RUN!
I HOPED THIS DAY WOULD NEVER COME. QUEEN IS A FOOL, BUT A VALUABLE ONE. HE'S BEEN AN UNKNOWING ASSET TO US ALL THESE YEARS. A TOTEM FOR THE BUSINESS.
WE'LL NEED TO HANDLE THIS CAREFULLY. KILLING HIM ISN'T A SOLUTION...
EMI!
EMI! I TOLD YOU TO GET OUT OF HERE.
EMI...

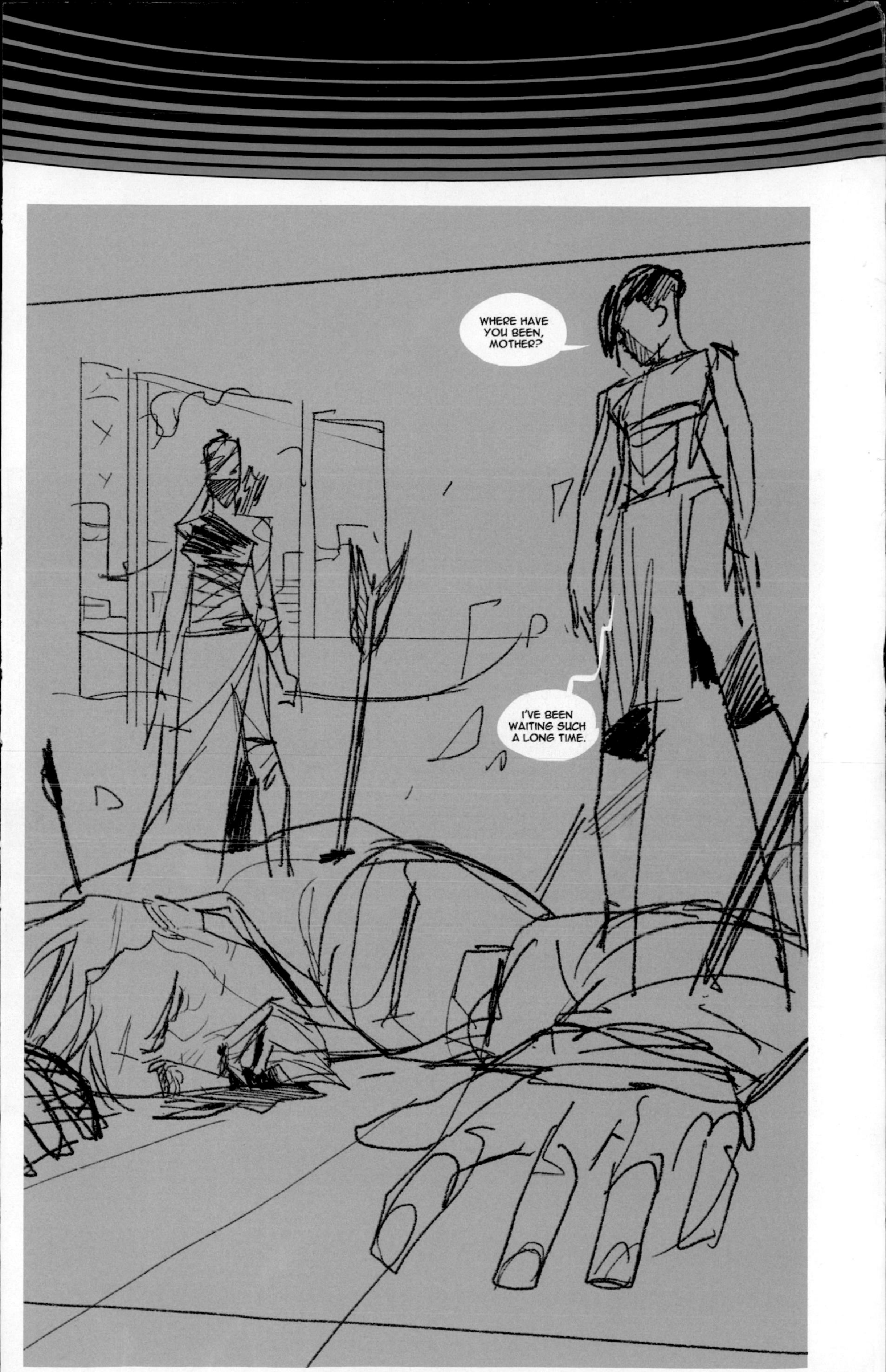
WHERE HAVE YOU BEEN, MOTHER?
I'VE BEEN WAITING SUCH A LONG TIME.

GREEN ARROW #3, Pages 4 & 5, Rough Layout
By JUAN FERREYRA

The floor is alarm-triggered,
its sensors communicating with chips nested in the guard's boots.
If anything else—heavier than a sheet of paper—touches the floor, the building goes into lockdown and blares with sirens.
DING!
There is at least one guard per floor.
And at staggered time intervals, they shift positions by elevator...
...their key cards resetting to match t heir new location.
The ventilation shafts are barred every twenty meters, so this is the only way up or down.
TUD!
For the next hour, my key card will trigger all doors in the floor below this one.
The location of Broderick's office.

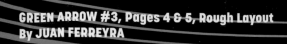

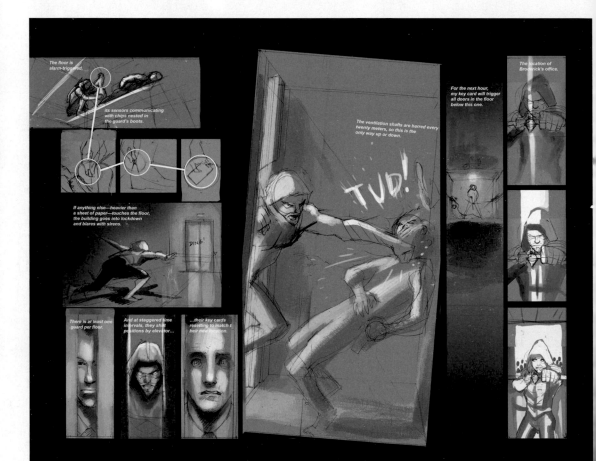